RURAL PROTEST: PEASANT MOVEMENTS AND SOCIAL CHANGE

*Other publications of the International
Institute for Labour Studies*

*

EMPLOYMENT PROBLEMS OF AUTOMATION
AND ADVANCED TECHNOLOGY
edited by Jack Stieber

COLLECTIVE BARGAINING IN AFRICAN COUNTRIES
*by B. C. Roberts and
L. Greyfié de Bellecombe*

AUTOMATION ON SHIPBOARD
edited by G. J. Bonwick

INDUSTRIAL RELATIONS AND ECONOMIC DEVELOPMENT
edited by Arthur Ross

THE LABOUR MARKET AND INFLATION
edited by Anthony D. Smith

WAGE POLICY ISSUES IN ECONOMIC DEVELOPMENT
edited by Anthony D. Smith

TRANSNATIONAL INDUSTRIAL RELATIONS
edited by Hans Günter

TRADE UNION FOREIGN POLICY
by Jeffrey Harrod

*Publication of the International Industrial
Relations Association*

*

INDUSTRIAL RELATIONS: CONTEMPORARY ISSUES
edited by B. C. Roberts

RURAL PROTEST:
PEASANT MOVEMENTS
AND SOCIAL CHANGE

EDITED BY

HENRY A. LANDSBERGER

BOOKS
10 East 53d St., New York 10022
(a division of Harper & Row Publishers, inc.)

Published in the United Kingdom 1973 by
THE MACMILLAN PRESS LTD

Published in the U.S.A. 1973 by
HARPER & ROW PUBLISHERS, INC.
BARNES & NOBLE IMPORT DIVISION

ISBN 06 494029 2

Printed in Great Britain

CONTENTS

PART 2

THE PEASANT AND FORMAL POLITICS:
EASTERN EUROPE BETWEEN THE WARS

PREFACE

UNTIL quite recently, most of the world's workers have been peasants. It was, however, possible during the first half of the twentieth century largely to ignore that fact. Attention tends to focus upon what is changing in societies, and what claimed attention then was the spread of industrialism, its consequences for industrial workers, and the progress and effects of trade unionism in ameliorating their conditions.

During the second half of our century, more attention is being given to peasant populations. The peasantry moves towards the centre of the stage of world history at the very time when the traditional rural way of life is in decline and the peasant economy is shrinking. Violence has often accompanied these changes. The great twentieth-century revolutions have been peasant-based. While the wars of the first half of the twentieth century were fought in highly industrialised countries, those of the second half of this century have been fought in areas of peasant population. The major social and political issues of Third World countries now arise from the continuing transformation of the peasantry, whether into a modern workforce or into a mass of unintegrated, poverty-ridden urban slum-dwellers. The way in which this transformation is carried out affects the prospects for peace.

The perspectives of social science, as developed in industrial countries, were initially ill-adapted to elucidating the issues in the transformation of the peasantry, and provided an inadequate basis for practical guidance to those seeking solutions. Preoccupation with the problems of development has, however, had a broadening effect upon social studies generally and in no area has this been more necessary than in the study of peasant populations. In the search for understanding of newly posed problems, the historical method has much to offer. The historian's task is to look at a complex problem in its fullness, not leaving any important facet out of account. Concerted attempts at comparative studies of specific aspects of different peasant movements may, by clarifying both differences and similarities, improve our understanding and ultimately help us to deal more effectively with the questions which now trouble us.

Foremost among these questions are: Under what circumstances have peasants become active in attempting to change their condition?

What are the origins of peasant movements? What have been their goals? What kinds of people have become their leaders? How have peasant movements related to other groups in society, such as urban workers and middle-class people? When have peasant movements been of lasting effect, and when merely ephemeral?

If the study of modern and even of some more remote peasant movements could give us any insight into these questions, it might be a step towards understanding how contemporary peasant communities may make the transition to full participation in national life.

Such considerations led the International Institute for Labour Studies to bring together a small international group of researchers on rural problems of development for a few days during the summer of 1967. This book grew out of contacts amongst scholars initiated through that meeting. The Institute's role in research is primarily one of stimulating studies of social problems of contemporary importance in its field. The opinions expressed by the authors and by Professor Henry Landsberger, the editor, are, of course, their own. The Institute does not, of itself, express views or advocate policies. I do hope, however, that the reader will agree that the contributors to this volume have demonstrated again that history written in a live concern for contemporary issues can help towards understanding and overcoming some of the gravest conflicts of the present.

ROBERT W. COX
*formerly Director, International Institute
for Labour Studies*

THE CONTRIBUTORS

Yu. G. Alexandrov, Asian Peoples Institute, U.S.S.R. Academy of Sciences, Moscow

D. Galaj, Polish Academy of Sciences, Warsaw

R. H. Hilton, Professor, School of History, University of Birmingham

E. J. Hobsbawm, Professor, Birkbeck College, University of London

G. Huizer, Visiting Professor, Institute of Social Studies, The Hague

G. D. Jackson, Jr, Professor, Department of History, Hofstra University, Long Island

H. A. Landsberger, Professor, Department of Sociology, University of North Carolina, Chapel Hill

P. Longworth, Centre for Russian and East European Studies, University of Birmingham

M. Molnár, Professor, Graduate Institute of International Studies, University of Geneva

R. Stavenhagen, Professor, College of Mexico

Chapter 1

PEASANT UNREST: THEMES AND VARIATIONS

by

Henry A. Landsberger

PEASANT[1] unrest, as this volume shows, has been so extensive both in time and in space that one is tempted to call it ubiquitous. Not only massive individual discontent, but organised protest have been an important ingredient of the history of the rural sector of many societies. This is true from Russia in the north to Indonesia in the south; from Latin America around the world to the Philippines; from at least the seventh century of this era until, of course, this very moment.

Yet differences characterise these episodes of unrest as much as similarities. Some uprisings, while very dramatic and bloody, nevertheless had no clear-cut effects, favourable or unfavourable, on the long-run position of the peasantry nor on the development of the society of which they were a part. Trends, visible before, continued with only slight modification afterwards. Such was the case, as Hilton's essay indicates, with most of the medieval revolts whether in France, England or Central Europe. By way of contrast, other uprisings have occurred in which the peasantry played a key role (albeit one shared with other classes) in events which constituted major breaks in the history of certain societies. Such was the case with the French and Russian Revolutions, or in that of Mexico from 1910 onwards and Bolivia some forty years later, as the paper by Huizer and Stavenhagen shows.

For further paradox and variation, in some societies intense peasant discontent has only rarely resulted in organised protest, whether successful or not.[2] Indeed, even in those societies where there has been frequent unrest and protest, long periods of relative quiet have been

[1] The problem of defining 'peasant', about which there has been much debate, is dealt with in the second part of this introductory chapter.

[2] Barrington Moore, Jr, has brought this out very clearly, contrasting India with China, in his *Social Origins of Dictatorship and Democracy* (Boston: Beacon Press, 1966).

as characteristic as brief but dramatic revolts, though it is the latter, of course, which have caught the interest of the historian and the social scientist.

There are many characteristics which some movements or some periods of peasant unrest have in common with others, however much they might be separated in space or time, while still others clearly do not share these characteristics. Nationalism, for example, played an important role in many peasant movements in North Africa and Asia in the period after World War II, as Alexandrov's contribution to this volume shows. This also occurred, in the incipient form of cultural regionalism, in Pugachev's Cossack Revolt of 1773 as portrayed by Longworth, in the Spanish Cantonalist Revolution of 1873 as described by Molnár and Pekmez, and in some of the East European peasant parties between the two world wars (the Croatian, for example). But neither nationalism nor cultural regionalism was found to have played a really substantial role in Bolivia in 1952; nor in certain other East European peasant parties, e.g. that of Bulgaria, as Jackson's essay shows.

Religion, too, or other explicit ideologies sometimes did (as in the case of Slovakia) and sometimes did not affect what happened. And many movements were clearly at least in part backward-looking, seeking to re-establish a past state of affairs, while others sought new arrangements in rural society, with little or no attempt to justify them by looking backwards. Given this intriguing panorama of similarities and differences, it seemed to us[1] of value to attempt a more systematic comparison of various periods of peasant unrest.

In this introductory chapter we present, first, the strategy followed to make such a comparison, together with a brief description of the cases on which the comparison is based, i.e., an overview of the following chapters of this book. Next, the key terms 'peasant' and 'movement' are defined and the utility of the definitions illustrated by references to various case-studies in those chapters. This is followed by a summary of the framework of topics, questions and hypotheses which the authors were asked to follow in writing their chapters. This Introduction ends with an examination of the results: a comparison of the individual contributions with the framework and the conclusions to which such a comparison leads.

---

[1] Here and elsewhere in this introductory chapter, the first person plural is used in a strictly editorial sense. The other contributors to this volume are not responsible for the ideas expressed here.

I. STRATEGY AND CASES

The strategy to accomplish the objective of systematically comparing peasant movements required two components, one more abstract, the other more concrete. The first will be described in greater detail below, after a section in which the concepts of 'peasant' and 'movement' are defined and the implications of their definitions explored. For the moment we will simply state that our purpose was to delineate a broad but comprehensive framework of topics for analysis. These dealt with, for example, the objective and subjective conditions preceding the movement; its goals; the nature of its membership, etc. Each of these broad topics was supplemented with certain more specific questions and hypotheses.

The utility of such a framework could, however, be evaluated only by actually using it and its specific hypotheses to analyse individual peasant movements. This constituted the more concrete part of the strategy.

An unbiased evaluation and a testing of the limits of the utility of the framework demanded, first, that the movements analysed be very different from each other. They should vary in the time at which they took place; their geographical location; the kinds of peasantry involved (including even landless labourers);[1] the presence in at least some of them of 'special' characteristics such as nationalism, anti-colonialism, or a religious element; and so forth.

Second, a severe test (as well as the obvious limits of our own competence) required that the cases be written for the most part by persons other than the proponent of the analytical schema, and that these authors should in turn represent a variety of orientations and disciplines. For it is all too easy for a single author to select examples which support his ideas from historical data which are frequently uncertain or even contradictory, and sometimes so voluminous that selection – though not necessarily biased selection – must take place. The distinguished group of scholars represented in this volume have produced this necessary series of 'case-studies'. The reader may find useful now a brief description of them.

Their order in the book, and hence here, is roughly that of their

---

[1] An unusal inclusion, by customary standards. which we will explain in the following section, dealing with definitions.

historic occurrence, though the internal organisation of the studies is not, of course, predominantly along time sequential lines.

The opening chapter by Rodney Hilton deals with a variety of peasant movements which occurred in western and southern Europe between the seventh century and what may be loosely termed 'the end of the Middle Ages'. Far from presenting a simple picture of enserfed peasants, rising up against a traditional, secular, feudal lord of the manor, this chapter describes and analyses an immense variety of situations. Among these, the simple picture mentioned is of course one, but in others the opponent may be newly enriched urban elements; taxes rather than exactions by the landlord may have triggered the revolt; free rather than enserfed peasants may have been the chief actors. The following chapter by Landsberger and Landsberger takes one of the best documented of the medieval uprisings, that which took place in England in 1381, and applies the proposed analytical scheme in great detail, and with suspiciously satisfactory results.

Eric Hobsbawm's essay on social banditry deals deliberately not with what would generally be regarded as a typical peasant movement, but with a phenomenon which arouses curiosity precisely because one suspects an affinity and relationship to the more usual kind of movement but is puzzled by the extent and nature of that affinity. In social banditry a precursor of, but separate from, a more full-blown uprising? – the actual beginning of a movement? – a replacement for one? – or is it sometimes one, sometimes another of these? From the point of view of the list of specific questions posed to the authors, a topic such as Hobsbawm's does not lend itself to a point-by-point answer. For example, the 'success' of social banditry is obviously of a very different kind from that of a typical peasant movement, the goals of which are more collective. Nevertheless, many of the topics raised by the framework – the kind of peasant involved, ideology, leadership, and preceding societal changes – can be and are in fact discussed by Hobsbawm.

The fate of the Spanish peasantry has been among the most tragic of any in Europe. It has been far more so than one might have been led to believe by the relatively few, localised outbreaks of unrest which occurred between the *comuneros* revolt of 1521 and the latter part of the nineteenth century.[1] The period of political turmoil between the overthrow of the Bourbon monarchy in 1868 and its

---

[1] Edward E. Malefakis, *Agrarian Reform and Peasant Revolution in Spain: Origins of the Civil War* (New Haven, Conn., and London: Yale University Press, 1970), pp. 133 et seq.

restoration in 1874 was one of those times during which part of the peasantry became highly active. They were animated at least to some degree by one of the more general revolutionary philosophies spreading through the new industrial working classes of Europe at the time. The extent of this influence, and the degree and nature of Spanish peasant unrest where it predominated are the themes of the chapter contributed by Molnár and Pekmez.

The second section of the book concludes with an analysis by Longworth of the Russian Pugachev Revolt of 1773, of particular interest because it had a regionalist–nationalist tinge, and was as much opposed to the state and its various means of extracting money and services as to landlords as such. This took place in a country where these three groups – state, landlords and peasants – and others, were inextricably interwoven.

With Jackson's chapter this volume begins its coverage of more recent, twentieth-century peasant activity. The intrinsic interset of the chapter is not, however, that it covers a further period of history and yet another geographic area. Rather, it lies in its analysis of the fate of a generic type of peasant movement – the peasant party – which flourished to any notable extent only in eastern Europe, and showed there in more crystalline form than anywhere else an idealisation of the agrarian way of life, and a hostility to the city, of which other movements show only traces. The paper by Galaj, like the Landsberger and Landsberger paper in relation to that of Hilton, takes the peasant parties of one of the countries (Poland) covered by Jackson's broader paper and examines in greater detail the history of these parties including their points of fundamental disagreement.

The final section of the book deals with peasant movements in today's Third World. Alexandrov's paper, focusing on post-war Asia and North Africa, shows particularly how peasant – indeed, national – unity at the early, anti-colonialist stage, may retard the crystallisation of intra-national conflicts. Such conflicts exist not only between the peasantry and those economically substantially superior to it both in the country and in the cities. Conflicts exist even within the peasantry itself: between those who have just a little more land and those who have less; between those who rent land and those who merely sell their labour. The underlying gap between these groups may well be widening. Consciousness of the gap, and organised action on the basis of such consciousness, seems to lag far behind.

The concluding chapter, by Huizer and Stavenhagen, analyses two classic Latin American peasant movements: those of Mexico and Bolivia respectively. In both countries a very substantial redistribution of land took place, partly as a result of peasant pressure. The question of particular interest raised here is this: are the characteristics of peasant organisations – and the power of the peasantry more generally, in all of its forms – dramatically different after a revolution in which they participated and made some gains, as compared with those societies where no major benefits have been formally bestowed on the peasantry?

These, then, are the historical cases covered in the subsequent chapters. Let us now, before presenting the analytical topics, deal with the definition of the two major concepts of 'peasant' and 'movements', since these are essential to an understanding of what follows.

II. 'PEASANTS' AND THEIR DEFINITION

The Present State of Uncertainty

To engage in long definitional exercises is to lay oneself wide open to the charge of sterile pedantry. Nevertheless, not to define the two central terms – 'peasant' and 'movement' – in a purportedly serious intellectual endeavour, especially when both terms are known to be ambiguous, would be regarded, and rightly so, as irresponsible. In this dilemma we therefore gladly choose the path of pedantry, hoping to make it as short as possible and perhaps somewhat exciting – in so far as this is possible within the always laborious confines of definition-mongering. For we propose to go against stated conventional definitions although far less, as we shall show, against actual and necessary practice.

Concerning the formal definition of the term 'peasant', it seems to us unchallengeable that there are considerable differences not only between outstanding authors, but even crucial variations for the same author within relatively short periods of time. In other words: the situation is so thoroughly confused that, first, we are unlikely to make it worse even if we err in our attempted contribution, and, second, the confusion itself is an indirect signal that something drastic and fundamental may be wrong.

Let us take, to begin with, but two of today's unquestionable authorities on the subject of the peasantry and their movements:

Barrington Moore Jr and Eric R. Wolf. These two writers, incidentally, have much in common in so far as their general points of view and
orientations toward society are concerned, so that one would expect
much agreement between them, as well as some degree of definitional firmness on the part of each. Moore states:

> it is impossible to define the word peasantry with absolute pre-
> cision because distinctions are blurred at the edges in social reality
> itself. A previous history of subordination to a landed upper class
> recognized and enforced in the laws . . . sharp cultural distinctions
> and a considerable degree of *de facto* possession of the land con-
> stitute the main distinguishing features of a peasantry.[1]

The reader should note these three characteristics: legal subordination, cultural distinctiveness and, especially, '*de facto* possession
of the land', because Wolf, in a well-known article written in the
mid-1950s, had likewise emphasised the characteristic of ownership
as being the critical one for definition.[2] But ten years later, in his
monograph *Peasants*, after referring to 'previously simple systems',
he goes on to say that peasants may be said to exist later, when the
simple systems:

> have been superseded by others in which control of the means of
> production, including the disposition of human labor, passes from
> the hands of the primary producers into the hands of groups that
> do not carry on the productive process themselves . . .

so that, 'peasants . . . are rural cultivators whose surpluses are transferred to a dominant group of rulers . . .'.[3]

Not ownership of the land, but loss of control over it – and of the
control of his own labour – seems to define the peasant (as contrasted
with Wolf's earlier article, and with Moore). Exploitation becomes
the central, defining characteristic. Yet, in Wolf's latest book, the
emphasis is on neither ownership nor exploited surpluses, and peasants
are defined as:

> populations that are existentially involved in cultivation and make
> autonomous decisions regarding the process of cultivation. The
> category is thus made to cover tenants and sharecroppers as well as

[1] Moore, op. cit., p. 111, note 1.
[2] Eric R. Wolf, 'Types of Latin American Peasantry: A Preliminary Discussion', *American Anthropologist*, vol. LVII, no. 3 (1955), pp. 452–71.
[3] Eric R. Wolf, *Peasants* (Englewood Cliffs, N.J.: Prentice-Hall, 1966), pp. 3, 4.

owner-operators as long as they are in a position to make the relevant decisions on how their crops are grown. It does not, however, include fishermen or landless laborers.[1]

There are, of course, several other characteristics which have frequently been mentioned as defining 'peasants', some of them implicit in – or even containing the germinal ideas for – one or other of the definitions we have cited above.[2] For example, Kroeber's early, classical stress that peasants are 'part-societies with part-cultures'[3] in a larger society is certainly congruent with later emphases on subordination and exploitation; and with the necessary existence of a state or of cities, beyond the peasantry. Kroeber's use of 'culture' is of course in line with all those definitions which likewise emphasise the cultural distinctiveness of peasants, including their values and perceptions, as did Redfield[4] and Foster.[5] Here we may note, however, that those who have used the concept of culture to define peasants have often thought of the peasant as living in a closed, isolated community (in which kinship played a great role), thus explicitly or implicitly contradicting those who have emphasised so much the external economic linkage, Moore and Wolf being examples.

But the difficulty with the definition of peasant society as ' in part autonomous, in part a part of a larger system' is that one never knows where the cut-off point comes. This was recognised by Erasmus, another major writer in the field, who felt, however, that this open-ended ambiguous nature of the definition could be used in a fruitful manner.[6] It will be recalled that Moore was likewise aware of 'blurring at the edges'.

The Nature of Definitions

When authors as thoughtful and as experienced in their substantive fields as are those whom we have cited differ and vacillate so much in their definition of a term (though they differ much less in its use),

[1] Eric R. Wolf, *Peasant Wars in the Twentieth Century* (New York and London: Harper & Row, 1970), p. xiv.

[2] These characteristics were discussed at some length in Henry A. Landsberger, 'The Role of Peasant Movements and Revolts in Development', in Henry A. Landsberger (ed.), *Latin American Peasant Movements* (Ithaca, N.Y.: Cornell University Press, 1969), pp. 1–4.

[3] A. L. Kroeber, *Anthropology* (New York: Harcourt, Brace, 1948), p. 284.

[4] Robert Redfield, 'The Folk Society', *American Journal of Sociology*, vol. LII (1947), 293–308.

[5] G. M. Foster, 'Peasant Society and the Image of the Limited Good', *American Anthropologist*, vol. 67 (1965), pp. 293–315.

[6] Charles Erasmus, 'Upper Limits of Peasantry and Agrarian Reform: Bolivia, Venezuela and Mexico Compared', *Ethnology*, vol. VI (1967), pp. 349–80.

then the problem is probably not located exclusively in the complexity of the facts each of them selects according to his disciplinary background – be it anthropology, sociology, or history. The difficulty probably lies in the basic approach to what a good definition, in principle, ought to look like.[1]

The difficulty in this particular instance arises, we believe, from the twin attempt (1) to classify concrete groups of human beings as being either 'in' or 'not in' some category: to type and categorise; and (2) to undertake such categorisation on the basis, preferably, of one criterion only, or as few as ever possible: ownership, or control of production process, or part-orientation to a market, or culture.

The opposite strategy is, first, to recognise that while categorisation may be indicated, yet it is not the only way to describe objects and is, in fact, less useful than thinking in terms of continuous variables. Thus, while it may be necessary to classify people as either male or female (and even here 'degree of masculinity versus femininity' has been found more useful on occasion) in other, indeed most, instances the use of typologies and categories is counter-indicated. People are not either tall or short, they have a certain height. 'Blurring' arises only if categorisation is attempted where it is not useful.'[2]

Second, a good strategy toward definition recognises that a whole set of such 'dimensions' may be necessary to characterise the phenomenon in which one is interested. While they should be kept as few as possible, it may be necessary to have a substantial number. Only when it was recognised that 'democracy' had to be defined in – at least – economic and cultural (especially, educational) as well as political terms could a modest beginning be made in a more balanced

[1] Max Black, 'Definitions, Presuppositions and Assertions', in his *Problem of Analysis* (Ithaca, N.Y.: Cornell University Press, 1954), pp. 24–45, deals with just a few of the host of problems which crop up – generally unrecognised – in formulating a definition.
[2] The reader may rest assured that we are not proposing some highly idiosyncratic innovation in a field about which we know little: epistemology. It is a mere summary, entirely unoriginal, of a position accepted as basically not subject to question. Carl G. Hempel's *Aspects of Scientific Explanation and Other Essays in the Philosophy of Science* (New York and London: Free Press and Collier-Macmillan, 1965) has sections of several essays devoted to such topics as 'From classificatory to comparative and quantitative concepts', 'Extreme types' (of which landless labourers would be an example), and how these belong to an 'early stage' in the growth of a scientific discipline' which become 'unnecessary' (p. 159), and so forth. On the essence of this point – as distinct from Hempel's more refined arguments about the nature of concepts – he is regarded as authoritative and pre-eminent. Moreover, his writings on this point go back to the early 1950s and have been accepted since that time (see his 'Fundamentals of Concept Foundation in Empirical Science', *International Encyclopedia of Unified Science*, vol. II, no. 7, pp. 1–93 (Chicago and London: University of Chicago Press, 1952). And Hempel acknowledges that he is merely elaborating the earlier ideas and terminology of Carnap.

discussion of the term, and a comparison begun of 'democracy' in the
so-called capitalist world as compared with that in the so-called
socialist countries. Indeed, the global and rather imprecise word
'democracy' tends to drop out of sight once one defines more con-
cretely in each sphere (economic, cultural and political) what he has
in mind. We think the same fate should overtake the term 'peasant'·

In sum: The epistemological starting-point for defining 'peasants'
needs to be the recognition that there are a series of important dimensions along which the positions people occupy in society can be
measured, and that these are continuous, and not of an 'either-or'
type. Attempts to categorise positions as either being 'peasant' or not
should be abandoned, and the furthest that one can fruitfully go is to
announce that he will focus attention on those 'rural cultivators' (for
on *that*, everyone is agreed) who occupy relatively low positions on
various critical dimensions. We will remove the remaining ambiguities from this last statement by addressing ourselves to the question: what seem to be the crucial dimensions?

Economic and Political Dimensions[1]

As one reads the major authors in the field, there seems to be
agreement – increasing, of late – that the key dimensions in the case
of 'the peasantry', especially for understanding their movements, are
economic and political ones. Technology and environment, rightly
analysed with great care by Wolf in his discussion of 'ecosystems',[2]
are important in determining what kind of peasantry arises. But for
that very reason they are not a part of the set of defining dimensions,
because they are among its causes, and the causes of a phenomenon
are never included in its definition. Similarly, such peculiarities of
culture as may or may not go along with being a peasant – mutual
mistrust, seeing 'the good' available in the world as limited – are
now generally regarded as being the effects of occupying a low
economic and/or political status. The possible effects of a phenomenon likewise are never included in its definition.

Now the crucial economic and political dimensions can each be
broken down into three equivalent sub-sets of dimensions. When
this is done I believe we shall automatically cover all the important

[1] The multidimensional description of status, power, etc., while perhaps seemingly
novel to some anthropologists and historians, is widely accepted in the field of sociology,
especially when it is made clear that there is *no* implication whatever that all status dimensions are equally important.
[2] Wolf, *Peasants*, esp. pp. 18–37.

criteria raised by each of the authors who have sought to define what 'the peasant' is. These three sub-dimensions are, respectively, those having to do with the control of the relevant economic and political 'inputs'; those having to do with the control of the 'transformation process' within the economy and the polity; and those having to do with the degree of benefit derived from the 'output' of each of these sectors of society.

To give an example: in the case of economic 'inputs', rural culti- vators can be measured on (1) the *amount* of the input they control (land, capital, labour); and (2) the *security* with which they control it. These are two 'sub-subdimensions' which it is well to keep apart in trying to understand peasant movements. Concerning control over the economic 'transformation process' (equivalent to Wolf's 1970 emphasis on making 'the relevant decisions on how their crops are grown'), we would convert this, too, into a 'more or less' kind of dimension. For in empirical fact peasants do not either 'make' or 'not make' relevant decisions, but may make more or fewer of them. In many parts of the world sharecroppers and tenants have often had little or nothing to say as to what crops they would grow. This was the case, for example, in the north-east of Brazil, where peasants of both kinds had to grow sugar, and where they were *forbidden* to engage in any kind of subsistence farming.[1] Once again this makes us question the very common definition of 'peasant' as being sub- stantially oriented toward subsistence farming. For surely no one would wish to exclude the 'peasant movements' of north-east Brazil, especially those of the early 1960s, from a discussion of peasant move- ments? Finally, with respect to benefiting from the economic 'out- put' of the rural economy: again it is the case that peasants can have (1) greater or less participation; and it may be (2) a more or less certain one. This is exemplified by landless labourers on modern plantations who may make up both in amount and in certainty of remuneration what they forgo on other status dimensions, in com- parison with other kinds of peasants.

Political status – surprising and novel though it will seem[2] – can be converted into dimensions very similar to economic ones. The 'resource inputs' of politics can be votes, but of course they can

[1] Ernest Feder, 'Societal Opposition to Peasant Movements', in Landsberger (ed.), op. cit., pp. 399–450, esp. pp. 428–32.
[2] We are following in very respectable footsteps, however, though we would not wish to hide behind these authors: Gabriel Almond and S. Coleman *et al.*, *The Politics of Developing Areas* (Princeton, N.J.: Princeton University Press), 1960.

also be family influence; money; the use of group values for leverage (as in the case of the élites of churches or ideologically dominant parties); and, of course, force, as in the case of the military. Peasants typically have few of these resources, just as they have few of the basic resources, or factors of production, of the economy.

As for 'transformation process': peasants can, more or less, participate in the actual formulation of political decisions, whether legislative, judicial or administrative. For us, a peasant – if one wishes to continue using the word at all, and we recommend against it – is 'more and more' of a peasant the 'less and less' he participates.

Finally, they can, more or less, benefit from the content of the decisions made – the 'output' of the polity: the tariffs and taxes approved or rejected; the employment and development programmes decided upon or not; the housing, welfare and land reform legislation enacted and adjudicated upon. Such benefits are possible, though not too likely, without the peasant's having had either political

Fig. 1. A Multidimensional Schema for the Measurement of the Economic and Political Status of Various 'Actors' and Groups including 'Low Status Rural Cultivators'.

Measured by	Economic status	Political status
I. Possession of critical 'resource inputs': (1) Amount (2) Security	Land Capital Managerial ability Labour quantity and skills	Votes Force, and threat of force Family influence Manipulation of affective 'value symbols': e.g., 'supernaturally ordained', 'basic human right' Political and adminstrative skills and knowledge
II. Participation in control over 'transformation processes'	Degree of control over: Combination of resources to be used, inputs to be bought and where Type and quantity of crops to be planted, marketing of the output, price	Degree of control over formulation and implementation of governmental policies in the economic, educational, political spheres, etc.
III. Participation in benefits, i.e., in 'output': (1) Amount (2) Security	As between low-status rural cultivators and all other beneficiaries including consumers, middlemen and the state, as well as landlords or employers: how is the yield from the product divided?	How far do economic policies and their administration, in executive, legislative and judicial branches, favour low-status cultivators? How far do educational policies and institutions favour low-status rural cultivators, etc.

resources or his having participated in politics. In Chile most recently, and also in parts of Bolivia and parts of Venezuela earlier, a good many observers believed that land reform came well before the bulk of the peasantry was really pressing for it. Working classes, too, have been granted benefits before they voted or sat in parliament. Sometimes this has been done to forestall their pressing for these rights, sometimes to assure their allegiance in advance, because it was recognised that they soon would become a political factor in their own right.

What do we gain and lose by this approach? First and foremost, the use of these dimensions permits the accurate, detailed description of the almost infinite variety of peasant positions, the difference between one kind of peasant and another, on the importance of which Wolf correctly places so much emphasis in his *Peasant Wars*.[1] This problem of distinguishing between peasants, that is within the peasantry, has always been so much more important (for example, in accounting for susceptibility to organisation) than the problem of 'delimiting' the peasantry. Our approach to the definitional problem puts the emphasis where the problem exists.

Moreover, because it consists of various dimensions, each of which implies a 'higher' versus 'lower', or 'more' versus 'less' aspect, this definitional approach automatically lends itself to making both qualitative (horizontal') and quantitative distinctions. This, too, seems to be congruent with the inherent nature of the subject-matter. The sharecropper, with his uncertain as well as reduced economic benefits, can at times be distinguished from the landless labourer, since the former may indeed have some control over the process of production while the latter by definition does not. The literature in the field often makes this kind of distinction categorically. But in many instances sharecroppers do not in fact have such control any more than do landless labourers, so that the use of even a relatively narrow concept like 'sharecropper', implying homogeneity within that group, may obscure reality as much as the use of the broader term 'peasant'. It is better to describe the real position in detail through the use of universally applicable, common dimensions, than to give it a categorical, misleading label.

No doubt there will be many who will find it difficult to accept a definitional approach which does not separate the landless labourer from everyone else. Provided the *dimensions*, which we think to be

[1] Wolf, op. cit., pp. x–xii.

really enlightening, are employed, we have no objections to adopting the linguistic convention of refusing to apply the word 'peasant' to landless labourers. The latter we regarded as, precisely, a linguistic convention, and therefore unimportant from an analytical point of view, either way. Whether one wants to include three-wheeled vehicles in the term 'automobile' really makes no difference, provided one does studies of greater or lesser accident rates, pollution emission, and cost per passenger for vehicles of different prices, size and durability.

In our scheme landless labourers (who, incidentally, may differ greatly among themselves)[1] are simply groups at a zero point in the control of the key resources of land and capital (though not necessarily at that point either in human skills or in managerial capacity). This lack of control may possibly make a critical difference with respect to such consequences as organisability and reaction to international market fluctuations. But whether or not, and how, it distinguishes him from other rural cultivators of generally low status is something best settled by empirical research. This implies including him (by whatever name) in the purview of the investigator, rather than excluding him simply on an assumption that differences exist.

It will be found that most major writers have had to include, and have in fact included, landless labourers within their purview, whatever name they have used. In the present volume, for example, Alexandrov subtly contrasts labourers with small owners, just as he contrasts the latter with sharecroppers and tenants. Huizer and Stavenhagen seem to regard the problems of those peasants who have some land, but an insufficient amount of it, as well as an insufficient amount of credit and technical aid, as one from a list of problems in which that of the growing mass of landless labourers is merely another, though perhaps the most severe one.

In another famous peasant movement situation, that of north-east Brazil in the early 1960s, to omit consideration of landless peasants would have been analytically very counterproductive. One key determinant of that tangled situation was precisely that some outside organising groups made an early decision to concentrate on that group, while others, who at first decided to ignore them and concentrate on tenants, later changed their minds and, as a result, collided with the

[1] Cf. Arthur L. Stinchcomb, 'Agricultural Enterprise and Rural Class Relations', *American Journal of Sociology*, vol. 67 (1961), pp. 165–76. Stinchcomb's approach is implicitly the same as ours: no greater categorical distinctions are made between landless 'peasants' and all others, than within the latter very heterogeneous, category.

other organising groups.[1]   To take another example, from working-class history: the new factory workers of the early nineteenth century may have been more or less organisable than the old craftsmen, established but endangered (carpenters, printers, tailors). And each of these was certainly very different from the others.   But both new and old would be regarded as part of the working classes, and, more important, the analyst would in fact keep his eye on the two groups.

The utility of continuous dimensions becomes even more apparent when one considers that the analysis of vertical stratification within the peasantry – the relation of those better-off to the worse-off – has often been a central issue for those who have concerned themselves with peasant movements and uprisings.   The writings of Marxist-Leninist writers are here of great interest.   In our opinion rightly, they have had no hesitation in using the term broadly, but they have specified crucial subcategories – easily convertible into dimensions. The writings of Lenin himself, and of Mao Tse-tung are of quite exceptional interest in this respect.   We can, of course, already find in Marx himself a peripheral interest in stratification within the peasantry, and in the likely changes–over-time in that stratification. Marx predicted that agriculture, too, would become capitalistic. Consequently property, for the same kinds of technological and economic reasons operative in industry, would also become highly concentrated and this would have the same result as in industry, including the generation of a propertyless, increasingly class-conscious, rural proletariat.

But understandably, it was a second generation of Marxists, above all Lenin and Mao Tse-tung, when faced with various tactical questions about revolution in societies more predominantly rural than England, Germany and France in the second half of the nineteenth century, who began to feel the need for a more precise delineation of the rural situation.   Given our interest here in defining which social groups might and which ones might not be fruitfully included in our study, the most important characteristic of the writings of these and of other authors writing in the Marxian tradition is that they invariably include a wide spectrum of groups in their analysis.

---

[1] For accounts of this complex situation, in which all relevant groups have to be considered in juxtaposition, see Cynthia N. Hewitt, 'Brazil': The Peasant Movement of Pernambuco, 1961–64', in Landsberger (ed.), *Latin American Peasant Movements*, op. cit. pp. 374–98; also, Clodomir Santos de Moraes, 'Peasant Leagues in Brazil', in Rodolfo Stavenhagen (ed.), *Agrarian Problems and Peasant Movements in Latin America* (Garden City, N.Y.: Doubleday Anchor, 1970), pp. 453–502

Lenin, already in the 1890s, saw clearly that quite apart from land-lords farming with both tenant and wage labour, there were three groups – by now a classic division – within the peasantry itself: (1) the well-to-do peasantry (including kulaks) who may themselves employ some wage labour but in any case could produce a substantial market-able surplus; (2) the 'middle' peasant, who is a tenant and/or has a very small plot of his own, in either case producing some but only a small surplus; and (3) the 'poor' peasant, who lives chiefly by selling his labour and is therefore a proletarian and a part of the toiling masses.[1]

Lenin wrote copiously on the agrarian question during the first decade of the twentieth century and up to the 1917 revolution, particu-larly on the complex issue of how much land was to be redistributed, and in what form. But in addition, and as a second topic of great importance, he sought to explore the position the three sub-classes of the peasantry would take, first, vis-à-vis the coming bourgeois revolu-tion to eliminate the last vestiges of feudalism and of disguised serfdom, and later, what position they would take relative to the revolutionary struggle for socialism against the bourgeoisie.[2] The distinction between poor, middle and rich peasants was maintained throughout his writings both before and after the revolution, with particular emphasis on the two extreme groups, since the middle peasant was expected to disappear. The failure of the Social Revolutionary (Populist) Party to see and analyse clearly these distinctions, and that party's implicit insistence on conceptualising the peasantry as a homo-geneous group, was one of the features distinguishing it from both the Bolshevik and Menshevik wings of the Russian Social-Democratic Labour Party. As Jackson points out in his chapter in the present volume, a similar homogeneous image of the peasantry pervaded the peasant parties of Eastern Europe between the wars, and this unrealism was one of the causes of their downfall.

Mao Tse-tung likewise became interested very early in his career in sub-classes within the peasantry. Indeed, according to Schram, his interest stems from a period during the early 1920s when he had not yet fully mastered the writings of Lenin, and while still a member of the 'left' of the Kuomintang (K.M.T.). Mao likewise omitted no one from the general category of 'peasant'. In his earliest systematic essay

---

[1] V. I. Lenin, *Development of Capitalism in Russia* (1899), as cited in Anna Rochester, *Lenin on the Agrarian Question* (New York: International Publishers, 1942) p. 17.

[2] E.g., in V. I. Lenin, *To the Rural Poor* (1905), as cited in Anna Rochester, op. cit., p. 28 et seq.

on the topic, he speaks of 'our work of organising the peasantry' as involving the gathering of 'five kinds of peasants into a single organisation: the peasant landholders, semi-landholders, sharecroppers, poor peasants, and farm-labourers and handicraftsmen'.[1] Each of the above groups was delineated with some care by Mao, and among the poorer sectors it was noted that there was overlap: that semi-landowners, for example, would of necessity also try to sell their labour or rent from large landowners, since the land they owned was no more than half of that needed for living. This breakdown was used by Mao not only for purposes of long-term analysis and policy formulation, but also for arriving at more short-term tactical conclusions, one of which was the desirability of avoiding alienating even the landowning peasants during the initial stages of the revolution.

More recent writers, Wolf and Moore among them, have also taken these divisions into account, and likewise include all rural low-status groups within their analysis. Their conclusions concerning specific topics, such as the relative militancy of various subgroups (to which we will refer at greater length in a subsequent section), may well differ from those of Lenin and Mao. For example, Wolf[2] sees the 'middle peasantry' as the most revolutionary, while for Mao it was the lowest strata. Moore decides, too, to diverge from Mao's position on this: 'The notion that a large rural proletariat of landless labor is a potential source of insurrection and revolution may be somewhat closer to the truth,' he says, but goes on: 'As a general explanation, this conception simply will not do.'[3]

There is, however, *de facto* agreement, even if not always explicit and conscious, that 'all rural cultivators of low economic and political status' be initially included in the concept 'peasant', and that differences within the peasantry then be analysed carefully by separating various economic and political subdivisions from each other.

Including *all low-status rural* cultivators under the term 'peasant', and using *various dimensions and sub-dimensions* to describe that status, enables one to delineate clearly, and to compare, three types of situations which have so often played a role in stimulating peasant (as well as working-class) discontent: (1) status inconsistency; (2) de-

---

[1] Mao Tse-tung, 'An analysis of the various classes of the Chinese peasantry and their attitudes toward revolution', extracted from an article of the same title in *Chung-kuo nung-min*, vol. I, no. 1 (Jan 1926) pp. 13–20, as reprinted in Stuart R. Schram, *The political thought of Mao Tse-tung*, rev. ed. (New York: Praeger, 1969) pp. 236–46 (p. 246).
[2] Eric R. Wolf, *Peasant Wars*, op. cit., pp. 290–2.
[3] Moore, op. cit., p. 455.

privation relative to some other comparable group; and (3) deprivation relative to one's own past status, or one's expected present status,
or a feeling of threat concerning one's future status.

(1) *'Status inconsistency'* [1] – a relatively favourable position on one
characteristic while remaining low on another – was, as Hilton and I
note in our papers, probably one of the immediate causes (note the
qualification) of peasant unrest in England in 1381, and in France in
1789. In both cases improvement in the peasant's lot had occurred
in many respects, but precisely this made the remaining disabilities
like marriage taxes and labour services seem all the more irksome.
(2) An unfavourable position relative to others – *'relative deprivation'* –
played at least some role in Mexico where, as Huizer and Stavenhagen
note, increasing contact with the United States enabled the peasant to
compare his lot with that of his neighbours to the north and, as a
result, become dissatisfied. Finally, (3) *deprivation relative to past, or
present-expected, or feared-future status,* is a common theme in many
of the essays of this volume. In particular, real loss during the preceding period and the threat of continued, uncontrollable loss in the
future gave rise to desperate reactions in the case of the Pugachev
revolt described by Longworth.

Making the concept 'peasant' broadly inclusive, and carefully
analysing the peasant's status on a series of separate economic and
political dimensions (as well as cultural ones like education, religion,
and prestige) will be fruitful, we believe, for studies deliberately and
systematically designed to be comparative.

III. 'MOVEMENTS' AND THEIR DEFINITION

The second definitional problem concerns the concept of 'movement'.
About this, more than the previous one, sociologists are likely to feel
strongly, while anthropologists and historians have been involved in
the controversy over the use of the word 'peasant'.

In the context of low-status groups such as peasants, we mean by
a movement any *collective reaction to such low status.* Here, again, it is
our position: first, that a broad, inclusive approach is desirable; and,
second, that the issue should not be posed in terms of whether some
assemblage 'is' or 'is not' a movement, but to describe it using certain

[1] This problem is extensively discussed in Gerhard E. Lenski's *Power and Privilege* (New
York: McGraw-Hill, 1966).

dimensions in order to go on to analyse their separate and joint causes, their interrelationships, and their effects.

Specifically, we propose using these four dimensions:

1. The degree to which there is a common consciousness of sharing the same fate.
2. The degree to which action is collective both in (*a*) extent of persons involved, and (*b*) in degree of co-ordination and organisation of action (up to a high point of being organised in complex ways).
3. The extent to which the action is 'instrumental': designed to achieve a goal outside of itself; and the degree to which it is 'expressive': undertaken because of the gratification inherent in the action itself.
4. The degree to which the reaction is based exclusively on low socio-economic and political status, as against being one in which other issues – religious, national – play a genuine, independent part.

Degree of Consciousness

The role of the concept of 'consciousness' in the movements of peasants is obviously going to be as critical as it has long been re-cognised to be in the movements of industrial workers. Marx and Engels, and later Lenin, were thinkers who most clearly recognised that the existence of certain movements, and especially the nature of their goals, were intimately related to the awareness of their members; and, further, that such awareness was problematic. Objective simi-larity of objective circumstances, and especially the physical proximity of factory life, and the 'emiseration' which could be expected from capitalist competition and ever-deepening crises: all of these would make workers aware of their shared fate and their common enemy. But, so Marxian thinking runs, the organisations they were likely to create – the trade unions, and hence the thinking of their individual members – were quite likely to take an insufficiently broad view of the causes of their plight and of the need for a fundamental revolution to remedy it. While potentially, and in fact also initially, unions are invaluable in increasing working-class consciousness, they are likely to be satisfied at a later stage with mere improvements in wages and work-ing conditions; and they are likely to ignore the needs of weaker parts of the working class who are unable to organise themselves, and so forth.[1]

Clearly, this kind of issue is equally relevant to the study of the

---

[1] Alexander Lozovsky, *Marx and Trade Unions* (London: Lawrence, 1935).

collective reaction of peasants to their particular position. The first
dimension to study would therefore be a rough assessment of *the
number of peasants* who *might* be conscious of the communality of their
problems, and the *quality* of that consciousness (e.g. is there a vision
of a societal system as a whole?) as compared with the number who
are thus conscious, and the highest level of quality possible.

Degree of Collectiveness of Action

The essence of a peasant movement is 'collective' (i.e., similar)
reaction to low status. Action may, however, be similar without
being co-ordinated. Thus, in many places – among them, countries
of eastern Europe before World War I – reaction has taken the form
of migration, rather than a frontal attempt to improve the existing
situation. While such migration may be a highly individual act, it
becomes more collective when each family group is influenced by
awareness that others, too, are migrating; and reaches a highly collective form if the group constituting a whole village migrates, as
Longworth points out was frequently the case in Russia. While it is
not our concern in this volume to deal to any extent with collective
reactions of this avoidance kind, it should be made clear that they are
to be regarded as one form of peasant movement (there is an unfortunate word-play here), and included in the general category.

The extreme, or 'high point' of this dimension occurs when co-
ordination of tasks and division of labour and some assignment of
authority is made explicit, not only among local family groups –
'simple organisations' – but when several such simple groups are co-
ordinated to form 'complex organisations'.

As we already indicated in our introductory remarks to this section,
measurement of 'degree of collectiveness' would, if one were to be
exact about it, take into account separately the *extensiveness* of collective action (of all peasants who could be reacting in the same way,
how many are doing so?); and the degree of *explicitness of organisation*
(of all those who are reacting in the same way, what proportion is
deliberately co-ordinating its reactions with those of others?). Both
of these are measures of the size of a movement, and it has long been
a convention in sociology not to regard as a movement any reaction
unless it is 'large-scale' and 'widespread'.[1] But instead of using some
arbitrary cut-off point for 'large-scale' (which would be absurd, and

---

[1] Kurt Lang and Gladys Lang, *Collective Dynamics* (New York: Thomas Crowell,
1961) p. 490.

scientifically quite unnecessary), it is best simply to regard 'size' as another one – or, as we have indicated, two – of these 'more or less' dimensions. Thus one does not attempt to regard certain collective reactions as being sufficiently widespread to warrant the use of the term 'movement' and others as too small, but adopts a 'more or less' position.

Again, labels should not be mistaken for reality. At first glance, the existence of regular peasant parties participating in parliaments might seem to indicate a good deal of organisation, certainly more than that of a movement like Pugachev's. But as Galaj makes amply clear in his discussion of the peasant parties of inter-war Poland, and as Molnár and Pekmez show in their description of the International in Spain, written constitutions and by-laws may be very different from organisational life. The rather loose and unstructured relationships between members and parties, the absence of paid officials and the wide range of activities which were quite spontaneously engaged in may make such a party *in fact* little better organised than a more 'typical' uninstitutionalised movement. And the opposite situation has been cited just above: the migration of families, which, though appearing to be a quite individualistic reaction is in fact, if not organised, at least a case of being influenced by the similar behaviour of others.

'Instrumental versus Expressive Orientation' and the Question of Rationality

A second tradition in sociology is to categorise even relatively formal voluntary associations (let alone collective behaviour with even less structure, such as 'movements' often are) as being *either* 'expressive' *or* 'instrumental'.

'Expressive' behaviour in collectivities is said to occur when members seek gratification in the very process of acting as members. These gratifications may be of a 'positive' kind – the sociability and recognition inherent in getting together – or they may be of a 'negative' kind. In the realm of peasant movements, an example is the *jacquerie*, a term originally used to name the revolt of French peasants in 1358, now used generically to describe peasant uprisings in which the prime motive is reputed to be to gain immediate relief from pent-up frustrations through destruction of property and the commission of violence against persons.

Various social gratifications are known to play a part, whether major or minor, in attracting the members of industrial trade unions to be more or less active. There is no reason to suppose that such motives might not also play *some* part in holding peasant movements together.

'Instrumental', on the other hand, is the adjective applied when an association or movement seeks goals which lie outside their own immediate activities, and where the activities are engaged in primarily because of the end result they will achieve: a change in the terms of land tenure, or higher wages.

There has been a strong tendency on the part of sociologists and social psychologists to see social movements, if not governed entirely by emotions, at least as possessing a strong irrational element: 'short-circuiting' in the logic of their belief system, as Smelser has put it, making it a defining characteristic of all collective behaviour, including the kind of social movement of concern to us here.[1]

We propose that these two characteristics be treated *not* in the way in which they usually are apprehended: namely, as the two opposed poles of a single continuum, so that the more instrumentally oriented an act or an entire movement is the less expressive it is bound to be. It is our suggestion that these be regarded, rather, as two quite separate dimensions. Even in the same act, expressive as well as instrumental elements may be present. Peasants burning cadastral rolls may admittedly be relieving their frustrations. But, simultaneously they may be very rationally destroying the landowner's evidence of ownership, and frightening him into abandoning his land. Even when both elements are not present in the same act – and often they are not – it is still very likely that a movement which in general is instrumentally oriented toward changing land tenure, rental and labour practices may on occasion have episodes of irrational hostility as well as moments of emotional, positive *cameraderie*. In this, peasants are no different from any other reputedly rational individuals. Certainly, peasant movements cannot be limited to those which have unusually severe 'short-circuits' in their belief systems, or are unusually addicted to activities immediately gratifying.

Low Status as the Movement's Basis

Finally, in defining a peasant movement as a collective reaction to low status, we have to recognise that a certain historical movement, though it may have been made up largely of peasants, may also have

[1] Neil J. Smelser, *Theory of Collective Behaviour* (New York: Free Press of Glencoe, 1963) p. 71.

other motives as a basis than reacting to low status. Nationalist motives may be at work, as in the case of the Croatian Peasant Party in the inter-war years; or religious motives may be present, as in Slovakia: both of these are described in this volume by Jackson.

The appropriate analytical task is, of course, not merely that of keeping these elements 'distinct', but to attempt to answer questions like these: To what extent is the national and the class question really the same, as in the case of expatriate plantation owners in Algeria and Kenya? To what extent, even when not the same, does the national or religious issue mobilise the peasants to that critical level necessary for action, in a way in which internal economic issues alone might not have been able to do, as some have maintained was the case in both China and Yugoslavia?[1]

With this we close our discussion of the four dimensions to describe collective reactions to low status: degree of consciousness; extent of similarity of reaction and degree of organisation; the 'instrumentality' and 'expressiveness' of reactions; and the degree to which a movement is based upon low status as distinct from other stimuli. There are certain points with respect to consciousness to be added when we consider movement goals, as will be seen below.

IV. PEASANT MOVEMENTS; SUMMARY OF A FRAMEWORK FOR THEIR ANALYSIS

We come now to the framework which we asked our authors to bear in mind in analysing their cases. It is presented in this section in relatively condensed form easily viewed as a totality. We make this account brief chiefly because finer points are discussed at greater length in the subsequent sections of this chapter (sections V through VIII). There, the authors' findings are compared with the framework, and we wish to avoid repetition. In any case, the framework and its hypotheses as submitted to the authors is available elsewhere, where it had been 'tested' by the author mostly against Latin American cases though already also, to some extent, against European and Asian experiences.[2] Obviously we could not expect all authors to pursue

[1] Chalmers Johnson, *Peasant Nationalism and Communist Power* (Standford, California: Standford University Press, 1962).
[2] Henry A. Landsberger, 'The Role of Peasants Movements and Revolts in Development' in Landsberger (ed.), *Latin American Peasants Movements*, op. cit., chapter 1. pp. 1–61, esp. pp. 22–61. A somewhat shortened version appears in the *Bulletin of the International Institute for Labour Studies*, no. 4, pp. 8–85.

exhaustively every one of the questions we posed there. Material such as Hobsbawm's on banditry does not lend itself to it too well in principle (though we are able to use a great deal of his material, as the reader will see), and in other instances, notably the medieval movements, the material was not available. Furthermore, intellectuals are not noted for their willingness to follow patterns planned by others, especially those working in the humanities and social sciences. In view of all of this, it is astonishing how many of the authors (e.g. Jackson and Longworth) were able to structure their contributions so as to follow the framework quite explicitly and in great detail; others in a somewhat looser form; while all essays in fact touch on the major points we suggested, whether they were formally so structured or not.

A. *Societal changes preceding the establishment of a peasant movement.* The beginning of a peasant movement not only in itself represents a change, but is the consequence of preceding changes as is, indeed, any historical event. From our own previous knowledge of various movements, it seemed advisable to ask authors to look for the following distinct kinds of changes which may, of course, not only occur simultaneously, but each may produce one or more of the others:

(a) Short-term precipitating events – a lost war, a new tax, a series of disastrous harvests – as distinct from long-term changes in social, economic or political structure: the decline of a feudally based aristocracy; the opening of commercial possibilities in agriculture; centralising tendencies in the national government.

(b) Changes which in the first place affect the class dominating the peasant and are only then passed on to the peasant (exemplified by the declining status of Peruvian hacendados in the *sierra* as compared with the semi-industrial plantation of the coast), as distinct from changes which affect the peasant directly: the introduction of new techniques and equipment which cause him to be left behind because he cannot afford them.

(c) Changes in the economic sector, as distinct from political changes, such as, for instance, the spread of the vote to middle classes stimulating peasant demands for the same right.

(d) Objective changes as distinct from subjective changes. The former concept is obvious. The latter refers to changes in aspirations, or in ideologies which at the least are necessary bridges between an objective change and an individual's reaction to it.

They also may occur independently of objective changes, as in the case of the spread of rising consumption aspirations.

Our own inclination at the time of drawing up the framework was to think that the most likely stimulus to a peasant movement would be a long-term (cf. (a) above) economic (c) decline in the position of some landed elite (b), leading to a squeeze on the peasantry. The reader will see below that we now believe certain other combinations to be equally likely.

B. *The goals and ideologies of the movement.* If low status along various status dimensions is the essence of being a peasant, and his movements are a reaction to his position, then crucial questions clearly are: what kinds of improvements do peasants seek, and how are these related to the nature of the changes preceding and stimulating the movement? These goals are generally connected with a broader view of society – how it functions and how it ought to function – which the peasant holds: his ideology. Thus, goals and ideology are best studied together. The five dimensions we asked the authors to bear in mind were these:

(a) The *breadth of goals* which the movement set itself. By this we mean to draw attention to the fact that while some movements concern themselves only with economic improvements – perhaps only with greater participation in the 'output' of the system, others press also for improvements in the political sphere (obtaining the right to vote freely), the cultural sphere (better education), etc.

We expected that the more the social institutions confronting the peasant were themselves interconnected – so that in order to tackle one, they all had to be dealt with – the broader would be the movement's goals.

(b) The *depth of goals*: How much change is sought along each of the status dimensions involved? To move away from the terminology of sociology, how revolutionary are the aims of the movement?

(c) Who is expected to benefit from the changes sought: how *parochial* are the aims? how *cosmopolitan*? It is particularly notable that in peasant movements the aim, however drastic, is formulated often only in local terms, just as industrial or regional trade unions may fight only for their constituents. The conditions under which such a parochial '*self-orientation*' occurred, as contrasted with a more altruistic '*collectivity orientation*', was to be explored.

In addition:

(d) Goals were expected to *vary both over time*, and *as between sub-groups*, especially between leaders and followers. Authors were asked to speculate why this might have been so if, indeed, it had occurred. We hypothesised, in particular, that radicalisation would occur if narrow, shallow goals met with frustration, and also if there were accord with any more general radicalisation of the social climate.

(e) The *clarity of goals* also seemed to vary considerably between movements. We thought this likely to be a reflection of the general level of education of the participants, but also related to whether there had or had not been some previously existing state of affairs – a 'golden age', real or imagined – to serve as a reference-point for the formulation of concrete demands.

C. The means and methods of the movement. More or less the same issues arise in analysing the means adopted by a peasant movement as for its goals. Here, too, there is the question of how *broad* a range of methods is employed (political organisation as well as economic pressure? self-education?). There is, too, the issue of the *'radicalism'* of means: is there a consideration of methods which the dominant group would define as illegitimate, especially violence? or only of those which would be regarded as legitimate? Once again, too, the question of *changes over time*, and *differences between sub-groups*, especially between leaders and followers, arises. It was our hypothesis that radicalisation of means would occur, just like radicalisation of goals, only after much frustration, and after violence had first been used by the dominant groups. Our conclusions about this appear in our summary of the cases in section vi, below.

D. The mass base of the movement. We have already dealt in the section on the definition of peasants (ii) with the critical issue of whether the better-off, the medium or the lowest subgroup among the peasantry is most susceptible to form the base of a movement, and also with the question: what are some of the conditions (status deprivation, etc.) under which they become active? We will therefore not deal with this topic again below, and note here only that it was one of the central questions in the framework submitted to the authors. Our hypothesis had been that the lowest groups would be proportionally under-represented, especially among the leaders of peasant movements.

E. Conditions facilitating organisation. Although groups of peasants may be deeply dissatisfied, such discontent may not be translated into behaviour – the kind of collective reaction we have defined as a movement – unless certain other conditions are present. Some of these are of a social-psychological kind, while others are more socio-political, or structural. Such factors as previous consciousness-arousing experience (service in armies would be one), or a history of communal co-operative effort might favour common reaction to low status; certain other social-psychological factors imputed to the peasantry might make such a reaction more difficult. We asked authors to explore such facilitating and retarding conditions.

F. The allies of peasant movements. Peasants, like industrial workers, have often been wooed by other groups who have had their own quarrel with the *status quo*, or with whatever changes might or might not have taken place in it. Such allies may bring much help, may indeed be essential to the establishment of a peasant movement. But they may also prove fickle in the heat of battle, may impart additional divisions, especially where internal unity is not very strong, and may in any case alter the nature of the movement, perhaps radicalising and broadening its goals. Our authors were asked which groups, in the cases they were examining, could be regarded as the peasants' allies; and in what ways they contributed to the strength of the movement and in what ways they might have weakened or at least changed it.

Similarly, consideration was to be given to the enemies of the movement, though this is generally a far less complicated matter.

G. Conditions of success and failure. Even when discontent eventuates in action, action does not, of course, necessarily imply success. On the contrary, success for movements which consist of individuals who are by definition low in economic and political resources is *a priori* likely to be rare. Establishing both the degree and the causes of success – and of the failure – of each movement are matters of great interest, and we asked contributors to attempt the task of doing so.

In short, we asked contributors to consider: (a) the sources and nature of the tensions, both objective and subjective, out of which a peasant movement might grow; (b) the conditions favouring the crystallisation of peasant discontent into collective action and protest, i.e., a movement; (c) the nature of that movement – its goals, means, ideology, membership, leadership and structure; and (d) the determinants of its success and failure, particularly in view of the allies of which it disposes, and the antagonists it faces.

A final note. Throughout the subsequent discussion, we will frequently compare the characteristics of peasant movements with those of urban working class movements, bringing out both the similarities and differences between these two. Both kinds of movements are based on large but disadvantaged classes, hence considerable similarity might be expected. Nevertheless, the worker's urban location, his association with an economic sector which is generally expanding, and his rather different relationship to the means of production (though this may be argued and certainly varies from time to time and place to place) are likely to produce differences in the movements in which he participates, as compared with those of the peasant. We hope readers will find that the comparison will shed light on both kinds of movements.

Indeed, we will also make occasional references to the movements of black people in the United States not, obviously, because we consider them to be 'peasants' or 'workers', but because all three kinds of movements have the underlying similarity of being based on persons of low socio-economic and political status, and their reactions to that status and to structural changes. This similarity in starting-points leads in turn to some enlightening similarities in the movements themselves. None of this denies that there are differences, equally profound. As the nineteenth-century economist and philosopher Jevons remarked: 'almost every classification which is proposed in the early stages of science will be found to break down as the deeper similarities of the objects come to be detected'.[1]

V. PEASANT UNREST AND SOCIETAL CHANGE

There is now substantial agreement that peasant uprisings are (a) invariably, but (b) in no way simply, related to economic and political changes far more profound than those affecting the peasantry alone: more profound even than developments in the agricultural sector as a whole. Changes occur in the objective conditions which govern society as a whole, and largely as a result of these changes there occur others which ultimately produce the kinds of status incongruities, relative status losses and the threat of further losses to which we have

[1] W. S. Jevons, *The Principles of Science* (London, 1892) p. 691, as cited in Abraham Kaplan, *The Conduct of Inquiry: Methodology for Behavioral Science* (San Francisco, California: Chandler Publishing Company, 1964) p. 53.

drawn attention previously. These discontents are, then, the immediate but of course not the more profound cause of unrest.

One is tempted to find a single, universally present ultimate cause, but unfortunately, this would seem to be mistaken. The economic integration of the society under consideration into a larger, possibly international, market; the consequent drive to commercialise agriculture; and the subsequent encroachment on peasant lands and peasant rights and status in general: this sequence is certainly the most promising candidate for the position of 'universal ultimate cause'. Asia as analysed by Alexandrov would be one example. Mexico as analysed by Huizer and Stavenhagen is no doubt among the classic examples. Its integration into world trade during the *Porfiriato* before 1910 resulted in the growth of a relatively small but wealthy farming elite (part of it foreign) engaged in the cultivation of sugar, cotton and other commercial crops. Opportunity tempted this élite to encroach ever more on the traditional lands of peasants, and, taking Morelos as an example, the uprising of Zapata occurred. How ancient and widespread the provocative effects of commercialisation are can be seen from the fact that Hilton reports a very similar situation in northern Italy in the early fourteenth century (the struggle between Fra Dolcino and the bishop of Vercelli).

But while this is no doubt one pattern of structural change, it is not the only one. Nor is it by itself sufficient. That commercialisation by itself is not sufficient is evident from the work of Barrington Moore, who brings out quite clearly that it is the nature of the reaction of the élite to its opportunity that is critical in determining whether or not there is large-scale unrest. It is not even the mere seizure of the opprotunity as such. The English landed aristocracy of the sixteenth and seventeenth centuries seized the opportunity firmly and simply drove out the peasantry. The East German Junkers successfully subjugated their peasants. In neither case did discontent – which surely there was – result in revolt or other collective forms of status unrest.[1]

Among the crucially needed additional conditions seem to have been structural characteristics such as:

(1) the conversion of the landowners into pure rent, tax and service collectors not engaging in farming or performing any other useful function apparent to the peasant;
(2) their failure to perform compensatory services for the peasantry,

[1] Moore, op. cit., p. 467.

e.g., protection: thus the relationship becomes purely one of economic exploitation;
(3) their generally becoming effete, weak and functionless relative to a growing central government (the cases of Russia and France);
(4) the partial survival of peasant communities 'damaged but intact', as Moore says,[1] which was true of Mexico, Algeria, the Cossacks, Spain, China – in fact, all cases in the present volume and those cited elsewhere.

Whatever the additional necessary conditions may be, commercialisation of agriculture leading to landlord encroachment is certainly a frequently underlying cause of revolt. Yet it is not, after all, even a truly necessary one. In the case of the Pugachev revolt as portrayed by Longworth, for example, no really major, dramatic change towards commercial crops seems to have played a part, although a long-term trend had begun several centuries earlier and was continuing. Nor does commercialisation seem to have played a major role in Poland specifically, as described by Galaj, nor in Eastern Europe generally as portrayed by Jackson either before World War I or after. Again, commercialisation had of course occurred, but much earlier, and landlord encroachment as a result of it was at the time of concern to us not a major factor in peasant unrest.

If one were to focus on landlord encroachment regardless of ultimate cause, thereby including the landlord's rising consumption aspirations or his response to negative pressures on him, e.g. for taxes, not only his response to positive opportunity, then certainly more cases would be included. For example, we could then account better for the encroachment of eighteenth-century Russian and fourteenth-century British landlords, squeezed by their Tsars and Kings respectively because of costly wars, and squeezed, too, by their own rising consumption aspirations as was the French nobility in the eighteenth century. (The peasants of Russia and England were also directly taxed more severely by the Crown: a substantial contributing factor in each case. But this, too, is not a matter of commercialisation.)

Very often, as Hilton points out, the structural change consisted of a shift of power within the elites. Such was the case of south-west Germany before the Peasant War of 1525. There, the higher-level territorial princes began to assert themselves over lower-level knights for reasons which had more to do with the technology of warfare, the

[1] Ibid., p. 460.

growth of administrative bureaucracies and of towns engaged in (non-agricultural) trade than it had to do with any commercialisation of agriculture. Agriculture in south-west Germany had been commercial for some time.

Nevertheless, these are all cases in which, as Hilton says, the basic differences of interest between landlord and peasant were involved and in which there occurred a change in the delicate balance of exploitation versus service.

But there remain a substantial number of instances which even this broadened net will not catch. In much of Eastern Europe between World War I and World War II, landlordism simply was not a problem, or, at least, it was not the main target on which the movement focused. (Of course, in other parts of Eastern Europe, e.g., Hungary, it *was* a problem.) Peasant movements, as Galaj and Jackson point out, were then not so much anti-landlord as anti-urban. There was indeed fear of encroachment on peasant power and economic status, but the threat was seen as coming from the town and from industrialism and urban capitalism, not from landlords.

There are a number of cases in which the encroachment on the peasant stemmed not from major changes within the society concerned, but from major changes in the relation between the society and other societies. These are the cases – China, Algeria, Asia as analysed by Alexandrov – in which nationalism fused with economic concerns. These are the cases in which the peasant's status was threatened by foreigners either semi-permanently (the French in relation to Algeria) or temporarily (the Japanese invaders in relation to China and the Germans in relation to Yugoslavia). The threat was either direct, i.e., through physical presence in the rural community, or indirect, through domination of the central Government (Czechs over Slovaks, Serbs over Croats).

Some allowance must be made for the independent effect of changes in ideology, values and aspirations. While these are generally roughly correlated with changes in social structure, they will also have some degree of independence from such changes. In particular, the world-wide spread of the values of the equality of man, and of the right of all to happiness and a minimal degree of material comfort, have surely played a role in stimulating unrest among the peasantry since the beginning of this century, as among other groups as well.

Thus, we lean towards a formulation which is, we recognise, distressingly general and vague in so far as the relation between peasant discontent and basic, structural societal change is concerned. It is true that such change precedes movements. As Wolf puts it, the peasant arises against wrongs which are 'but parochial manifestations of great social dislocation'.[1] But it need not be the introduction of commercial agriculture. It may well be a major change not in economic structure at all but in the political, e.g., a change towards the centralisation of power, perhaps related to external warfare or to change in the technology of war and only rather indirectly linked, if at all, to any basic changes in the productive system. Indeed, the change may be one in which the whole society moves in relation to others, of course accompanied by economic effects and partly economically caused, but with very complex causal interrelationships between the political, economic and ideological (i.e., the rise of nationalist sentiment).

Finally, we would not even wish to link peasant discontent only to changes which can be called 'developmental'. In the abstract, a meaningful definition can certainly be given to the latter concept. It is usually defined in terms of greater institutional adaptability and flexibility; the capacity to perform a wide range of functions; greater productivity; specialisation together with more effective co-ordination between the specialised parts, etc.

But there is no clear evidence that the changes which preceded the peasant movements described in this volume are developmental in this sense. The process of power centralisation which, indirectly, was one of the ultimate causes of the Pugachev revolt: was it really development? did the political system function better as a result? To what extent had Spain been 'developing' in the mid-nineteenth century prior to the Cantonalist revolt of 1873? And even if there was development in one sense, e.g., the greater productivity of the Mexican economy in the years before 1910 as a result of commercialisation, to what extent was south-west Germany in 1525 rapidly modernising (as distinct from already having been, for some time, more modern in some respects than other parts of Germany)?

One distinguished author has recently announced that he is no longer using the concept of political development[2] in view of its great ambiguities and complexities. We propose to follow suit at least in this instance, and not to link the occurrence of peasant movements with changes exclusively of a developmental kind.

[1] Wolf, op. cit., p. 301.
[2] Samuel P. Huntington, 'The change to change: modernisation, development and politics', *Comparative politics* (April 1971), vol. 3, no. 1, pp. 283–322. See esp. note 42, p. 304.

As far as the peasantry itself is concerned, the restlessness which attends any and all of the different changes we have described above links up with the status dimensions which we proposed in our definition of 'peasant'. That restlessness (1) may be based upon and due to real objective deterioration in some or all status dimensions; (2) it may be due to 'status inconsistency' or uneven improvement (improvement in some aspects, no change or a deterioration in others). Peasants may become increasingly discontented (3) through changes in their position 'relative' to that of others, and (4) because a rise in aspirations occurs faster than the improvement in objective status: the spread of egalitarian ideas and conceptions of the right of everyone to happiness. Finally, (5) combinations of these may occur. The English peasant of 1381 had been subject to uneven improvement *and* some recent deterioration; the Russian peasant of 1917 had been subject to uneven improvement: after all, he *was* no longer a serf, as well as to some deterioration.[1]

VI. GOALS, MEANS AND IDEOLOGIES OF PEASANT MOVEMENTS

'What do peasants really want?' is an obvious question to pose. What underlies it, unspoken but generally present, is the further question: 'How different would society be if these goals were realised and their consequences permitted to work themselves out?' Posed in this way, the question still leaves out of account whether the peasant *consciously* wants major social change or wants certain specific changes of the full consequence of which he is unaware. But that, too, is often in the mind of the questioner: 'Are peasants likely to be moved by a revolutionary mood? Under what circumstances are they likely to be explicitly desirous of changing major social institutions, the groups who wield power, and the rules by which and the objectives towards which that power is wielded?' Finally, the question: 'In what direction is change desired: back towards a past state of affairs, or towards some new institutional design?' is also behind the interest in the goals of peasant movements.

The interest in these and other related questions basically centring around the revolutionary propensity of the peasant is understandable

---

[1] For a schematic treatment of objective versus subjective, improvement versus deterioration; economic versus political, etc., see 'The role of peasant movements and revolts in development', Chart 1–2, p. 29, in Landsberger (ed.), op. cit.

in Western society, which has been much concerned, ever since 1789, with the prospect of revolution: its desirability or otherwise, and its inevitability or otherwise. Posing such questions with respect to the peasantry is even more understandable when we take into account the obvious parallel which once again suggests itself with the industrial working classes. The latter are, or were at one time, also low in status, and were also dissatisfied. It hardly needs to be pointed out that the extent to which they were or could become revolutionary has been of extreme importance, both practically and theoretically. And on both practical and theoretical counts, it has been a subject of debate for over 120 years. Is it late, as Marx thought, or early in the process of industrialisation that revolutionary fever reaches its highest pitch? Are persons from outside the working class needed to fully arouse workers to revolutionary consciousness? Are working class movements limited in aim? Are they revolutionary but in an essentially conservative and counter-revolutionary direction?

The complex but certainly active role of the peasantry in several of the great revolutions from 1789 onward (the French, Mexican, Russian, Chinese and Cuban) has, of course, heightened interest in exploring its revolutionary potential, i.e., in clarifying what its goals are and what means it is prepared to adopt. Hence the debate surrounding the writings and policy positions of Mao Tse-tung on the revolutionary potential of the peasantry, and the writings of Guevara on the relation between peasants, organisation and outsiders, transferred to the rural sector a set of questions which in a very similar manner had long been posed in the urban-industrial.

Taking this into account, the framework used by the contributors to this volume was formulated so as to focus much attention on: (a) whether the goals of the peasantry were *narrow or broad*, i.e., concerned with many different sectors of society, such as the educational and religious as well as the political and economic; and (b) whether they were relatively shallow, or whether they were *profound and 'radical'*, i.e., likely to have a substantial effect on social structure. Demanding longer leases and lowered taxes would obviously have less effect on the distribution of power and wealth than the demand that all holdings above eighty hectares be abolished. In the light of the authors' contributions and our own further thought, we would now add a third dimension for the analysis of goals: (c) the extent to which they are *'self-' rather than 'collectivity-oriented'*, i.e. the extent to which changes are sought on behalf of others than the participants themselves.

Looking not so much at the contributions to this volume as to the general literature on the topic, there seems to be a good deal of agreement on the issue of the potential radicalism of the peasantry. It is subscribed to by writers as unlike each other as Mao Tse-tung and Huntington. All tend to see the peasant as revolutionary. This is a position, however, which we believe needs to be more carefully worded in order to make it fit a greater variety of known facts. Indeed, several authors either do provide their own qualifications and *caveats*, or clearly mean something special with the word 'revolutionary'.

The most extreme position is perhaps that of Huntington, who believes that because ownership and systems of property are involved in the dispute between landlord and peasant, the tensions in the countryside are 'potentially so much more revolutionary than those of the city', where only a more quantitative dispute over the distribution of income is at issue. In the countryside, the nature of the system is inevitably in question, not only the distribution of its rewards.[1]

Lenin, especially after the 1905 Revolution and once again during the summer of 1917, clearly felt that at least the poorer peasants and labourers had very definite revolutionary potential although not of the same spontaneous vigour as that of the urban proletariat. However, to abolish the remnants of feudalism and therefore, at least temporarily, Lenin felt, as does Huntington, that even the richer peasants would be revolutionary.

Mao's thought runs in much the vein, but is even more emphatic. In one of his most frequently cited statements, he sees the poor peasant as being due 'seven points' out of ten, while urban dwellers and the military rate only 'three points' towards the 'accomplishments of the democratic revolution'. Like Lenin, he believes that even the richer peasants can be enticed to participate in the early phase of the revolution, when the abolition of feudalism is the issue.[2] Guevara and Debray in turn merely orchestrate these basic points, though they are chiefly concerned with issues with which we deal later and which are, in any case, somewhat peripheral to this study: the kind of organisation needed to make revolution in the countryside, the extent to which these organisations should be those of a particular party, etc.

There is of course, no question that peasants played crucial roles in

[1] Huntington, op. cit., pp. 298–9.
[2] Schram, op. cit., p. 252. The quotation is from Mao's famous 'Report of an investigation into the peasant movement in Hunan'. The original report has undergone a variety of interesting changes in the course of later official publication.

France, Mexico, Russia and China. The events in France during the summer of 1789 and in Russia during the summer of 1917, are particularly instructive, because while a bourgeois parliament deliberated and agonised, the peasantry, independently and not necessarily led by urban elements, rose up and simply took over the countryside, thus erasing the old order. But we already need to note that in China the revolution, while also based on the peasant, was not peasant-led. And in Mexico, the agrarian struggle was much more protracted and in so far as it was won, the help of the central Government and of urban elements was essential to the victory. Moreover, the peasants' victory up to (say) 1915 was erased by their later defeat by Carranza's troops in the period 1915–18.

But by thus focusing on the violent and dramatic *means* used by the peasantry, and the genuinely revolutionary *consequences* these had, one runs the three important dangers of: (a) forgetting to look carefully at the ends subjectively sought: (b) the relative rarity of large-scale peasant uprisings; and (c) the particular conditions under which the uprisings took place.

Our own position is to divide these reactions carefully into two kinds, depending on the stage of vitality or disintegration which the existing system has reached, i.e., on the stage at which encroachment, uneven improvement or rising aspirations occur.

If encroachment or uneven improvement occur at a time when the peasantry still has a vivid memory of an earlier, communal existence, then we would agree with what Wolf so much emphasises in the concluding chapter of his book, that the 'rebelliousness' of peasants is for the sake of the ultimate aim: 'to remain traditional'.[1] We would, however, emphasise, in addition to this stress on the conservative – in fact, reactionary – element, that to achieve their aim, the kinds of demands made by peasants are quite *limited and specific*. For they are indeed only a reaction to a previous series of events in which the peasant's traditional way of life has been assaulted in specific ways: his economic status reduced, certain new taxes imposed, etc. They are the reactions to the highly negative economic effect of, e.g., emancipation in Russia from 1861 onward and the peculiar buffeting the Russian peasant community, the *mir*, received as a result, and later as a consequence of the Stolypin reforms. They are the results of the encroachment on Mexican communities during the period prior to 1910; on the Spanish peasant during the eighteenth and nineteenth centuries as

[1] Wolf, op. cit., p. 292.

portrayed by Molnár and Pekmez;[1] and to similarly deteriorating conditions in many cases of peasant revolt in the Middle Ages as portrayed by Hilton.[2]

It seems to us important to note that when these assaults on the peasant and his community begin, his reactions, i.e., the means used by the peasantry, are generally not violent, nor – and this is even more to the point – are the goals at all revolutionary. The urban *narodniki* – students going forth into the Russian countryside to channel the supposed revolutionary fervour of the peasant – were notoriously badly received by them in the 1860s and 1870s. Zapata's original Plan de Ayala did not at all categorically look for the expropriation of large landholdings in order to break once and for all the societal power of the *hacendados*. It claimed only the restoration to villages of such land as had been unjustly taken. And Moore draws attention to the fact that the demands of the peasantry in the 1525 uprising in south-west Germany began 'with the moderate demands of well-to-do peasants and became more radical . . . (P)artly . . . due to the refusal of early moderate demands'.[3]

A careful reading of both Huntington and Lenin – admittedly two peculiar names to link together, as we have already pointed out – make it apparent that they were aware of this limited scope of peasant demands, as well as the initial tendency to use non-revolutionary means. But they do not make as clear as one would like the distinction between forward- and backward-looking demands, and the conditions under which each are made.

Huntington recognises that peasant revolts 'have typically aimed at the elimination of specific evils and abuses'. They were, in 'Russia as well as elsewhere', almost 'inevitably directed at the local landlords and officials, not at the authority of Tsar or Church nor at the overall structure of the political or social systems' so that 'a government can, if it is so minded, significantly affect the conditions in the countryside so as to reduce the propensity of peasants to revolt'. Reforms 'may be a substitute for revolution in the countryside' (whereas they are a 'catalyst' for revolution in the cities).[4]

[1] See also ch. vi, 'The agrarian question', pp. 87–130, of Gerald Brenan, *The Spanish Labyrinth* (New York: Cambridge University Press, 1960).
[2] Huntington is well aware of these losses suffered by peasants in the course of 'modernisation' (cf. pp. 296–7: though we have already stated that we are reluctant to use either the words development or modernisation for these changes). In any case, Huntington does not, for some reason, link them to his discussion of the peasant revolutionary position.
[3] Moore, op. cit., p. 464.
[4] Huntington, op. cit., pp. 374–5. The widespread desire to preserve some of the basic authority structures of their societies, and eliminate only their most oppressive aspects –

The fact that peasants, at least down to the 'middle' level of prosperity, are thus assuaged with some ease was recognised also by Lenin. He feared the agrarian reforms being instituted in Russia at the end of the first decade of this century which were designed to establish a large class of small and medium proprietors, thereby breaking up the *mir*. He feared them for precisely the reason that Stolypin instituted them: because it would make the peasant a part of the bourgeoisie.

The Stolypin reforms, however, which were intended to establish a class of independent farmers, took place at a totally different stage from the *narodniki*, even though separated from it by only forty years. For the early twentieth century was a time when the *ancien régime* was clearly on its way out and disintegrating. At this stage, we maintain, the demands of all but the poorest peasants, while still limited and concrete just as before, now look to a *new order* – that of bourgeois proprietorship. They no longer look to the restoration of previous communal rights.[1] If these middle and rich groups achieve this new position then, as Lenin, Mao Tse-tung and, again, Huntington[2] recognise, they become once more conservative, and the point of support for the new *status quo*.

But it is most important to note that this 'conservatism' is with respect to a new society, one to be established, and is not a backward-looking one. Thus, it seems to us that Wolf's emphasis on 'traditionalism' may cover only half of the logically possible, and empirically extant, cases.

The situation in which the better-off peasants ask for an expansion of new rights is most likely one to which we have previously referred as 'status incongruity': one in which their position may have improved in many respects, but may have stood still – or even declined – in others. In sum: situations of *decline of status*, in the *early stages* of still vigorous feudalism, result in specific demands for a return *to the old communal life* in those spheres where deterioration has taken place.

---

regarded in any case as illegitimate and usurped – is manifested in the frequency with which peasant proclamations state that true royalty would be supported, e.g., in the Pugachev Revolt, with its claim that the leader was Tsar Peter III; or in England, where the crown as such was never attacked.

[1] Of course, elements of *both* forward- and backward-looking may be present simultaneously, and demands be mixed accordingly. This seems to have been the case in England in 1381 and in Germany in 1525: the old rights were still very much remembered and were used as one point of reference. But a new, richer, independent peasant had also grown up, and some demands were tailored to his desire to establish himself more firmly, freely and independently. Both types of demand were hostile to feudal impositions, but were oriented in different directions.

[2] Huntington, op. cit., pp. 435 et seq.

Situations of *uneven increase in status*, usually in *the later stages of feudalism*, result in demands for *movement towards a new type of higher status*, e.g., peasant proprietorship, and the abolition of the remnants of old status depressants (feudal obligations), but these are so much 'in the air' that they can hardly be called 'revolutionary'. In any case, there is no vision of, no striving towards, a totally different kind of society which might be called genuinely revolutionary.

As for the 'poor peasant' – the landless labourer, whom Wolf does not regard as revolutionary while Mao and Lenin do so regard him – we think it important to make a distinction between his availability for drastic behaviour, i.e., for revolutionary means on the one hand, and on the other his adherence or non-adherence to basic revolutionary long-run goals. Revolutionary in the former sense – available as a recruit for those engaged in revolutionary activity – he may well be under certain circumstances. And that is actually all that both Lenin and Mao claim, and are ultimately interested in. They take no position beyond the fact that poor peasants have no positive investment in *either* feudalism *or* bourgeois farming. They do not claim that the landless labourer is a positive adherent of the idea of a new society whether conservative or otherwise. In this latter sense, then, no one is really claiming that the poor peasant is a 'revolutionary', and we would strongly agree with not making any such claims.

Whether either kind of demand – backward- or forward-looking (or both simultaneously) – are *successful* depends, of course, on the strength of the system, and will be discussed later.

What, however, of those cases where there do seem to be glimmerings of a totally different society being sought, i.e., of demands being both broad and profound, and in that sense generally revolutionary? These cases are best illustrated by the agrarian ideologies prevalent in Eastern Europe, and described by Galaj and Jackson, though there clearly was a utopian element also among the peasant and working class elements who participated in the Cantonalist Revolt in Spain in 1873. First, it is noteworthy that in the case of Eastern Europe, the original demands were moderate, though forward- and not backward-looking. They envisaged the use of new, modern institutions with their request for education, state credit, improved agricultural techniques and parliamentary representation. There is nothing profound and revolutionary in this.

But later, the goals of these movements did become tinged with a broader conception of social change. They involved not only specific economic, political and cultural rights, but also movement towards a different kind of society which seemed to have elements of both new and old. What was envisioned was a society controlled not by the hated cities and their oversophisticated intellectuals, especially lawyers and politicians, but controlled by small-scale rural villages. Co-operation would be emphasised, not competition; a uniform culture and set of values rather than moral relativism and pluralism; physical work on the land rather than urban occupational specialisation; and communalism would reign rather than individualism, except for property, which would be individual, unlike the pre-feudal village.

This is what apparently characterised the East European agrarian 'state of mind', as Jackson calls it, since it was not a fully articulated theory and ideology. But it also characterised some of the medieval movements, as the reader of Hilton's essay will see: less so Hobsbawm's bandits, who seemed to be generally backward-looking.

There seem to be two sources of this kind of ideology. First, the source may be the existence of ideological innovation in other parts of society. As Hilton notes, it is generally in urban centres, not in the country, that ferment of this kind begins. Wolf notes precisely the same thing; Marxists would of course agree; and we noted the same in our framework: 'changes in the degree of radicalism of goals will occur in accord with more general changes in social ideology',[1] and it is 'Its leadership, particularly its outside leadership, [which] imparts to peasant movements such ideologies as they have, particularly in the case of radical ideologies.'[2]

Secondly, susceptibility to radical ideologies is likely to be a function of the structure of rural society at any given moment of time, i.e., we see ideology as a part of the rural social superstructure, with new ones spreading according to the degree to which previously current ideologies do not fit the actual social facts. A peasantry which finds itself increasingly economically exploited by superior groups and institutions providing it no services in return, and with an ideology which provides no plausible justification for this, will be more susceptible to other ideal designs for society. In particular, anarchism – envisaging abolition of the exploitative and oppressive state – will be attractive under these circumstances, as has been noted by Wolf[3] and by Hobsbawm in his essay in this volume and in his previous writings.

The condition of East European society, while perhaps objectively not as miserable, was still one in which strange and seemingly hostile

[1] Landsberger, op. cit., p. 38. [2] Ibid. p. 52. [3] Wolf, op. cit., p. 294.

forces – the rise of industrialism and urbanism – gained momentum. These objective, visible phenomena, together with ideological egalitarianism and other currents of thought we have previously noted, agreed poorly with the orthodox ideologies previously available to the peasantry, particularly orthodox religion. They stimulated the peasant's aspirations without satisfying more than a fraction of his demands. Puzzled and frustrated, and taking some strands from various brands of socialism which came to the countryside from the cities themselves, a vague peasantist ideology began to take root.

Movements of industrial workers have been subjected to very much the same kind of analysis, with results which seem to us to differ only in degree but not in kind: fundamentally, because the underlying phenomena, the movements, have much in common. For example, early labour movements such as those of skilled workers in the U.S. but especially in the United Kingdom in the eighteenth and early nineteenth centuries often sought not only higher wages, but the restoration of the actual mechanisms of wage and labour supply regulation and of work apportionment which had existed in the period of the corporate city, and was still remembered through oral tradition. These movements were conservative or, more accurately, ' reactionary', but at the same time quite concrete and limited in their demands. Observers such as Frank Tannenbaum have noted this conservatism not only as an early, but as a continuing underlying theme in labour movements,[1] just as observers of today's peasant movements are often uncertain of the degree to which they may not be basically tradition oriented.

As the fundamental economic and technical situation has changed, some worker demands have changed with them. Gradualistic demands such as those for higher wages, shorter hours and better working conditions, all concrete and limited in their general social impact, have continued to be made, of course. But in addition, new demands, e.g., for participation in management, have arisen which are predicated on the existence or furtherance of an entirely new system of technology and organisation. They are in that sense forward looking, though in some cases (e.g., worker participation in management) still not overly profound. Profound or not, the debate over worker ownership and control (essentially, a form of syndicalism) versus ' municipal socialism' (early Fabianism) versus full socialistic control, roughly parallels the

[1] Frank Tannenbaum, *A Philosophy of Labor* (New York: Alfred A. Knopf, 1951).

argument in the rural sector over individual proprietorship versus co-operative versus state collective farms.

But from the beginning of the nineteenth century, in addition to these relatively concrete demands, more radical utopian schemes have been formulated. Their originators and chief propagators were usually not workers, but their ideas were attractive to some members of the working class, faced by a new system of industry and new urban surroundings. These utopian schemes, too, have had some elements in common with agrarian ideologies because both have had to some extent the same basic common enemies: urbanism, industrialism, large-scale technology, bureaucracy and, in some cases, competitive capitalism. Counter-themes such as egalitarianism, co-operation, small-scale communalism, simplicity, a degree of rusticism as in Fourier's *phalanstères* have therefore been basic to most of these schemes: the rebuilding of a community with both new and old elements, and an end to individual exploitation. We doubt that the difference between agrarian utopias and utopias attractive to the industrial working classes are larger than differences within each of these two groups of proposed utopias.

Scientific radical analyses such as Marxism, while of course totally different from utopian visions, have in their own manner portrayed the goals of working class and peasant movements in terms which are partly comparable. Just as Lenin saw the peasant as easily diverted from a revolutionary path by being made into a proprietor, so in the case of working class movements, the worker's own organisation – the trade union – was seen as all too easily neutralised through success in gaining its too limited goals of higher wages, shorter hours and better working conditions. And the fundamental process of proletarianisation was under capitalism predicted as likely to occur both in agriculture and in industry.

Hilton and Longworth deal in some detail with one especially intriguing topic under the more general one of ideology: that of religious heresies and the 'deviant' movements to which they some-times give rise on the one hand, and on the other, the growth of peasant movements. This topic is, in principle, a familiar one to students of working class movements, e.g., the British in the first half of the nine-teenth century. Did Methodism and other kinds of religious dissent defuse protest by ideologically emphasising transcendentalism, the acceptance of the *status quo* and the personal responsibility of the individual for his fate? Did it lure away leadership potential? Or did it, on the contrary, ideologically reinforce protest by condemning material greed, emphasising the equality of all before God, and strengthen trade unions organisationally by training leaders in its chapels?[1] The same kinds of questions have also been posed with respect to the civil rights movement in the United States, and whether black churches and sectarian movements did or did not facilitate it.

Issues very similar to these are dealt with in the two contributions to which we have referred. Both authors seem to lean toward the mutual reinforcement view of religious dissent and social protest. This view of religion is clearly not shared by Alexandrov, who regards religion as an important obstacle to the formation of peasant and other democratic movements in Asia and North Africa, nor is it shared by Huizer and Stavenhagen discussing the role of the Catholic Church in Mexico. But the contradiction is more apparent than real and is easily explained. Alexandrov, as well as Huizer and Stavenhagen, deal with an established religion and church, while Hilton and Longworth deal with newly established, dissident movements. The chances are greater that the latter will be compatible with the protest movements of low status groups, than that the former will be.

We might summarise as follows a large part of the preceding discussion of the relationship between societal change, peasant discontent and the goals and ideologies of different strata of the peasantry.

1. *Peasant discontent* can be usefully divided into feelings of: (a) absolutely declining status; (b) relative declining status, or 'relative deprivation'; (c) status incongruity; and (d) insufficiently met rising aspirations.

2. Among the *societal changes* most likely to produce each of the above are the following:

    (a) Encroachment on peasants and pre-existing peasant communities and their rights by landowners or the State, in a process of enfeudalisation, will lead to feelings of declining status. Such policies of encroachment might be prompted by positive incentives such as the desire to take advantage of new commercial or technical opportunities, or by negative pressures on political or economic elites, such as the loss of a war.

    (b) The ascent of new groups, e.g., the growing importance of

[1] See E. P. Thompson, *The Making of the English Working Class* (New York: Vintage Books, 1963), especially ch. xi, 'The transforming power of the Cross'.

commercial and industrial centres and their urban middle classes will give rise to feelings of relative deprivation.

(c) The break-up of a feudal type of economic and political structure will give rise to feelings of status incongruity among others, because the break-up is likely to be uneven so that some aspects of status will improve more than others.

(d) The diffusion of new general ideologies (such as visions of an egalitarian or socialist society) and of ideas about specific rights (such as the rights to education, a higher standard of living) will give rise to the discontent of insufficiently met rising aspirations.

3. Propositions concerning *goals and ideologies* of the resulting movements:

(a) Encroachment on existing rights will initially lead to relatively narrow, specific, backward-looking demands for the preservation or restoration of the *status quo*. If these demands are not met, more radical demands, blending old and new, will be formulated and their corresponding ideologies welcomed (Mexico, 1910; industrial Britain, 1810–40).

(b) Relative deprivation due to the rise of new classes will lead more immediately to the formulation of comprehensive, though still backward-looking demands and the acceptance of supporting ideologies (as in the case of the peasantry in interwar Eastern Europe and of the French utopias for industrial workers in the period 1820–60).

(c) The break-up of a feudal society and its halting change towards an individual, private property system will lead to relatively specific forward-looking demands that private property rights be universally established and the remaining feudal impositions abolished (rural France in 1789, Latin American peasant demands for private property today).

(d) The diffusion of new ideologies will, by definition, stimulate movements with specific or general demands, depending on the nature of the ideology. There seems to be no agreement on the circumstances under which new ideologies spring up, except that they flourish at times of change and strain. And of that, there seems to be no lack at any stage in history.

(e) The more interconnected are various institutions opposing the low-status group – religion, state authority, economic status –

the more likely it is that demands will also be broad and comprehensive, as well as profound. Typically in European feudal society, Church and State were intertwined with the agrarian economic property structure, and as a result, peasant demands would often cover all three institutions. Blacks in the U.S. South, while moderate as to means, had a wide range of demands. European labour movements, facing the remnants of feudal status in which religious, property and political power interlocked, were more radical and broader in their demands than their U.S. counterparts, facing no Church and a practically absent State.

The following general points concern the evolution, over time, of radicalism in goals and means:

(a) On the whole, the early spontaneous demands made by peasants (and industrial workers) are specific and limited to their own situations, 'self-oriented' rather than embracing society-wide changes, and are not overly 'radical'.

(b) Initially, too, collective peasant reactions are not violent, 'radical', in means.

(c) Prolonged frustration will, however, radicalise all low-status groups, probably more with respect to means than to goals. Only a small group within each will have visions of a 'new' society. A larger proportion may tacitly support violent means.

(d) It is possible that the lower, propertyless strata of each group, e.g. of peasants, are more easily radicalised with respect to means; while the better-off strata, when they do become radicalised at all, are more likely than the former to become radicalised with respect to goals. By virtue of education, the higher strata are more likely to grasp the interrelation between institutions and the need to change them simultaneously.

VII. ORGANISATION: FACILITATING CONDITIONS

So far, we have in effect discussed only the potential for peasant movements: the nature of discontents, their structural sources and the goals envisioned by those who are dissatisfied. What converts feelings of discontent with status into collective behaviour either expressive of discontent or designed to remedy the situation? Again, we will find a substantial number of areas of agreement, as well as certain unresolved issues.

Community

First, there seems to be agreement that the existence of strong communities with previous experience in co-operation, or at least with knowledge of each other, facilitates the organisation of peasants. Hilton stresses this point; so do Wolf [1] and Moore.[2] Some authors believe that movements based on existing communities are more likely to be backward looking. But no one seems to question that they facilitate the establishment of movements as such.

Peasant communities before the advent of a movement are generally not organised beyond the level of the individual community. Or they were so organised only in the long distant past, e.g., the Inca empire which preceded the Spanish conquest and therefore does not constitute a helpful model for Peruvian peasant organisations in the 1960s and 1970s. Hence the critical organisational obstacle faced by a new movement may well be that of creating a viable organisational structure – authority, communication, decision-making mechanisms, etc. – beyond the level of the community. Where larger organisational units did exist, as in the case of the Cossacks, described by Longworth, far less difficulty is encountered in establishing a co-ordinated movement of substantial proportions. But such situations are rare.

In the case of working class movements, the local guild and craft organisation also served as an organisational model, e.g., in the case of printers and carpenters in the U.S. and the United Kingdom. But even where it did not, the fact that any given industry is often highly concentrated spatially in one or a very few areas (the automobile, coal and steel industries are examples) or that its members are drawn into a quasi-community through life styles (railroad) or through working for one or a very few employers: all these factors make it much more easy to establish working class organisations beyond the factory than it is to establish peasant movements beyond individual farm or village. Indeed, the geographically scattered manner in which individual peasants may live even at the local level may be a severe handicap to organisation, a point which Hilton discusses in his paper. We believe these to be among the most important reasons why peasant organisations are likely to be weaker than those of industrial workers: problems

---

[1] Wolf, op. cit., p. 294.
[2] Moore, op. cit., p. 460.

of geographical scatter, and the objective and subjective obstacles they create.

Leadership

Another facilitating element is, clearly, leadership. Here, too, there is a good deal of consensus among various authors, though not unmixed with some disagreement on relatively minor issues.

One important question is: Can the peasantry produce its own leadership? I believe the answer is fairly clear: The more extensive and national, and the more permanent the movement becomes, the less likely is it to be, or at least to remain, in the hands of peasants.

There is a definitional problem here which needs to be clarified. A person who devotes much of his time to any organisation necessarily, of course, ceases to devote his time to tilling the land, or operating a machine or being a lawyer. If no more than this were meant by saying that few peasants are the leaders of large-scale movements, the statement would be trivial. What is meant, rather, is that few persons become leaders who at an earlier stage of their lives were working peasants. Indeed, not many leaders – although clearly more – were brought up in the homes of working peasants, i.e., in the homes of low status rural cultivators.

We believe that there is a substantial quantitative difference in this area of leadership potential between industrial working class movements on the one hand and peasant movements on the other. Indeed, we believe that this difference is in turn partly the cause of differences in the structure of the movements themselves. The working class movements of different countries, very soon after they have reached a certain level of maturity, generally consist of at least two distinct branches, both active and vigorous: an economic branch, the trade union movement; and a political wing: a labour, communist, socialist or other party. There may be, of course, all manner of rivalry between and within each of these 'wings'.

Now while the political emanations of working class movements have always had heavy representation from middle class intellectual elements, the trade union movement has generally been staffed even at its top national levels by ex-workers. (This is, however, less true in many of the Third World countries, where even trade union movements are often run by persons from outside the working class.) Generally, however, trade unions have been organisationally vigorous with working class leadership, disposing of a complicated hierarchy of active grass-roots organisations, typically organised on an industry basis and culminating in a national confederation uniting all trade unions. In other words, the industrial working class can provide its own national leadership although in fact it has often been supplemented by representatives of other classes, particularly in the realm of politics.

In the case of the peasantry, there seems to be a substantially different situation. The only organisations of truly national scope seem to be the kinds of East European peasant parties described by Galaj and Jackson. The impression one has is that these were possibly even more dominated by non-peasants than the parties of the urban proletariat by non-workers. For in such countries as Germany and England, a substantial number of erstwhile workers reached positions of eminence not only in the trade union movement, but in the more nationally oriented political arm of the working class movement. Robert Michels, for example, examining the social origins of socialist deputies in the German Reichstag in the period 1903–06, found that 65 per cent (53 out of 81) were of 'proletarian origin'.[1] Compare this, for example, with Jackson's description of the Croatian Peasant Party. Only 50 per cent of its parliamentary delegation was peasantist even during the brief period in the early 1920s when peasant influence was at its height, and before this party – as so many others – drifted into being substantially controlled by bourgeois elements.

Peasant movements of national scope – whether in the form of parties as in Eastern Europe, or armies composed largely of peasants, as in China – are, therefore, rare. And when they occur, they are held together by leaders who are, at best, from peasant homes but who never tilled the land themselves, turning very early to other pursuits, especially intellectual study. Outstanding examples range from as far afield as Mao Tse-tung in China to the Radić brothers in Croatia and Stamboliiski in Bulgaria. By way of contrast, Emiliano Zapata, who was certainly in part a working peasant, may be taken as symbolic of the maximum that can be expected of a peasant movement (save the customary 'rare exceptions') if it remains genuinely peasant-led. Zapata's concern, as has been stressed by all who have written about him, ended at the boundaries of the state of Morelos, and with the solution of the problems of its peasantry. Those who in the 1920s and 1930s, after his death, led a truly national agrarian movement, doing

---

[1] Robert Michels, *Political Parties* (New York: Dover Publications, 1959; originally published 1915) pp. 271–2. For the very substantial proportion of trade unionists among British Labour Party M.P.s, see J. A. Banks, *Marxist Sociology in Action* (London: Faber 1970), esp. pp. 155 et seq.

political battle at the level of the central government over the terms of a nationally applicable agrarian reform programme, were all – like Antonio Díaz Soto y Gama and Gildardo Magaña – of urban, generally middle or upper class background, and of a high level of education.[1]

Moreover – and this, too, is very frequent – Zapata's family had a long history of leadership not only in its own village but beyond,[2] and his father was by no means the poorest in the area. Peasant leaders – Mao is another example – are disproportionately drawn from its better-off strata as is, indeed, the case also with leaders of industrial workers.

At the local as distinct from the national level, and in the case of movements confined to a certain region, peasants can and do provide leadership. In some cases, all leaders were peasants, as Hilton makes clear. But in many other movements, persons from outside the peasantry played important leadership roles even at the local level: local intellectuals (clergy and teachers); local merchants, artisans and innkeepers; and even local members of declining élites. Especially interesting, perhaps, is that lower-level clergy occasionally played supportive roles in Eastern Europe, especially during the early, education – and co-operation – oriented phases of many movements in the late nineteenth and early twentieth centuries; just as one knows them to have done in Latin America more recently.

We still believe this – the presence, even at the local level, of leadership from outside as well as from within the peasantry – to be the more typical situation, especially where the peasantry did not have a tradition of some literacy, and of internal authority and a certain degree of autonomy. It frequently did have such a tradition in medieval Europe, especially in England, France, the low countries and Germany. In these countries, the peasantry readily produced its own leaders. But outside of these areas, e.g., in Latin America and Asia, with their tradition of extreme oppression and submission, and with no tradition of peasant literacy and participation in self-governing institutions, supplementation of leadership cadres from outside the peasantry was and is very frequent.

Homogeneity of Interests

While the question: 'Which level of the peasantry is the most radical: is it the highest level? the middle? the lowest?' did not lead

---

[1] Robert A. White, S.J., 'Mexico: the Zapata Movement and the Revolution', in Henry A. Landsberger (ed.), *Latin American Peasant Movements*, op. cit., pp. 149–51 and 162–6.
[2] Robert A. White, op. cit., p. 132.

to a simple, uncomplicated answer, there is another approach to the phenomenon of stratification within the peasantry which is more successful. It takes as its starting-point the axiom that the peasantry, even as a whole, is not very powerful – certainly not by itself and without allies. A corollary then is, that unless the peasantry is at least united within itself, it stands little chance of achieving anything, at least by its own efforts. It is for this reason that a 'divide and conquer' policy has been adopted by perceptive traditionalists all over the world. This is true of countries as far apart as Russia on the one hand, with its Stolypin reforms of 1906, designed to create a prosperous upper and middle peasantry of non-revolutionary temper, to Mexico on the other hand, where today a very large group of post-reform *ejidatarios*[1] is just prosperous enough – relative to the growing number of landless labourers – to remain relatively tranquil. The economic interests of the *ejidatarios* are actually opposed to the interests of the landless labourers. The latter may want either higher wages (in part from the *ejidatarios*, for whom they often work) or they may want some of the scarce remaining land (presently occupied by the *ejidatarios*, or desired by them, as Huizer and Stavenhagen point out) to augment their own insufficient plots. Thus is the peasantry divided within itself. However, it is in Alexandrov's analysis of Asia and North Africa, and Galaj's analysis of Poland, that the reader will find the clearest expression of the theme that one of the greatest inhibitors to the build-up of strong organised pressure for rural change are antagonisms within the peasantry itself or, at least, differences in goals which make one sector relatively uninterested in whatever may be vital to the other. Alexandrov in particular, aware that a landless labouring class is emerging in Asia (as it is in Latin America), notes that its ties to the land-owning peasantry are still too strong for it to attempt to exert against it all the power it might.

The parallel with industrial working class movements is somewhat less pronounced in the case of this characteristic than in that of others. Lack of unity there has often been, of course, in the sense of one group failing to lend full support to struggles which were vital to another. In particular, the better-off sections of the working class, as of the peasantry, have often not been much concerned about their less well-off brethren – as in the case of the American Federation of Labor in the

---

[1] Peasants given usership rights to land under the agrarian reform programme. Ownership itself is vested in the village, not in the individual, but is in any case highly regulated by national statutes.

mid-1930s, for example, thereby giving rise to the establishment of the Congress of Industrial Organizations (C.I.O.). Such lack of unity had been one – but only one – of the reasons for the failure of general strikes, such as that of Britain's in 1926, when the coal miners in the end had to fight by themselves, and lost. But genuine conflicts of interest between one sector of the working class and another because one group is, in fact, in an employing and capitalist relationship to the other, is very rare because, in that sense, the working class is structurally not as heterogeneous as is the peasantry.[1] This profound structural hetero-geneity of the peasantry is an important reason, in addition to the factor of leadership potential which we have already noted, why the latter movements are generally less 'extensive' (i.e., embrace a much smaller percentage of potential adherents) and are generally far weaker than the movement of industrial workers.

In a more general sense, and regardless of local details, all movements whose ultimate source of energy is the individual's attempt to improve his status – and this is the source of the energy of both working class and peasant movements – can be expected to show some organisational weaknesses and a lack of cohesiveness, even when explicit internal conflict can be avoided. Key individuals may find ways to improve their lot which are not beneficial for the movement; and sub-groups within the movement may likewise go their separate ways. While this may ultimately be self-defeating for the majority, the individual and the small group are in fact likely to behave in such a manner.[2] The stress which some writers have put on the need for a vanguard which would be more clearly aware of the interests of the deprived classes as a whole is a recognition of this point, as is the stress by other writers that the objective situation needs to be allowed to mature considerably so that a large majority of the masses spontaneously becomes aware of their common interests.

[1] In the view of some, however, even the extreme accusation is justified that skilled workers exploit the unskilled as do capitalists. Thus William D. Haywood, one of the leaders of the Industrial Workers of the World (I.W.W.), wrote: 'As strange as it may seem to you, the skilled worker today is exploiting the labor beneath him, the unskilled, just as the capitalist is'. See his *Autobiography* (New York, 1929), p. 187. Louis C. Fraina, another U.S. radical leader, described the skilled workers as 'a reactionary mass whose interests are promoted by the more intense exploitation of the proletariat of unskilled labor, the overwhelming mass of the workers, and by imperialistic adventures'. See his *Revolutionary Socialism: A Study in Socialist Reconstruction* (New York: Socialist Propaganda League, 1918), p. 50.

[2] This point and others are elaborated in Henry A. Landsberger and Cynthia N. Hewitt, 'The sources of weakness and cleavage in Latin American peasant movements', in Rodolfo Stavenhagen (ed.), *Agrarian problems and peasant movements in Latin America* (Garden City, N.Y.: Doubleday-Anchor, 1970) ch. 16, pp. 559–83.

Modernisation Experience

In the 'framework' submitted to the contributors to this volume as a possible aid in ordering their material, we indicated that those sectors of the peasantry, and those individuals, would be most likely to participate in movements who had been most exposed to what in today's jargon are called 'mobilising' or 'modernising' experiences. These concepts cover not only education, i.e., that better educated groups and individuals would be most likely to participate in and lead peasant movements. They refer equally to the experience of living in towns and even in other countries, where new ideas and the idea of association in particular, may be acquired; or to army service, where skill in the disciplined use of force is acquired, the fruits of organisation and co-operation observed and often the incompetence of the upper strata demonstrated. Indeed, wars in general are associated with, and often precede the outbreak of peasant unrest: for one thing, they impose additional burdens on the peasantry and they undermine the strength of the ruling class. But in addition, and of more relevance here, wars teach peasants to fight.

The essays in this book provide additional support for the above hypothesis. Pugachev, for example, had been a soldier, as was Emiliano Zapata in Mexico. José Rojas, in Bolivia, had resided outside his own country: and so, as Huizer and Stavenhagen point out, had Primo Tapia of the State of Michoacán, in Mexico. The mobilisation – opening to new ideas, breaking with traditional and customary ways of submission – experienced by whole groups through, e.g., war, is of course a central point in the early section of Alexandrov's essay on peasant movements in Asia after World War II. It is important, too, in Huizer and Stavenhagen's analysis of Bolivia prior to 1952; Hilton's discussion of several medieval movements, especially those of England and the French *jacqueries* of 1358; and Jackson's and Galaj's analysis of the increasing political awareness of the peasantry of Eastern Europe after World War I. The awakening effects of war, and its undermining of existing élites, is indeed one of the universal themes in these papers.

More generally, we can assert that the awakening of consciousness and militancy, through education, or through the experience of living or fighting outside the area in which the movement later occurs, all facilitate the process of organisation. More recently, of course, the penetration of mass media, especially radio, into rural areas, has had a stimulating effect. Both media and education, e.g., literacy campaigns, have on occasion been employed quite deliberately in efforts to make the peasantry politically conscious of its situation, as in the case of the *conscientizaçáo* movement in Brazil, conducted by a progressive Catholic group, M.E.B.[1]

Reinforcing Cleavages

It is clear from several of the contributions in this book that peasant organisation is facilitated if, in addition to the clash of purely economic interests, the antagonists are divided by other cleavages. National, religious and ethnic-cultural divisions are potentially the three most important of these.

Alexandrov's paper emphasises heavily how important for the origin and beginning of peasant movements throughout the huge area covered by him – North Africa and Asia – was the almost universal presence of alien, colonialist regimes. These brought with them colonial settlers as in Algeria, or large-scale capitalist plantations as in Sumatra, or even foreign money-lenders and merchants who came, not from the mother country, but from other dependent territories, such as the Indian *chettyars*–money-lenders–in Burma, who owned an impressive percentage of the best land. The addition of demands for national independence and cultural autonomy to those for economic improvement added significantly to the total force of a movement which was therefore neither purely national nor purely economic, but a fusion of several elements, the importance of which varied from class to class and, of course, from case to case. That economic cleavages alone may not be sufficient to establish a radical and extensive, i.e., nation-wide peasant movement, and that nationalism is needed as a reinforcing agent, has been argued in greatest detail by Chalmers Johnson.[2] But Alexandrov, in a more qualified form, partially supports the thesis in the present volume. For he draws attention to the fact that the clamour for agrarian reform temporarily subsided immediately after World War II even though little if any improvement took place in the lot of the peasant, but merely because aspirations for national independence were satisfied. The emphasis is, however, on the temporary lessening of social tension due to the achievement of political goals.

[1] Emanual de Kadt, *Catholic Radicals in Brazil* (London and New York: Oxford University Press, 1970).

[2] Chalmers Johnson, *Peasant Nationalism and Communist Power* (Stanford, California: Stanford University Press, 1962).

Europe, however, provides us with a number of highly interesting examples of the inhibiting rather than the stimulating effects which religious, national and cultural cleavages can have on peasant movements. Jackson's paper well illustrates the point, and so does the chapter by Molnár and Pekmez, with its stress on Spanish 'cantonalism'. On the one hand, many East European peasant parties, for example, gained critically needed strength at the time of their establishment before World War I from the fact that they were founded as part of the political and cultural opposition to alien governments dominating the region, specifically the Russian, Austro-Hungarian and German empires. Nevertheless, once the new nations were established, their internal cultural and religious differences had two important negative effects. First, they prevented the peasantry from establishing a unified front. Thus, as Alexandrov points out, caste divisions are having a debilitating effect in India, while between the two world wars, nationality differences kept apart the peasants of Serbia from those of Croatia; and the Czech, Slovak and Slovene peasants in the case of Czechoslovakia. Secondly, these cleavages directed several agrarian movements from their original peasantist goals altogether, and directed them into nationalist and cultural-religious channels, Croatia and Slovakia being once again the outstanding examples. In some cases – of which the Czech is perhaps the most clear-cut, though Poland also qualifies – the agrarian party softened its agrarian programme not so much in order to engage in nationalist and religious struggles against external elements, but in order to participate in broad coalitions with a view to maintaining internal political stability.

We conclude, therefore, that cleavages other than economic ones may be of critical importance both in strengthening and weakening peasant movements, depending simply on whether or not they coincide with, or cut across class lines.

Once again there is a parallel here with the movements of urban workers. The nationalist-cultural element was an important reinforcing agent in the establishment of many a trade union movement, e.g., those of India, Kenya, Guinea and many other African, especially North African, countries.[1]

But nationalism and more specifically tribalism, as well as religious differences, have also served to weaken urban labour movements in Africa, not only to strengthen it. Nigeria, even during its pre-

[1] For Africa, see Ioan Davies, *African Trade Unions* (Baltimore, Md.: Penguin Books, 1966).

independence period, was a baneful example of the debilitating effects of ethnic and tribal differences, while in Holland and France religion has in the past deeply divided labour. Indeed, such divisions have been present even in the U.S. (blacks today, the Irish and other immigrant groups in the nineteenth century) and in the United Kingdom, though to a far lesser degree. But no doubt the most widely cited example of nationalism triumphing over class unity is represented by the relationship between the German and French labour movements in the first decade of this century and up to the outbreak of World War I in 1914. Galaj ruefully refers to the widely prevalent, and all too descriptive slogan 'Polish peasants with the Polish gentry'. Suitably transposed, it described much of the French and German urban working classes in 1914. Once again, therefore, we find considerable parallels between peasant and working class movements.

Peasant Personality

There is one set of themes found very widely in the literature on peasant movements which is for good reasons not found to anything like the same extent in the literature on urban working class movements. It is that of the 'peasant personality', and the possible obstacle to organisation which it poses. The closest urban parallel is the current debate in the United States over whether or not the concept, 'the culture of poverty' has some basis in reality or not, i.e., whether or not the pitiful situation of the poor, including their failure to organise and participate in community organisations, might be due in part to the kinds of motivations and general personality characteristics which they might have or which they might lack, as the case may be. Attributing to the poor themselves some of the immediate responsibility for being poor is, of course, as old as the Elizabethan Poor Law in England. But for various reasons, the pros and cons of this kind of analysis have recently come to the fore in the U.S.

The traits attributed to the peasantry and supposedly militating against their forming successful organisations, can be grouped conveniently under five headings: (1) apathy; (2) resistance to change and innovation, including the innovation represented by the establishment of new organisations; (3) suspiciousness towards all, including fellow peasants; (4) submissiveness to traditional authority, and to traditional norms in general including those norms which result in the peasant's own exploitation; and (5) lack of knowledge. The latter is an intellectual characteristic which, on the face of it, is more subject to change

as compared with the more permanent motivational attributes represented by characteristics (1) through (4). Among those who have
written specifically about peasant personality attributing one or other
of the above characteristics to it, are Banfield[1] and Foster,[2] but Marx's
well-known reference to peasants as 'a sack of potatoes' is, in fact, a
colloquial formulation of the same point.

While some writers have questioned altogether whether peasants
possessed these characteristics, most of the argument has been over
whether these traits are deeply engrained cultural characteristics, or
whether they are rational, behavioural responses to difficult situations
likely to evoke similar responses from anyone placed in them, and
therefore very likely to change once the situation is changed, i.e., once
scarcity of resources is removed and peasants are no longer pitted one
against the other.[3]

But many of those who have analysed specific movements have
directly or indirectly, and without attempting to generalise because
this was not their interest, noted the same basic point. Among the
contributions in this book, for example, those by Jackson and Galaj,
dealing with peasants in Eastern Europe, give some of the most direct
evidence that the attitudes of the peasantry may be a severe handicap
to organisation. Galaj in particular draws attention to the need which
early peasant leaders felt, no doubt realistically, to make it their first
order of business that peasants overcome their 'slave mentality' and
'feelings of inferiority and insecurity'. Hence the enormous emphasis
placed by these movements on education. The very same emphasis
was encountered by this author at the other end of the world, in the
course of a historical study of a small but symbolically significant
agricultural workers' movement in Chile, whose (outside) leaders
referred with humanity and pity, not with contempt, to the mentality
of the *campesinos* as 'almost animal-like'.[4]

This theme, however, is not a universal one in the contributions to
this volume, and Hilton, for example, makes no reference to it. It may
therefore be a conditional rather than a universal phenomenon:
prevalent where particularly severe and prolonged oppression have

---

[1] Edward C. Banfield, *The Moral Basis of a Backward Society* (Glencoe, Ill.: Free
Press, 1958).

[2] George M. Foster, 'Peasant Society and the Image of the Limited Good', *American
Anthropologist* (April 1965), vol. 67 no. 2 pp. 293–315.

[3] For a discussion of some of these issues, see *Human Organisation* (Winter 1960–61),
vol. 19, no. 4, which contains a debate between Foster, Lewis and Pitt-Rivers.

[4] Henry A. Landsberger, 'Chile: A Vineyard Workers' Strike', ch. 5, pp. 210–73, in
Henry A. Landsberger (ed.), *Latin American Peasant Movements*, op. cit.

reduced the peasant to apathy and fatalism, or where the play of the market or a growing scarcity of resources have led to suspiciousness. Where it does occur, however, it clearly is an obstacle to the formation of cohesive peasant movements.

We may summarise this section by stating that the following factors are conducive to channelling felt discontent into an active peasant movement: (1) prior community organisation; (2) the existence of leadership 'resources' outside of the peasantry to supplement those from within it since the latter will exist only if the peasantry has had organisational experience, but will even then not be plentiful enough nor will it have national vision; (3) homogeneity of interests within the peasantry; (4) reinforcing cleavages such as national, ethnic or religious differences dividing the peasant from his antagonist; (5) the absence of cross-cutting cleavages of the same kind, which might divide the peasantry and join a part of it to its antagonist; (6) the relative absence of personality characteristics such as apathy and suspiciousness which might hinder the establishment of cohesive movements; and (7) the exposure to modernising experiences which would have the effect, among others, of overcoming the negative personality characteristics to which we have just referred.

But even the establishment of a movement does not explain its success, and to this problem we now turn.

VIII. ALLIES AND ANTAGONISTS, SUCCESS AND CONSEQUENCES

Before exploring the conditions determining the success and failure of peasant movements, one ought first to be sure that he can recognise and measure 'success' and 'failure' where they exist. For a variety of reasons, this is often tremendously difficult.

In the case of movements which took place long ago, and occurred at times or at places where systematic records were either not kept, or else not preserved, there may be little evidence on which to base a judgement. This is particularly the case where any improvement or deterioration is modest in size, since small differences quite especially require systematic information before one can be sure that they are not an accident of the particular cases one happens to have at hand. Logically, this scarcity of reliable and systematic data would be one of the difficulties in assessing the effect of medieval movements: was there really a significant diminution in the obligation and restrictions placed on serfs and villeins fifty years after the English Peasant Revolt of 1381 ? As Hilton points out, it is difficult to obtain the facts concerning this and other early peasant movements.

Next, there is the danger of falling into the fallacy of *post hoc, ergo propter hoc*: changes in the condition of the peasantry – whether positive or negative – which may occur after the establishment of a movement are not necessarily due to it, but might have occurred in any case. Thus, a general improvement in the economic condition of agriculture might be more responsible than elite concessions to a previous outbreak of peasant unrest for an improvement in the situation of the peasantry. But the two causes may be difficult to separate from each other. Perhaps the most clear-cut example of this confusion of causes is Eastern Europe between the wars, where the deteriorating condition of the peasantry must have been due more to overpopulation and, later, to the world depression than to governmental reaction to the pressure of peasant parties, since this reaction was often favourable.

Thirdly, long-run, medium-run and short-run effects should be distinguished from each other if success and failure are to be assessed, and they should be balanced against each other. But this, too, is often very difficult to do. Obtaining an increase in the agricultural minimum wage, for example, which is of immediate benefit to many people, may be followed by a long-term substitution of labour by machinery or land. How can one balance the increased welfare of those who do permanently benefit from any such improvement with the misery of those who may be eliminated or never hired. This is a very real problem in assessing the situation in the U.S. rural South today.

Fourthly, since improvements are sought simultaneously along different dimensions – power, prestige, economic welfare – how can one balance gains along one of these dimensions with losses along another? This is a very real problem, as is apparent from the paper by Huizer and Stavenhagen and other studies of the Mexican situation, which indicate that Mexico's peasants feel more free today, and feel that they have more power than before the revolution – psychic benefits which cannot be ignored – while it is clear that their economic situation may not have improved much, certainly not relative to that of other groups. Under these circumstances, has the movement succeeded or failed?

Finally, and perhaps most important, what is often most apparent is that a profound, qualitative change in the position of the peasant has taken place. For example, ten years after a revolution many peasants may work in communes, state farms or collective settlements: entities which have never before existed. But it is very difficult to evaluate in what respect, and to what degree, such fundamental change does or does not constitute improvement.

Some, but only some, of the above problems in the evaluation of the success or failure of peasant movements will be eased if the kind of universal dimensions for the measurement of status are employed which we have suggested above, thus making comparable, on a piecemeal basis, situations which in their totality appear to be non-comparable. It is possible, for example, to measure and therefore to compare, as between a semi-feudal and a collective form of agriculture, the degree of control which peasants have over the use of the factors of production; their standard of living; the prestige their position enjoys, and so forth, even if a single global comparison of their positions is not possible. Nevertheless, even such comparisons along separate 'analytical dimensions' do not resolve all problems. Hence it may be wiser to speak of 'the consequences' of peasant movements than of their success, which conjures up a rather simplistic picture of 'good versus bad'. With these reservations in mind, let us proceed.

As is implied by linking 'success and consequences' with 'alliances' in the title of this sub-section, we believe that the effects of a peasant movement are as much determined by other struggles which may be taking place in society at large at the same time, as by the efforts of the movement as such.

Let us compare the movements described in this volume which, basically, failed to alter greatly the state of the peasantry (the medieval movements, the Pugachev Revolt, the Spanish peasant revolt in 1873) with those which resulted in a substantial change in the position of the peasantry: the Mexican and Bolivian movements, for example – or those of France in 1789, Russia in 1917–18, and China later.

Two general differences stand out, dividing the latter group of countries from the former.

The first of these is that the peasantry in the latter countries disposed of very powerful allies who were very active, essentially on their own behalf, though often courting the peasantry. The peasantry in the societies in which its movements were successful was able to change its status very substantially because its antagonists were being successfully assailed by powerful groups in addition to the peasantry itself.

Placing successful peasant movements in a context of a movement by other classes to improve their status, fighting against a common antagonist, is not to deny that the peasantry also played a crucial role. But in the France of 1789 it was the middle class and Paris who were the initial critical actors in a more general revolution in which the peasant's change in status was only a part. The middle class had already defied Louis XVI and the aristocracy in June 1789, and Paris had stormed the Bastille on 14 July, before peasant unrest forced the aristocracy to abolish feudalism on 4 August. In Mexico, it was again the middle class and the early working class without which the revolution in that country, and the agrarian reform that followed it, would have been as unthinkable, as it would without the peasantry. Middle-class Madero designated November 1910 as the time for a revolutionary uprising: Zapata's forces got under way in Morelos only in March 1911. In Russia it was the working and the middle classes, together with a war-weary army and navy of peasants, who removed the old elites from power from February 1917 onward. Peasant disorders on a major scale broke out only in the middle of the year.[1] In Bolivia it was likewise the middle and the working classes which overthrew the old regime in the spring of 1952, and once again peasant disturbances did not begin until later, though peasants were to benefit by sweeping land reform as a consequence.

In all the above cases, therefore, the peasantry did not begin to act until after the more general revolution had already begun, initiated by middle class and working class elements, not by the peasantry. China alone is the exception, but so much of the specific sequence of events there was affected by the prolonged war with Japan, and the Kuomintang's inability to wage it successfully, that no general lesson can be drawn from the fact that peasant armies played an almost exclusive role there. The Cuban Revolution can also not be regarded as spearheaded by the peasantry but rather, as a situation which the countryside was hospitable to a revolutionary guerrilla movement led by urban middle class elements.

This brings us to the second difference separating the countries in which peasants changed their status from those in which they failed to do so. It is a specific application to the peasantry of a point made by Crane Brinton over three decades ago about successful revolutions:[2] that success is due as much to the weakness of the established elites, as

[1] Launcelot Owen, *The Russian Peasant Movement 1906–1917* (New York: Russell and Russell, 1963) pp. 145 et seq.
[2] Crane Brinton, *The Anatomy of Revolution* (New York: Vintage Books, 1957; first published 1938).

to the strength of the revolutionary forces. Barrington Moore likewise warns against unduly focusing on the peasantry when attempting
to explain their participation.[1] As we think about the English crown
and the feudal aristocracy surrounding it in 1381, it is clear that although
there were divisions, and although weakening had occurred as a result
of the Hundred Years War, the elite system was more cohesive, and
more capable of a vigorous response to threats from below than were
the Romanovs in 1917, the Bourbons in 1789, Porfirio Díaz in 1910, the
Bolivian regime in 1952 and Batista in 1958. In all of the latter cases,
the remnants of the central Government were separated from their own
chief supporters, who were, in turn, weakened and unenthusiastic about
supporting the regime. Hence peasant movements, and the larger
revolutionary movements of which they were a part, succeeded in
these countries.

The East European peasant parties after World War I would seem
to be an interesting set of cases intermediate between success and
failure. Collapse of the three great empires in 1917–18 had temporarily
created a vacuum. Into this void, popular forces – necessarily chiefly
peasant, given the nature of East European societies – could move in.
Hence in many countries parties came to power which represented the
peasantry, at least in part. But as time went on, landowning and upper
middle class elements for the most part recovered, and the peasantry,
without major allies, lost out. Drastic change in their position came
only after the dominant groups lost power in the aftermath of World
War II. In addition, however, as Jackson and Galaj emphasise, the
restricted success of the peasant parties of Eastern Europe must also be
attributed to an underlying imbalance between land and people. It is
well to remind ourselves, at the conclusion of an analysis which has put
much stress on class relations, that factors incidental and random to
such an analysis – technical and natural causes – can greatly influence
the course of events.

Finally, there is the case of the modern 'farmers' of Western Europe
and the North American continent whose situation is not discussed in
this book. The very word 'farmer' – and the fact that use of the
alternative word 'peasant' would not be appropriate[2] – indicates that
we are no longer dealing with persons of very low status. However,
in England, France and Germany the old powerful landed elite has also

---

[1] Moore, op. cit., p. 457.
[2] The difference corresponds reasonably well with that between *agricultor* and *campesino*
in Spanish.

practically disappeared. Hence the farmer is, in essence, a status inter-mediate between the two old extremes. It seems clear, however, that in all the above countries the farmer's political power, and the economic benefits he obtains from the system, are in excess of his real *economic* bargaining power. Often, the poorer farmers obtain fewer such benefits than the rich – as in the case of U.S. farm subsidies. But they nevertheless obtain more than they would if left to fend for themselves.

What appears to be happening is that these benefits are granted by social forces which are relatively to the right of the political spectrum (the Republican Party and Southern Democrats in the U.S.A.; the Conservative Party in England) in return for the political support by all farmers, large and small, of these right-of-centre forces. Naturally, such an alliance between rural poor and rich is fragile, and the small farmer may break away in a more 'populist' direction, as he has often done in the U.S., Canada and in France in the 1950s.

From the point of view of our more general analysis of the deter-minants of success and failure, what is demonstrated by the West European case is once again that the poorer farmer obtains his success, or his change in status, more from the efforts of his allies – whether these be politically 'left' or 'right', whether urban intellectual or rural aristocratic – than through his own direct efforts. In that sense, the situation in Western Europe and North America would seem to be similar to that of poor farmers elsewhere. It is what his allies do, and their success – which, of course, he seeks to help to achieve – that is critical for the poorer farmer.

We arrive, therefore, at some paradoxical conclusions concerning the success and failure of peasant movements. Peasant demands are generally not radical and sweeping. Yet, except for the North Atlantic countries, they have generally been resisted. In the face of such resistance, and in the absence of such gradual improvement, changes in the peasant's status have not come about except as part of general, revolutionary change. Peasants generally do not take the initiative in these revolutions, though they play a crucial role in them shortly after their outbreak by sweeping away the old regime in the agricultural sector. At that point, the peasantry is temporarily truly revolutionary. If the peasantry does take the initiative and has no allies, it is generally unsuccessful. By itself, it is too weak and its antagonists are too strong, for the peasantry to gain its objectives.

The above implies – and the history of Latin America and Asia bears this out – that voluntary concessions by their opponents to low-status groups such as the peasantry are unlikely even though, at the beginning, the concessions required to maintain the *status quo* might not be very large. There seems to be a substantial quantitative difference here between the development of working class and peasant movements. Of course, both are resisted in the early stages of their development by those classes who evidently have most to lose from their potential success. The persecution suffered by the early working class movements both from employers, and by the State and legal system, are too well known in the cases of England, Germany, France, Russia and the United States to be detailed here. The same was true in the Asian and African Territories dominated by these countries when trade union movements attempted to establish themselves in the inter-war period and after World War II. However, it is clear that the extent of repression was no longer as fierce in the colonies as it had been in the mother countries fifty or a hundred years earlier. For by the middle of the twentieth century the idea of a working class movement with both a political and an economic expression had become accepted in many – but, of course, still not in all – countries.

Peasant movements, however, seem to have benefited far less from this trend towards greater acceptance, although it would be wrong to assert that there has been no such trend at all. In the industrially developed countries, as we have already noted, today's farmers' organisations, which are well developed and powerful, are indicative of the fact that rural cultivators have indeed been upwardly mobile, as a class and as a whole. Their interest groups and associations are little different from those of doctors, merchants, industrialists, as well as trade unions.

But in the Third World, peasant movements seem to be far more systematically kept in check than the movements of industrial workers, to whom substantial concessions are often made. In Latin America – in Chile and Peru (until 1964 and 1968), in Brazil, in Colombia – landowners, with the support of the State, were much more inclined and more able to resist peasant organisation than the desire of the working class to establish trade unions.[1] Even in countries such as Mexico, where peasant organisation is formally allowed in ways similar to that permitted industrial workers, the real force of such organisations seems to be far less than that of the latter. Concomitantly, the concessions

[1] For a full description of the whole range of techniques used by landed élites against peasant organisations in Latin America, see Ernest Feder, 'Societal opposition to peasant movements and its effects on farm people in Latin America', in Henry A. Landsberger (ed.), *Latin American Peasant Movements*, op. cit., ch. 10, pp. 399–450.

made to the peasantry are fewer. As a result of continual frustration, this large sector of society, as it becomes mobilised through education, through the media of mass communication, and through the efforts of interested external classes (already Lenin foresaw clearly a race between the middle classes and the working class for the allegiance of the peasantry) may become available for dramatic revolutionary action, just as have been the peasants of other centuries. Certainly their ties to the present system are few.

So far, peasant activity has failed to realise its objectives in most of the Third World countries, as it has throughout history, because other classes have not been ready to support common action against existing regimes. But this is no indication that in the future such alliances may not occur, and be successful. Two questions will then become critical. The first, in terms of time sequence, is whether outside powers will attempt to prevent such revolutions: and the support of the People's Republic of China for Pakistan over Bangla Desh indicates that 'left' as well as 'right' outsiders may support established regimes against a (partly) rural revolution. But, secondly, even if revolutions are successful, there is the question as to whether the dramatic change contemplated for the peasant is really an improvement or not, and whether he will then be allowed freely to seek the improvement he wants. We referred above, briefly, to the historical trend of the greater acceptance of working class and peasant movements as organised representatives of their class interests. It is possible that this trend has reached its zenith, certainly in the case of the new nations. Convinced that the enormity of the problems facing these countries requires that a strong central government formulate and execute development plans, there may well be less tolerance for movements which, though based on large masses, still do not represent society as a whole, and whose immediate objectives may be seen as opposed to the long-term interests as a whole. The days may well be over in which mass movements, whether of peasants or of industrial workers, are allowed to confront governments, whether of the left, the right, or the centre. Since the kinds of major changes in the status of the individual peasant which are contemplated in a post-revolutionary phase are often difficult to evaluate in terms of whether they constitute an improvement or simply a change in the peasant's status, the outlook for the peasant – whether as individual, or as member of the movement – looks cloudy, to say the least.

PART 1

PEASANT REVOLTS AND THE DISINTEGRATION OF 'FEUDALISM'

Chapter 2

PEASANT SOCIETY, PEASANT MOVEMENTS AND FEUDALISM IN MEDIEVAL EUROPE

by
Rodney H. Hilton

I. THE PEASANT ECONOMY

THE European peasantry has been a disappearing class since the dawn of industrial capitalism and the overwhelming majority of peasant economies today are to be found in Africa, Asia and Latin America. However, an examination of peasant economies within the framework of European feudalism is not altogether beside the point when we are considering the general problem of peasant movements. First, the characteristics of the peasant economy in certain parts of medieval Europe are very well documented. The evidence confirms that its fundamental characteristics are found widely separated in time and place, an indication of the strength, almost the indestructibility, of this type of social organisation. Second, we must recognise that, owing to the great influence of European science and culture, at any rate until recently, the ways of looking at peasant economies and at the relationships between peasants and other classes (especially landowners) have been greatly influenced by the historical experience of medieval Europe. This is true of terminology – the terminology associated with feudalism, for example. It is also clear from the writings of modern sociologists and social anthropologists that they frequently have the institutions of medieval feudalism as a framework of reference when they are discussing modern peasants, in Europe or outside. Third, some of the actual institutions and social attitudes of medieval feudal society were transferred by European conquerors to other parts of the world. The Spanish and Portuguese colonies in South and Central America are obvious illustrations of this point.

Peasant economies varied considerably in detail from region to region of medieval Europe. The Mediterranean zone, with its warm dry climate and light soils, was able to support such crops as the vine and the olive, which could not be easily cultivated in Northern, Central and Eastern Europe. Central and East European agriculture on the other hand was given its special characteristics, not merely by the long winters from which these parts of Europe suffered but also by the importance of the forests until well after the end of the Middle Ages. Within contrasting climatic zones there were other contrasts, between mountains, plains and river valleys. These were chiefly important in determining the balance between arable and pasture in agricultural systems.

But in spite of the differences between peasant economies, which were determined by differences in the natural environment, there were similarities which, from our point of view, were much more important. These similarities arose from the fact that the peasant economy was essentially self-subsistent. Peasant households were family-based, and whether the family was nuclear or extended, its labour was the principal labour force on the holding; the bulk of the produce on the holding was used to sustain the family; and the year-by-year reproduction of the economic life of the holding was based mainly on seed, implements, livestock, and so on, derived from within the holding. Grain provided the cheapest foodstuff for the medieval peasant and consequently, even in areas which were favourably situated for the production of such cash crops as wine, wool, flax, and so on, there was always a strong element of arable farming for subsistence.

A striking illustration of the near-indestructibility of this type of economy in the Middle Ages is provided by the way in which villages which seem to have been completely blotted out of existence during the Hundred Years War in France reappeared after the restoration of relatively peaceful conditions. Crops and livestock had been stolen by marauding soldiers, the buildings had been razed to the ground, the inhabitants had been killed or dispersed, but after the war new immigrants rebuilt the houses and occupied the same arable fields, meadows and pastures which had been allowed to revert to scrub during the fighting.[1]

The fact that the peasant economy of the Middle Ages was largely self-subsistent meant that peasants could have existed without the help – or interference – of the other classes of feudal society. Village com-

[1] J. M. Pesez and E. Le Roy Ladurie in *Villages désertés et histoire économique* (1965), p. 213.

munities were conscious of being immemorial institutions, older than the lords who exacted rents and other payments from them. It is, however, true that lordship in peasant society was also very ancient, and of varied origins, sometimes resulting from conquest, sometimes from social differentiation within peasant communities, sometimes from assertions of power involving the imposition of 'protection' when military force openly regulated social relationships. The peasants often accepted overlordship as a natural fact of their existence, but there was always another tradition which corresponded better to the facts: that lords were an unfortunate and unnecessary imposition upon them. The medieval peasant world was, therefore, very self-contained, so that although production for the market by peasants is found very early, it was always possible to make a clear distinction between the product which remained on the holding at the disposal of the direct producers, and that which was taken directly as tithe, or rent in kind, or sold in order to pay rents in cash, taxes, ecclesiastical dues. The amount of cash spent on purchases of luxury was negligible – even peasants with vineyards drank water[1] – and the amount spent on farm equipment or building materials was very small. In other words, when the peasants turned an important part of their product into cash, that cash left their hands almost immediately and they had very little to show for it. Why else is it that, in contrast to Roman villas, excavated medieval village sites hardly ever yield any number of finds of coins?

The settlement pattern of medieval European peasant society was by no means homogeneous. In flat or gently undulating terrain, as in the English Midlands or north-eastern France, where conditions favoured extensive grain production, the characteristic settlement was the large nucleated village. In mountainous or broken terrain where pastoral activity was relatively more important, dispersed settlements in hamlets, or even isolated farmsteads, were to be found. Dispersal was also facilitated where, instead of open fields and intermixed parcels of land, peasant holdings were consolidated and enclosed, so that the farm house could be built on the holding instead of in the village. But these patterns did not invariably result from the conditions described. In Italy and other Mediterranean countries peasants who might be primarily pastoralists often lived together in fortified villages which were almost urban in character, for the sake of protection. Where cash crops, such as the vine, predominated, common rights over the arable were eliminated and dispersal was facilitated.

[1] R. Dion, *Histoire de la vigne et du vin en France* (1959) pt. III, chap. xiv.

In spite of all this, probably the majority of peasants inhabited villages and hamlets rather than isolated farms and lived from a combination of arable and pasture farming. This type of mixed farming involved at least some degree – sometimes a considerable amount – of communal regulation of vital aspects of economic life, such as access to common pastures and woodland, routine of ploughing, harrowing, sowing, reaping and harvesting on arable fields, control of quarries, fisheries and other natural resources. These necessary functions of economic life were the basis of the cohesion of the village community. The capacity for organisation in pursuit of social and political demands arose naturally from the day-to-day experience of peasants. So although peasants were much weaker than feudal lords in many different ways – lack of armed force, lack of support from other social groups, inability to fight battles far away from their holdings and over a long period of time – they should not be regarded as completely powerless, for they were capable of tenacious common action. Wace, the twelfth-century writer attributed a consciousness of this capability to the Norman peasants in his verse chronicle of the Dukes of Normandy:

> Et s'il nus velent guerrier
> Bien avum contre un chevalier
> Trente a quarante paisans . . .[1]

II. PEASANTS IN FEUDAL SOCIETY

The European feudal society in which medieval peasants comprised the majority of the population had many specific features not found in other societies based on a peasant economy. All the same, the types of possible relationship between landowning minorities and peasant majorities are fairly limited, so that in spite of the specific features of medieval European feudalism, varying much, of course, from one region to another, many of its characteristics are to be found elsewhere and in other epochs. The term 'feudalism' has, of course, provoked much debate. Many medieval historians prefer to reserve it for the institutions which arose from the spread of the hereditary military fief (*feudum*) in certain West European countries between about the ninth

---

[1] 'If they want us to fight, we have 30 or 40 peasants for each knight'. The part of Wace's chronicle describing the revolt is partly printed as an appendix in L. Delisle, *Etudes sur la condition de la classe agricole et l'état de l'agriculture en Normandie au Moyen Age* (1851); see also Hugo Anderson's edition of 1879 for the complete account.

and twelfth centuries.[1] This method, by which great landowning lords – kings, dukes, counts, even bishops and abbots – exchanged land for the military service of armed horsemen, gave rise to many social practices and beliefs, in brief the culture known as 'chivalry', which lasted much longer than the original mechanism for mobilising military force. But feudal institutions defined in this way involved only the ruling groups of medieval society, feudal rulers at the top, the knights at the bottom.

'Feudalism', however, is a term which has a much wider and still valid meaning. This wider definition is the one which lays stress on the relationship between all classes of society, not merely on certain relationships within the ruling class. It is therefore useful when discussing the position of the peasantry. In this sense, feudalism is a system of economic and social relationships based on the legalised and institutionalised claim of a ruling group to a substantial part of the surplus of peasant production. The members of the ruling group usually appear as landowners, though the concept of landownership is by no means precise, for it often appears as the ownership of rights over the working occupiers of the land, rather than of ownership of the land itself. Since, as mentioned earlier, the ruling group was not economically necessary to peasants, who already effectively possessed their own means of subsistence (contrasted, for instance, with propertyless wage workers), the element of coercion in the transfer of the peasant surplus to the lord was quite open. It was guaranteed by the possession by the lords of military force – that armed cavalry which was associated with feudal institutions in the narrower sense. But, since the exercise of force is best legitimised by legal sanction, lords from high to low developed rights of private jurisdiction for the regulation of their relations with the peasant communities. At a time when population was scarce and there were great tracts of uncultivated wood and waste, it was necessary to restrain peasant migration, as well as to have a legal basis for demanding personal services, rents in money, in labour and in kind. As far as possible, therefore, peasants were enserfed. In the historical context of early medieval European society this meant the extension to free peasants of laws of slavery derived partly from Roman law, partly from Germanic law and partly newly worked out for the varying circumstances of different European territories.

Although the relations between the lords and the peasants were the

[1] R. Coulborn (ed.), *Feudalism in History* (1956).

most important determinants of the general character of medieval European feudal society, there were many complicating factors. Other classes grew in importance with the expansion of the European economy. The most important of these, naturally, were those connected with production for the market, merchants interested in international and regional trade, manufacturing artisans and all the other groups, such as victuallers, who were inseparable from urban growth. But urban specialisation was not the only consequence of growth. Concentrations of political power involved increasing numbers of persons in administrative activity, the beginnings of bureaucracies. These were at first mainly ecclesiastics, the only literate persons. The increasingly complex public and private jurisdictions enlarged the legal profession. Out of a combination of administrative needs and intellectual activity came abbey and cathedral schools, then universities. War, even then, made enormous demands on the resources of the State, giving rise to elaborate taxation systems, credit arrangements with bankers, demands for war supplies, and so on, further complicating the social structure. The political interests of medieval merchants, bankers, lawyers and administrators normally coincided with those of the feudal lords, but this was not invariably the case. Artisan interests would usually be closer to those of the peasant class from which many of them sprang. But again this was not invariably the case. Hence, when there was a confrontation between peasants and lords, other social groups might adopt attitudes which one might not have expected and which, on the surface, might seem contrary to their class interests.

Further complications arose from the fact that neither lords nor peasants were homogeneous social groups with simple aims. The most important divisions within the ranks of both lords and peasants were economic. Lords of great estates whose incomes depended on the exploitation of large numbers of servile peasants could be expected to have a different attitude to the peasants from the lesser gentry, who are often found to be more dependent for their incomes on the use of hired labour on their demesnes than were the greater lords. They would therefore be more interested in low wages than in maintaining unfree peasant status. It is sometimes suggested that there was a division of attitude as between lay and ecclesiastical lords. This was not normally the case. Old-established monasteries whose income came from the big estates of traditional structure shared the lay aristocrats' distrust of the peasants. Sometimes they were even harsher than the laity. It is not among the great ecclesiastic landlords that we find more sympathetic attitudes to the peasants, especially not among the monastic landlords. Sympathy was more often found, as one would expect, among the lower clergy, the parish priests. It could also be found among the clerical intelligentsia in the universities, who were perhaps aware of the egalitarian strand in the Christian tradition. A critical attitude towards unfree legal status is also found among some lawyers.

The peasant class also was socially divided.[1] As early as records exist we are aware of the contrast in the medieval village between the rich peasants, the *laboureurs*, and the smallholders, the *manouvriers*, who supplemented their incomes by wage labour, hunting or the practice of a craft. Again, by no means all peasants were reduced to serfdom. Free peasants are found in varying numbers in all European countries throughout the Middle Ages. Some of the free peasants were rich but many were poorer than serfs. Naturally, different social situations affected the attitudes of different groups among the peasants. On the whole, however, it is remarkable that social differences within the peasantry had fewer political consequences than one might expect. This is due to many factors. For one thing the style of life of rich peasant families with big holdings was always much nearer to that of poorer peasants than it was to that of the gentry. For another, peasant holdings tended to be impermanent. The rich peasants of one genera-tion might be the poor of the next. And even the richest peasants did not hire wage labour on a big scale. Hired labourers were often younger sons of other peasant households. There was no sharp and permanent conflict in peasant society between employers and hired men. The social division between peasants and lords was that which mattered most in rural society, as the history of peasant movements shows.

III. THE CHRONOLOGY OF PEASANT MOVEMENTS

Peasant movements, varying in intensity from armed rebellion to almost imperceptible pressure on seigneurial administration, occurred during the whole of the medieval period. Owing to the uneven distribution of the surviving evidence it is dangerous to compare the

[1] The best and most recent survey of the medieval European peasantry is by G. Duby *L'économie rurale et la vie des campagnes dans l'occident médiéval* (1962), translated into English (1968) as *The Rural Economy and Country Life in the Medieval West*.

amount of peasant discontent in one region with that in another, or in one epoch with another. The general impression given in surveys of medieval social history is that the fourteenth and fifteenth centuries were the epoch *par excellence* of open conflict between lords and peasants,[1] as though their relations had been quite idyllic before then. One writer even contrasts the period of peasant war in Germany, in the early sixteenth century, with the situation during the whole of the previous period, which he refers to as the epoch of *la bonhomie médiévale*.[2] This view of medieval society, though by no means uncommon, is surely unjustified. Not only were there bitter conflicts between lords and peasants in the last two centuries of the Middle Ages, but there are good reasons for supposing that this was also the case in early times as well. It may well be, in fact, that our chief reason for supposing an exacerbation of the situation in the later Middle Ages is simply that the surviving evidence is more abundant. It is tempting, of course, to associate the increase in social tension with the crises of the later Middle Ages, whether this is seen in terms of economic stagnation caused by falling population and falling demand for agricultural produce or in terms of increased seigneurial exploitation resulting from the undoubted crisis of the seigneurial economy. An examination of the facts will, however, without necessarily leading us to underestimate the social tensions of the later Middle Ages, show that these were by no means without precedent.

Although Alfons Dopsch insisted that peasant discontent was by no means unknown in the Dark Ages,[3] the documentary evidence is imprecise. Just as the historians of the Late Empire can say little more than that the revolts of the Bacaudae seem like peasant wars against the State, so Gregory of Tours' story of the violent reaction of the people of the region of Limoges in 579 against heavy land taxes indicates little more than general rural discontent. But in the Lombard Edict of Rothari (643) there is already more precise evidence. Chapters 279 and 280 of this edict are entitled *De concilio rusticanorum* and *De rusticanorum seditionem* (sic) and refer to organised, armed movements by serfs or slaves under the leadership of free men. Conspiracies (*coniurationes*) of serfs in Flanders and elsewhere are mentioned in an

---

[1] This is the case even in the survey by G. Duby mentioned above.

[2] H. Dubled, 'Aspects sociaux de la guerre des paysans notament en Alsace', *Annales Universitatis Seraviensis* (1956) p. 71.

[3] A. Dopsch, *Economic and Social Foundations of European Civilisation* (1937), p. 237. E. A. Thompson, 'Peasant Movements in Late Roman Gaul and Spain', *Past and Present*, no. 2 (1952).

imperial capitulary of 821, and the serf owners are instructed to suppress them. Such scattered references not only show the existence of peasant discontent, but indicate that elementary forms of common organisation were already present. These had an important future with the later development of rural communes capable of negotiating on equal terms with the feudality. A better documented example of an early peasant movement comes from northern Italy between 882 and 905. It resembles closely those of a much later date, revealing many of what one might call the classic features of peasant grievances and peasant action against the territorial overlord. It was a quarrel between the peasants of Limonta on Lake Como with their lord, the abbey of St Ambrose, Milan. The main point at issue was the labour services of olive gathering and pressing which the abbey was claiming, and which the peasants resisted. As happened later in other lands, they not only objected to the labour services as such, but brought in the issue of personal status as well, claiming first to be imperial *aldiones* (freedmen), later to be at least imperial serfs. These claims to a protected status, well short of freedom, are analogous to the claims of some English peasants to certain privileges of tenants on alienated crown lands, the 'ancient demesne' of the crown. In both cases they hoped to use the authority of the sovereign to restrain the demands of the immediate lord.[1]

Peasant movements of all sorts occur during the formative period of feudal society during the period of expanding trade and urbanisation in the twelfth and thirteenth centuries, during the period of extreme population pressure before about 1350, as well as during the critical years of the later Middle Ages. We have a peasant war in Normandy at the end of the tenth century as well as in the prosperous regions of maritime Flanders and possibly in northern Italy at the beginning of the fourteenth; rebellions after 1350 in war-ravaged France and in peaceful England; more peasant wars at the end of the Middle Ages in declining Catalonia and in booming southern Germany. It would appear from these facts that, while local or short-term economic and political difficulties could well be precipitating causes of peasant movements, the basic factor must be found in the nature of the relations of the principle classes concerned, peasants and lords.

---

[1] Gregory of Tours, *Historia Francorum* v, xxi (28); *Monumenta Germaniae Historica, Legum* iv i 67–8; *Capitularia,* i 301. P. S. Leicht, *Operai, artigiani, agricoltori in Italia dal secolo VI al XVI* (1946) pp. 73, 83–6; R. H. Hilton, 'Peasant Movements before 1381', *Economic History Review,* (1949). C. Violante, *La società milanese nell' età precomunale* (1953) pp. 85–6.

IV. PEASANT DEMANDS

What happened when peasant movements, violent or not, were pre-
cipitated was that peasants or their spokesmen articulated demands for
the fulfilment of traditional peasant aims. These can almost entirely
be summed up as the demand for land, for freedom, and for the reduction or abolition of rents and services – demands which are by no
means confined to the medieval peasantry.

The demand for land, for the division and redistribution of big
estates, is familiar in modern and contemporary movements. It is
seldom found in the Middle Ages as a peasant demand, at any rate as
far as arable land is concerned. Proposals for the confiscation, secular-
isation and redistribution of monastic estates occurred, of course, but
the social backing for these usually came from the lesser and middling
nobility. There was, however, a medieval equivalent to later demands
for estate confiscation. This usually took the form of a demand for the
abolition of lords' monopoly of hunting and fishing rights and control
of access to common pastures. This is quite understandable. Fishing
and hunting, important survivals of the pre-agricultural gathering
economy, were regarded as natural resources to which all should have
access, at any rate all with a stake in the land represented by the arable
holding. An aspect of the assertion of seigneurial rights by lords from
the tenth century onwards was their claim to overriding property
rights in the undivided woods, pastures and rivers within their lordship.

One of the earliest (though not abundantly) documented examples
of an outright war between peasants and lords is that which took place
in Normandy in 996 at the beginning of the reign of Duke Richard II.
The matter at issue seems to have been, according to the earliest
description by the chronicler William of Jumièges,[1] the peasants'
assertion of their free hunting and fishing rights. It is unfortunate that
the chronicler is not strictly contemporary, since he wrote nearly a
century after the events described. He is, however, regarded as one of
the most accurate of the historical writers of this period. The rising is
described in much greater detail by an even later chronicler, writing in
the middle of the twelfth century, the Channel Island versifier, Wace.
He emphasises other aspects of peasant resentment at the extension of
seigneurial jurisdiction and these may of course represent an interpola-

[1] *Gesta Normannorum Ducum*, ed. J. Marx (1914) bk v cap. 2.

tion of what Wace knew to be twelfth-century grievances into a tenth-century context.

But this competition for the resources of wood, waste and water continued. It was an issue in movements of peasant discontent in northern Italy between the tenth and the twelfth centuries. It has been suggested that the fierce and implacable war between the heretical Apostles under Fra Dolcino and the armies mobilised by the bishop of Vercelli in 1304–7 was the consequence of the deprivation of peasant common rights by the growing urban communes.[1] The demand for hunting and fishing rights occurs again in England in 1381, especially as embodied in the charters of liberties briefly extorted by peasants of the villages on the estate of the Abbot of St Albans. And it occurs in terms which echo previous medieval demands in the Twelve Articles of the German peasants in 1525, where the demand is for hunting and other common rights, not for a re-division of the arable. In fact the nearest approach to a claim for the arable part of landowners' estates would seem to be the demand by peasants in Catalonia, at the end of the fourteenth and beginning of the fifteenth centuries, that holdings abandoned as a result of population decline (the *casas ronecs*) should not be resumed by lords into demesne, but reissued to the peasants.[2]

The two other staple demands of most medieval peasant movements were normally closely connected, though it is not always easy to see which had priority. It was normal to argue that rents and services could not be arbitrarily increased, or indeed increased at all, at the expense of men of free condition. Which did peasants prize most, freedom or low rents? If these were mutually exclusive alternatives the historian could observe which choices, in practice, were made. But precisely because freedom and low rents went together, we cannot always tell which, at any given time, was the crucial issue. And of course in most cases it might be wrong to separate the one from the other.

[1] S. D. Skaskin, *Le condizioni storiche della rivolta di Dolcino* (Rapporti della Delegazione Sovietica al X Congresso Internazionale di Scienze Storiche a Roma) (1955); E. Werner, 'Popular Ideologies in Late Medieval Europe: Taborite Chiliasm and its Antecedents', *Comparative Studies in Society and History* (1960). But a closer examination of the evidence collected by A. Segarezzi in Muratori, *Rerum Italicarum Scriptores* IX, v, in connection with other evidence of agrarian conditions, is necessary to test the suggestion of Skaskin and Werner.

[2] *Gesta Abbatum Monasterii Sancti Albani*, III (1869) pp. 318–31; Articles 4, 5 and 10 of the German peasant demands are in *Translations and Reprints from the Original Sources of European History*, II (Univ. of Pennsylvania); P. Vilar, 'Le déclin catalan du bas Moyen Age', *Estudios de Historia Moderna*, VI. For J. Vicens Vives, however, the quarrel of the *remensas* concerning the *casas ronecs* was that the landowners tried to make the remaining peasants pay the rents from the abandoned holdings.

Here again, the agitation of peasants, often non-violent, but not seldom breaking into violence, seems to differ little in essential character from one medieval epoch to another. In the conflict we have mentioned between the peasants of Limonta and the abbey of St Ambrose, at the end of the ninth century, it will be remembered that status was the plea on which the peasants resisted increased labour services. In his account of the 996 peasant rising in Normandy, Wace puts into the mouths of the peasants, as a justification for their war against the whole range of seigneurial exactions, the statement *nus sumes homes come il le sunt*. The whole of the fluctuating battle between lords and peasants in England between the beginning of the thirteenth century and the beginning of the sixteenth century was fought for freedom as the guarantee of fair distribution of the product of the peasants labour. *Nulli servire volumus* was one peasant cry at the end of the thirteenth century in a conflict over increased services;[1] the end of bondage was the first article of the Mile End and Smithfield programmes in 1381; the end of servitude was linked with the abolition of the *malos usos* in fifteenth-century Catalonia; abolish serfdom, said the German peasants in 1525 for 'Christ has delivered and redeemed us all without exception, the lowly as well as the great'; as late as 1549 the rebels of Norfolk under Kett asked 'that all bondmen may be made free for God made all free with his precious blood shedding'.[2]

V. FUNDAMENTAL CAUSES OF CONFLICT

The nature of the social and political programme of medieval peasants is to be explained, then, in very general terms by the pressures resulting from the lords' attempts to maximise their incomes. It is of course a commonplace that at least from the tenth century onwards the market for an increasing range of the luxury commodities which were the main staple of international trade was expanding. This market was almost entirely composed of lay and ecclesiastical landowners, the overwhelming bulk of whose incomes was derived directly or indirectly from peasant rent in money, in kind or in labour. As more goods become available, customary expectations in aristocratic living standards rose. At the same time costs of war, of politics and of

[1] R. H. Hilton, 'A Thirteenth-Century Poem about Disputed Villein Services', *English Historical Review* (1940).
[2] F. W. Russell, *Kett's Rebellion in Norfolk* (1859) p. 51.

administration also increased. Demands on peasants for rent and service were therefore not only always present, but tended always to be growing. Thus, the basic antagonism of landlord and peasant was a permanent element in the situation. This did not, however, exclude the establishment of an accepted equilibrium between the two sides. Peasant movements therefore occurred, not so much because of the permanent antagonism (though without this, there would, of course, have been no reason for them), but because of disturbances from time to time of uneasy equilibrium.

The tendency for demands on the peasant surplus to grow, being a function not only of the needs of individual estate owners but also of the growing needs of governments, was expressed not only as rent, or labour service or tithe but also as an ever-increasing tax burden. But from time to time the pressure could slacken, and peasant conditions could temporarily improve. When an equilibrium which embodied recent improvement of the peasants' conditions of life was disturbed, this could be a serious precipitant of peasant protest movements. Not that this type of disturbed equilibrium was the only one possible. The denial of improvements which might reasonably have been expected consequent on the improved bargaining position of peasants, could also lead to trouble. Too obvious a flouting of the expected social role of the lords as the military protectors of rural society also represented a form of equilibrium disturbance. Political disturbances which would seem at first to be internal to the ruling class as a whole could lead to a general breakdown in social equilibrium, stimulating the formulation of traditional peasant aims.

VI. PRECIPITATING CAUSES OF INDIVIDUAL MOVEMENTS

(1) *Conflicts over Rents, Services and Taxes*

Many peasant uprisings, or movements of protest not necessarily involving violence, were caused by lords increasing their demands for rent of one sort or another. Disturbances in English villages in the thirteenth and fourteenth centuries resulted from these circumstances. The peasants concerned almost always alleged a departure from customary practice by the lords. It is true that lords also riposted that they too were simply taking what was their customary right. Where custom ruled, innovations could only be justified by being shown to be old-established. Who then was speaking the truth? There can be little doubt that in thirteenth-century England the innovators, the disturbers of equilibrium, were the lords. The upward trend of agricultural prices, rents, taxes and other burdens on agriculture is too well documented for us to question the general correctness of peasant complaints about increased services. In fact lords not infrequently took their stand on their customary right to increase rents and taxes arbitrarily. In 1261, peasants in Northamptonshire claimed as freemen the right only to pay a fixed tallage, while a new lord, shortly after acquiring the manor on which the peasants lived, had tallaged the whole village arbitrarily. Arbitrary as against fixed tallage was the issue between the Prior of Harmondsworth (Middlesex) and his tenants in 1278, when the peasants unsuccessfully tried to claim royal protection as former tenants of the crown. In 1279 the Abbot of Halesowen (Worcestershire) imposed an enormous fine in his private court on a servile tenant who had been the leader of a movement of resistance to arbitrary increases in both labour services and other dues (entry fines and marriage fees).[1]

The small-scale actions of English villagers in the thirteenth century were usually defeated. Supported by the greatest of feudal landowners, the King, the lords normally won in the royal courts, for the tide was running too strongly against peasant interests. This does not seem to have been the case in parts of France, Italy and other European countries. The period was, for some peasants in these countries, an era of stabilisation, marked precisely by gains which the English peasants failed to achieve, namely the fixing of customary rights at an acceptable level.

In the Paris region and northern France, village communities of *vileins* acquired charters which emancipated them from the obligations of *mainmorte* (death duty), *chevage* (poll tax) and *formariage* (payment for permission to marry) which were considered servile in character. The charters frequently stabilised, without abolishing, other lordly exactions such as tallage, and even gave limited rights of self-administration. In some cases these charters were acquired by fierce struggle. Seventeen villages of vine cultivators near the wine capital of Laon found themselves, like the burgesses of Laon itself, in conflict with the bishop, who in 1177 had revoked a charter they had already acquired. In 1185 the King intervened. The level of tallage was fixed, as were certain rents, and right of self-government by twelve *échevins* (judges) was given.

[1] Hilton, 'Peasant Movements . . .'

Attempts by the bishop to revoke these privileges were countered by threats of mass emigration, and by allying with the cathedral chapter, also the bishop's antagonist, the villagers regained their privileges.[1] Not for long, however, for the monarchy went back on its support for the peasants, and after seventy years (1190–1259) of fluctuating fortunes, only one of the seventeen villages emerged with even minor privileges.

Sometimes collective privileges had to be bought at a heavy price, so that it could be that the gain was the lords' in the short run.[2] The fixing of conditions could, of course, only benefit peasants when the general level of rents and prices was rising. In reverse circumstances, fixed rights could only benefit the lord, particularly when he held jurisdiction and the power to enforce it. Even in the middle of the thirteenth century when the fixing of obligations was preferred by peasants to obligations which fluctuated arbitrarily at the will of the lord, such stabilisation of conditions was not always welcome. The 1247 *custumal* (statement of customary dues) of the village of Verson, belonging to the abbey of Mont St Michel, fixed peasant rents and services for a century and a half to come. But a contemporary poem written from the standpoint of the monks makes it clear that the background to this fixing of customs was one of peasant protest against the level of rents and services. It suggests that the *custumal* was imposed on them following the defeat of their protest.[3]

On the whole, however, the charters granted to peasant communities seem to represent gains by peasant movements. The movements were not by any means always violent, but all made use of the built-in solidarity of the peasant community to get concessions from the lords. It should be emphasised, of course, that the lords were often in financial need and were prepared to sell privileges for money. Hence the chief beneficiaries on the peasant side were the well-to-do who had accumulated cash gained from production for the market. It is significant that the earliest of the European peasant communal successes were acquired where a market element in the economy was most advanced: in Italy P. S. Leicht saw the outcome of the dispute between the peasants of the Limonta region and the abbey of St Ambrose at the beginning of the tenth century (mentioned above) as heralding the achievement of

---

[1] M. Bloch, *Caractères originaux de l'historie rurale française* (1931), V, 2; A. Luchaire *Les communes françaises* (1890) pp. 81–96.

[2] Duby, op. cit., p. 479.

[3] Delisle, op. cit., Appendix viii for the 'Conte des Vileins de Verson'; for the custumals, R. Carabie, *La propriété foncière dans le très ancien droit normand*, I (1943).

communal rights, through the acceptance by the lord of fixity of obligations. In the eleventh and twelfth centuries, by a combination of pressure and purchase, the rural commune in central and northern Italy had already come into existence, a century or more in advance of the chartered rural communes of northern France.

In some countries, the gains made by the rural communes were long lasting. In spite of the devastations of the Hundred Years War, French peasant rights lasted at any rate until the sixteenth century. In other places there were earlier reversals of fortunes. If it is true that the incredibly bitter struggle in 1304–7 in northern Italy between Fra Dolcino and his followers and the armies of the bishop of Vercelli was the consequence of the usurpation of the rights of the rural communes by the politically and economically dominant urban communes, it would seem to show that previous peasant gains could not be maintained in the face of new and more formidable enemies than the rural lords. It has been observed that the rights of the Italian rural communes in the tenth, eleventh and twelfth centuries were (in spite of the relatively advanced level of market production) essentially a feudal-manorial phenomenon, representing the striking of a balance between lord and peasant. But in the thirteenth century the expanding urban communes introduced a new element into the situation. Their policy now aimed at dissolving the older ties between landlord and tenant so as to eliminate all intermediary power between the city government and the inhabitants of the rural *contado*. This was a situation unique in medieval Europe and undoubtedly resulted in a deterioration of peasant conditions. In abolishing serfdom and proclaiming the equality of man, the rulers in the towns intensified their hatred and contempt for what they considered to be rural brutishness.[1]

Peasant movements which had as their objective the stabilisation or reduction of the level of rent (rent being broadly interpreted here) necessarily involved primarily a confrontation with the lord. But though the historian can make distinctions between public and private authority, it is doubtful whether the peasant of medieval Europe was able to see much distinction between the agents of the State and those of the landed aristocracy. This is well illustrated by an early fourteenth-century English poem known as 'Song of the Husbandman'. Composed perhaps by some cleric close in social condition to the peasants, it lists quite indiscriminately those who take away from

---

[1] See Philip Jones, 'Medieval Agrarian Society in its Prime: Italy' in *Cambridge Economic History of Europe*, I (2nd ed. 1966) pp. 401, 404, 419.

the peasant the product of his toil: the collectors of the King's taxes, the lord's bailiff and other manorial officials. But the emphasis of the poem is heavily on the baleful effect of state taxes, to pay which the peasant has to sell off his corn, his stock and the agriculture equipment, for the tax collector 'hunteth as hound doth the hare'.[1]

It should not be a matter of surprise, therefore, that tax impositions were as important as demands for increased rents or services as precipitants of peasant discontent, or that the movements resulting from these impositions led to attacks by the peasants which ranged much more widely than assaults on tax collectors. One of the bitterest peasant wars of medieval Europe was that which occurred in the maritime provinces of Flanders at the beginning of the fourteenth century. This was the conflict which only ended with the defeat of an army of rebellious peasants and artisans by the French King, overlord of Flanders, at Cassel in 1328. The region had been a focus of discontent for a quarter of a century at least, and there must have been memories of the plebeian victory of Courtrai in 1302 against the combined forces of the French monarchy and the Flemish nobility. One of the main subsequent grievances had been the collection of indemnity taxes, begun as early as the Capitulation of Athis shortly after Courtrai (1304) and most recently renewed in 1322. But although densely populated, the area was not poor. The dead rebels after Cassel were well-to-do peasants, not serfs but freemen who hated the apparatus of power represented by the judges of the local courts of the Count of Flanders. By 1324 these officials and the tax collectors were being imprisoned and tithe payments were denied. A further attempt (at Arques 1326) to impose another indemnity rekindled the revolt, and led to a terror against the pro-French nobility. By this time, to quote Henri Pirenne, it was '*une guerre de classes entre les paysans et la noblesse*'. The King of France intervened not only to punish an anti-French rising but to save the class on which French interests depended.[2]

It was the repeated imposition of an unaccustomed tax, the poll tax, levied in 1377, 1379 and 1380–1 which sparked off the rising in southeast England in the summer of 1381. As in Flanders, this disturbance of the equilibrium at one point led to a vast extension of the field of action, so that once the rebels had dealt with the tax collectors they turned on the lawyers, the corrupt local jurors, burnt the manor court

[1] R. H. Robbins, *Historical Poems of the Fourteenth and Fifteenth Centuries* (1959).
[2] H. Pirenne, *Le soulèvement de la Flandre maritime* (1900).

records and sacked the properties of persons such as the Duke of Lancaster who symbolised for them the evils of the regime. The social strata represented in the rising, including (as in Flanders) both peasants and artisans, were also by no means desperately poor or exceptionally underprivileged. It is probable that there had been attempts at a seigneurial reaction against the consequences of the population collapse – attempts to keep rents up and wages down to an unrealistic level – but these, though unsuccessful, had raised the temperature as far as relations between the ruling and the ruled classes were concerned, so that an extraordinary imposition like the poll tax would inevitably provoke a violent reaction.[1]

The second and most serious of the wars of the Catalan *remensas* in 1483 was sparked off in a not dissimilar manner. There had been for many years a seigneurial reaction against the consequences of the population collapse in the second half of the fourteenth century. The lords had attempted to step up rents and services, of which the most recently introduced were the most resented, the *malos usos*. With support even from the crown of Aragon and some of the crown lawyers the peasants arranged to buy out these exactions. But in 1481, the long drawn out negotiations were suddenly broken off and the lords tried to reimpose the *malos usos*. This brought about a confrontation between lords and peasants. Peasant leaders like P. J. Sala were no longer content simply to beg for the abolition of the *malos usos* on condition of compensation for the owners, but to demand the end of all rents and services. This they did not, of course, achieve but the successful waging of war by the militants was probably the necessary condition for the achievement of the demands of the 'moderate' wing of the *remensas* who were prepared to negotiate but not to fight. By the Sentence of Guadalupe the *malos usos* were abolished – after a century of agitation ranging from threats of death to the lords to armed struggle against them.[2]

(2) *Wars and Political Crises*

The military organisation of the Catalan peasants and their participation in the civil wars in the second half of the fifteenth century are a unique feature of medieval peasant movements. More frequently peasants were passive sufferers in the wars that were waged over their land by contenders between whom they were unable to make any

[1] R. H. Hilton, *The Decline of Serfdom in Medieval England* (1969).
[2] J. Vicens Vives, *Historia de los Remensas en el siglo XV* (1945).

distinction. The peasants in France in the areas devastated in the course of the conflict between Plantagenet and Valois Kings submitted to burning and looting by French and English soldiers and freebooters of varying origin for many years before the outbreak in 1358 of the famous *Jacquerie*. The situation since the defeat of the French nobility at Poitiers in 1356 had been one of social and political chaos, but there seems to have been a sharp deterioration in the situation in 1358. The few authors who have studied this movement disagree about the precipitating causes. S. Luce thought that it was provoked by an order from the Regent allowing castellans (lords of castles) to requisition peasants' goods to victual their fortresses; J. Flammermont disagreed and suggested that the most likely immediate cause was a fight between peasants and brigands; G. Fourquin, the most recent interpreter of the *Jacquerie*, draws attention to the consequences of the developing civil war between the supporters of the Regent and the Parisians, allied to the King of Navarre. According to this view there was in fact an intensification of requisitioning as of pillaging by the rival armies who were living off the country. But Fourquin points out that the rising was generalised over the whole of the Ile de France, including relatively untroubled and prosperous areas. The background of discontent here may, he suggests, have been an economic crisis caused by low grain prices and high industrial prices. However, he sees this as a crisis which dates back to 1315. In this case, the search for a precipitating cause to explain the events of 1358 is imperative. In view of the capacity of peasants even in the Parisian basin to live off their own, market factors hardly seemed to be an adequate explanation for the revolt breaking out.[1]

Apart from the reaction against the brigandage of a noble class which had shown itself militarily incompetent, the existence of sharp conflict within the French ruling class cannot be ignored as a predisposing factor to this widespread but short-lived uprising. Similar splits in the upper ranks of society are found on the eve of other peasant movements. There is no need to look for this factor in the case of occasional village movements such as one finds in thirteenth-century England, nor perhaps in the case of the type of slow peasant pressure which culminated with the purchase of communal privileges. But it is noteworthy that violent rebellions involving large numbers

---

[1] S. Luce, *La Jacquerie*, 2nd ed. (1894); J. Flammermont, 'La Jacquerie in Beauvaisis' *Revue Historique* (1879); G. Fourquin, *Les campagnes de la région parisenne à la fin du Moyen Age* (1964) p. 233.

of peasants over a wide area often follow periods of political crisis which one would have thought would only have been the concern of governments, the landed aristocracy and the merchant capitalists in the towns. The rising of maritime Flanders must be seen in the context, not merely of local class antagonisms, but of the division of those elements among the nobility who had supported the anti-French actions of the Courts of the House of Dampierre, the Clauwaerts faction, and the pro-French Leliaerts, comprising the bulk of the nobility, the Francophile Count Louis de Nevers, who succeeded in 1322, and the patricians of the big towns. The English rising of 1381 in some respects could be seen partly as an outcome of the conflict between the Lancastrian faction of the aristocracy and those who were outside the influential circles at Court, a conflict which came out into the open in 1376 but which was by no means disposed of by 1381. As we have seen, the *remensas* in Catalonia actually participated, on the side of the crown, in the civil wars of the 1460s. These were political crises with their origins within the ruling groups of society. But there were other crises, too, perhaps even deeper, which also had the effect of releasing the energies of peasant communities and focusing their attention on the possibility of realising long-standing objectives. These crises, very important in a Europe dominated by a powerful institutionalised church, were partly political, but also emotional, spiritual and ideological, usually manifesting themselves as heretical movements.

(3) *Religious Crises and Heresy*

The relationship between social protest and heresy was by no means simple. No study of heretical movements which were supported by masses of poor people in town and country will get far if the heresies concerned are treated as changing currents of thought and feeling about the purposes of religion, in isolation from a social context. On the other hand, it is insufficient to treat such heresies as if the beliefs proclaimed were simply a more or less consciously assumed expression of social and political aims, thinly disguised in theological terms. All the same, beliefs are often taken up by people for other reasons than those which moved their originators, or early propagators. The acceptance and elaboration of fragments of the beliefs of Joachim, early thirteenth-century abbot of Fiore in Calabria, by the disoriented urban poor of the late medieval Low Countries throws no light on Joachim, but much on the social mentality of such movements as that of the Brethren of the Free Spirit. On the whole, extreme millenarian or chiliastic beliefs in the Middle Ages seem to belong to urban rather than rural settings.[1] This is not surprising. A kingdom of God on earth in which property was held in common and in which love between the sexes was a matter for free choice was unlikely to appeal to peasants. The peasant communities were rooted socially and economically in the individual family holding which was passed from generation to generation by customary rules of inheritance. These things they wanted to strengthen. They might welcome the abolition of tithes, the expropriation of church property, the abolition of the ecclesiastical as well as the lay hierarchy. These ideas fell short of chiliastic dreams.

The Twelve Articles of the German peasants in 1525 repeat the substance of many peasant demands made in other countries throughout the Middle Ages – the abolition of serfdom, of excessive services, of heriots (death duties), the reduction of rents, enjoyment of common rights. The religious clauses of the Articles, emphasising the way of life of the gospels, demanding an elected priesthood and popular control over the disposal of tithes, shows how important had been the church reformers in influencing the thoughts of the rebels, perhaps in providing an opportunity and a stimulus comparable to the political upheavals which preceded other peasant movements. There is a long history behind these religious attitudes. The evangelical heresies which stressed the study and imitation of the life of Christ and the Apostles as seen in the gospels, and which minimised the sacramental and sacerdotal aspect of Christianity to the extent of advocating the virtual abolition of the institutionalised Church, go back at least as far as the eleventh century. It is not necessary here to answer the question: Did social radicalism precede and determine religious radicalism, or the other way round? The facts simply are that peasant aspirations arising out of their social and economic situation are at least as old as evangelical heresy; that this type of heresy was supported mainly, though not exclusively, by the poor of town and country; and that influential heretical movements sometimes acted as mobilising forces for peasant movements which might otherwise never have begun.

Various twelfth-century movements in which heresy had an obviously plebeian social basis – those associated for instance with Pierre de Bruys in the south of France, with Eon de l'Etoile in Champagne, Flanders and the Rhineland – are not well enough documented for us

[1] G. Leff, *Heresy in the Later Middle Ages* (1967); N. Cohn, *The Pursuit of the Millennium* (1957); M. Reeves, *Prophecy in the Later Middle Ages* (1969).

to identify them with rural rather than urban discontent. The movements associated with Arnold of Brescia and Peter Waldo almost certainly were, to begin with, primarily urban. The word *tixerant*, weaver, became a synonym for heretic during this period. But the Pastoureaux in mid-thirteenth-century France were possibly of rural origin, if the biased reports of Adam Marsh are to be believed. There is no indication, however, of a specifically peasant programme; simply the determination to extirpate the clergy, uproot the monastic orders and attack the knights and the nobles. The Apostles of Fra Dolcino who, by the time they were crushed in 1307 seem to have numbered over a thousand, had been in existence as a heretical sect for some forty years. Yet, for all that has been written about the revolutionary character of their movement, they have left no programme with recognisable peasant demands. This is not to deny the relevance of the movement to our theme, since they were certainly a revolutionary element in the society of the time. It was the religious message which brought them together, but it is most unlikely that they could have been mobilised for the apostolic message were they not suffering from the social upheaval in north Italian rural society to which we have already referred.

The same is true of the radical wing of the Hussite movement. The Taborites and their militant millenarian temporary allies, the so-called Pikarts, were called on to the stage, so to speak, by the politico-religious crisis of early fifteenth-century Bohemia, and through the organisation which religion gave them expressed their social aspirations. As we know, the social struggle was merged into the national war against the Catholic church, the Emperor and the Germans. The so-called extremists were crushed by the knight Jan Zizka and eventually, as the Unity of the Czech Brethren, the peasant evangelicals adopted so extreme a form of pacifism and quietism that it has been thought that their submissiveness encouraged the deterioration in peasant conditions which took place in post-Hussite Bohemia.[1]

In many cases these peasant movements were triggered off by religious as well as by political crises. It is not surprising that the egalitarian implications of evangelical heresies should seem to fit their social aims, not to speak of the more direct social and political appeal of religious programmes which included the expropriation of the great

---

[1] J. Maček, *The Hussite Movement in Bohemia* (1958); F. G. Heymann, *Jan Zizka and the Hussite Revolution* (1955); P. Brock, *Political and Social Doctrines of the Unity of the Czech Brethren* (1957). H. Kaminsky, *A History of the Hussite Revolution* (1967).

ecclesiastical landowners. But the ideology of all medieval peasant movements was not uniformly expressed in terms of religion. J. Vicens Vives noted that the ideology of the Catalan *remensas* movement came, surprisingly enough, from lawyers rather than from churchmen. He quotes the jurist Mieres, who is said to have influenced the peasants with the view that all men are free by natural law and have the right to be protected by their king against the nobles. There is no indication of the direct influence of lawyers in England on the peasant movement of 1381, though some of the pleaders hired by peasants to fight cases for them in the courts put forward arguments about all men being in origin free. Such ideas could not be kept in watertight compartments. Hence the rebels' outlook in England in 1381 was not unlike that of the Catalan *remensas*. There was the same stress on free status and a clearly held though naïve political conception of a popular monarchy (or regional monarchies) with no intermediaries between the king and his people. In spite of what has been said about the influence of Wycliffe in 1381, the religious attitude of the rebels did not (like the later Lollards) involve doctrinal heresies (with regard to the Eucharist, for instance); they did, however, recommend the expropriation of the church hierarchy, a radical enough measure. The same predominantly social and political character of the ideas of rebels is found during the period of the revolt of maritime Flanders, linked with anti-clerical feeling, though not with heresy. It is perhaps of some significance that in these two last cases (the English and the Flemish risings) where the religious element was least marked, the participants do not seem to have come from disrupted peasant communities, but – and this applies particularly to the leadership – to have been, on the whole, successful producers of agricultural commodities for an urban-industrial market.

VII. LEADERSHIP AND ORGANISATION

The problem of the ideology of peasant movements is closely connected with that of leadership. The egalitarian and libertarian outlook which is strongly marked in most movements, whether social-political or religious in overt motivation, could, partly at any rate, have been introduced from outside the peasant class. The socially radical strand in Christian thought must, it is often thought, have been brought to the illiterate peasant masses by priests or other members of the clerical order. Dolcino was the son of a priest; priests such as John Ball and

John Wrawe were prominent in England in 1381; inevitably in Bohemia leaders and ideologists like Zelivsky and Koranda were drawn from the clergy; and after all Thomas Munzer, the early sixteenth-century German revolutionary was a cleric. Other leaders of peasant risings, not clerics, seem to have come to the peasantry from outside. Such were the members of the gentry at the time of the *Jacquerie* and in East Anglia in 1381, men who may afterwards have pretended to have been forced to assume leadership, but who in fact may very well have seen good reasons for throwing in their lot with revolt at the time. The greatest leader of the Bohemian Taborites was the knight Jean Zizka. Sometimes other classes provided leadership; the artisan Wat Tyler is often cited. But are there enough examples of leaders from outside the peasant class to entitle us to make it a rule that peasant movements cannot throw up their own leadership?

One difficulty, naturally, is the vagueness of the descriptions of the origins of rebel leaders to be found in the medieval evidence. Artisans were probably not far removed from peasants even in the towns, not to speak of village artisans who were often enough also tillers of the soil. The lower clergy were often recruited from the younger sons of the lesser gentry, but boys of free or even unfree peasant families could occasionally achieve clerical status. But apart from the possibility of close family links between leaders from other groups and the peasants, there is in any case plenty of evidence that peasants themselves assumed the leadership of these movements. Wace's detailed description of the Norman rising of 996 gives no indication of any others than peasants being involved in the affair – and this is significant whether the chronicle reflects authentic tenth-century tradition or the social conditions of the twelfth century. Osbert, the leader of the peasants of Verson in their struggle against the abbey of Mont St Michel, was *un vilein felon*. The isolated village rebellions in thirteenth- and fourteenth-century England were normally led by a man or a group of men from the village community, the sort of people who were capable of organising a common fund and hiring a lawyer to plead for them. Zannekin, leader of the peasants of maritime Flanders, was a peasant, although one of the relatively well-to-do, as was Guillaume Karle, the principal leader of the Jacques in 1358. For all Verntallat's *hidalgo* connections, he and Sala, leaders of the Catalan *remensas*, were essentially peasants.

The origins of the leaders of peasant uprisings were, then, mixed. For various reasons, clerics, townsmen and members of the gentry might identify themselves with these movements and emerge as leaders. But the peasants were not an inert and unthinking mass. They were capable of producing their own leaders whom they would probably trust more than they would trust outsiders, in spite of the fact that the leading peasants were almost certainly drawn from the ranks of the village rich. But such persons, as has already been suggested, were not divided by any great gulf from the poorer members of the community and were in any case those who were accustomed to the direction of village affairs in the local courts.

And so we find that an outstanding feature of many revolts in the Middle Ages was the firmness of organisation. Let us take the rising in maritime Flanders. Here was no undisciplined or easily dispersed mob. The existing administrative structure of the maritime regions of the county of Flanders were kept in being, the counts' *baillis* simply being replaced by captains chosen by the peasants themselves. There was a proper military organisation, discipline was maintained and there was no drift to anarchy. But this should not surprise us. Stable village communities, even when not formally given rights of self-administration (as in some of the French or Italian charters), had a long tradition of common management based on the collective routines of husbandry. Even where village or manorial assembles were presided over by the lords' officials, the conduct of affairs was normally in the hands of the villagers, those, that is, who knew and could declare local custom. Therefore, although peasant rebels might not wish to operate far from their home base or during periods when they had agricultural work to do, their capacity for organisation would be greater than that of uprooted persons who had lost their village base, or of urban artisans or journeymen whose life had less of collective routine about it.

During the English rising of 1381 various forms of organisation can be discerned. In a number of cases the subdivision of the shire, the hundred, appears faintly as the organisational basis of peasant mobilisation. In the Isle of Thanet (Kent) the parish organisation was used. The confederate townships in Hertfordshire who supported the townsmen of St Albans against the abbot were no doubt those owing suit to the abbey court under the ash tree; here, therefore, the organisational framework was seigneurial. But this was not all. New forms of organisation developed. It seems that, after the first mobilisation by village, parish and hundred, the movement was kept going by militants who organised themselves into companies operating on a regional basis. These are referred to in the judicial records as *magnae societates*, a phrase which gave rise to the legend of the whole rising being planned by a 'Great Society'.

These fairly well documented examples of coherent organisation based on existing, even official, institutions are striking enough. However, they cannot match the organisation of the Catalan *remensas*, which were more effective and longer lasting. This was partly because one of the main issues throughout the fifteenth century was the redemption of the *malos usos* by means of a money payment as compensation to the lords. This could only be discussed and eventually assessed at meetings of peasants. It was the policy of the Crown of Aragon and the jurists who were its advisers to promote this redemption in the interests of social peace. Peasant assemblies, therefore, had a legal basis derived from the patronage of the monarchy. In 1448, for instance, assemblies of fifty peasants, attended by royal officials, were to elect syndics for the discussion of the redemption payment. The nobles, of course, were hostile to the very idea of peasant assemblies, the monarchy's attitude was not always favourable, but from this moment on peasant assemblies became unavoidable. By 1462 armed mobilisation was beginning which the monarchy had to accept in view of its difficulties with the nobility. The peasant leader Francisco Verntallat organised his army in the Montana on the basis of one man from every three households, and both politically and militarily the peasant forces kept their independence of the royal administration. This army was in existence until the nobles were defeated in 1471 and was capable of re-mobilisation in future periods of crisis, as in 1475 when sworn associations (*sacramentales*) of peasants refused to pay dues demanded by the church of Gerona, and of course in the 1480s under P. J. Sala.

When we move back in time we rely on chroniclers' accounts rather than on the judicial and administrative records which illuminate fourteenth- and fifteenth-century movements. Now chroniclers who describe peasant movements were normally so appalled by the enormity of these subversions of the established social hierarchy that they paid little attention to forms of organisation. Fra Dolcino and his lieutenants must have had exceptionally good organisation and discipline to keep a large force in embattled existence for two or more years. But the writers describing the movement were more interested in denouncing it than in describing it accurately, so we get no convincing picture of organisational forms. However, the description by William of Jumièges of the movement of 996, short as it is, gives a brief insight into a quite sophisticated form of organisation. There were several assemblies (*conventicula*) in each of the counties into which Normandy was divided. From each of these, two delegates were elected to represent their decisions at a central gathering. It was these delegates who were captured by the agents of the Duke, mutilated, and sent back to their districts as a result of which 'the peasants returned to their ploughs'. The exact social background of the rising is unknown; D. C. Douglas thought it might be a last anti-feudal stand of freemen of Scandinavian descent.[1] This was a guess. However, it seems likely that here again we have an organised movement of established peasant communities quite different from the wandering bands of disoriented millenarians found in France in the following century.

It is an obvious difficulty for the historian of peasant movements in the Middle Ages that the evidence is unreliable in the sense that he cannot know whether or not it is complete. Apart from the fact that much evidence must simply not have survived, what does survive has not yet been systematically collected together. We are not therefore in a position to prove that conflict between peasants and the many persons and institutions who claimed a share in the product of their labour was as constant and inevitable as (say) strikes in modern capitalist industry. Some historians who recognise the disturbed and violent tenor of medieval life in general hesitate to accept that this violence, so easily resorted to by aristocratic rivals for land, power or even wives, could enter (regularly at any rate) into the relationships between rulers and ruled. Our assessment of the situation must, for the time being, be qualitative rather than quantitative. But, as has been shown, this takes us quite a long way. Whilst not underestimating the rich variety of the various situations in which lords, governments and peasants found themselves in conflict, it would seem clear that the basically unchanging character of peasant society over many centuries was matched by a consistency of type of peasant movements, underlying which were simply demands for freedom, for lower rents and services and for access to agricultural resources that were withheld from them. The variety between one movement and another is provided by differences, not in fundamental but in immediate or precipitating causes; by variation in ideological motivation; by differing relationships with other contemporary social or political movements; by changes in the balance of social power between the contending parties, and so on.

[1] 'The Rise of Normandy', *Proceedings of the British Academy* (1947).

It is because there are basic underlying similarities between the problems of peasant societies at all times, in the early or late Middle Ages, in the modern or contemporary epochs, that a study of medieval movements may be suggestive to the student of the contemporary underdeveloped world. No perceptive historian would, of course, wish to oversimplify the consistencies observable in peasant movements in widely separated centuries. The variations are as interesting and as important as the similarities. However, the differentiating factors between one movement and the next are not without their own pattern, especially if seen over a long period and over a wide area.

Chapter 3

THE ENGLISH PEASANT REVOLT OF 1381

by

Betty H. Landsberger and Henry A. Landsberger

I. INTRODUCTION

So impressive was the uprising of English peasantry in 1381 that it has continued to be a focus of scholarly attention in social, economic, political and constitutional histories, as well as in general history, throughout the nearly six centuries since its occurrence. Our own interest in it, and our re-analysis of it, stems from our belief that its characteristics are timeless, and that the lessons it contains are nearly as applicable to events today as they are to the time in which they occurred. Some of these lessons have figured in the discussion in the opening chapter of this book.

Granted its importance in the history of peasantry, the question arises whether, in view of its early date, we know enough about it. Is the kind of information available to us which we need in order to analyse this uprising as a peasant movement? To make an analysis in order to compare one movement with others makes greater demands on the reliability and validity of information than does the writing of a credible story of the revolt.

Surprisingly enough, in view of the relatively undeveloped state of literacy in fourteenth-century England, there exists quite a body of first-hand information. This is in the form of descriptions of the happenings, prepared almost entirely by monks whose job it was to record events. G. R. Kesteven[1] lists the better-known of these accounts,

---

[1] *The Peasants' Revolt* (London: Chatto and Windus, 1965). The works listed by Kesteven include: The *Anonimal Chronicle* of St Mary's, York, written by an anonymous monk and generally accepted as the most reliable source (and translated by Sir Charles Oman in his *Great Revolt of 1381*); The *Chronicon Angliae* by Thomas of Walsingham, a monk of St Albans abbey; *Knighton's Chronicle*, a record of events before and during the revolt that is likely to be based largely on hearsay; and *The Chronicle of Sir John Froissart*. Froissart, a French knight, had earlier written a lively, if not always accurate, account of the opening phase of the Hundred Years' War. His account of the Peasants' Revolt tends to favour Richard II.

and his evaluations of them are consistent with those of other scholars. Inasmuch as the chroniclers were on the side of the Government and/or landowners and were writing for that part of the public (few on the other side were literate in any case) these reports give a necessary, but inadequate, narrative of the revolt. To these accounts must be added primary sources such as parliamentary statutes, letters patent of the King, local archives, and, most important of all, court records of the trials against offenders. Our task in this study has been to select among the available sources on the basis of the degree to which they are documented from the primary sources, and especially from the second class of primary sources, the official documents.

There is a scarcity of information on some of the points most interesting to the present investigation, especially on the peasants' organisation and on their ultimate goals. Many questions will always go unanswered because the revolt was never recorded from the peasants' side. Nevertheless, there has been enough thorough investigation of the rising and its historical context to merit analysis as a significant movement of peasants. The studies are listed and discussed in a Note on Sources at the end of this chapter.[1]

A brief description of what took place is the necessary starting-point for our study. The following summary is based on the account presented in the *Cambridge Medieval History* and on Oman's description of events in Cambridgeshire.[2] As a preface to the account of the revolt itself, it should be explained that a poll tax (a flat tax per person), universally agreed upon as the spark which set off the flame of revolt, had been voted by Parliament during 1380, the year preceding the revolt, as a means of raising money urgently needed because of the continuing war against France. Since there had been gross attempts at evasion on every hand, the Government, hard-pressed for cash, had made repeated attempts at collection and had sent one set of authorities after another into the country districts.

The *Cambridge Medieval History* reports that by May 1381 troubles over collection of the poll tax had grown to the point that three Essex villages resisted authorities by force, first rioting and then murdering court officials sent to punish rioters. In the first week of June riots spread throughout the county. The Government, which did not respond to the rebel challenge with notable strength of arms, was

---

[1] See pp. 138–141.
[2] *Cambridge Medieval History*, VII, 461–3; and Sir Charles Oman, *The Great Revolt*, pp. 124–5.

unable to control the situation. In north Kent, across the Thames from Essex, another rising began, and on 6 June armed rebels moved from Dartford to Rochester and plundered the castle there. On 10 June rebels 'occupied' Canterbury and opened the prison.

Throughout these events a modicum of order among the rebels was maintained by their leader, Wat Tyler (of either Essex or Kent), who had the spiritual and, perhaps more important, oratorical support of a priest named John Ball. Ball, who might be considered the foremost ideologue of the rising, had preached for some twenty years against social inequality and wickedness on the part of the aristocracy. These activities had kept him in trouble with the hierarchies of both Church and State, and, finally, led to his imprisonment.

On 11 June, the *Cambridge Medieval History* continues, the Kent rebels set out for London, reaching Blackheath the next day and promptly released prisoners, including Ball, at the Marshalsea and King's Bench prisons, and sacked the archbishop's manor house at Lambeth. At the same time, rebels from Essex approached London.

The mayor of London, Walworth, was prepared to defend the city and, except for indecision by the royal council, might have successfully done so. While the council gathered at the Tower of London for safety, there occurred, according to the *Cambridge Medieval History*, 'definite treachery in the city government itself'. After one unsuccessful attempt to parley with the rebels, and with the apparent aid of several aldermen, two entrances to the city were opened and the rebels entered to find substantial support among city dwellers. Disturbances ensued and more prisons were opened. The people focused their rage on three hated symbols – John of Gaunt, Hales, the treasurer, and the lawyers – by sacking and destroying buildings connected with those men.

The royal council finally decided on a strategy of conciliation. In a meeting between Richard II and the rebels it was agreed that villeinage and feudal services would be abolished, and that land held by villein tenure would be rented as freehold. Monopolies and restrictions on buying land were to be ended.

But before this meeting, held at Mile End, was over, rebels elsewhere in the city vented their anger on the two men they hated most. Chancellor Sudbury and Hales, both of whom had remained behind at the Tower, were dragged into the streets and beheaded on Tower Hill. Other murders followed, including the massacre of many Flemings living in London. *The Cambridge Medieval History* describes the state of London with the terse sentence: 'Anarchy reigned in the city'.

Despite the danger, Richard, only fourteen years old, met again the following day with Tyler and the rebels. It was at this meeting that Walworth struck and mortally wounded Tyler, setting the stage for Richard to ride forth among the rebels, claiming that he was their chief, promising to fulfil their demands and calling upon them to follow him. The combination of this leadership by Richard, who had never been a focus of rebel discontent, and the confusion wrought by the death of their leader were sufficient to move the rebel band north to the open fields of Clerkenwell, from which they dispersed.

Knowledge of the Kent and Essex rebels' apparent success in London spread into the countryside; riders sped through the villages claiming that the King had freed all serfs and that no one would henceforth owe services to his lord. In East Anglia on 12 June, in Cambridgeshire and Hertfordshire on 17 June, and in some areas further from London on later dates, risings occurred. Oman describes the disturbance in Cambridgeshire. Although it occurred after Tyler's death in London, it is worth recounting because the events paralleled closely what happened at the earlier risings in Kent and Essex as well as the later ones in East Anglia, Hertfordshire and other areas.

According to Oman, there was intense dissatisfaction with manorial dues throughout Cambridgeshire and in as many as twenty villages bonfires were set to burn documents belonging to unpopular land-owners. In some of these villages manor houses were sacked and destroyed. In the country, much as in the city, the rebels' anger was directed at officials who represented the collection of the poll tax and the oppressive aspects of the feudal system, including sheriffs, clerks, justices and lawyers. In Cambridgeshire, Oman notes, there were apparently two deaths, those of a wealthy justice, Edmund Walsing-ham, and a lawyer named Galon. Walsingham was decapitated and his head placed on the town pillory. Apart from these two, no other deaths are known to have occurred in Cambridgeshire with certainty, 'though every other form of violence abounded'.

In the following section we shall go on to consider the broader setting of the rising.

II. PRECEDING TRENDS

The feudal system in thirteenth- and fourteenth-century England was not a very stable one, according to both Vinogradoff[1] and Petit-Dutaillis.[2] Many peasants had enjoyed at least relatively free status in Anglo-Saxon times; it was after the Norman conquest that the whole group was pushed down into the legal status of serfdom. That they did not rest easily there is evidenced by the many instances where they banded together in a legal fight to try to establish their former pre-conquest status, claiming the right of 'ancient demesne'.

This already unstable structure of feudal arrangements on the manors was made even more unsteady by changes in the general economy brought by the fourteenth century. *The Cambridge Economic History*[3] cites among others: the development of trade and industries and corresponding growth of towns; the development of new farm lands and new types of farming, the raising of sheep being especially important; the growing move to the cities (especially to London) by the landowners, increasing their need for money and their readiness to substitute rent for the customary services due from their villeins. In so far as the landowners left their country residence, the social situation on the manors, of course, changed.   *174707*

These changes brought with them equally great changes in the make-up of the peasant class itself chiefly a much greater differentiation than had existed during the preceding century. Hilton[4] has described this development, pointing out that even in the twelfth and thirteenth centuries there were 'poorer' and 'richer' peasants, depending on the size of their holdings. As the lords decreased their personal control over their manors and were willing to let more land for rent, gradually 'the rich got richer', and peasants themselves became employers of labourers to help work their increased holdings.

One of the most powerful institutions and centres of influence in medieval England was the Church. There was division and dissension here, too.

---

[1] Vinogradoff, *Villeinage in England* (Oxford: Clarendon Press, 1892).

[2] Petit-Dutaillis, 'Introduction historique', *Le soulèvement des travailleurs d'Angleterre en 1381* (Paris, 1898).

[3] *Cambridge Economic History*, vol. i, pp. 493–527.

[4] R. H. Hilton and H. Fagan, *The English Rising of 1381* (London: Lawrence and Wishart, 1950) pp. 28–30. Eileen Power, in the *Cambridge Medieval History*, has described the same development in many European countries.

One-third of the land of England was held by ecclesiastical orders; thus the Church was of prime importance as a landlord. Though there was of course, variation, the church holdings were generally run in a very reactionary fashion, and old rights and privileges vis-à-vis their labourers and economic activities in neighbouring towns were jealously guarded and insisted upon.

'The Church' of course included a great many social levels. For the men at the top it was a source of great wealth as well as power. But the same structure included many very poor friars. The village priest was often on a par economically with the serfs – indeed, many of the lower-level clergy came from peasant families.

Because the Church was in many respects the centre of village life, the clergy were important and influential persons. Part of their power rested upon the fact that they were among the very few literate persons in the lower levels of the society.

It is easy to see how it happened that the clergy were at the same time among the chief targets and the chief instigators of the revolt. The chief targets were wealthy and prominent in the hierarchy, and were associated especially with the abbeys and priories where feudal services were strictly exacted. The poorer clerics were among those who knew best and resented most the evils of the Church. Because of their role they were in a position to instigate rebellious ideas, to spread ideas from one place to another, and to become leaders when peasants began to react against oppression.

As we now narrow our focus to the quarter-century before the revolt itself, we note Vinogradoff's[1] remark that 'The customary system which represented the average requirements of the thirteenth century was entirely unable to do justice to the competition of the fourteenth, to the rise of wages and to the new openings in industry and trade. . . . The customary system was eminently disqualified to meet critical emergencies and sudden changes of conditions.'

'Critical emergencies' occurred during the generation preceding the revolt. In the first place the war with France became less and less profitable; in fact, it became costly and grew less and less popular. The nobles themselves suffered reverses and lost hope of gains. The populace had to keep paying taxes to support an army which failed to win victories. But an even more critical emergency occurred at home, and in every region: the Black Death, the plague which killed off a large

---

[1] This is from his review of the book by T. W. Page, *The End of Villeinage in England*, in *English Historical Review*, xv (1900) p. 779.

proportion of the population. Estimates of the loss of population range from one-third to one-half.[1]

The effect upon agriculture of the loss of such a tremendous proportion of the population can readily be imagined. In the *Cambridge Medieval History* we read:

> Labour, whether rendered in the form of villein services or free and paid for in cash, became suddenly much more valuable. For work which had been done previously by hired labour landlords were asked to pay perhaps twice as much as before the pestilence, while to get the same number of days' work done by feudal dues they had now to press much harder on the smaller population that remained.[2]

In their desperation, the landlords reacted in many ways at once. And whatever they did, trying to procure labour from the scarce supply, they managed in one way or another to aggravate grievances, stimulate discontent and pave the way to the 1381 revolt.

Some paid more, tried to attract workers from other landowners, leased out more land; in short, made concessions to get what they could. Where this happened, the workers became more independent, in a stronger position and ever more ambitious to improve their bettered condition. The contrast between themselves and the workers still unfree became a source of discontent for the latter. Other landholders who still held a large number of men in villeinage – and here Dutaillis mentions especially various church holdings – bore down harder than ever on their workers.

Above all – and this step was to bring about the most discontent of all – landowners turned to the Government, that is, to the Crown, and to the Parliament which was so constituted as to represent their interests, for legislation to help them meet the crisis.

Thus began the series of King's ordinances and Acts of Parliament which are known as the Statutes of Labourers, and which form a never-to-be-forgotten chapter in the history of repressive legislation. However correct it may be that the Government was acting to deal with a chaotic and disastrous economic condition, it is none the less true that the workers resented it thoroughly as a means to make them pay for the country's troubles and, above all, as a hindrance, arbitrarily im-

---

[1] Petit-Dutaillis, *Studies and Notes on Stubbs' Constitutional History* (Manchester: University Press, 1930) p. 256. Other estimates are somewhat smaller. The *Cambridge Economic History* estimates between one-third and one-half.

[2] *Cambridge Medieval History*, VII 463.

posed, to keep them from taking advantage of existing conditions in order to improve their lot.

We turn to Dutaillis for information about the Statutes. He mentions this very early one, 'To restrain the malice of servants', and another 'To obviate the outrageous dearness of victuals'. Then:

> While the plague was still raging and it was impossible for parliament to assemble, the royal council had taken measures. An ordinance had been published on 18 June 1349. It compelled men and women under sixty, having no means of support, to work when they should be required; they and all other labourers had to accept the wages paid in 1346, or in the five or six years before. Breaches of contract were forbidden. Penalties were imposed on all those who offered wages above the legal rate. Retailers of food and innkeepers were to charge reasonable prices.[1]

Hilton continues a description of the ordinance as follows:

> ... Their lords were to have the first refusal of their services. Contracts by the day were forbidden, only contracts for six-monthly or yearly periods being legal ... Officials had the right to put into stocks those who [did not submit] ... Bodies of justices, chosen from amongst the local nobility and gentry of the counties, were appointed to try ... delinquents, and to fine or imprison.[2]

This was followed by an Act of Parliament.

The statute of 9 February 1351 made the law more precise, and fixed a definite amount for many kinds of wages. It was afterwards reissued and made more severe. A statute of January 1361 ordained that labourers who went from county to county seeking higher wages should be branded on the forehead with a red-hot iron.[3]

Dutaillis indicates a special reason for the resentment displayed over the Statutes. He explains that the legislation was in many ways a novelty: wages and prices had indeed been controlled by municipalities before this time, but 'agricultural workers had never been subject to an official limitation, and free labourers had never been forced to reside in a certain district'.[4]

The attempt to turn back the clock and place restraints on workers'

[1] Petit-Dutaillis, *Studies and Notes*, pp. 264.
[2] Hilton and Fagan, *The English Rising*, p. 26.
[3] Petit-Dutaillis, *Studies and Notes*, p. 264
[4] Ibid., p. 265.

finding work where they pleased was a severe hardship, particularly for peasants who had more land and depended upon hiring workers themselves. Hilton points out that this intervention drove these richer peasants into the rebel cause against the Government.[1]

The generally outraged reaction to the Statutes made necessary further Acts of Parliament. One kind of measure was directed against the concerted opposition on the part of the villeins. Other measures had to do with the administration, the enforcement, of the Statutes. It was to the advantage of the nobility, in order to be granted fines, if cases came before royal tribunals. Usually, therefore, offenders were tried by 'justices of labourers' (who had been set up specifically for the Statutes) or by commissioners appointed to preserve the peace. In 1368 these functions were entirely transferred to the justices of the peace by a statute. Dutaillis notes that this could only have the effect of further irritating the workers, since these justices came from the middle class of the rural districts, 'the most conservative class in the country', who already were in control of local administration and, in effect, of the House of Commons.

It is in the story of the court actions that the record of opposition to the Statutes is most dramatic. The research of Putnam was devoted to exactly this matter, and Dutaillis bases his discussion of the enforcement of the Statutes largely on her work.[2]

The inferior courts, under the justices mentioned above, dealt most frequently with excesses of wages and prices, though they concerned themselves with all of the issues covered in the Statutes, even taking labourers from one employer to give to another. Dutaillis comments: 'It is evident that the commissioners were very active and very tyrannical.'[3]

The superior courts dealt with actions for breach of contract, more difficult to decide. According to Dutaillis: 'Miss Putnam conjectures that from 1351 to 1377 the two supreme courts (King's Bench and Court of Common Pleas) dealt with 9,000 of these actions, brought by employers against men who left their work before the end of their contract, or against other employers who had enticed their labourers from them.'[4] Dutaillis points out how widely interpreted the Statutes

[1] Hilton and Fagan, *The English Rising*, p. 28.
[2] Bertha Putnam, *The Enforcement of the Statutes of Labourers* (New York: Columbia University Press, 1908).   [3] Petit-Dutaillis, *Studies and Notes*, p. 266.
[4] Ibid., p. 267. From Hilton and Fagan we learn that 'in almost every case for which there is evidence, the jury's verdict or the court indictment was in favour of the employer'. *The English Rising*, p. 27.

were: 'Schoolmasters, chaplains, bailiffs and squires were regarded as bound to their masters.'[1]

Almost all of the students of the rising comment upon the large increase in the number of outlaws after the Statutes were passed. To run away from one's district in search of higher wages was, for a very large number of peasants, worth the price of becoming liable to be 'shot on sight'. Hilton[2] reminds us that in the tales of Robin Hood, mentioned in *Piers Plowman*, and well known in the fourteenth century, the heroes are outlawed yeomen – the freemen among the peasantry. Obviously, outlaws made not only good recruits for the rebel bands but, on the move as they were, spread word of rebellion from one place to another.

Power notes a new spirit making its appearance, pointing out that *Piers Plowman* (which is believed to have first appeared in the 1370s) sounds a new note in literature. It was an idealisation of the peasant himself: 'The labourer and not the priest was the type of holiness whose sweat quenched hell fire and washed the soul clean'. She finds this spirit 'half religious and half socialistic'.[3] Class-consciousness among the peasantry was growing, together with the rise of egalitarian and socialistic doctrines. The Germans marched with the wooden Bundschuh for their banner and the English repeated a doggerel couplet:

> When Adam delved and Eve span
> Who was then the gentleman?[4]

Joseph Clayton, in his study of the revolt, which he regarded as the first great national movement towards democracy, refers to this same spirit as the gospel of brotherhood, and comments: 'It may be said that today [he wrote in 1910] the idea of political and social equality is generally accepted and that of brotherhood denied. In the fourteenth century, brotherhood was esteemed, but equality was a strange, intruding notion.'[5] Lindsay, too, notes that men of that day had caught a vision of an England where new problems were to be solved in co-operative association rather than to allow self-advancement and greed to continue unchecked.[6]

---

[1] Petit-Dutaillis, *Studies and Notes*, p. 267.
[2] Hilton and Fagan, *The English Rising*, p. 86.
[3] *Cambridge Medieval History*, VII, 'Peasant Life and Rural Conditions', p. 739.
[4] Ibid. The couplet was coined by the priest and rebel leader, John Ball.
[5] Joseph Clayton, *Leaders of the People* (London: Martin Secker, 1910) note p. 143.
[6] Philip Lindsay and Reginald Groves, *The Peasants' Revolt, 1381* (London: Hutchinson, 1951) p. 175.

The urban centres of England still were not very numerous nor large. Dutaillis describes them in this sentence: 'At the accession of Richard II, London had 40,000 inhabitants, York and Bristol 12,000, Plymouth and Coventry 9,000, Norwich, Lincoln, Salisbury, Lynn and Colchester between 5,000 and 7,000.'[1] As the centres of trade and industry, they were the nuclei of the changes taking place in the economy of England, and political power and activity were becoming important as well. Dutaillis states: 'Industries were multiplying and becoming more specialised. The guilds of artificers (craft guilds) were developing by the side of merchant guilds. There were forty-eight of them in London at the end of the reign of Edward III.'[2]

Towns, like countryside, lost in population because of the plague, and wages and prices jumped greatly; masters and workmen, who actually worked closely together in most instances, according to Dutaillis, found mutual profit in the situation. When the Statutes were passed,

> the artisans offered violent resistance to the statutes of labourers. They refused to serve those who would not give them high wages. They broke their contracts in order to work for those who would give them more. They formed 'leagues, confederacies, and conspiracies' to keep up the price of labour. They forcibly opposed the execution of corporal punishments imposed by the justices on labourers.[3]

There seems to have been none of the opposition between towns and surrounding rural areas that existed, according to Power, during this period in various countries on the Continent. On the contrary, the swift and ready participation of townsmen of various classes with the peasantry, from the earliest outbreaks in Kent to their welcome to and their common actions in London, points to the fact that there was a thorough identification of interests on the part of townsmen with countrymen. Wilkinson, whose article on the revolt contains much reference to London, speaks of the powerful support which Londoners gave to the revolt.[4] Wilkinson's description of the development of the political sense of the London population[5] seems in some ways to parallel, as well as to supplement, the

---

[1] Petit-Dutaillis, *Studies and Notes*, p. 268.
[2] Ibid.
[3] Ibid., p. 270.
[4] B. Wilkinson, 'The Peasants' Revolt of 1381' in *Speculum*, 15 (1940) 29–30.
[5] Discussed below in section v on the organisation of the movement.

development of the new spirit among the peasants, mentioned earlier. It was probably Londoners who were responsible for directing the general hostility against the Government towards particular leaders, termed 'traitors'. Possibly without their 'political sense' the revolt would never have taken the turn towards the central Government.

The war with France has been credited by all of the students of the period with profound effects on conditions within the country: political, economic and social. The war had been going on sporadically for decades and had been the important project of Edward III, the predecessor of Richard II. In 1369, under Edward III, there occurred a period of renewal, and from that point it dragged on with temporary interruptions and truces until 1389. The *Cambridge Medieval History* tells us that by the time Richard came to the throne at the age of ten, in the year 1377,

> he found the country in a false position with respect to the war. Public opinion had not yet learned to distinguish between winning battles and conquering a state; it insisted on the continuance of campaigns from which no government could win credit, but which served only to make taxation necessary and to keep England in frequent fear and in occasional danger of the horrors of a French invasion.[1]

One main effect of the unsuccessful war effort was that it contributed to the unpopularity and instability of the Government. In accordance with precedent, an advisory council was established upon the succession of the ten-year-old Richard to the throne.

> The method of government by a continual council to advise the great officers of State lasted only till 1380. It was not a great success. The expeditions made each year in France or Brittany cost money and brought no credit . . . Constant changes of chancellors indicated the instability of the government . . . Trouble with London – itself a sign of weak government – was to be a constantly recurring feature of the reign.'[2]

Still another effect of the war on the population of the country was, at least, to instruct the population in the ways of war, and, at the worst, to brutalise the nation. Dutaillis is one who claims that the latter had occurred:

[1] *Cambridge Medieval History*, vii 457.
[2] Ibid., pp. 458–60.

In the years immediately before the rising, the rolls of Parliament, the statutes, and the royal letters leave the impression that great disorder prevailed in the country. Crimes of violence were very frequent. Armed bands were organised, not only for robbery, but to gratify private ambitions, to abduct 'heiresses', to take possession of a manor, or to terrorize the justices.[1]

He notes also the development of lawless habits on the part of the nobility, pointing out that they were accustomed as individuals to keep troops of swashbucklers in order to defend their interests by force. Comments Dutaillis: 'There can be no doubt that in 1381 bands of rebels were frequently led by old soldiers, both English and foreign, accustomed to pillage and bloodshed, whether for gain or for the gratification of their brutal passions.'

And now, to focus on events immediately preceding the revolt: 'The brand which suddenly kindled the fire was the poll tax,'[2] stated Dutaillis, and all students of the revolt agree that it was the reaction to this tax which set the populace ablaze. Aside from the general fact of the unpopularity of taxation, there are special reasons why the levying and the inept collection of this tax epitomised the corruption and inefficiency of the Government, and symbolised to the populace all that which they had come to hate about it.

For several years the Government had been short of funds and the continuation of the costly war against France had made the condition worse each year. In 1377 funds had been raised for the first time by a poll tax. This tax, amounting to a groat (4 pence) a head, was collected so far as can be determined without special reaction on the part of the population. When Parliament met in April 1379, they were confronted with serious financial problems in the form of a deficit together with the fact that 'ordinary financial expedients were exhausted'.[3] These, according to Trevelyan, were the taxation on imported wool and those taxes known as the 'fifteenth and tenth' on particular lands and tenements. The idea of a poll tax was popular with the upper classes: '"The wealth of the kingdom is in the hands of workmen and labourers" was a saying that took the fancy of the lords, knights, and burghers of Parliament.'[4] But in setting the tax, Parliament at least had the grace to base it on ability to pay.

Nevertheless, the Parliament of 1380 was given a financial report even worse than before: all taxes had proved hopelessly inadequate;

[1] Petit-Dutaillis, *Studies and Notes*, p. 273–4.   [2] Ibid., p. 275.
[3] Trevelyan, *England in the Age of Wycliffe*, p. 99.   [4] Ibid.

they were in arrears on the payment of troops; Chancellor Sudbury confessed to Parliament that 'he had even pledged the King's jewels which would soon be forfeited if not redeemed'.[1] As Oman and others remarked, it was astonishing that through it all Parliament was determined to continue waging the unfortunate war. To meet the crisis they again voted a poll tax, partly as a bargaining measure against the wealth of the Church which was forced to come up with one-third of the total of £160,000 that Sudbury demanded. Though there were provisions that in each township the wealthy should aid the poor, this time 'every lay person in the realm, above the age of 15 years, save beggars, should pay three groats (one shilling)'.[2] This represented a week's wages for many a villein.

Oman reports that the response to the new tax was a widespread effort to falsify census figures in each village, either through the co-operation or coercion of the constables responsible for collection.

> The result was that every shire in England returned an incredibly small number of inhabitants liable to the impost . . . [Between the listings of 1377 and 1381] the adult population of the realm had ostensibly fallen from 1,355,201 to 896,481 persons.[3]

'The main body of the returns bear witness to a colossal and deliberate attempt to defraud the government.' The Government was not only angry but desperate for funds. The ministers were driven into 'an inquisitorial research' into the details of the returns to discover and punish the persons who had endeavoured to deceive them.

Oman gives this account of the Government's second attempt at collection. On 22 February 1381 the Council issued a writ calling for instant efforts to collect the whole of the tax. On 16 March an additional writ created a fresh body of collectors, and by April and May the second collection began.[4] Initial surveys revealed how wide the evasion had been, e.g., 'in Suffolk no less than 13,000 suppressed names were collected in a few weeks'.[5] Oman continues that 'the revision had not gone far when [the] explosion of popular wrath occurred'.[6]

Powell, as well as Trevelyan, adds the insight that 'it appears that it was the action taken under this fresh commission, regarded as it may

---

[1] Oman, *The Great Revolt*, p. 23.   [2] Ibid., p. 25   [3] Ibid., p. 26
[4] Ibid., p.29. Oman remarks that for unascertainable reasons, the commissioners were sent only into fifteen shires, 'including all those of the south-east and, in addition, Somerset, Devon, Cornwall, Gloucestershire and the West Riding of Yorkshire'. Petit-Dutaillis notes that these fifteen were the counties in which revolt occurred most widely and with greatest ferocity. It should also be noted that the collection commissioners were *not* backed by armed force.   [5] Ibid., p. 30.   [6] Ibid., pp. 30–31.

possibly have been by the people rather in the light of an attempt to extort a fresh tax without the authority of Parliament, that was the more immediate cause of the outbreak'.[1] He points out a related fact, as does Oman: 'It is said that this [second] commission was suggested to the ministers by John Legge, one of the king's serjeants-at-arms. The reputation of having done so cost him his life.'[2]

III. AGRICULTURE AND THE PEASANT COMMUNITY

There has been a great amount of careful research into England's rural life and its agricultural population during the thirteenth and fourteenth centuries. The student who wishes to obtain a complete and trustworthy picture may go to the writings of Homans, Vinogradoff, Maitland, Coulton or Rogers, to name only the best known and most frequently quoted of the scholars.[3] Our purpose here is to single out only a few points of relevance to the development of the peasant movement.

There had been a development towards urbanism which Dutaillis regarded as phenomenal during the half-century before the revolt.[4] Nevertheless up until that point – and still so by comparison, say, with Flanders – England was an agricultural country. The estimate is that about half of the population of 1,350,000 were villeins and serfs at the time of the rising.[5]

The pattern of agriculture, rural life and village communities throughout England was immensely varied.[6] Isolated sheep-farming

[1] Powell, *The Rising in East Anglia*, p. 6.
[2] Oman, *The Great Revolt*, pp. 29–30.
[3] G. C. Homans, *English Villagers of the Thirteenth Century*, (New York: Russell and Russell, 1941); Sir Paul Vinogradoff, *Villeinage in England* (Oxford: Clarendon Press, 1892); F. W. Maitland, *Manorial Courts, The Court Baron*, and other works; G. G. Coulton, *The Medieval Village*, and other works; Thorold Rogers, *A History of Agriculture*.
[4] Petit-Dutaillis, 'Historical Introduction', pp. xli and xlii. He notes that it was during the fourteenth and fifteenth centuries that the cities of England reached the high point of their wealth and independence, thanks to their economic activity. During the half-century before the revolt smaller cities, as well as large ones like London, Bristol, York and Plymouth, had doubled or tripled their municipal budgets.
[5] See Oman, *The Great Revolt*, p. 27.
[6] In a note on p. 445 of *English Villagers*, Homan extracts from an article by Kominsky information regarding the diverse ways in which farms were organised and worked. 'He finds (1) that in the shires described in the Hundred Rolls 'out of 650 vills described and investigated, 336 are not identical with manors'. The majority are manors only in Oxfordshire. (2) That the Hundred Rolls 'show that about 60 per cent of the territory examined is represented by demesnes with dependent villein land (i.e., the typical manorial elements), while 40 per cent, a considerable proportion, is non-manorial in character'. (3) That there are two kinds of non-manorial arrangements: (a) a complex of free

regions, for example, differed greatly from market farms. According to Trevelyan: 'There was less homogeneity of law and custom throughout England in the fourteenth century than there is today'.[1] Nevertheless, throughout the Midlands, East Anglia, and south-east England where, especially in the latter, the population of the country was concentrated, the rural pattern was sufficiently similar to warrant a description.

The manor was the unit of land division and agricultural activity, and the land was in the hands of the lord of the manor. The arable land of the manor consisted of the lord's portion, the demesne farm, whose produce belonged to him, and the small holdings which were the portions of the peasants. These latter were held 'of the lord', i.e., they were not the property[2] of the peasants who tilled them although they were held permanently by a single peasant and his descendants, passing on to his widow or to a son on his death.

The villeins and serfs 'paid for' their holdings by giving a certain and specified amount of labour services to the lord for the farming of the demesne farm. The number of 'work weeks' per year varied directly with the size of holdings. However, this was no ordinary contract because the villein was tied to the soil by law. 'He could not sell his land nor leave his farm without permission (of his lord)', Trevelyan tells us.[3] Even in cases where the customary labour services of the villein had been commuted, he still was likely to remain a serf, 'unfree and bound to the soil of the manor by the law of the land'.[4] The land itself was classified as 'free' or 'unfree', and the same classification applied to persons. It is evident that this practice would make for great stability in the rural population.

Homans,[5] describing thirteenth-century villagers, furnishes us with a detailed picture of the arrangements on farm and in village. The villeins, together with a number of landless labourers, lived in a small

---

tenants, in feudal relation to their lord, paying rent, (b) demesne without villein land. (4) That the amount of land in villeinage varies roughly directly as a size of the estate. (5) That according to investigations in the *Inquisitions Post Mortem* of the thirteenth century, labour services are valued at something like 40 per cent of the total render of tenants in the eastern counties of the Midlands where the proportion is highest.

[1] Trevelyan, *England in the Age of Wycliff*, p. 221.

[2] Eric Wolf explains that there was no private property, in the sense we know it today. Even the lord of the manor ultimately held 'of the King'. He has described the system in North-west Europe in medieval times as 'patrimonial domain'. 'Patrimonial domain over land is excercised where control of occupants of land is placed in the hands of lords who inherit the right to the domain . . . and where this control implies the right to receive tribute from the inhabitants in return for their occupance' (*Peasants*, p. 50).

[3] Trevelyan, *England in the Age of Wycliff*, p. 195   [4] Ibid., p. 186.

[5] Homans, *English Villagers of the Thirteenth Century*, pp. 68–106.

village, as often as not together with the workers from one, or more than one, other manor. That is, each manor did not have its separate village by any means, even though these villages were typically very small communities.

Each villein had the land (a yardland or half-yardland) on which his house was located and his animals and poultry were housed; and, in addition, alongside those of other villeins, strips of land on the fields which were farmed almost always on some kind of rotation system. On his yardland often lived one or more families of cotters, or cottagers, themselves holding either little or no land, who owed a certain amount of service to him as well as to the lord.

A part of the manor and the village population were also the freeholders, usually (but not always) few in number but holding somewhat larger parcels of land than the villeins. They were free in the sense of being free of the labour services which the villeins had to render. In place of the services, they paid rent to the lord.

The point to appreciate is that the whole working population associated with the manor stood under the power of the lord from whom, in one way or another, they held their land. Both the law and customs, however varied, defined the relationship in this way.

The crux of the changes away from the traditional feudal arrangements lies in the changed situation of the peasant as a producer. In a very real sense, this was where the revolution occurred, and the three- or four-week revolt itself was but a public dramatisation of the fact that the peasants had now achieved new power and status.

It is important here to distinguish two periods of time: at least a hundred years preceding the revolt, during which peasants began to play a new role as they acquired greater amounts of land; and (of tremendous importance) the agricultural crisis brought on by the sudden rise in the value of their labour due to the population loss occasioned by the Black Death. Without either of these, one cannot imagine the occurrence during the fourteenth century of the revolutionary changes away from feudal arrangements.

In the traditional picture, the centre of production on the manor was the demesne farm, the produce of which belonged to the lord. Indeed, in theory, the produce of the peasants belonged to him, too. But in practice, manorial customs did not allow enforcement of this to its extreme. Production for the lord, however, was the *raison d'être* of the manor as an enterprise.

The fact that this was no a simple, uncomplicated social arrangement is attested by the variety of other duties, obligations, institutions, and even sentiments which went along with it. In the important events in the peasant's life – his marriage, his children's marriages – he was related to the lord by needing to secure permission and to pay special dues. The overabundance of ways in which the villein's dependence upon his lord was demanded in the culture of the manor suggests that, because in point of fact the lord was completely dependent upon the work of the peasants, a whole network of customs was devised to create the impression that the opposite was the case. But the lord's 'sharing' in the enterprise of the manor was hardly on a face-to-face basis with his villeins. The steward and the bailiff were the administrative officers who 'ran' the manor, and the foreman, or reeve, chosen from and often by the villeins themselves was the only administrator with whom the peasants were likely to be in close contact. Nevertheless, it is beyond doubt that there was a bond of sympathy between a lord and his villeins.

Changes outside manor life were to bring about change in this important aspect of the economy of the manor. Probably the most decisive factor which brought the 'loosening' of the manorial system was a change in the lords' interests, habits and needs.[1] As urban centres grew in size and in power, especially London; as involvement grew in the war against France; as money began to creep into the picture replacing traditional exchanges; as sheep-farming to feed the growing wool market came to look like the most profitable agricultural enterprise – the lords tended to leave the country districts, in spirit if not in body. More and more, they were satisfied to settle their bargain with their villeins in money terms, by accepting rent for the holdings; to hire the labour needed on the demesne farm; or even to lease out the domain farm itself. As need – and/or greed – increased, they could, and did, increase the money returns by hiring out the 'bordland' or areas not previously cultivated.

Dutaillis states that 'under the reigns of Henry III and Edward III, was born the middle class of molmen, later called copy-holders, villeins who did not perform work services and, in practice, were hardly distinguishable from freeholders'. He observes how the lords were contributing to their own downfall by renting out all they could, because they were, in so doing, helping develop 'the robust and ambitious yeomanry'.[2]

---

[1] See Lipson, *The Economic History of England*, vol. I, ch. 3.
[2] Petit-Dutaillis, '*Historical Introduction*', pp. xxviii and xxix.

Then came the great crisis in agriculture occasioned by the loss of population due to the Black Death. We have noted the effects of this event in a previous section. The opportunities for the peasant as a producer increased suddenly and enormously, on the one hand to increase his holdings, on the other hand to increase his wages. (Dutaillis points out that rural wages rose almost 50 per cent – and 'reapers frequently received 5d. or 6d. a day instead of the 2d. or 3d. which they earned before the plague'.)[1]

But with this opportunity came the frustrations which led to increased unrest, constant strikes and hostile outbursts, and finally to the revolt itself. The lords insisted upon legislation – the Statutes of Labourers – to help them regain the control over their labour which they had bit by bit been abdicating and selling away. And although their repeated cries in Parliament for new efforts at enforcement bespeak the lack of success the Statutes enjoyed, there was enforcement enough to arouse much resentment.

The men who had risen to the top of the peasant-producer class, having extended themselves far beyond what they could work with their own hands, were hard-hit. Their usual labour supply – other villeins who could spare some time to hire out some of their labour, and landless labourers – had decreased in number as much as any other group because of the Black Death. And the Statutes not only gave the lords 'first refusal' of the services of those who were available, but prohibited the peasant producer from bidding for needed labour by offering higher wages – and fined those who did do so. Furthermore, the Statutes, in the regulations against price rises, forbade the villein's taking advantage of food scarcity in order to add to income from the sale of his produce.

Those who had not fared so well as these large holders were at the same time equally frustrated. The villein who still had to perform work services – by far the majority[2] – was prevented from earning the wages which farmers were crying to offer him for whatever periods he had to devote to work on the demesne. He had to stay on his own manor, being forbidden by law to leave it to seek whatever wages he might be able to command elsewhere. And the profit from his relatively small amount of marketable produce was limited by the price regulations.

---

[1] Petit-Dutaillis, *Studies and Notes*, p. 259.
[2] Petit-Dutaillis, in the 'Historical Introduction', p. xxxiv, says that for the country as a whole, the movement to replace work services by money rents had only begun.

The fact that freedom to buy and sell in open markets was one of the demands at Mile End indicates that the peasant producers needed and knew they needed access to markets. This, like the fixing of their land rent, was a necessary corollary to their freedom, and the demand reflects their stage of development as producers by the time of the revolt.

'The peasant as consumer' is a point on which little reliable information is available. Undoubtedly along with growing incomes and growing commerce, the material wants of the better-off members of their class had been rising. The growing greed of the peasant was certainly referred to frequently enough, in records of Parliament and in popular literature. Although these were undoubtedly prejudiced perceptions, a portion of *Piers Plowman*, translated into today's English by Oman, is worth reading. As will be seen, the peasant here described is a landless labourer:

> The Labourers that have no land and work with their hands deign no longer to dine on the stale vegetables of yesterday; penny-ale will not suit them, nor bacon, but they must have fresh meat or fish, fried or baked, and that hot-and-hotter for the chill of their maw: Unless he be highly paid he will chide, and bewail the time he was made a workman . . . Then he curses the king and all the king's justices for making such laws that grieve the labourer.[1]

That their material wants had been increasing is a condition we must assume to have been true.

We turn now to look at the peasant's legal status and his role as a citizen.

Vinogradoff as well as the several other scholars of villeinage have pointed out the distinction which needs to be made between the legal status and the actual status of villeinage. The actual condition probably never corresponded to the legal definitions of an almost slave-like status of the unfree man. Lipson[2] tells us that personal serfdom lasted through the fifteenth and sixteenth centuries, surviving 'as an instrument of extortion . . . Manumission was a source of profit.' Actually 'serfdom lost all economic significance in the moment it ceased to be the basis of compulsory labour and the keystone of medieval husbandry.'

Homans cites various items of evidence for the fact that the personal

---

[1] Oman, *The Great Revolt*, p. 9.
[2] Lipson, *The Economic History of England*, I (London: A. & C. Black, 1929) 112–4.

aspect of serfdom – even the name 'villein' – was repugnant to thirteenth-century villagers.[1] Homans[2] distinguishes for us the village from the manor organisation, pointing out that the village government was in some respects a unit of the royal authority and administration. The reality of the villagers' tie to the authority of the Crown is attested by their linking themselves to the King in their fight against their lords and the restrictions of the manorial system.

It is important to recall, too, the citizenship training they received as members of the jury – or as 'litigants' – in the hallmote, the manor court. Attendance at this court and jury service were among their duties as villeins of the lord. This in turn should be seen as related to one of the grievances connected with the villeins' status as unfree men. As such they had no access to the King's courts and thereby no place to bring suit against the lord.

When it came to politics, 1381 saw the debut of the peasants on the national political stage. Dutaillis emphasises that the rebels had no political programme,[3] and, indeed, it is hard to see how they could have been expected to have one. They demanded the removal of 'traitors' from the King's Council and in fact saw to the permanent removal of some of them by the act of murder. Dutaillis's observation, nevertheless, is only partly correct, because they in fact had a platform, in the shape of very definite demands, as we shall see in the next section. But there, the strategy came to an abrupt halt. They did not have ready a new slate of officers who were to take over and implement their programme. After all, it was only their debut, and they could not have been expected to give a completely professional performance.

IV. GOALS AND MEANS

A clear political goal was the rebels' wish to express hatred against the Government by punishing officials high and low. Whether or not it was at Mile End that the rebels asked the king for permission to punish the traitors who had sinned against him and the law, and how Richard answered, are subjects not generally agreed upon by students.[4] It is

[1] Homans, *English Villagers of the Thirteenth Century*, pp. 236–7.
[2] Ibid., ch. 21.
[3] Petit-Dutaillis, *Studies and Notes*, pp. 275–6.
[4] Neither Dutaillis nor Trevelyan records this as one of the demands conceded at Mile End. Oman reports it as such, as does very specifically Kriehn in his article, 'Studies in the Sources of the Social Revolt in 1381', *American Historical Review*, VII (1902) 254–85, 458–84.

agreed that there was, especially among the Londoners and Kentish-men, a strong hatred directed against the Government. The person of the young (14-year-old) Richard II was excepted but – beginning with the Duke of Lancaster, the uncle of the king and long the most power-ful figure in the Government; then the chancellor; and going down through other court officials and men of law at all levels to local func-tionaries – they wanted to kill or to destroy the homes and possessions of those who had come to symbolise for them 'the Government'. Many, in fact, lost their lives. Hatred against officialdom was also attested by the burning of court records, tax lists and other official documents, though these acts also served to destroy proof of liability.

Freedom from serfdom headed their social goals. It was primarily the Essex men who led the fight for this, the goal for which the movement is best remembered. It was the principal goal shared by rebels through-out the counties. They demanded not only legal freedom (charters of manumission) but the necessary economic right to implement this: the right to hold their land at a fixed rent (4d per acre) and the right to buy and sell freely elsewhere. These, together with the declaration of amnesty for acts of the rebels, were the demands made to and granted by the king at Mile End, where, according to Dutaillis, primarily bands from Essex met with the monarch. Ironically, the existence of these demands is only known through the letters of revocation issued by the king between 30 June and 2 July. The burning of manor rolls and registers and the manor court records again attest to this demand, these records being the symbols of their feudal relationship.

Kriehn believes that at Mile End demands were made and granted for repeal of the Statutes of Labourers and for freeing of prisoners and abolition of outlawry. He notes that not a word was said as to Parlia-ment and its rights, saying that in its persistence in legislation hostile to the lower classes (since the first Statute of Labourers in 1349) it had completely estranged them. He believes that their ideal of a popular absolute monarchy – the king to rule on the advice of the 'true commons' – simply left Parliament out of the picture.

Kriehn is one student of the revolt who chooses to accept the reports of some of its chroniclers (principally the Anonimal Chronicle) to the effect that a group of demands was presented to the King by Tyler at Smithfield, at the meeting where Tyler was killed. These included not only a further expression of dislike of the law enforcement they had been experiencing from their governors and a demand for a return to the law of Winchester (local enforcement only), but for the free use of woods – for hunting, fishing, and for wood itself.

Also allegedly demanded here was the disendowment of the Church and abolition of its hierarchy: that the goods and the land of the Church be divided among the parishioners, keeping out only that needed for the sustenance of the clergy, and that there be henceforth only one bishop and one prelate. Wilkinson, whose view is that Tyler was trying for 'shock' and extremity in his demands at Smithfield, adds another: 'that all lordship should be abolished, save that of the king'.[1]

The large admixture of local quarrels and grievances in the total revolt is responsible for the demands of a purely local character which appear as a part of the revolt.[2] Obviously these include the several instances of a demand for ousting of the oligarchies from control of municipalities – at Beverley and York in Yorkshire, as well as Northamptonshire, for example. In Cambridge, the university was a special target and a promise was exacted that it would ever remain submissive to the city. But probably most often the people of the locality rose up against a church holding and demanded freedom from the special privileges of the ecclesiastical order: abbeys and priories from East Anglia to counties far to the west and south were attacked by bands including townspeople as well as the villeins and serfs. The risings at St Albans and at Bury St Edmunds are the most famous single instances.

The depth of change indicated by the demands is a matter subject to various interpretations. It depends on the perspective from which it is viewed. When the terrorised cries of the moment itself – reflected in some of the chronicles – had subsided so that the motives of the rebels could be assessed a little more clearly, it appears that few of the leaders had in mind sweeping changes in the social order. That the majority seemed to have had only rather limited changes in mind is reflected by the fact that after receiving their charters of freedom from the king at Mile End, many of the bands were ready to and did return to their localities, apparently satisfied.[3] Lest manumission itself appear as more profound a change than it actually was, it should be noted that changing

---

[1] B. Wilkinson, 'The Peasants' Revolt of 1381', p. 27. This demand appeared in the Anonimal Chronical, the translation of which is given by Oman in *The Great Revolt*, pp. 186–205.

[2] Oman after surveying many of the uprisings inspired largely by local grievances remarks: 'As at Scarborough and Beverley, indeed the same as Bury, Cambridge and St Albans . . . during the anarchy of 1381, every man and every faction strove to win what could be won by the strong hand' (p. 147).

[3] See Petit-Dutaillis, 'Historical Introduction', p. lxxxviii.

from feudal services to money rents had already been going on for a
long time, for many villeins in the manors bordering their own.
Though it may appear, long afterwards, that had they been able to
deal a mortal blow to serfdom, the change would have been indeed
profound, this was surely not what they had in mind. It was an extension of a desirable condition, not a completely new condition, which
they sought. Likewise as to changing the Government: there was no
cry for a complete overthrow, but rather for the removal of specific
officers[1] felt to have been responsible for failure and repression; and,
throughout, complete allegiance to the King. Trevelyan and Oman
refute charges – first made by Froissart – that the rebels held com-
munistic goals. Trevelyan points out.:

> it may be questioned how much stress was really laid by the agitators
> on the project of 'having all things in common'. When the Rising
> took place, no such request was put forward. Personal freedom,
> and the commutation of all services for a rent of 4d. an acre, were the
> very practical demands then made. When this had been granted,
> most of the rebels went home; even those who stayed, produced no
> scheme of speculative communism, but confined their further
> demands, at most, to disendowment of the Church, free use of
> forests, abolition of game-laws and of outlawry. The attempt to
> picture the Rising as a communistic movement ignores the plainest
> facts. It was, as far as the bulk of the peasantry was concerned, a
> rising to secure freedom from the various degrees and forms of
> servitude that still oppressed them severally. Whenever there is a
> labour movement, a few will always be communists, and the con-
> servative classes will always give unfair prominence to the extreme
> idea.[2]

The degree of homogeneity of the rebel's goals is likewise evident
from the foregoing description: some – liquidation of traitors and
freedom from serhfood – were shared broadly; many were specific
to the locality. Opinion among scholars of the revolt seems almost
unanimous that both as to goals and as to participation, the bands of

---

[1] The leaders meeting in London on 13 June made a list of the 'traitors' for whom
they ordered beheading. Oman, on p. 60 of *The Great Revolt*, names these: 'John of
Gaunt, Archbishop Sudbury, Treasurer Hales, Bishop-Elect of Durham, Chief Justice
Belknap, Chief Baron Plessington, Sir Ralph Ferrers, John Legge, the King's Serjeant
who was supposed to have advised the sending out of the poll-tax commissioners, Thomas
Bampton, and Sir Thomas Orgrave, Sub-Treasurer of England'.
[2] Trevelyan, *England in the Age of Wycliffe*, pp. 197–8; see also Oman, *The Great
Revolt*, p. 21.

each locality operated as units. Wilkinson, for instance, states: 'Our records consistently described the main bands of rebels as operating mostly apart. The rebels achieved an astonishing degree of unity, but it is necessary to remember the very strong local loyalties they displayed.'[1] There was 'county-unity' as well as 'village unity': Wilkinson agrees with Dutaillis that it was Essex men with whom the King met at Mile End, while those who remained and were present at the next meeting were Kentishmen and Londoners.

There is evidence that there was persistence over time in the goals held by the rebels. Hilton's research into peasant movements before 1381 has shown the many instances of combinations to refuse feudal services as early as the thirteenth century: he cites a case 'in 1278 brought by villein tenants of the Priory of Harmondsworth'[2] and another, even earlier, in Northampton in 1261: 'The tenants of Mears Ashby [claimed] to be free men, to have the right to buy and sell land freely, to be amerced [fined] only by the judgment of their peers, and to pay a fixed tallage [annual tax to landlord].'[3] Such instances, of course, increased during the fourteenth century to the point where Parliament in 1377 put the matter before the King.

After the revolt, Oman tells us that 'the terms of the charters which they [the peasantry] had won in Tyler's time now served as ideals which they hoped someday to achieve . . . At St Albans, [the tenants] are accused by their abbot of having made copies of the document which they had extorted from him, "as evidence that they should have said liberties and franchises in time to come."'[4] Oman states, further: 'The theory that the fair rent of land should be 4d. an acre . . . also reappears regularly in the subsequent demands of the villeins of manors when a strike or an agricultural union was on foot'.[5]

With respect to the durability of the goals among the rebels at the time of the rising, however, Wilkinson has this to say: 'It was with regard to this particular grievance [hostility to John of Gaunt, the Duke of Lancaster] most of all, that the Londoners and rebels from Kent and Essex met on common ground.'[6] This hostility, as he notes, was the symbol of a more general hatred against the Government based on wider discontents – failure of the French war, and the poll tax. After the sack of the Savoy palace and the murder of Sudbury and

---

[1] Wilkinson, 'The Peasants' Revolt of 1381', p. 25.
[2] R. H. Hilton, 'Peasant Movements before 1381', *Economic History Review*, 2nd ser., II 2 (1949) p. 125.   [3] Ibid., p. 126.   [4] Oman, *The Great Revolt*, p. 155.   [5] Ibid.
[6] Wilkinson, 'The Peasants' Revolt of 1381', p. 31.

Hales, 'The movement inevitably began to ebb because it had few other realizable aims common to all'.[1]

Briefly stated, the means employed by the rebels were, first, to organise as many as possible; second, to use force against persons and property (including official documents) symbolising the destruction of that which they hated; third, to go to the king to obtain the changes they wanted to see occur.

These were the means actually employed. How much they were results of chance, as opposed to how much they were chosen after some amount of thought and discussion, we will never know: there was so little literacy among the rebels and, indeed, throughout the lay society, that recorded information on this, as well as other items internal to the movement, does not and never did exist.

It is certain that rebels all over wide regions followed more or less the same plans of action. In many instances – especially was this frequent in East Anglia – they forced people to join their bands by threat of death or destruction of property, sometimes other peasants, sometimes large property owners. It seems correct to say that there was not a county where any action occurred – and this included a majority of the counties of England – where manor rolls and court records were not destroyed. Almost everywhere sheriffs, escheators, justices and tax collectors were sought out for threats and actual punishment; although the majority of the rebels joining the march to the King were from Kent, Essex and London, the documents show that also in attendance there were the leaders of local uprisings from other East Anglia counties, Winchester, and more distant points. Furthermore, the records show that some of these latter returned – as is well documented in the case of Cambridge – pushing their demands 'in the name of the King'.[2]

To what extent were the means of the rebels violent outbursts, or, on the other hand, instrumental acts?

The small amount of 'violent outburst' and the large proportion of 'instrumental acts', especially on the part of the rural folk, is one of the most striking aspects of the rising. This is not to deny that in some localities, on the part of some of the bands, there was simply pillage and robbing or blackmail. But these instances are relatively few and isolated parts of the whole.[3]

[1] Ibid., p. 32.   [2] Powell, *The Rising in East Anglia*, p. 42.
[3] Trevelyan discusses the relatively small extent of violence on pp. 214–16 of *England in the Age of Wycliffe*.

It will be recalled that a particular type of destruction did occur everywhere: namely, the tearing up and burning of manor rolls, court records and tax lists. This, we would contend, is to be regarded more as an instrumental than as an expressive outburst. In itself, it was a way of destroying evidence of serfdom and what they considered to be unjust taxation without inflicting harm upon persons.

It was in London, where thousands had entered and been joined by many of the 40,000 inhabitants, that we find deliberate violence. There were the executions of the 'traitors' at the Tower: the Chancellor Sudbury, the Treasurer Hales, and (according to Kesteven) seven others. There was the subsequent murdering of citizens, largely the hated foreign group of Flemings, to the tune of some 140 or 150 persons, according to the estimate of a reliable chronicler.[1]

Possibly even more instances of violence involved the destruction of property in London. This included the sacking of the rich furnishings and the dramatic burning of the Savoy (the palace in London of John of Gaunt, Duke of Lancaster), the destruction of establishments of Hospitallers (the religious order of which the hated Hales was master in England), and the attacks on courts.[2] But with the great numbers involved at the time of the climax of the revolt, taken together their actions are probably not to be regarded as wanton violence nor a mob gone wild.

There are further indications that the violence which did occur in London arose more from the city-dwellers than the rural bands. The careful law-abiding behaviour of the latter as they entered the city on Thursday, 13 June, is described by Kesteven: 'The entry of the rebels was not, at first, nearly as terrifying as the more well-to-do citizens had feared. It is reported that many of the rebels paid for the food and drink that the citizens offered them, and they apparently did no damage to private property that afternoon.'[3]

Further, when the murder of citizens did occur, on the day and night of Friday, 14 June, the chief targets, as we have already stated, were the Flemings. It is well established that the hatred of this group belonged to Londoners, not to the men from the country.

---

[1] Kesteven describes the violence in London on pp. 56–9 of *The Peasants' Revolt*. It is his opinion that 'the violence done to the Flemings and other foreigners was more the work of the London rabble than of the country folk.' (p. 59).

[2] A vivid account of these attacks appears on pp. 230–1 of Trevelyan, *England in the Age of Wycliffe.*

[3] Kesteven, *The Peasants' Revolt*, p. 50.

V. THE MOVEMENT AS ORGANISATION

It is the organisation of the peasants at the local level which is the sturdy and incontrovertible fact behind the movement. Hilton reports evidence of organisations of peasants to voice disputes about their status as early as 1278.[1]

Completely verified is the fact that by 1377 there was sufficient organisation into leagues of farm workers to cause concern in the ruling class. We have already referred to the Act passed by Parliament in that year against the leagues and conventicles being formed by the peasants. Reville presents a record which shows that there existed conspiracies to resist services, customs and the like after 1377, and before the revolt itself.[2] Dutaillis cites numerous instances continuing many years after the revolt where the Crown responded to calls for help in various districts to combat leagues of peasants demanding freedom from services.[3]

Dutaillis also gives instances of organisations of workers in London which had begun to develop in various crafts and trades before the time of the revolt.[4] Even more important in London, however, was the fact that there already existed factions struggling for political power. Wilkinson notes that 'London citizens were politicians in the modern sense long before the citizens of other less favoured communities had any real appreciation of, much less influence over, national policy as a whole'.[5]

There is clear evidence of the participation of Londoners in inciting the revolt at its earliest stages, and when it comes to the 'general movement' – national, or, at least, regional uprising – the leadership function was performed by these men. The detailed description of the first instances of uprising in the south-east which Dutaillis gives in his 'Historical Introduction'[6] suggests that the Londoners directed their efforts very cleverly. The county of Kent, just south-east of London, where very few instances of villeinage existed, was already 'with them' in spirit – a spirit of revolution against the leaders of the Government,

---

[1] Hilton, 'Peasant Movements in England before 1381', p. 116.
[2] Cited by Dutaillis in 'Historical Introduction', p. xxxiv.
[3] Ibid., p. cx.
[4] Ibid., pp. xlv, xlvi.
[5] Wilkinson, 'The Peasants' Revolt of 1381', p. 30.
[6] Petit-Dutaillis, 'Historical Introduction', pp. lxxi et seq.

that is. It was therefore Essex – where the grievance of the population was primarily the burden of serfdom, but which was not yet so politicically awake as Kent – where we have instances of inhabitants of London going to incite the population. (Essex is just north-east of London.) According to the Sheriffs' Report, later made for the King, on activities of Londoners during the revolt, two butchers from the capital, Adamatte Well and Roger Harry, had, since 30 May, been travelling all over Essex giving the call to arms: 'To London!' On 13 June Thomas Farringdon, apparently of an illustrious family, coming after these two, regaled the Essex population with the story that the Treasurer, Hales, had taken away his rightful heritage. He later led the attack of Cressing-Temple and contributed to the destruction of establishments of the Hospitallers at Clerkenwell. 'If these Londoners did not create the revolt in Essex, they at least organised and directed it and gave it the precise objective which their hate had chosen.'[1] Between these two levels of organisation – the small, village-size leagues of villeins seeking to throw off their serfdom, and the energetic citizens of the big city anxious to rid the country of certain officials – there was what we might refer to as the 'middle management' group out of which, at the moment of revolt, emerged the men who led the army of peasants into London, and, elsewhere, directed campaigns throughout their counties, as did Wrawe in Suffolk and Lister in Norfolk.[2]

The man by whose name the revolt was afterwards known – Wat Tyler – was one of these, and he rose to the occasion not only by leading his army of thousands into London but of directing them once there, acting as their spokesman before the King, and giving orders for the conduct of groups returning from London to their localities to secure their positions under the charters of freedom given them by the King.

As far as we have been able to determine, neither Tyler nor a single one of these many leaders, was himself a peasant.[3] Many undoubtedly had peasants in their not-too-far-off backgrounds, but, by the time of the rising, like Tyler, they were artisans. (Lister, for example, was a dyer.) Or, like Wrawe and Grindcobbe, of St Albans, they were priests, chaplains, curates or other men of the Church. In all localities

---

[1] Ibid., p. lxxii.

[2] See Powell, *The Rising in East Anglia*, for a description of these activities, pp. 9–14, 26–30.

[3] Oman, speaking of chiefs of bands in Kent, says, 'there is a sprinkling of wealthy yeomen and priests, but the great majority are artisans and peasants of the poorest class' (p. 45). The leadership to which we refer is of a level higher than the chiefs of individual bands.

heavy participation of lower clergy in the leadership of the revolt has been noted by almost all scholars.

As to the degree of contact and planning before the revolt among the men who became leaders, no real evidence is available. It is interesting – because we see similar reactions to present uprisings of minorities – that many chroniclers report that the rebel leaders were organised into a 'Great Society' with extreme changes as their goals. Later scholars for the most part dismiss this, believing that in their fright, the chroniclers accepted rumours as fact.[1] That it is an open question is indicated by the fact that Trevelyan,[2] as well as Powell, took the position that they were organised beforehand.

It is clearly verified that one man was doing all he could to organise the peasants, to get them moving, and to make radical changes in the unjust distribution of wealth and power in the land. That man was the itinerant priest named John Ball. Later, under 'Ideology', we shall consider his role at greater length. Here we note only that for twenty years preceding the revolt he had preached the gospel of equality to the villagers in the south-east counties, and had urged them to act.

It may well have been, as has been suggested by Trevelyan, that he was but one of the many doing the same thing. Their energetic carrying around from manor to manor and from village to village of the news of discontent and conspiracies among groups of peasants probably did much to help build a vision of the achievement of a better society than the present one. Priests then, as well as wandering run-away villeins, outlaws and other refugees created by the Statutes of Labourers, formed the principal lines of communication existing among farm and small town dwellers.[3]

The short life of the revolt – a matter of less than a month except for local forays in outlying districts – made no real test of loyalty given nor discipline exacted by the leaders. Most historians consider that both are evidenced when one considers the speed with which Tyler was able to gather together his army of thousands, lead them into London and keep them in some order once there.

Reville considered that Tyler's sense of leadership was evidenced by his response when the people of St Albans came to him for instructions

[1] An example is Oman. See pp. 12–13 of his *Great Revolt*.
[2] G. M. Trevelyan, *England in the Age of Wycliffe*, pp. 202–3. The author's contention that the revolt was 'planned long before' is supported by references to several original sources.
[3] Petit-Dutaillis, 'Historical Introduction', p. lxviii.

about how to carry out their revolt: he reports that Tyler gave them a very detailed plan of action to follow, and promised them his help should they need it, on condition that they swore to omit none of his orders nor his system.[1] The rumour (reported by Froissart) that Tyler was able to command and receive obedience due to a term of military service in France is neither confirmed nor denied by other evidence. But the loyalty of the people to him is attested to by one of the chroniclers, the St Albans monk, who says that, by 14 June, Tyler had become, for the insurgents of London and for all the neighbouring counties, 'King of the people'.[2]

What psychological characteristics of the peasant group made possible this willingness to join with their neighbours in a common cause, a cause which meant rebelling against their masters and others, like public officials, with power over them? For this meant leaving the safety of their homes to join in a march under leaders whom few could have known personally, in a band which quickly grew to hundreds and then thousands, and led them into acts of pillage, arson and even murder against the most powerful figures in the land. In particular, how much could the ideals of freedom and equality have meant to them?

Reville in his book *Peasants of the Middle Ages*, discussing peasants from all of Europe, had this to say about the mind of the peasant: 'It is a mirror. Without instruction, he believes what he is told, he submits to the wisdom of the other person provided that what he hears does not contradict his own interests too much . . . Simple and naïve, rude and violent, these peasants could become the most brutal, the most indomitable, the most ferocious of enemies.'[3]

How do our fourteenth-century British peasants correspond to this view of peasantry in general? They had, for something more than two centuries, been accustomed to living under a rule of law and followed customs which had in them the elements of active and even democratic citizenship. This is to say that they were not 'without instruction': rather, they had been instructed through everyday experiences to manage the problems of their community by regularised procedures. Homans in his *English Villagers* describes and discusses what these were.[4] They served – they were forced to serve regularly – as jurors in manor courts. They made the by-laws which

[1] Reville, *Le soulèvement des travailleurs*, p. 11.
[2] Petit-Dutaillis, 'Historical Introduction', p. xciii.
[3] Quoted by Petit-Dutaillis in 'Historical Introduction', p. lxix.
[4] Homans, *English Villagers of the Thirteenth Century*, pp. 102–6, 309–38.

governed various aspects of their behaviour as villagers, and they elected their fellows and themselves served as groups to enforce these by-laws. They participated in elections of their 'foremen' or reeves. There were some who, individually or in groups, brought suits in royal courts petitioning their freedom from servile status on the basis of descent from tenants on 'ancient demesne' (royal property) at the time of Edward the Confessor. Oman comments on the sophistication of this petitioning.[1]

In the introduction to *Villeinage in England*, Vinogradoff demonstrates that many authorities agree that originally, i.e., under the Saxons, after they had rooted out most of the Romanised Celtic population of English Britain, there was a free community. He tells us that 'the main idea' of Stubbs, the authority on the constitutional history of England,

> seems to be that the English constitution is the result of administrative concentration in the age of the Normans of local self-government formed in the age of the Saxons . . . Even after conquest and legal theory had been over the ground, the compact self-government of the township is easily discernible under the custom of the manorial system, and the condition of medieval peasants presents many traces of original freedom.[2]

Further, on Saxon times: 'Most of the arable land was held separately, but the woods, meadow and pastures still remained within the village groups. The township with its rights and duties as to police, justice and husbandry was modified but not destroyed by feudalism.'[3]

Vinogradoff mentions that 'Toqueville in France has done most to draw attention to the vital importance of local self-government in the development of liberal institutions'.[4]

Dutaillis notes as an important underlying historical development the fact that the lords, since the twelfth century, had used their power to reduce the status of all the peasants to the rank of serfs. Whereas at the time of the Domesday Book there had been two different ranks, villeins and serfs, they had all come to be treated as serfs. The only trace left of 'the old villeinage' was in the 'ancient demesne' and in the county of Kent where it had been kept almost intact. Dutaillis comments: 'When G. L. Gomme [in an article in the *Antiquary*, XI,

---

[1] Oman, *The Great Revolt*, p. 10.
[2] Vinogradoff, *Villeinage in England*, pp. 23–4.
[4] Ibid., p. 24.   [4] Ibid.

pp. 97–100] considers the revolt of 1381 as an effort made by the peasants of England to re-establish the community of the Anglo-Saxon village, he is only expressing in paradoxical form an undeniable truth'.[1]

Another relevant aspect of the psychology of the rebelling farm workers, joined here by the working population of the towns and cities who were equally oppressed by the Statutes, has also been well appreciated by Dutaillis. Because of steady increases in production and commerce during the fourteenth century, 'all workers for a half-century or more had seen a betterment of their conditions and had become jealous of their well-being. Villeins, free peasants, artisans, merchants all wanted to acquire more comfort and material luxuries or at least safeguard the advances they had obtained'.[2] The poets – Gower, Langland and Chaucer – as well as the prose of Parliament made references to the rising aspirations of the ordinary people.

A further psychological characteristic of importance to the movement was the apparent willingness to bow to the authority of one person they chose to adhere to as chief. The authority of Tyler, the leader of the rebel armies, and of Richard II, the King, was a force coming from below at least as much as superimposed from above. Perhaps the rudiments of nationalism were behind their unquestioning acceptance of the King: 'Hold ye with King Richard and the true Commons' was certainly their motto.

VI. IDEOLOGY

The ideology of the movement was in many ways its most interesting aspect. Perhaps the lasting contribution of the movement was the expression of commitment to this ideology by the common people in their rebellion.

The content of this ideology has already been suggested as we have viewed the development and the goals of the movement. In a word, it was their right to freedom and equality of status and an end to the unjust oppressions of the many by the privileged few. Trevelyan has said that 'The rising of 1381 sets it beyond doubt that the peasant had grasped the conception of complete personal liberty, that he held it

[1] Petit-Dutaillis, 'Historical Introduction', p. xxxix.
[2] Petit-Dutaillis, 'Historical Introduction', p. xlviii. Eileen Power in the *Cambridge Medieval History*, vol. VII, also writes about the improving condition of peasantry all over Europe for more than a century before (pp. 735 ff.).

degrading to perform forced labour, and that he considered freedom to be his right'.[1]

Various aspects of the context in which this ideology grew among the peasantry should be noted again: the rise in the economic value of peasant labour and increased holdings on the part of many; the breaking-up in many areas of the old self-contained manorial system; the development of 'a new spirit' among landless peasants regarding the value of the peasant and his work (all of this in the setting of a system where they participated as active citizens and where there were roots, back in Saxon days, of a peasant population with relative freedom); and their growing dissatisfactions with those who held power over them, both as employers and as governors.

It was in relation to the verbalisation of these dissatisfactions with the powerful and their own growing aspirations that the folk literature – *Piers Plowman* and *Robin Hood* are notable examples – and the sermons of the day became important forces.

The extensive research by G. R. Owst on the sermons of the thirteenth, fourteenth and fifteenth centuries has established the fact that social criticism was the content of sermons preached over a long period of time and by some of the most prominent churchmen in England. His examples come from many sources, with particular attention given to sermons and writings of John Bromyard, Chancellor of Cambridge University. He contends that their attacks against the sins – especially the sins of avarice and pride – of the upper classes, Church and laity alike, were long enough and strong enough to have caused the revolt.[2] He notes, too, that these sermons went right on in the same tone in the years following the revolt.

Owst makes it clear – as does Trevelyan with respect to Wycliffe —that it was not the intent of the churchmen to incite the lower classes to punish the wealthy and powerful for their sins, nor to appropriate their goods. They intended to prophesy *divine* vengeance for the carefully and vividly detailed sins of the nobility, the merchants and the lawyers.

Their effect, however, differed from their intent.

Sacred orators of the Church, as hostile to class war and social revolution as any Luther, were here themselves unconsciously formulating a revolutionary charter of grievances. With the one

[1] Trevelyan, *England in the Age of Wycliffe*, p. 185.
[2] G. R. Owst, *Literature and Pulpit in Medieval England*, p. 307.

hand they were really instructing the rebels of tomorrow how to present their case and prepare for the struggle, while, with the other, they sought to restrain them from taking any action in the matter. Everyone can guess which hand was likely to prevail.[1]

Owst has built a good case for the importance of the social criticism made by prominent churchmen in unwittingly causing the rebellion. But it was churchmen of much lower rank who brought their words and doctrine to the peasants. In fact it was the 'poor friars' and the 'wandering priests'. The scathing attacks on the wealthy clerics and the selfish nobility originating in Cambridge, Oxford and London lost nothing in the translations these low-level clergy made in their deliveries to the rural folk.

The heavy participation and the leadership taken in the rebellion by the lower clergy has already been pointed out. Among these there was the outstanding one, John Ball, whose contributions as a leader of the people were equal to his contributions to the development of their ideology.

Ball was active for at least twenty years as a preacher. Hilton[2] tells us that the authorities feared him already as early as 1362, when the Archbishop of Canterbury excommunicated him. His effectiveness even then may be judged from the fact that the successor to that archbishop instructed a subordinate to threaten with excommunication those who listened to him.

A famous account of his activities and preaching was given by Froissart:

> A crazy priest in the county of Kent, called John Ball, who for his absurd preaching had thrice been confined in prison . . . was accustomed to assemble a crowd round him in the market place and preach to them. On such occasions he would say, 'My good friends, matters cannot go well in England until all things be held in common; when there shall be neither vassals nor lords; when the lords shall be no more masters than ourselves. How ill they behave to us! For what reason do they thus hold us in bondage? Are we not all descended from the same parents, Adam and Eve? And what can they show, or what reason can they give, why they should be more masters than ourselves? They are clothed in velvet and rich stuffs, ornamented with ermine and other furs, while we are forced to wear poor clothing. They have wines, spices, and fine bread, while we

[1] Ibid., p. 295.   [2] Hilton and Fagan, *The English Rising*, p. 97.

have only rye, and the refuse of the straw; and when we drink, it must be water. They have handsome seats and manors, while we must brave the wind and rain in our labours in the field; and it is by our labours that they have wherewith to support their pomp. We are called slaves, and if we do not perform our service we are beaten, and we have no sovereign to whom we can complain or would be willing to hear us. Let us go to the King and remonstrate with him, he is young and from him we may obtain a favourable answer, and if not we must ourselves seek to amend our conditions.[1]

It is likely that his famous letters were written from prison in order to keep in touch with his followers. Just as the pot was beginning to boil, in April 1381, he was incarcerated in the Archbishop's Prison at Maidstone, and it is certain that he wrote many of the letters then. He wrote in an allegorical style and often (but not always) under an assumed name.

Ball knew as well as the authorities the size of his following. He had threatened when put into prison in April that he would soon be released by an army of 20,000 armed men. The breaking open of the prison at Maidstone was indeed one of the first acts of the rebel bands. He could and did accompany them, then, on their march to London, and it was he who addressed them when they were gathered at Black-heath, poised for their encounter with the rulers in the metropolis.

Oman tells us that, when the Blackheath sermon was over, 'the multitude cried with a loud and unanimous voice that they would make him both archbishop and chancellor, for the present primate was a traitor to the Commons and the realm, and should be slain as soon as they could lay hands on him'.[2]

Trevelyan has referred to their ideology as 'Christian democracy', and Oman comments: 'It is notable that Ball is made to preach democracy and not communism – the insurgents wanted to become freeholders, not to form phalansteries and hold all things in common'.[3]

VII. OPPONENTS AND ALLIES

It appears that the rebels' aggression met first with surprise and shock rather than with resistance. The holders of power who finally rallied to oppose the rebellion were mainly concerned to get the rebels to go

---

[1] Ibid., pp. 98, 99.
[2] Oman, *The Great Revolt*, p. 52.   [3] Ibid.

home so that peace would be restored and things could go on as before.

We have seen that the rebels excluded the person of the King from those they deemed responsible for the wrongs their Government had visited upon them. They named as 'traitor in chief' the man who for many years had been the leading figure in the Government – the Duke of Lancaster (John of Gaunt). Very early in June, at the meeting at Maidstone when they named Tyler as their chief, the rebels issued the proclamation which Hilton reports as follows:

1. Continued allegiance to King Richard and the Commons.
2. That they would accept no king named John.
3. To agree to no tax that might be levied henceforth in the kingdom; no consent to any except it were a fifteenth.
4. To be ready when they were called upon.[1]

Actually, because he was away on a military campaign against Scotland, the hated John was spared involvement. Perhaps for this fortuitous reason – because no other particular cause is clear – they made Sudbury a particular target. He was a natural symbol of power, being at once the Chancellor in King's Council and chief prelate, the Archbishop of Canterbury. Robert Hales, the Treasurer, shared with him the position of the chief target within the governing group. We have seen above the reasons for Hales as a choice: not only as Treasurer was he the figure logically associated with the poll tax, but one of the agitators from London, Thomas Farringdon, due to a personal grievance, had thrust his name forward as an enemy.

These men, together with a group of dukes, earls, and court and city officials who happened to be on the scene, formed the council of the opposition and advised the young King as to how the rebels were to be dealt with. These may be termed the opposition to the *action* of rebellion. We shall see that it was Parliament who were apparently the chief opponents of the rebels' *programme*.

All accounts of the revolt present one version or another of what went on in the Council in order to meet the crisis of the sudden rebellion and invasion of London. However it was arrived at, the strategy finally followed was one of making concessions in order to get the rebels to go home. It is not clear whether or not the opponents actually plotted the killing of the chief, Tyler, who, with many others, stayed on in London. Kriehn subscribes to the theory of a plot;

---

[1] Hilton, *The English Rising*, p. 104.

Wilkinson rejects this, feeling on the contrary that it was to Tyler's interest as leader to promote conflict. In any case, there had been enough 'stalling action' between Friday's conference at Mile End and the meeting with Tyler on Saturday for Walworth, mayor of London, to have been able to round up a sufficient number of men-at-arms to escort the confused and disheartened rebels out of London after the death of their chief.

Was Richard an opponent or an ally of the rebels? Young as he was, he was a very important figure in the events. Though most students of the revolt hesitate to credit him with planning the strategy which the Council followed,[1] all of them accept the fact that he played an active role in meeting with the rebels and a courageous and decisive one thrusting himself forward as their 'Chief' after Tyler had fallen.

If indeed there was any substance to Richard's alliance – even in sentiment – it was quickly dissipated after the reverse in the rebels' fortune. Though the brutality following the *Jacquerie* was avoided, there is no record that Richard himself showed particular reluctance to pursue and to punish the rebels during the repression which followed the revolt, and he is reported some days after the revolt, to have flung at them the remark: 'Serfs you are, and serfs you shall remain'.

We have mentioned that the chief opposition to the programme of the rebels was located in Parliament. There was a session in late 1381 and early 1382. We quote from Oman on what occurred here:

> It was Seagrave (the new Treasurer) who . . . laid the problem of the day before the House of Commons. The King had issued, under constraint of the mob at Mile End, many charters enfranchising villeins and abolishing manorial dues. Such charters were null and void, because the sovereign had no power to publish, without the consent of Parliament, any such decrees, which granted away the rights of many of his royal subjects, before the consent of their representatives in Parliament had been obtained. Knowing this, he had revoked all the charters by his proclamation of July 2. But he was informed that certain lords were willing to enfranchise and manumit their villeins of their own free will; if this was so, the King would have no objections to sanction such emancipations.[2]

---

[1] Wilkinson credits the luckless Sudbury and Hales with having counselled the policy of patience and concession which prevailed over the 'hawk' policy championed by Walworth.

[2] Oman, *The Great Revolt*, p. 150.

There is speculation about the reasons prompting the King and his council to make this suggestion. Some believe it ties in with the afore-mentioned semi-sympathetic attitude towards the rebels with which they credit the King. None the less, it was completely rejected by the members of Parliament.[1]

In spite of this harsh attitude to the rebels' demand for freedom, it should be noted that Parliament did demand by petition that the King grant a general amnesty to those who had taken part, save for certain important leaders and mischief-makers. (Of the 287 excluded from amnesty, in fact nearly all were allowed, during the next few years, to go free. These included Thomas Farringdon and the 'traitorous' London aldermen, Tonge, Horne and Sibley.)

In spite of relative tolerance towards the participants in the act of rebellion itself, Parliament maintained steadfastly its anti-peasant attitude in relation to their work and status. Oman remarks: 'Parliament continued to harp on its ancient theme of violations of the Statute of Labourers. So far from being cowed or converted by the recent insurrection, it continued for some years to devise new remedies for the perversity of the working classes. The session at Cambridge in 1388 was singularly fruitful in futile devices of the usual sort.'[2]

Although little opposition was to be found in the countryside at the time of the rebellion itself, there are records of some individuals who dared to oppose. Reville presents a lengthy record[3] of how the prior at St Albans hedged and bargained with the rebels there in order to maintain control. The targets of the rebels in various of the munici-palities did what they could to fight back. Oman describes the successful single-handed drive against the rebels in East Anglia on the part of the bishop of Norwich.[4]

Who may be named as allies of the rebels? It will be remembered that the rebel bands themselves consisted of many in addition to peasants. Artisans, lower clergy, and even a few prominent land-owners – as for instance, Sir Roger Bacon in Eastern Norfolk – were in some places as intimately connected with the uprising and as much a part of the movement as the rural workers themselves.

In the role of allies the principal names seem to be the prominent citizens of London, especially three aldermen – Tonge, Sibley and Horne. The help they could and did give the rebel leaders in opening

[1] Ibid., pp. 150–51.   [2] Ibid., p. 154.
[3] Reville, *Le soulèvement des travailleurs d'Angleterre en 1381*, ch. 1.
[4] Ibid., pp. 129–34.

the gates of London to them – and to counsel with the leaders, planning their entrance – was formidable.[1]   Oman speaks of the traitor-aldermen as 'a bitter and unscrupulous minority, ready to stir up trouble in order to get rid of the existing office-holders, and install itself in their places'.[2]   Hilton traces this political division in London to the conflict between the different economic interests of the drapers and the victuallers.[3]   The former, supported by John of Gaunt, the Duke of Lancaster, were in favour of free trade and consumers' interests, against the interests of the food trade.

Regardless of motivation, the fact is clear that several aldermen allied themselves with the rebels, especially against Mayor Walworth of London, and gave aid and counsel which may well have been crucial in getting the rebels into a position where they could demand their interviews with the king.

VIII. THE ENDING OF THE UPRISING AND ITS RESULTS

The ending of the uprising, like its beginning, was sudden. It had begun in late May and reached its maximum intensity on 15 June when, as Dutaillis states in a short summary:

> it had taken over London and all of eastern England up to Norfolk and perhaps still farther; to the west it was felt to Bridgwater. That very day in London it was brought to a sudden halt, but only there; elsewhere it continued its upheavals; it spread even farther, feeding old feuds . . . in several cities in Yorkshire until the end of July. But one can consider that as of the last days of June the revolt of the workers of England had ended.[4]

Dutaillis raises the question as to how it could have been checked with this rapidity. Naturally the loss of the leader, Tyler, on the

---

[1] Oman tells us that on the evening of 12 June, when Horne together with other aldermen, had been sent by the Mayor to warn the rebels not to come closer to London, he separated himself from the other aldermen and sought an interview with Tyler. 'He told him that the whole of London was ready to rise in their aid, and urged them to demonstrate against the bridge and the gates, promising them help from within. When night fell, he took back with him to his home three of Tyler's lieutenants, and put them in touch with the malcontents of the city, for the purpose of concerting a tumult on the following morning. Horne then had the effrontery to go to the Mayor, and assure him that the insurgents were honest folks and that he would wager his head that if they were admitted within the walls, they would not do a pennyworth of damage.' *The Great Revolt*, p. 51.   [2] Ibid., p. 50.
[3] Hilton and Fagan, *The English Rising*, pp. 39–41.
[4] Petit-Dutaillis, 'Historical Introduction', p. cx.

fifteenth contributed to the collapse. But Dutaillis, feeling there was never much coherence in the action, doubts that, had he lived, Tyler could have maintained success long. He believes that in many counties 'only the most flagrant selfishness had been the guide of the rebels'.[1] In the settling of old quarrels energy and purpose were frittered away. 'Since the interest was not the same everywhere, it was enough for the nobility to draw the sword on the government and to send judges in order to make the majority of the people bow down where they were directed.'[2] And he notes that 'once the principal leaders were gone, seeing the weak cohesion of the bands, the governors and the nobles took courage'.[3]

The first task was to restore order to London, and Walworth and a few aldermen were given extraordinary powers to do this. On the night of the fifteenth and the day following, they arrested a number of insurgents. Oman tells us that 'a certain proportion of these prisoners were beheaded, without being granted a jury or a formal trial'.[4] Among them were two notable leaders from Kent and a principal lieutenant of Tyler's, Jack Straw. The confession which he was bribed by Walworth to make, in order to know 'what the designs of his friends had been'[5] is not accepted at face value by any students, though others agree with Oman that it may have contained an element of truth. Straw is reported to have told of designs by Tyler to kidnap, and later kill, the King to establish himself and other rebel leaders as chiefs over their respective counties.[6]

Peace was restored in London with few executions, imprisonment being chiefly the fate even of such dangerous characters as Farringdon and the traitorous aldermen. According to Oman the executions during the first phase of the repression were not nearly so numerous as might have been expected – nor as they were reported by the chroniclers, whose figures reached into the thousands. He accepts a total somewhat higher than Reville's count of 110 persons for whom documents existed attesting to capital punishment.

'When the government had recovered from its panic,' states Oman, 'every prisoner without exception was proceeded against under the normal processes of law, with the co-operation of a jury.'[7] This was true 'even of such a notorious offender as John Ball', who was located after he had fled London and tried before the Chief Justice, Tresilian,

[1] Ibid., p. cxi.   [2] Ibid.   [3] Ibid., p. cxii.
[4] Oman, *The Great Revolt*, p. 87.   [5] Ibid., p. 81.
[6] Ibid., pp. 81–2.   [7] Ibid., p. 87.

in St Albans. He fearlessly admitted his guilt in taking a leading part and acknowledged his authorship of the 'incendiary letters' which had been distributed in Kent. His punishment was the severe form which a few others suffered: he was condemned to be hanged, drawn and quartered. Most of the leaders, like Ball, died proclaiming their pride in their part in the movement. Only one, John Wrawe, turned 'state's evidence' and informed against his fellow rebels.

The Government, with the King himself leading his army into Essex, then turned to the repression of the rebellion in the surrounding shires. Disorder continued in Kent, where charter-burning and pillage were still in progress on 20 June, and where it was late in July before order had been restored in all the localities.

Oman, like Dutaillis, refers to harshness and 'judicial errors' in the court proceedings, and, indeed, on 30 August Richard, upon advice, ordered all further executions and arrests to cease, and all cases awaiting trial to be transferred from local courts to the King's Bench. 'This practically brought the hangings to an end, for one after another the surviving insurgents were pardoned and released.'[1]

It is clear that the results of a movement like this one need assessment on a long-run as well as a short-run basis. About the latter, in the case of the uprising of 1381, it is easy to arrive at a certain answer.

There is no doubt that during the years immediately following the revolt there was only a picture of failure.

Apparent gains were quickly and decisively withdrawn. The charters of freedom 'extorted' from the King on 14 June were annulled on 2 July, and Dutaillis states that during the following weeks several orders were issued, 'obliging tenants of various manors to abandon their new pretensions'.[2] The same author tells us that the records 'so thoroughly destroyed by the rebels – register and rolls of manors, judicial acts, charters, etc. – were ordered reissued, the new to have the effect of the old'.[3] Money which had been extorted had to be repaid, and the fines levied against offenders were many and heavy.

Succeeding Parliaments not only reaffirmed the old duties of serfs, but found new ways to harass them. One of these, in 1388, forbade children of peasants to leave the manor after twelve years of age. In 1391, they demanded that villeins be forbidden to send their children to schools. It was 1392 before the Statutes of Labourers were finally repealed.

---

[1] Oman, *The Great Revolt*, p. 88.
[2] Petit-Dutaillis, 'Historical Introduction', p. cxxvi.   [3] Ibid.

Nor were city dwellers any more forgiving. After the revolt, states Dutaillis, several cities – among them London and York – refused access to citizenship to persons born in serfdom.

Dutaillis stoutly defends his contention that there was not a bit of difference after the revolt in the conditions of peasants nor in their relationships with their lords. He cites not only documents of Reville, but later studies of particular manors, like Maitland's and Vinogradoff's, to show that at the end of the reign of Richard II, as in the time of Edward II, labour services continued and the villein continued to pay a fee when his daughter was married. He refers to Powell's discoveries of instances after 1381 where energetic efforts were made to fortify rights of property owners to enforce villein labour services. He also contends that the severe attitude towards heretics which was manifest by the Government after the revolt was part and parcel of the reactionary policies inspired by fear created by the uprising.

But if the opposition – Parliament, the landlords, city dwellers – stiffened after the revolt, so did the rebels. There were numerous instances of renewed 'conspiracies' to refuse services and demand increases in wages after the revolt, on manors in many districts. In the towns and cities workers continued their efforts to form leagues to raise wages.

What then of the long-run? For many years the conclusions of the agricultural economist Rogers were accepted – by the constitutional historian Stubbs, for example – that the movement brought the end of villeinage in England, that money rents were now substituted for old services, the old serfs went on to be yeomen, etc.

But the substantial research of many prominent scholars – T. W. Page, Vinogradoff, Maitland, as well as that of Reville and Dutaillis – has led to the refutation of this theory and the view that the revolt made little difference to the ending of villeinage. Commutation of services for money rent, leasing of new lands and manumission continued to go on after the revolt just about as before. And it continued to occur after the revolt because of changes in agriculture. As Lipson has said: 'The alienation of the demesne or its conversion into a sheep-run were the real forces which dissolved the economic fabric of medieval serfdom;' and 'The abolition of villeinage as a tenure prepared the way for its abolition as a status'.[1]

The forces of history were on the side of the rebels, at work before as well as after their revolt towards the throwing off of servile status

---

[1] Lipson, *Economic History*, p. 110.

and greater independence. Lipson makes the same point which has been made earlier in this study:

> The Peasants' Revolt was not an isolated episode, but only an example on a larger scale of occurrences which were taking place in many parts of the country both before and after the insurrection. It has attracted attention because it was more dramatic, more widespread, and more violent, but we need not minimize its importance to recognize that its true significance is likely to be misinterpreted ...
> It is clear that the struggle between the landlords and the serfs was protracted for at least two generations beyond the Peasants' Rising, and that the revolt itself was but one symptom of a malady which continued to afflict rural society until villeinage completely disappeared.[1]

Though it is not a proposition subject to proof, common sense points towards the conclusion that the rebellion was a step towards freedom and a wider spread of the rights of democracy. Trevelyan asserts that the rights of the peasants could never again be ignored nor overridden after the revolt as they had been before. Though they saw none of the benefits themselves, the rebels had put force behind their demand for equality.

NOTE ON SOURCES

The best documented and the most solid study of the revolt was the work of a Frenchman, André Reville – published after his death by another French historian, Charles Petit-Dutaillis. Dutaillis used the wealth of documents collected by Reville in the preparation of the 'Historical Introduction' to this book[2] which supplements Reville's own completed account, itself representing only a portion of that which he had prepared to write himself. This work has amazingly enough never been translated into English and is a book almost impossible to obtain.[3] Dutaillis for that reason devoted a good-sized part of another work of his[4] to an abridged version of Reville's book. Both of these have been drawn upon greatly in this research.

[1] Lipson, *Economic History, p. 110.*
[2] André Reville and Charles Petit-Dutaillis, *Le soulèvement des travailleurs d'Angleterre en 1381* (Paris, 1898).
[3] For this study we were fortunate enough to obtain a copy from the University of Pennsylvania library.
[4] Charles Petit-Dutaillis and Georges Lefebvre, *Studies and Notes Supplementary to Stubbs' Constitutional History* (Manchester: University Press, 1930).

An Englishman, Edgar Powell, did a study comparable to Reville's in procedure (i.e., relying on official documents) though less extensive in the area covered: his *Rising of 1381 in East Anglia*[1] deals specifically only with Suffolk, Norfolk and Cambridgeshire, almost the very area covered in the account which Reville did manage to complete.

Sir Charles Oman based his study of the revolt on the work of Reville and Powell and the documents uncovered by them. He states in his Preface: 'If André Reville had survived to complete his projected study of the Great Revolt in 1381, this book of mine would not have been written . . . Reville's collection, together with the smaller volumes of documents published by Messrs. Powell and Trevelyan in 1896 and 1899, and certain other isolated transcripts of local records, lie at the base of my narrative.'[2] While his study has been criticised – by a later scholar, Wilkinson, as 'not adding anything of great value' as well as by others – most of the statements in his account are soundly based on careful comparison of the chronicles and on generous references to the official documents collected by Reville and Powell.

The other great British historian who devoted major attention to the revolt is G. M. Trevelyan who in fact collaborated with Powell in publishing some relevant documents.[3] In his *England in the Age of Wycliffe*[4] appears his very cogent presentation of the revolt. This we have drawn upon, with a little caution since the citing of evidence is sacrificed occasionally to elegance of style. The sweep of his historical knowledge gives Trevelyan's work a dimension and judgement which adds greatly to its value.

In addition to these book-length studies, there are several articles of the same sturdy, well-documented calibre. Several students (Trevelyan and Wilkinson among them) have alluded to the article by an American, G. H. Kriehn[5] as an important addition, his work having been devoted to the careful comparison of the various chronicles in order to establish the more valid among these accounts. The article by Wilkinson[6] is a similar sort of checking of contemporary sources, in this case, the Sheriff's Reports made at the instigation of Richard II, on the activities of Londoners involved in the uprising. The article

[1] Edgar Powell, *The Rising of 1381 in East Anglia* (Cambridge University Press, 1896).
[2] Sir Charles Oman, *The Great Revolt of 1381* (Oxford: Clarendon Press, 1906).
[3] Edgar Powell and G. M. Trevelyan (eds.), *The Peasants' Rising and the Lollards, Unpublished Documents* (London, 1899).
[4] G. M. Trevelyan, *England in the Age of Wycliffe* (London: Longmans, 1899).
[5] George Kriehn, 'Studies in the Sources of the Social Revolt in 1381', *The American Historical Review*, VII (1902) pp. 254–85, 458–84.
[6] Wilkinson, B., 'The Peasants' Revolt of 1381', *Speculum*, 15 (1940) pp. 12–35.

by R. H. Hilton on 'English Peasant Uprisings Before 1381'[1] should also be included since its subject-matter is so immediately related to the formation of the 1381 movement and since it is carefully documented.

With the exception of Wilkinson's article, recent studies of the revolt have made less contribution to our knowledge than those done at the turn of the century. The most recent, *The Peasants' Revolt*, by G. R. Kesteven,[2] one of a series entitled 'Studies in English History', though carefully written, is a very short account, making no additions to previous knowledge. Very entertainingly written, and not at all devoid of documentation, is Philip Lindsay's and Reginald Groves' *The Peasants' Revolt of* 1381.[3] But the idealisation of the peasants (a wide swing of the pendulum from Froissarts' idealisation of the nobility in his accounts[4]) has led them to make many unsubstantiated assertions and conclusions. The small volume by Hilton and Fagan[5] relates the rising to Marxist ideas, providing us with several stimulating interpretations. Hollis' *The Hurling Time*[6] is a poorly documented account.

To all of the foregoing must be added materials from studies either wider in scope or of topics closely related to the setting of the revolt and the issues around which it revolved. The relevant volume of the *Cambridge Medieval History*[7] and the *Cambridge Economic History*,[8] as well as Stubbs' *Constitutional History of England*[9] have much to contribute to placing the revolt in its historical context. Detailed studies of manor life[10] and village life[11] of the period are necessary in forming a picture of the peasants who participated and the social arrangements under which they lived.

Owst's work[12] provides material from the sermons of this period.

[1] R. H. Hilton, 'Peasant Movements in England before 1381', *Economic History Review*, 2nd ser., II 2 (1949) 117–36.

[2] G. R. Kesteven, *The Peasants' Revolt* (London: Chatto and Windus, 1965).

[3] Philip Lindsay and Reginald Groves, *The Peasants' Revolt of 1381* (London: Hutchingson, 1951).

[4] See Kriehn on the Froissart account, for instance.

[5] R. H. Hilton and H. Fagan, *The English Rising of 1381* (London: Lawrence and Wishart, 1950).

[6] Christopher Hollis, *The Hurling Time*.

[7] *The Cambridge Medieval History*, VII (Cambridge University Press, 1941).

[8] *The Cambridge Economic History*, I (Cambridge University Press, 1941).

[9] William Stubbs, *The Constitutional History of England*, II (Oxford: Clarendon Press, 1896).

[10] See, for example, Maitland, 'History of a Cambridgeshire Manor', *English Historical Review*, IX (1894).

[11] Homans G. C., *English Villagers of the Thirteenth Century* (New York: Russell and Russell, 1941).

[12] Owst, G. R., *Literature and Pulpit in Medieval England* (Cambridge University Press, 1933).

The issue of overriding concern in the revolt was freedom from villeinage. Relevant, therefore, are the many studies, some of them, like Vinogradoff's,[1] excellent, which have addressed themselves specifically to the development and the decline of this aspect of feudal life and medieval times.

[1] Sir Paul Vinogradoff, *Villeinage in England* (Oxford; The Clarendon Press, 1892).

Chapter 4

SOCIAL BANDITRY

by
E. J. Hobsbawm

AN Austrian, then employed in the Turkish service, has left us an account of the events which preceded and announced the outbreak of the great peasant insurrection in Bosnia, which led to the detachment of that region from the Ottoman Empire in 1878. There had been a dispute about tithes. The Christian peasants of Lukovac and other villages gathered, left their houses and went up into the mountains; the Christian peasants near Gabela and Ravno went on strike and held meetings. While the dispute was under negotiation, a caravan from Mostar was attacked by a band of armed Christian robbers and seven Moslem carters killed. The Turks thereupon broke off discussions. The peasants of Nevesinje thereupon took arms and went into the mountains, where alarm-fires were lit. In Ravno and Gabela the peasants also took arms. To the well-informed it was clear that a major insurrection was at hand.[1]

The case is cited here because it illustrates three aspects of social banditry, which is the subject of this paper. First, it illustrates its character as a phenomenon of social discontent, or closely connected with it. Second, it illustrates the curious but significant coexistence of banditry with more ambitious or general movements of social insurrection. Third, it illustrates the rather backward and primitive situations in which banditry is found to play the role of a movement or phenomenon of social protest and rebellion. The third aspect is almost self-evident. It is mentioned here only to remind the reader that the study of social banditry throws little light on the great majority of agrarian social movements likely to occur in the last third of the twentieth century. It throws light rather on certain characteristics and problems of traditional social structure in rural areas, which, in so far as they persist, may today normally find quite different forms of expression. The second is not obvious at all. It is indeed not at all common to find

[1] Dr J. Koetschet, *Aus Bosniens letzter Tuerkenzeit* (Vienna-Leipzig, 1905.) pp. 6–8.

it mentioned in the literature, admittedly sparse, about banditry.[1] The first is familiar in the form of folklore or popular culture: after all, the myth of Robin Hood, who robbed the rich to give to the poor, has survived a good many centuries and social changes to become the subject-matter of newspaper strip cartoons and television serials. On the other hand, the nature of the phenomenon is not well understood, though it has begun to attract scientific attention in recent years.

What is social banditry? It consists essentially of relatively small groups of men living on the margins of peasant society, and whose activities are considered criminal by the prevailing official power-structure and value-system, but not (or not without strong qualifications) by the peasantry. It is this special relation between peasant and bandit which makes banditry 'social': the social bandit is a hero, a champion, a man whose enemies are the same as the peasants', whose activities correct injustice, control oppression and exploitation, and perhaps even maintain alive the ideal of emancipation and independence. Hence, in the extreme – and historically almost certainly exceptional – case of the genuine Robin Hood, the social bandit is the very opposite of a criminal, in the public mind. He represents morality: Jesse James, in popular anecdote and romance, was a devout Baptist and Sunday school teacher.[2] He may actually have a moral authority superior to that of the official system: the Brazilian *cangaceiro* Lampião (c. 1900–38), according to a ballad, when setting out on his career around 1917–20, received a formal document appointing himself captain and his brother lieutenant, not from the State, but from Padre Cicero, the accepted Holy Man of the north-eastern back country.[3] The women of the Aspromonte (Calabria) pray to the saints to protect the great Musolino (1875–1956).[4]

Consequently also the ideal social bandit, as represented in the popular image of ballad and story, does not transgress the rules of what the peasants accept as morality. He becomes an outlaw for some

[1] For a general discussion, cf. E. J. Hobsbawn, *Primitive Rebels* (Manchester, 1959), ch. 1 and *Bandits* (London, 1969). The latter work contains a select guide to further literature in languages accessible to me. Among regional monographs of value, the following are notable: C. Bernaldo de Quiros, *El bandolerismo en España y México* (Mexico, 1959), Joan Fuster, *El bandolerisme Catalan*, 2 vols. (Barcelona, 1963), E. López Albujar, *Los caballeros del delito*, (Lima, 1936), M. I. P. de Queiroz, *Os cangaceiros, les bandits d'honneur brésiliens* (Paris, 1968), F. Molfese, *Storia del brigantaggio dopo l'unità* (Milan, 1964), G. Rosen, *Die Balkan-Haiduken* (Leipzig, 1878).

[2] Kent L. Steckmesser, 'Robin Hood and the American Outlaw', *Journ. Amer. Folklore* 79 (Apr–June 1966) 312.

[3] *Lampeao, O rei do cangaço*, by Antonio Teodoro dos Santos (O Poeta Garimpeiro) (São Paulo, 1959). This is one of numerous verse romances about the celebrated bandit.

[4] *Il ponte* (1950): Special issue on Calabria, p. 1305.

infraction of the official law which the peasants do not consider to be a crime – a conflict with the rich, the State or the foreigners, a case of legitimate revenge, or the like. This 'honourable' origin of his outlawry is insisted on, and in fact, represents not only image but also, to a very great extent, fact.[1] He 'takes from the rich to give to the poor', a characteristic which may also belong to reality as well as to myth, if only because bandits who take from the poor cease to be heroes and risk being regarded as mere criminals, and because generosity and lavish spending are both morally obligatory for genuine 'nobles' (including 'noble robbers') and because they win friends and influence people. It is recorded that the impoverished highwaymen of Piura (Peru) in the 1920s and 1930s were less popular than one might have expected members of their trade to be, because they were too unsuccessful to give away much loot.[2] Thirdly, the ideal Robin Hood 'never kills but in self-defence and just revenge', i.e., limits his use of force and violence. Though this is patently a point where reality and image are likely to diverge, often quite sharply, the ballads and stories very generally insist that Robin Hoods do, or at any rate should, accept such limitations. Fourthly, of course, he 'rights wrongs', that is to say he represents the ideal of justice against the reality of injustice.

In so far as the social bandit thus represents the opposite of crime, he is not regarded as a law-breaker, or sinner, by anyone except the official system of power and morality; nor even as an outsider. If the State and the ruling classes let him return to ordinary life, he is immediately reintegrated as a respectable member of the community which he has never really left. The evidence on this point is conclusive.[3] Conversely, public opinion takes a very different view of bandits who are not regarded as being on the side of the peasant, and some dialects have entirely different words for them. Similarly, the public attitude to bandits who do not live up to the moral standards of the Robin Hood image is much more complex, even when in some ways they too are regarded as heroes or champions. The true 'noble robber' has nothing to reproach himself with, but ballads about other types of popular or celebrated brigands may well conclude with a scene of death-bed repentance for the sins they have committed. In a word,

---

[1] Cf. Hobsbawm (1959) pp. 15–16.

[2] López Albujar (1936) p. 184.

[3] Perhaps the most impressive testimony to the moral standing of the 'good' bandit is provided by a former sergeant of police, now a farmer in the Argentine Chaco, who spent an entire morning praising the deeds of the bandit *Maté Cosido* whom he had once spent a great deal of time vainly pursuing, and insisting that he was *not* a criminal. ('It was his calling to be a bandit, mine to be a policeman'. Personal information, 1968).

the idealisation of social bandits is not that of criminals and law-breakers as such, as sometimes expressed in the milieu of Bakuninist intellectuals or the urban sub-culture of disorganised poverty. It is the idealisation of a certain stance of social protest and the actions deriving from it.

It is appropriate to begin the discussion of social banditry by thus sketching its myth or public image, because it is rarely a conscious movement of social protest. It is a form of dissent and rebellion by a – generally small – number of individuals who, as individuals, reject the subjection of the ordinary peasant or the constraints of his social role, and by so doing, automatically – so long as they do not actually join the peasants' enemies – adopt another role for which the mental drama of peasant society makes provision, and which implies social protest. The bandits may or may not set out to be exemplars or leaders of protest, but if they do not become landlords' bandits (e.g., guards or other armed followers of the rich) or government bandits (e.g., soldiers), they may adopt the role of peasant bandit both because it comes natural and brings prestige and admiration, and because, like all other peasants, they are themselves familiar with it. They may become robbers, because there is no other way for an outlaw to earn his living except by appropriating the surplus of someone else's labour. They may become social bandits, because they share the moral judgements of the rest of the peasantry, not to mention the fact that their survival depends on the refusal of the peasantry to give them away to the police.

The kind of social protest which banditry represents is therefore normally neither very conscious nor highly organised. Nor are its objectives very ambitious. They are, essentially, the maintenance or restoration of a stable pattern of traditional social relationships; not a call for the abolition of exploitation, but a protest against its abuses. Their aim is not 'freedom' (except for the outlaw himself) but 'justice'. Hence in the legends and songs the bandits are rarely found in conflict with the supreme authority of the land, if this authority is represented as legitimate and therefore the fountain of both a stable order of social inequality and of 'justice'. It is not the King who is Robin Hood's enemy but the local authority, the local oppressors – abbots or lawyers. It is not poverty that he wishes to abolish, but the excessively unjust treatment of the poor.

Nevertheless, the modest aims of the bandit, which are also the modest aims beyond which in normal conditions the ordinary peasant scarcely allows his dreams to stray, are curiously intertwined with more ambitious movements and ideals. This is why social banditry may be regarded as a precursor, and a primitive form of, wider peasant agitations. Banditry has three kinds of relationships with such wider movements and aspirations.

First, banditry and more ambitious types of peasant movement tend to flourish in the same areas, if not actually to live in symbiosis. The area of intensive *bandolerismo* in Andalusia in the mid-nineteenth century was to turn into the area of mass rural anarchism some decades later,[1] and conversely, in Andalusia the guerrilla resistance to General Franco's regime after the Civil War tended often to echo the style of the traditional *bandolero*.[2] North-eastern Brazil, between 1890 and 1940, was simultaneously the classic territory of the *cangaçeiros* and of backwoods messianic movements, to which the bandits subordinated themselves, when they did not actually provide them with their armed forces. 'In this world', the ballad makes the great Lampião declare, 'I respect only Padre Cicero (the greatest of these messiahs) and no one else'.[3] Areas of endemic peasant insurrection, like Banten in north-east Java, are also areas notorious for endemic banditry.[4]

Second, at times when mass unrest grips the peasantry, banditry merges with these larger movements, and notable increases in banditry may indeed prepare and announce them. We have already seen such a combination in the Bosnia of the 1870s. Similar phenomena have been observed on a large scale in Java during the 1940s, when bands increased in number, size and activities before merging with gigantic millennial mobilisations of peasants abandoning their labours to await the imminent transformation of the universe.[5]

A somewhat less archaic version of this phenomenon is the absorption of banditry into revolutionary movements of a modern type. This is familiar both in Latin America and in the Balkans and the Far East. Pancho Villa in Mexico is the most celebrated example, though the history of Cuban independence furnishes others who took the side of revolution.[6] The participation of *haiduk* chieftains in the nineteenth-century Balkan movements of liberation may or may not have been

---

[1] Bernaldo de Quiros (1959) pp. 250–1.
[2] Tomás Cossias, *La lucha contra el 'Maquis' en España* (Madrid, 1956) pp. 73–6.
[3] R. Rowland, ' "Cantadores" del nordeste brasileno', *Aportes* 3 (Jan 1967) p. 138.
[4] D. H. Meijer, 'Over het bendewezen op Java', *Indonesie* III (1949–50) pp. 179–82.
[5] P. M. van Wulfften Palthe, *Psychological Aspects of the Indonesian Problem* (Leiden, 1949) pp. 30–34; S. Kartodirdjo, *The Peasants' Revolt of Banten in 1888* (Hague, 1966).
[6] F. López Leiva, *El bandolerismo en Cuba* (Havana, 1930) pp. 24, 30; M. Barnet, *Cimarrón* (Havana, 1967) pp. 85–6.

effective, but there can be no doubt that several of them – and notably Panayot Hitov, who has left us an invaluable autobiography[1] – were accessible to the appeal of the urban revolutionaries. The brigands of Banten, accustomed to the archaic insurrections of their society, appear to have been readily mobilised for the first of its modern ones, the Communist rising of 1926.[2] However, the most important example of the mobilisation of bandits for revolutionary purposes is undoubtedly that of China, where the young Mao Tse-tung deliberately set out, not only to copy the guerrilla tactics of classical Chinese bandits (as described in the famous Water Margin Novel and other pieces of literature) but also to recruit marginal elements in rural society for the new Red Army. 'These people fight most courageously', he had observed a few years earlier. 'When led in a just manner they can become a revolutionary force.' At all events it seems that in 1929 the bulk of the Red Army was composed of such 'declassed elements'.[3]

Third, banditry may itself provide the model or cadre of certain kinds of primitive peasant insurrection or guerrilla activity. When the Ukrainian peasants of the sixteenth and seventeenth century arose, it was by imitating the minority of free cossacks, i.e., by declaring themselves to be cossacks.[4] The resistance of continental southern Italy to the new unified kingdom (1860–5) took the form of an expansion of traditional brigandage into a form of guerrilla war, and earlier resistance movements against the French had done the same.[5] Admittedly such a development of banditry is likely only in rather archaic situations. What is much more common is the integration of bandits into more modern revolutionary movements, organised in other ways and by other leaders, such as has already been mentioned. What is even more likely is the systematic use of bandit tactics and experience for the technically very similar activities of guerrilla warfare. This is, once again, commonest in situations familiar with social banditry. The Internal Macedonian Revolutionary Organisation (I.M.R.O.) of the early twentieth century – and its opponents – both modelled their

[1] Published in German by Rosen (1878).
[2] H. Benda and R. McVey, *The Communist Uprisings of 1926–7 in Indonesia. Key Documents* (Ithaca, 1960).
[3] S. Schram, *Mao Tse Tung* (London, 1966) p. 141.
[4] Cossacks themselves were not, or only marginally, social bandits in our sense, but formed one variant of a fairly widespread species of which social bandits were another, namely minorities of independent armed peasants sprung from the ordinary peasantry. See I. Racz (1964).
[5] Molfese (1964), A. Lucarelli, *Il brigantaggio politico del Mezziogiorno d'Italia, 1815–1815* (Bari, 1942).

fighting units on the bands with which every Macedonian was familiar, and, undoubtedly, recruited them largely from their members. Yet even when this is not so, the tactics of bandits and guerrillas and the terrain on which both operate are essentially the same, and the latter must inevitably take lessons from the experience of the former.

II

Social banditry of the kind discussed in the previous pages, is an extraordinarily widespread phenomenon. It can, or could, be found in very much the same forms throughout Europe, the Mediterranean region, the Islamic world, South-East and East Asia, Australasia and the post-Columbian Americas. Indeed, the only large regions in which it cannot easily be traced are sub-Saharan Africa and India. Though the latter area is familiar with the comparable phenomena of dacoity, the fact that dacoits appear to belong to separate communities, castes and tribes to their victims, makes it difficult to establish the intimate relationship between bandit and non-bandit within peasant society which characterises social banditry, and makes it preferable to exclude dacoity, like other forms of raiding by one community against another, from the present discussion.

Speaking socially, rather than geographically, banditry is found throughout the wide belt of rural societies which lies between the tribally organised and the modern industrial,[1] excepting only, it would seem, formalised caste societies. It is unlikely to be found within societies organised primarily around kinship, since in these the horizontal socio-economic stratification does not yet prevail over the vertical division between kinship groups, nor are 'states' and 'governments' in the modern sense found. In the clan society of the old Scottish highlands the Macgregors may have specialised in the family occupation of outlawry, but their victims were not the rich as such but the other clans (including their poor). It is equally unlikely to be found in the modern industrial era, partly for social reasons – their rural structure is very different from that of the traditional peasantry, partly for technical and administrative ones – they have far better communications and law-enforcement angencies, partly for political ones – they have new, and probably more effective, mechanisms for articulating social protest. Thus in England which has given the world the classic stereotype of the 'noble robber', namely Robin Hood, there is

[1] Readers are at liberty to substitute some other terminology, if they prefer it.

no recorded case of a real Robin Hood since, at the latest, the early seventeenth century. However, there is good reason to believe that social banditry is unusually prevalent at two moments of historical evolution: that at which primitive and communally organised society gives way to class-and-state society, and that at which the traditional rural peasant society gives way to the modern economy. At such times the desire to defend the old and stable society against the subversion of its values, the urge to restore its old, threatened or disintegrating norms, becomes unusually strong. At such moments the social bandit appears to undertake the task for which he is so ill-fitted.

Though we can sketch the broad distribution of banditry in space and time, it is much more difficult to analyse its precise distribution either synchronically or diachronically, for information about it is defective, remarkably scattered, and it has so far never been systematically collated and compared.

Synchronically, it is obvious that banditry is very thinly and unevenly spread. At a rough guess, one would not in normal circumstances expect to find more than 0.1 per cent of the rural population who actually are bandits,[1] though in times of revolution or social breakdown the number might greatly increase. For obvious reasons it has always flourished best in remote and inaccessible areas (e.g., mountains, forests, and complexes of islands and waterways), and under inefficient administration. The combination of both, as in the Balkans under the Ottoman Turks, or in frontier zones, was certain to produce banditry. As a matter of observation, certain kinds of economic and social environments have been far more bandit-prone than others, e.g., pastoral economies than tillage ones. However, the distribution of banditry has simply not been sufficiently well established to allow us even provisional generalisations about it.

Diachronically, there is very little doubt that banditry varies with the peasants' poverty, insecurity and the severity of the tensions of their society. However, though these may often feel exactly alike to the peasantry, they may be due to entirely different mechanisms. They may reflect the periodic, more or less irregular, hazards of any traditional society, such as harvest failure, epidemic, war, conquest and administrative breakdown, or the more or less recurrent disturbances of equilibrium such as the 'dynastic cycle' of imperial China, after

---

[1] Calculated on the basis of the data for the bands active during the Colombian *violencia* in G. Guzmán, O. Fals Borda, E. Umaña Luna, *La violencia en Colombia*, vol. II (Bogotá, 1964), and some information about Macedonia kindly provided by Dr Douglas Dakin of Birkbeck College, University of London.

which such societies return, sooner or later to 'normal', which includes the normally expected degree of poverty, oppression and social or other banditry. On the other hand they may reflect the disruption of an entire society, the rise of new classes and new social structures, based on a new economy, in a word, historical development. Hence the significance of the moments of historical transformation which we have already noted.

Two examples of such transformations may illustrate the argument. The first is that of the Sardinian highlands, perhaps the last region in Western Europe where banditry remains endemic today. Here we may observe in the second half of the nineteenth century how a primitive pastoral society, organised in kinship groups whose relations were regulated by blood-feud, began to be drawn into the networks of modern government and the modern market economy. Changes in the character of the violence within this society appeared. The collective raiding of the plainsmen by community expeditions from highland pastoral villages ceased around 1900, to give way to individual raiding by their inhabitants. The purely lateral feuding between family-complexes began to give way to vertical disputes: of families which have become collectively 'poor' (i.e., lacking in sheep and pastures) against those who have become collectively 'rich', or, what is much the same, of families lacking 'influence' by their relations with the Italian authorities against those which have acquired it. In brief, and more particularly from the time of the agrarian crises of the 1880s and 1890s, we observe the birth of something which has affinities with social banditry; affinities which are vaguely recognised in the communist-influenced rhetoric of some of the bandits after World War II.[1]

The rapid economic transformations of the 1950s and 1960s brought a new wave of brigandage, which still continues at the time of writing. This time, however, the social-revolutionary element seems less marked, though it is still clear that the bandits are primarily recruited from the poorer shephards, and the annual bandit-cycle reaches its peak when rents for pasture-lands are due. Banditry remains a socio-economic phenomenon. The decline of the post-war wave of social radicalism in the Italian South and the direct penetration of wealth and economic development in their more advanced forms into Sardinia, have opened up new economic perspectives to robbers, e.g. (as witnessed in

[1] Hobsbawm (1959) pp. 176–9. For a full bibliography of Sardinian banditry, cf. F. Ferracuti, R. Lazzari, M. E. Wolfgang, *Violence in Sardinia* (Rome, 1970) pp. 147–64.

1966) the kidnapping of landowners who had become rich by selling their hitherto valueless land for tourist development, in order to extract some of the profits of the transaction.

The second illustration is north-east Brazil, where both banditry and backwoods messianic movements were epidemic between about 1890 and 1940, and both have since ceased, though their memory is of course very much alive both locally and among the emigrants from the region who have flocked into the big cities. Here the correlation with historical change is clear. The *cangaceiros* develop, as a specific phenomenon, when the old Brazil begins to give way to the new – and there was indeed a strong element of deliberate conservatism about them. Antonio Silvino tried to stop the mail and the building of railroads. As in Sardinia, banditry appears to have developed out of the family feuding of the primitive pastoral society of the *sertão*, and most *cangaceiros* began their career with some incident of blood-vengeance. The era of epidemic banditry was the period when the economic conditions of the back-country peasantry deteriorated, but *before* industrial and urban development in the more advanced sector of Brazil began to provide a serious possibility of emigration, and it ceased after the 1930s, when urbanisation and industrialisation appeared on a large scale. In brief, it occurred at a time when the impoverished backwoodsman could not yet emigrate, and his only non-agricultural prospects in the region were to become a minstrel – or a bandit. During the same interval between the beginning of socio-economic disruption and the appearance of new economic, social and political possibilities, the wider rural movements of millennial or messianic character developed, and they too have since declined.

III

We must next consider the problem of the recruitment of bandits, for it affects the nature of the social protest they embody, and its effectiveness. Essentially, as has already been observed, banditry is not in itself a social movement, but the personal rejection by a number of individuals, of the role of poverty and subjection assigned to the peasant. This rejection is both a matter of social and of individual choice. Socially, certain types of rural society tend to produce a larger surplus of unemployed able-bodied men than others, and hence a larger proportion of potential bandits. Thus highland pastoral societies, with their relatively low labour requirements, tend to have a persistent surplus of men, which may be – temporarily or permanently – drained off by emigration, often as soldiers or policemen (as from pre-industrial Switzerland, from Corsica or Albania). It probably also produces bandits in greater quantities than elsewhere. Again, certain age-groups – most obviously the young men between puberty and marri-age – are both more mobile and less shackled by the responsibilities of land, wife and children, which make the life of the outlaw almost impossible for most adult peasants. It is indeed well established that social bandits are normally both young and unmarried.[1] Men marginal to the rural economy, or not yet absorbed or reabsorbed into it, will be drawn to banditry; notably ex-soldiers, who, with herdsmen, form probably its largest single occupational component. So will certain occupations which maintain a man outside the framework of constant social control in the community, or the supervision of the ruling group – e.g., herdsmen and drovers.

However, in addition to such predictable sources of potential bandits, most rural societies contain a certain proportion of individuals who, for one reason or another, are unwilling to accept the constraint of their social position: the *insubordinate*. It is from among these 'village Hampdens'[2] that many rural trade union leaders are selected, and they too, if nineteenth-century British experience is any guide, were often forced into economically marginal or independent occupa-tions by victimisation, or choose such occupations in order to escape subordination. It is from among these that, in more archaic periods and environments, bandits are readily recruited, or who are forced into outlawry. However, it would be quite mistaken to assume that men who in one era are likely to become bandits, are the potential trade union cadres of another. The history of English rural social movements – and no country has a longer history of trade-union-like agitations among farm-labourers – suggests that their leading cadres were most likely to be drawn from among those with recognised social standing within the informal community of the rural poor, including the heads of families, village artisans, innkeepers and the like. As we have seen, except perhaps in regions so remote from landlords and State that local community structure is unaffected by them, people like these do not provide many bandit chiefs; indeed, rural craftsmen are usually rare among bandits. On the contrary, the *insubordinates* who

---

[1] Hobsbawm (1969) ch. 2; López Albujar (1936) p. 126.

[2] For non-English or non-literary readers, the reference is to Gray's 'Elegy in a Country Churchyard' and the famous hero of the English Revolution of the seventeenth century.

find themselves most naturally drawn towards banditry are those who can, to use the proverbial phrase of such environments, 'make themselves respected', by strength, courage, aggressiveness and threats: the rural 'tough'. Unlike the potential union cadres, such men are probably less educated and skilled than the average. (There is no doubt about the high degree of illiteracy of bandits, but comparisons with the education of non-bandit peasants have not been made.) They are most likely to capitalise on their toughness by becoming armed guards of landlords, soldiers, or policemen, outlaws or bandits – or, in special situations, *mafiosi*. All these careers emancipate them from the subjection of the ordinary peasant. All may give them not only more respect but a higher income and more comforts than ordinary peasants. But only one or two of the ways which open out to the insubordinate rural tough lead him to social banditry.

Banditry is thus, for those who take it up, not so much a social protest on behalf of all peasants, though it may acquire this function. It is the personal emancipation of strong individuals, drawn from some socio-economic sources rather than from others. It is the acquisition of freedom for themselves by a minority, who, by virtue of this very fact, are different from, and may well feel themselves superior to, the rest of the passive and the obedient.

Freedom and a rough equality rule within the band, and it may be prepared to share them on occasion with the rest. Nothing is more touching than the joy in the life of liberty and simple festivities which the Brazilian *cangaceiros* led, and which, fortunately for the student, is recorded by a number of competent observers. But their own backwoods pastoral was not a model for the rest of the peasantry, and their activities were not supposed to emancipate those who did not join them. It was the messiahs and not the robbers who provided a model for general social change. At the same time, the personal success of the bandits could – and perhaps usually would – eventually tempt them to join the rich and powerful, though not to forget their popular origins.

IV

For all these reasons banditry is not so much a form of peasant movement as a symptom of peasant unrest, and when it becomes part of a peasant social movement or a movement of national liberation, its effectiveness is limited. For these reasons also the genuine 'noble bandit' of the Robin Hood type is probably rather rare – though cases have been recorded[1] – so that his social role may have to be projected onto less suitable candidates for idealisation such as the eighteenth-century highwaymen of England (Dick Turpin), France (Cartouche) or the German Rhineland (Schinderhannes), who belonged to the entirely different class of the pre-industrial criminal underworld or out-group,[2] or the Billy the Kids and Clyde Barrows of the twentieth-century United States.

There is, however, a variant of banditry which, however ineffective by modern standards, is or was more overtly a movement of protest and revolt. We may call it *haidukry*, after the Balkan outlaws of this name, though it is also found in East and South-east Asia, and possibly else-where. What distinguishes haidukry from other kinds of social banditry is that its social function is consciously recognised, permanent, and to this extent it is much more institutionalised and structured than the common type of brigandage, in which men become bandits because they happen to fall foul of the official law, and bands form casually around prestigious outlaws. This does not mean that the motives which produce haiduks rather than bandits are more overtly political. The evidence of the numerous ballads about the Bulgarian haiduks strongly suggests that their individual motive was mainly economic: outlawry was a better job than hill-farming.

Nevertheless, whatever the private motifs which made men into haiduks, in doing so they took a step recognised as having political implications. The Bulgarian word for becoming a haiduk literally means 'to put oneself in a state of insurrection'. Unlike the Robin Hoods, the haiduks were always there in the mountains, to be joined by a man (and in the Balkans sometimes even by a girl) of spirit, just as the analogous bandits in imperial China were always there, as a recognised nucleus of potential dissidence. Unlike the Robin Hoods, who exist as celebrated individuals or not at all, the haiduks exist as a collective entity and the songs about them celebrate the haiduk life rather than particular leaders, though of course these also receive admiration. (It may be no accident that the famous Water Margin Novel, the classic of Chinese bandit literature, traces the fortunes of

[1] For example, Angelo Duca, Vardarelli in Italy, Doncho Vatach in Bulgaria, Janošik in the Carpathians.
[2] A convenient criterion for differentiating between bandits belonging to peasant society and those who are outside it: pre-industrial criminal robbers spoke a special esoteric language (cant, caló, argot, rotwelsch, etc.), while social bandits spoke a version of the local peasant dialect.

well over a hundred men who are its collective heroes.[1]) Unlike the ordinary Robin Hoods, the leaders of Javanese bandit groups are men driven into banditry by a sense of mission, a religio-magical duty, and sometimes claim to be pretenders from a former ruling family.[2]

Conversely, though the redistribution of wealth, the righting of wrongs (except in the form of vengeance) and in general the championship of the poor as such, normally do *not* form a significant part of the public image of haiduks, who often have a reputation for cruelty and terror, the attitude of the peasantry towards them is one of respect and admiration and not only of fear. In the Balkans they were recognised as the champions of the orthodox against the unbelievers, in China as the potential bases of rebellion against excessive oppression or even against a dynasty whose heavenly mandate to rule had been exhausted by injustice, in Indonesia for similar reasons.

Permanence of existence and social function may have helped to give this form of banditry a stronger institutional structure, such as the elaborate social hierarchy of the Chinese bandits in the Water Margin Novel, the assemblies and hierarchies of the cossacks, the functions of captain (*voivode*) and standard-bearer (*bairaktar*) which were normal in Bulgarian haiduk bands, each with assigned formal duties, or the similar military structure and terminology in some Indian dacoit communities. Being essentially an abnormal social unit, at least during the banditry season – which had its formally fixed starting and finishing dates in the Balkans, normally from May to September – haiduks could not easily copy the model of the family- and farm-based peasant community. In Europe they seem to have adopted the forms of voluntary kinship groups, male brotherhoods, possibly also influenced in some cases by military Islamic sects such as the Bektashi. Certain groups of this kind – perhaps in China, probably among the Cossacks – also seem to have been able to maintain fighting organisations on a much larger scale than the ordinary brigand band, which is almost invariably and everywhere composed of between six and twenty men, with fifteen as the usual size for a largish group,[3] larger operations being undertaken by coalitions of such groups. However, the subject has not been adequately studied yet.

Haidukry is perhaps the closest that social banditry comes to an organised, conscious movement of potential rebellion, but in the nature

[1] A translation by Pearl Buck exists under the title *All Men Are Brothers* (New York, 1937).
[2] Wulfften Palthe (1949) pp. 27–8.
[3] Larger bands are, however, reported from the thinly populated frontier of NE Brazil.

of things it belongs to the past. That past may not be very remote in some parts of the world – the nineteenth century in the Balkans, the twentieth in parts of Asia – but, except for the temporary revival of ancient traditions in periods of social disorganisation, such as the aftermath of wars and revolutions, we can hardly regard it as retaining serious significance in the era of modern peasant movements. Moreover, haiduks collectively were subject to the same temptations as bandits individually. Their power often made it necessary for the rulers and the rich, especially in the remote areas in which they flourished, to come to terms with them, perhaps to hire them for their own purposes. Like the bandits, such 'military strata sprung from the free peasantry'[1] might easily become the servants of lords or governments. If the Bulgarian haiduks were peasant bandits, the Hungarian ones became seignorial or government haiduks, like the Russian cossacks.

V

A note on the effectiveness of the bandit element in modern peasant movements may conclude this paper. Two general observations about this may be made.

First, the technical and ideological limitations of banditry make them relatively ineffective even as fighting forces, unless absorbed into movements of the modern type, with a modern cadre of leadership, and the capacity to organise and to operate on a scale far beyond the essentially localised field of activity of the grass-roots bandit.[2] Conversely, bandits without such an *encadrement*, or who are abandoned by their 'modern' supporters, are not successful. This was the case of the brigand-guerrillas of continental southern Italy in the 1860s, and of the famous Giuliano after the Second World War in Sicily. In the long run it is doubtful whether, even in alliance with, or absorbed by, modern revolutionary movements, bandits are a very valuable asset for revolutionaries, though initially they may be useful allies.

Second, the social ambiguity of banditry, on which we have insisted in this paper, makes them an uncertain element in social movements

---

[1] I. Racz, *Couches militaires issues de la paysannerie libre en Europe orientale du XVe au XVIIe siècle*. Publicationes Institi Philogiae Slavicae Univ. Debreceniensis, 48 (Debreczen, 1964).

[2] Evidently even for traditional bandits this scale of operations may be much larger where conditions of transportation or settlement permit or require it – e.g., in prairie, steppe and *llano* country, or on a thinly populated but not too mountainous frontier.

which must sooner or later challenge both traditional society and the existing structure of wealth and power, towards which successful bandits, however popular in origin, belong to are drawn. We know too little about the fortunes of bandits, haiduks, etc., after the triumph of the movements with which many of them may have sympathised, or to which they may have contributed. However, a glance at the history of nineteenth-century Greece, where the heroic and national *klephtic* tradition of the liberation era degenerated only too often into a system of gangs hired against the people and against rivals by rich and corrupt politicians, suggests strong doubts about the reliability of the populist convictions among such outlaws.[1]

One final example may illustrate the limitations of banditry in peasant movements. The Mexican revolution contained two important peasant components, one strictly derived from the tradition of social banditry (Pancho Villa), one altogether lacking the bandit element (Zapata). In military terms it may be argued that Villa was a much more formidable force, but his intervention in the revolution neither changed its social character nor produced any lasting effect on the conditions of the peasantry even in the areas of his direct influence. It was the influence of the Zapatista movement which gave the Mexican revolution that agrarian-revolutionary turn which has determined its fortunes ever since. Nevertheless, Villa is not to be entirely neglected. He survives as a hero, a myth, and even in a minor way as a catalyst of popular aspirations. Perhaps it is characteristic that these aspirations are today not those of social justice, but of national mobilisation against the *gringos*.

[1] Cf. Romilly Jenkins, *The Dilessi Murders* (London, 1961).

Chapter 5

RURAL ANARCHISM IN SPAIN AND THE 1873 CANTONALIST REVOLUTION

by

Miklós Molnár and Juan Pekmez[1]

I. THE SETTING

'"Do you see that dust cloud, Sancho? It is being churned up by the approach of a mighty army formed of untold multitudes of different nations." "Then there must be two armies," replied Sancho. "For over there, look, another dust cloud is rising . . ."'

'The dust clouds they had seen were caused by two large flocks of sheep moving towards the same road from the opposite direction, but so well concealed by the dust that it was impossible to make the sheep out until they had come quite close.'

Whether or not he drew his inspiration from these lines of Miguel Cervantes, the British writer Gerald Brenan was to depict Andalusia in the same terms 400 years later.

'During the next four centuries [after the *reconquista*] sheep farming not merely took precedence over agriculture, but to a great extent displaced it through all the lands ruled over by the Crown of Castile. So much was this the case that a large part of the sparse population of the country lived on the verge of starvation. The sheep passed the summer on the great plateaux of northern Castile and descended in autumn to Extremadura. Similar migrations took place in other parts of the peninsula. The huge clouds of dust that accompanied their movements became one of the characteristic sights of Spain . . . Agriculture declined so rapidly that by the end of the seventeenth century the French Ambassador was reporting that the area of cultivated land around Seville, which was then the largest and most prosperous city in the country, had shrunk to one-twentieth of what it had been a century before.'[2]

[1] Abridged version of a longer study to be published in French.

[2] Gerald Brenan, *The Spanish Labyrinth* (London: Cambridge University Press, 1943) pp. 105-6.

Here again the same countryside appears, seemingly unchanged since the days of the knight of the sorrowful countenance, with the same shepherds enveloped in the same dust clouds making their way across the vast arid plains with their migratory flocks. Who knows, the wandering knight, the knight in search of the vanished past, may still be there questing anew for adventure against windmills.

Be that as it may, the setting has changed little over the last four centuries, and as far as the countryside is concerned the change has been even less noticeable than in the case of the infrequent urban centres in expansion since the mid-nineteenth century. Thus Gerald Brenan, author of the excellent *Spanish Labyrinth*, found the land of Don Quixote still there after the Spanish Civil War, a land that was also that of the man who inspired Brenan's work, the Spaniard Juan Díaz del Moral, a notary at Bujalance near Cordova, whose hobbies were history and sociology and who, in 1923, published the first definitive history of rural social movements in Spain.[1]

Yet throughout the latter half of the nineteenth century this static and archaic scene, the principal geographical setting for this essay, was traversed by a succession of social upheavals. For Spain too, in spite of its isolation and backwardness, compared to industrial and middle-class Europe, stood at the great crossroads of contemporary history. Don Quixote's windmills had yielded place to mills powered by steam. Modernisation was on the march in the north and east of the country. The disentailment of land was disrupting the old established rural structures in the centre and south. New classes sprang up, and more and more sectors of the population came under the sway of progressive ideas. Was Spain, this mixture of archaism and modernity, to become an industrial and middle-class nation such as Britain, France or Germany, or was it to slumber for a further century upon the gilded shores of its past? Was its transformation to follow the pattern of the Western democracies or was it to pass through the convulsions that threaten all social systems entering the industrial age without having solved the major social conflicts of the old order?

The Spanish peasantry appeared, indeed, still to be at the stage of the French Revolution when the contemporary proletariat of Barcelona was already under the influence of the First International and the Paris Commune.

In 1868, the crisis endemic in Spain for half a century began

[1] Juan Díaz del Moral, *Historia de las agitaciones campesinas andaluzas*. (Madrid: Alianza Editorial, 1967); new abridged edition of the original Spanish edition, 1929.

gathering momentum to reach a climax in 1873. The tide of history surged forward as if Spain wished to encompass in a single sweep what other nations had taken two stages or even several centuries of struggle to achieve. In a single year, the country passed from constitutional monarchy to a parliamentary republic, and from a centralised state through disintegration into quasi-autonomous 'cantons', to its final end in the restoration. At the same time, social groups and movements shifted places, roles and positions at a rate no less bewildering than that of the political parties. At different times, leadership of the movement was in the hands of the industrial middle class, the army, or the proletariat. Their various revolutionary endeavours by no means always reflected their proper economic interests. Ideology too played its part. Regionalism cut across class consciousness, status-seeking across material considerations. Social divisions were unclear.

The historian setting his course by a compass calibrated on the Western model will have a difficult, if not impossible, task ahead of him. He will search in vain for class struggles opposing well-defined groups whose positions in society could be explained, as they ought to be, by relationships dependent on production. Everything overlapped. Spain had its 'Girondins' in favour of centralisation and its 'Jacobins' who were federalists when they were not anarchists. There were, in addition, middle-class liberals of wildly revolutionary tendencies and socialist proletarians who were astonishingly level-headed and moderate. The terms liberal, democrat, radical, intransigent, socialist, republican, etc., had no hard and fast meanings, and did not match the socio-economic trends it is tempting to read into such political catchwords.

One important factor in the metamorphosis of these ideas from one region to another was the fragility of national unity. Another was the overlapping of the old and new social structures. According to the 1887 census there were only 243,867 industrial workers in Spain as opposed to 4,854,742 agricultural workers and a few thousand in other occupations. Including their families, this gave Spain a total population of 17,565,632 inhabitants. Thirty years earlier, there had been 150,000 industrial workers, 26,000 miners and 600,000 small craftsmen as opposed to 2,390,000 agricultural workers.[1] For the crucial year of 1873, which fell between the two censuses, no figures are available.

---

[1] Angel Marvaud, *La Question social en Espagne* (Paris: F. Alcan, 1910) pp. 81–2; Eduardo Comin Colomer, *Historia del anarquismo espanol (1836—1948)* (Madrid; Editorial RADAR, n.d.–1948–50?)

Judging from the 1887 statistics, however, even with industrialisation forging ahead, the proletariat were still certainly numerically weak and the small craftsmen diminishing in number. The small craftsmen, who were still numerous in 1860, had almost completely vanished from the 1887 census. This is probably because the statisticians lumped a large number of these small craftsmen together with the industrial population or with the agricultural workers.

The 'Rural Question' and Anarchism

This arbitrary selection is not over-important, however, since the general trend is obvious. The Spain of 1873, the Spain of the First Republic and of the Cantonalist Revolution, was almost exclusively agricultural, with a relatively unimportant industrial proletariat mainly concentrated in Catalonia. The peasantry was the dominant factor in Spain, particularly the agricultural labouring class, which was more numerous than in any other West European country. This class must have had a population of approximately four million families, the most politically active elements of which were concentrated in the south: in Andalusia, in Estremadura, and in the Levante (but in Catalonia, too, it is true).

The Spanish peasantry, particularly in the south, formed a constantly disturbing and agitated element of the Spanish political scene from the revolt, immortalised by Lope de Vega, at Fuente Ovejuna in 1476,[1] through the Cantonalist insurrection of 1873 to the Civil War of 1936-9. Gerald Brenan has used political maps to show the persistence of these political movements. It is evident from these that Andalusia, Valencia and Catalonia, which were hotbeds of federalism and cantonalism as well as of anarcho-internationalism in 1873, remained the wellsprings of similar movements during the Civil War of 1936-9. Even trade union membership reveals this political identification, for, while the workers of Castile and the centre of Spain belonged as a general rule to the socialist U.G.T., those of the southern and south-eastern regions supported the anarcho-syndicalist C.N.T.

Nowhere else in modern times has such constancy and such revolutionary ardour been found in the rural sector, and nowhere else has it

[1] In April 1476 the whole village of Fuente Ovejuna rose in revolt against the master of the Order of Calatrava, Gómez de Guzmán, bailiff of the King, who used them harshly and in a humiliating manner. The bailiff was murdered and his corpse dragged in the dust. The incident led to an intensive investigation to find and punish the criminals, but the King's agents came up against a population as unanimous as it was resolute. Each question received the single reply: '*Fuente Ovejuna*', the whole community in this way assuming responsibility for the acts committed.

shown so many points of resemblance to the urban workers' movements, be they socialist or syndicalist, liberal or vaguely anarchist.
Historians and sociologists have been unanimous, or practically so, in
taking this as due to two factors: the influence of a historical heritage
going back to the *reconquista*; and the anarchism imported by the First
International around 1870 which was grafted on to it. This is merely
hypothesis, however, and as such has often been weakened or distorted
by the attitudes taken up by the historians themselves. Certain authors
(among them the most brilliant, such as Brenan) have assumed the
existence of a more or less vague and widespread 'rural anarchism',
without attempting to discover its origins and actual extent, nor its
true relationship to the organised workers' movement of 1860–80.
On the other hand, the historians of the workers' movement, whether
anarchists such as Max Nettlau or Marxists such as Stieklow, showed
little interest in the 'rural question'.[1] They approached the history of
the International strictly from the urban workers' point of view, even
where they were not unaware of the spread of the movement into the
countryside. As a result, the 'anarchist question' was never in fact
correlated to the 'rural question' as regards the upsurge of revolution
in 1868–74 even though this marked the starting-point of both the
workers' movement and rural unrest in modern Spain. Indeed,
neither was the 'revolutionary question' itself ever related to the social
movements of the urban or rural proletariat.

Yet the historians of the 1868 revolution did not lose sight of either
question. At times they even gave an unwarranted importance to the
agitators of the International, as did certain historians of the Paris
Commune. With the exception of Díaz del Moral, however, who,
moreover, limited himself to the study of the province of Cordova,
there is no work which tries to lay bare the interaction of the political
parties and social forces in the revolution. Laying stress on the part
played by the International groups in the insurrection is, as a rule,
intended as a criticism of their aims; from this point of view, the
Internationalists were mere bomb throwers. Yet the intent to revolt is
specifically denied by those social historians who are authorities on the
matter and whose theories are based on the study of certain official
texts of the International. Before examining in detail the role of the

[1] Max Nettlau, *Miguel Bakunin, La Internacional y la Alianza en España (1868–1873)*
(Buenos Aires, 1925); Idem. *La Première Internationale en Espagne (1868–1888)* (Dordrecht:
D. Reidel Publishing Co., 1969); George Stieklow, *Die bakunistische Internationale nach
dem Haager Kongress* (Stuttgart: J. H. W. Dietz Nachf., 1914) (Ergänzungshefte zur
Neuenzeit no. 18).

International in the events following the 1868 revolution, it is advisable to take a closer look at the evolution of Spain's agrarian structure, and of the peasantry within it.

The Political Background: 1868–75

From 1868 to 1875, Spain passed through a particularly turbulent phase of its history. In September 1868 a *pronunciamiento* ended the rule of the Spanish Bourbons, Isabella II left the country, and power fell into the hands of General Serrano as Regent and General Prim as Prime Minister. In June 1869, the Constituent Cortes adopted a constitution that was both monarchist and democratic and sprang from a compromise between the Liberal Unionists and the Progressive Democrat parties. Spain was thus on the look-out for a constitutional monarch and unwittingly found itself involved in the Franco–German rivalry over Bismarck's candidate, Prince Leopold Sigmaringen-Hohenzollern. In the end, neither the Prince of Hohenzollern nor the Duke of Orleans, nor even Ferdinand, ex-King of Portugal, was to occupy the vacant throne, but a fourth candidate, Amadeo of Savoy, who was elected King of Spain on 16 November 1870. His reign lasted only two years and a few months. The assassination of General Prim deprived the young King of his main supporter, and the country was further weakened by the Carlist War. Amadeo, finally abandoned by General Serrano and 'handed over' to the radicals, abdicated in February 1873. The Republic was proclaimed at once. It lasted for a year and was succeeded by a military dictatorship that lasted until the restoration of Alfonso XII in January 1875. Spain, after eight years of troubles (preceded, moreover, by two revolutions and a civil war in the space of fifty years), was once more under the rule of the Bourbons and was to remain so until 1923. In the meantime, she was to lose her American Empire as well as any hope, a hope that had still been strong in the mid-nineteenth century, of catching up with the developed countries of Europe.

In this vast panorama, the Spanish Republic of 1873 was no more than an episode and the Cantonalist revolt an incident. Nevertheless, short as it was, the 1873 episode was extremely important.

It was significant because the modern Spain that had been struggling to emerge since the Napoleonic era, through the turmoil of its civil wars, finally succeeded in finding a system, albeit a very imperfect one, which expressed its most profound (though often contradictory) aspirations. In the same way, several trends converged in the 1873

Republic only to peter out in the chaos of the Cantonalist movement.

This is not the place to go into the distant origins of the Spanish attitude that anything is preferable to centralisation. Many works have dealt with this question and various explanations of it exist. The 'centrifugal tendency' is none the less a fact. It is an obvious and permanent factor that turns up in one form or another throughout the contemporary history of the oldest centralised state in Europe. The 'centrifugal tendency' is apparent in Catalan and Basque separatism. It appears in federalism as opposed to monarchism, or, at other times, as opposed to a Jacobinism of centralist leanings, and also as a bulwark against the levelling and standardising effects of liberalism. The 'Catalonia versus Castile' explanation which is most often put forward for the federalist phenomenon is insufficient, in spite of the skill of certain analyses using this antagonism as a basis for argument.[1] In finding a way through the revolutionary turmoil of 1873, account must also be taken both of the autonomist leanings of the 'intransigent' *petite bourgeoisie* of south and south-east of Spain, and more particularly, of the 'spontaneous' anarchism which was encouraged and organised by Bakunin and the First International.

Anarchism and the International

It should first be made clear that in the Spain of 1868–74, anarchism, the International and extreme federalism made up a single whole that was not separable into its component parts. It is true that their 'spheres of influence' did not match completely. An untutored or 'spontaneous' anarchism in the widest sense of the term covered a more extensive area than the network of sections of the International Workingmen's Association (I.W.A.) in Spain, which itself was probably anarchist in the majority but included a small fraction (the New Madrid Federation founded by Engels' Spanish correspondents and by Lafargue) that was termed 'centralist' or 'Marxist', or even 'authoritarian'.[2] Lastly, the federalist 'sphere of influence' covered a much wider area than the International. At the centre, however, their 'spheres of influence' overlapped, covering a mass that was simultaneously internationalist, anarchist and federalist. What is the explanation?

It is often taken to be a fortuitous coincidence. The first cells of the

[1] See Salvador de Madariaga, *Spain: A Modern History* (New York: Praeger, 1958), pp. 143–55.

[2] Some provincial groups, particularly in Valencia, Lérida and Toledo, were also under the influence of the centralists.

International in Spain were founded by the emissary of the Russian anarchist Michael Bakunin, the Italian Giuseppe Fanelli,[1] during his stay in Madrid and Barcelona between November 1868 and February 1869, that is in the very midst of the revolution which broke out in September 1868. Apart from eye-witness accounts,[2] some documents and the manifestos and by-laws of the First International groups bear witness to the success of Fanelli's mission. However, it is also evident that there was some confusion among the members of the first founding cells as to whether they belonged to the International Workingmen's Association (the International) or the Bakunist organisation, the Alliance of Social Democracy, or to both at once.[3]

Be that as it may, no mere coincidence, error or confusion (whether deliberate or accidental) can explain such a tenacious and deep-rooted phenomenon as the Spanish workers' double attachment to anarchism and to the International. Any coincidence there may be lies not in the confusion created by Fanelli but in the receptivity of his hearers to the ideas he brought from Bakunin.

In any case the 'confusion' continued. The International, which was soon to spread over the whole of Spain, drew up a programme that was international, proletarian and revolutionary as well as federalist and anarchist. Its newspapers, *La Solidaridad* and *La Federación*, its manifestos, the records of its first congresses (the 1870 Congress at Barcelona and the 1871 Congress at Valencia) found no difficulty in reconciling the principles of the I.W.A. as directed by Marx and his friends from London, the headquarters of the General Council of the International, and the ideas of Bakunin and his friends in Geneva and the Jura.

This happy spirit of compromise was, however, soon to become impracticable for reasons which had nothing to do with Spain. From 1868 on the General Council of the International in London, and Karl Marx in person in particular, suspected Bakunin in Geneva of intriguing against the London centre with the aim of imposing his own policy and direction on the International Association. Finally, in September 1872, the Fifth General Congress of the I.W.A. at the

[1] The first contacts between the I.W.A. and various Spanish organisations such as the Iberian Legion and the Central Office of the Workers' Societies of Barcelona have not been mentioned. In this connection see the works of Nettlau cited above and José Termes Ardévol, *El movimiento obrero en España, La Primera Internacional (1864–1881)* (Barcelona: Publicaciones de la Cátedra de Historia General de España, 1965).
[2] See principally *El proletariado militante*, by Anselmo Lorenzo, cited above, vol. I pp. 21–77.
[3] Ibid., pp. 25 and 39.

Hague decided to exclude Bakunin from the International. The breach was thus complete. However, even before the Hague Congress, as the controversy deepened, the various sections found themselves forced to take a stand either in favour of 'centralist' resolutions from London or in favour of the 'anti-authoritarian' doctrines held by the opposition led by Bakunin.

In Spain the conflict between Marx and Bakunin only served to emphasise the anarchistic leanings of the Spanish Internationalists. The centralising bias of the resolutions passed at the London Conference of 1871, and later the exclusion of Bakunin by the Hague Congress of the I.W.A. in 1872 acted primarily as a catalyst. It made conscious what had until then been instinctive, that is the hostility of the Spanish members of the International towards the 'authoritarian' General Council which wanted to organise them from London . . . rather as their authoritarian governments had always done from Madrid. Anything coming 'from above', from an administrative centre, whether governmental or revolutionary, appeared to them to be equally contaminated with authoritarianism. After the Hague Conference, a significant play on words to this effect may be seen in several texts. Making use of Marx's first name, the Spanish anti-authoritarians applied the same disrespectful epithet to the followers of the German communist as they did to their most reactionary monarchist opponents, they called them 'Karlists'.

The struggle between the federalist and centralist (or 'authoritarian' and 'anti-authoritarian') tendencies became particularly violent during 1872 and 1873. Friedrich Engels' feverish activity in support of the Spanish groups who were loyal to the Marxist cause was, no doubt, a major factor in this. Engels, in fact, sent a continuous stream of advice and instructions from London to Paul Lafargue. He was, in addition, the author or co-author of several publications castigating anarchism, Bakunin in person and the Alliance, as well as the harmful effects of their influence in Spain.[1]

However powerful the ideological and intellectual contribution of personalities such as Marx and Engels might have been, it proved ineffective in Spain in the unequal combat between the small Marxist

[1] See in particular *L'Alliance de la démocratie socialiste et l'Association internationale des travailleurs*. Report and documents published by order of the International Congress of The Hague (London, 1873). This booklet was reproduced in *La Première Internationale. Recueil de documents*, published under the direction of Jacques Freymond (Geneva: Droz, 1962), vol. II. Volume III of this collection (1971) contains two texts by Engels which appeared in the *Volksstaat* in 1873: 'La République en Espagne' (p. 365) and 'Les bakounistes au travail, Mémoire sur l'insurrection d'Espagne de l'été 1873' (p. 379).

group and the overwhelming majority of anarchist sections. The end came at the Cordova Congress with complete victory for the views held by Bakunin's Spanish friends. In December 1872, the Spanish Federation, consisting of approximately 29,000 members grouped in ten trade unions, 236 local federations, 119 mixed trade sections, and 484 trade sections, joined the 'anti-authoritarian pact' of Saint-Imier, a pact which for a decade was to remain the fundamental anarchist programme for the whole of Europe. At following congresses, in Spain as well as at the international congresses (Geneva, 1873, and Brussels, 1874) the Spanish Federation scored even more resounding successes in spite of government persecution. With almost 50,000 members in 1873, the Spanish branch of the I.W.A. was one of the most powerful and certainly the best established and organised.

It seems undeniable that the International in Spain was above all an industrial workers' movement. The organisation of the movement began in the great urban centres such as Madrid and Barcelona, and these two cities remained its strongholds during the whole period covered by this study. Here, as also in the provincial towns, the majority of local sections and federations were made up of industrial workers. Its leaders came almost exclusively from industry, the crafts or the professions. Its ideological bases were those of the international socialism of the time which drew its inspiration from three main sources: Proudhonism, the British trade union system and German communism.

Yet the peasant element was much more heavily represented than in any other national group of the International. In addition, the extreme rapidity with which the Association spread through the southern districts in 1873 (in Andalusia especially) gave it a genuinely rural character. In Catalonia, the most highly industrialised region, there were also a very large number of agricultural workers' and peasants' sections.

The history of these sections and their place in the International will now be examined, after a brief description of the underlying causes of social unrest.

II. THE AGRARIAN STRUCTURE

The timeless problems of rural Spain, which are generally laid at the door of the land tenure system of large estates (*latifundia*) in the southern, and small holdings (*minifundia*) in the northern half of the country descend in a direct line from the remote past and have been constantly exacerbated by population growth.

During the nineteenth century a new factor, the disentailment of civil and church land, combined with the population problem to lead to the total overthrow of traditional agrarian structures.

In broad terms, disentailment can be defined as a process inspired by economic liberalism at its purest, whereby land owned by the Church and the nobility, as well as unoccupied arable land and land belonging to the communes, was put back into circulation.

1. *Economic liberalism*: this drew its inspiration from the ideas of Jovellanos (1744–1811) and was expressed in the legislation of the Cortes of Cádiz (1811–22) which passed a series of measures designed to reorganise the land tenure system. This was a very cautious first step that was brought to a halt by the return of Ferdinand VII, thus putting back the application of reformist doctrines by as much as thirty to fifty years. It is interesting to note that during the eighteenth century, men preoccupied by the agrarian problem, such as Aranda, Floridablanca, Olavide and Campomanes, recommended solutions that accorded the State a large share of control while respecting certain traditional types of land tenure. In contrast to the liberal tendencies of Jovellanos, they therefore represented the pre-liberal collectivist trend.

2. *Land belonging to the nobility and the Church*: over the centuries the land, secured by legal privilege, became to an ever greater extent concentrated in the hands of the nobility and the Church (monasteries and different orders, institutions, etc.). The property owned by these two groups remained, in practice, outside the circulation of national wealth, and the civil and ecclesiastical accumulation of land was thus a one-way process of adding to the inherited wealth of the two aristocracies. Legal barriers of all kinds such as *mayorazgos* and *vinculaciones* prevented any return of this property to the common people.

The process of disentailment was not actually set in motion until the Napoleonic invasion and the first measures taken by Joseph Bonaparte (closure of monasteries, nationalisation of church property). This process was to gain momentum throughout the nineteenth century in a sporadic (due to the alternation in power of the liberals and the moderates) but irreversible manner. It was particularly marked from 1836 to 1854 under the energetic action of personalities such as Mendizabal[1]

---

[1] Mendizabal nationalised church property in order to solve the financial difficulties provoked by the first Carlist war and to deal a decisive blow to the clergy who had taken up arms in defence of the cause of the pretender Carlos I.

and Pascual Madoz.[1] The lands of the nobility and the Church were put back into circulation in the name of the economic liberalism that was one of the features of the nineteenth century, but this recirculation was chiefly to benefit a class that had become wealthy but had had no opportunity as yet to acquire ownership of land. This was the middle class. The landless peasantry and the agricultural labourers (that is, the majority of the rural population) were excluded from the reform. Thus Spain let slip the opportunity of creating a class of small independent landowners, and, once the monopoly of the establishment was broken, allowed the land tenure system to relapse back into its former condition as large new estates grew up (neo-latifundism). There is no doubt that the new system was much more prejudicial to the interests of the mass of the peasantry for the reasons that are given below.

3. *'Baldíos' and common land*: Before the disentailment, the worst-off agricultural classes were able to make a living by directly working the common land[2] which belonged to the communes, by renting a plot of land at extremely unfavourable rates (this due to the fact that it was a seller's market and to the existence of middlemen who made their profit from the difference between the rent charged for land 'wholesale' and the amount paid by sub-tenants when the plots were distributed), or else by hiring out their labour to the great estates (agricultural day labourers). The hiring of day labourers was seasonal and extremely uncertain as it depended on whether the local landowner, be he aristocrat or churchman, wished to put his land under cultivation, and this was not always the case. Under these conditions, the existence of common land that could be cultivated free of charge served the majority of the peasantry as a guarantee against famine.

Too great an importance, however, should not be attributed to communal institutions, for their collectivist character has often been overemphasised. In point of fact, although the common land fulfilled an important function, from the eighteenth century onwards it no longer represented an effective barrier against destitution because of the increase in population (which rose from 5·7 million in 1700 to 12 million in 1808). This explains the abnormally high number of beggars and tramps, which stood at 100,000 *families* as a rough estimate. The *baldíos* or ownerless arable lands might have been used to solve this crisis if they could have been progressively assimilated into the

---

[1] General Land Reform Act of 1 May 1855.
[2] Four million hectares before the disentailment. Vicens Vives (ed.), *Historia social y económica de España y América*, IV 30.

common land system by being put under cultivation by the impoverished peasantry, or even if they had been divided into plots with the
grant of a legal title of ownership. In practice, until the nineteenth
century, the *baldíos* remained the hunting preserves of the influential
families of the cities and, particularly, was at the disposal of the *Mesta*,
the great sheep farmers' guild, which used it at will to pasture their
flocks. It was only during the first part of the nineteenth century, after
the War of Independence and the appropriation of land that resulted,
that the legislature undertook to ratify[1] such appropriations by measures that Vicens Vives considers 'more revolutionary than most of the
disentailment decrees', since they set up a precedent under cover of
which the *roturadores de baldíos*[2] increased in number. It is undeniable,
however, that such appropriations of land did little to resolve the
agrarian problem, particularly as in most cases the poverty of the
squatters rapidly led to their land passing into the hands of the middle
classes anxious to increase their ownership of land. Disentailment also
put common land on the market and this fell directly into the hands of
those with the money to pay for it.

The middle classes, moreover, as their ownership of land increased,
became in Hennessy's words, 'a second aristocracy'.

The British Consular Reports kept in London at the Public Record
Office serve to complete the picture:

> Landed proprietors in Spain have the custom to let out their lands
> either to single tenants or to a company of labourers for a term of
> three to four years at so much per annum, free of taxes – especially
> those who own a large extent of land such as in Andalusia, La
> Mancha, Ciudad Real, Toledo.
>
> In Castile and Aragon, properties are smaller and many pro-
> prietors cultivate their own lands – others let them to small tenants
> who pay rent either in kind or in cash.
>
> The same is true for Asturias, Valencia, León, Galicia . . . Average
> amount held by each tenant: one to two acres . . .
>
> Extreme disorder in the administration of property (separate codes
> in each province, etc.) prevents the creation of *bancos hypotecarios*,
> which would prevent capital being lent at usurious rates (10–15 per
> cent; even 40–50); this system inhibits both proprietors and tenants.
>
> The habits, customs, laws, etc., have accumulated from the earliest

---

[1] The problem raised by the appropriation of the *baldíos* was not finally settled until
the Act of 24 August 1865.

[2] Occupiers of ownerless land.

ages: Gothic, Christian, Jewish and Moorish forming an inextric-
able web which no legislator has attempted to unravel . . . The
consequence is that most Spanish proprietors are perpetually involved
in law-suits which are lost and won and lost again, going from one
province to another, and appealing to different courts . . .

[In Andalusia] the position of the labouring classes . . . is morally
and physically bad. Pay is generally insufficient, the food scanty and
the clothing bad. The people are generally very ignorant albeit
intelligent. Eighty per cent are unable to read or write. They are
prone to idleness, proud and independent as well as very excitable,
but generally speaking not disaffected towards their employers . . .[1]

The Spanish middle classes thus became land based and it was their
attainment of the right to own land that, upon the disappearance of the
last traces of common land, pushed the mass of the peasantry once and
for all into the ranks of the proletariat.

In addition, there was a serious crisis in Spanish agriculture in 1866
resulting in widespread famine and a considerable increase in the death
rate among the worst-off sections of the population. The Spanish
peasant also had a long millenarian tradition of appropriating land in
the *latifundia* districts, sharing it out and destroying the ownership
records. The history of Spain is studded with many such violent
demonstrations of peasant fury: the events following the 1868 revolution were critically influenced by them.

III. THE SPANISH INTERNATIONAL AND ITS AGRICULTURAL SECTIONS, 1870–73

As a starting-point, it is essential to have a rough idea of the apparatus
the Spanish International intended to set up to carry out the social
revolution. At the base of the structure were the living and active
cells, the trade sections, which grouped together the workers of the
same occupation living in the same locality. The different trade
sections in the same locality were united in a local federation which
elected a local council to deal with administrative matters, correspondence and propaganda. The trade section was linked to other sections
of the same trade situated in other districts through the intermediary
of the trade federation which appointed a council. Complementary

---

[1] Extracts from a report by Percy ffrench on the tenure of land in Spain in *Layard to Granville No. 218*, London, Public Record Office, FO. 72/1327, and FO. 83/333.

trades, or trades participating in the production of the same product amalgamated their sections on the local level into a grouping[1] and on the national level into a federation of trade federations or trade Unions. The different trade federations that were members of the same union sent representatives to the council of the Union. At the apex of the organisation was the Federal Council (or Commission) of the Spanish Regional Federation, which was elected by the workers' congresses. The Council was a liaison and communications centre and symbolised the unity of the movement. Through it, contact was kept up with the General Council of the I.W.A. in London, thus fulfilling the dual purpose of the movement: to achieve international as well as national solidarity among the workers so as to combat capitalist oppression more effectively, and to bring about the social revolution.

Following the example of the other trade sections, the agricultural sections of the International were to evolve within this extremely complicated, tentacular and unwieldy framework.

The bulk of the agricultural sections[2] were located in Catalonia and Andalusia. A few were scattered throughout the rest of the country, mainly around Valencia and in Estremadura.

The character of the agricultural sections was determined by the region in which they were located. In Catalonia, the agricultural section formed only one of several sections for different trades. This meant that local federations in Catalonia were not dominated by the agricultural workers' sections, as happened in Andalusia. Take the agricultural workers of Mataró, for example. In August 1871, their section had a membership of thirty. The local federation for the same area consisted of five sections with membership as follows:

The '*Tres Clases de Vapor*'[3] (Cotton Spinners) section	700
The Builders' section	40
The Basketmakers' section	48
The Potters' section	36
The Agricultural Workers' section	30
Total membership	854

[1] *Agrupación local.*

[2] Our principal source is the nine volumes of manuscript carefully preserved for a century and containing practically all the documents produced by the Spanish Federal Council of the First International from 1868 to 1874, as well as copies of its correspondence: *Asociación Internacional de los Trabajadores. Actas del Primer Consejo Federal de la Región Española. 5 julio 1870– 9 marzo 1874. S.l.t. – 2 vols.* (referred to henceforth as *Actas*); and also *Asociación Internacional de los Trabajadores. Comunicaciones y Circulares del Primero, Segundo y Tercer Consejo Federal español y de la Primera Comisión Federal*

Thus, out of a total of 854 members of the International, there were only 30 agricultural workers. This table also shows the agricultural section to be the smallest. However, generalisations should be avoided since even in Catalonia there are cases (much rarer than the Mataró type, it is true) where there was a majority of agricultural workers in the local federation: at Olot, for example, where in October 1871 'the local federation . . . had just organised an agricultural workers section, which had more members than any of the others'.[1] It was, moreover, from the agricultural section at Olot (which also had the highest rise in membership over the ensuing months) that the initiative came to convene a congress to set up the Union of Rural Workers. Yet it should be noted that the practice in Catalonia was, with few exceptions, for the local federations to be amalgamations of various trade sections and this led to a more even distribution among industrial and rural workers, with the former in the majority, especially in areas where the textile industry was dominant. In the mountainous regions of the interior the proportions were reversed. Lastly, it should be observed that in Catalonia the agricultural sections were usually the last to be set up and the last to join their local federations. In other words, the Internationalist seed first took root in an urban workers' and craftsmen's environment and from there spread to the rural sectors.

In Andalusia, on the other hand, as a result of the uniformly rural nature of life outside important centres such as Cádiz, Seville or Málaga, the local federation might consist of an agricultural section only. This gave rise to true agricultural federations. In other cases, such as at Sanlúcar de Barrameda (province of Cádiz), it was the local peasant councils that took the initiative in forming new trade sections, even the non-agricultural ones. Thus at Sanlúcar, the agricultural and vineyard workers' section that was set up as a local federation in August 1872 helped to found other sections, such as the bakers' section, the cobblers' section and the seamen's section. In the three major regions selected for study, the agricultural sections were distributed as indicated in Table 1.

---

española. 18 septiembre – 21 abril 1874. S.l.t. 7 vols. (referred to henceforth as *Comunicaciones*).

Outside Spain, the Archives in Berne, the Archives of the Canton of Neuchâtel, and the various papers belonging to the Amsterdam Institute, to name only the richest sources of material, form an essential basis for research.

[3] *Federación de las Tres Clases de Vapor de Cataluña.* This is left untranslated in the English language histories. It was apparently a cotton spinners union (see Brenan, p. 138).

[1] *La Federación*, no. 114, 22 Oct 1871.

TABLE 1

REGIONAL DISTRIBUTION OF LOCAL FEDERATIONS OF THE INTERNATIONAL
SUBDIVIDED ACCORDING TO WHETHER FORMALLY CONSTITUTED AGRICULTURAL
SECTIONS DEFINITELY EXISTED (CATEGORY 1) AND WHERE THEY POSSIBLY
EXISTED, BUT EVIDENCE IS NOT CONCLUSIVE (CATEGORY 2)

	Catalonia	Andalusia	Rest of Spain	Total
Category 1	66	22	11	99
Category 2	14	21	11	46
Total	80	43	22	145

The local federations have here been divided into two categories.
Category 1 includes all federations in which agricultural sections were
definitely in existence according to the documentation used in this
study. As regards category 2, although a first document search points
to Internationalist agitation among the peasantry (whether as propaganda or in another form), there appears to be insufficient evidence to
warrant the conclusion that such sections existed in a properly *con-
tituted* form.

The table shows the agricultural sections that were in existence
during the fairly long and troubled period stretching from 1870 to
1873. During these four years, agricultural sections were founded,
struggled to survive, and often vanished without trace. This means
that this static picture shows only a part of the truth, the actual foundation of rural sections. It makes no allowance for the ups and downs
suffered by such sections nor for their possible dissolution.[1] However,
a more precise idea of the situation may be obtained by comparing the
list given by the Spanish Federal Commission's memorandum to the
1873 Geneva Congress with the preceding table.[2]

The Union of Rural Workers (U.R.W.)

In the short description given of the social organisation of the
International in Spain, it was mentioned that the unions of like
trades were to be true confederations of trade federations. In prac-

---

[1] Many agricultural sections were dissolved or died out gradually at the end of the
period, particularly during the government repression that followed the Cantonalist
rising.
[2] See *La Première Internationale*. Recueil de documents publié sous la direction de
Jacques Freymond. Tome IV: Textes présentés et annotés par Bert Andreas et Miklós
Molnár, Publications of the Graduate Institute of International Studies (Geneva: Droz,
1971).

tice, while such unions did actually exist[1] there were practically no trade federations, with the result that an essential piece of the machinery was missing. The trade union really representing a confederation of trade federations was practically non-existent, and (according to Lorenzo)[2] the ten unions extant were founded in violation of the regulations adopted by the workers' congress. He gives the following proof of this: 'Article 10 of Regulation No. 4 provides that "The Council of the Union, made up of one representative from each trade federation, shall carry out the resolutions of the Congress of the Union and those of the Federal Commission of the S.R.F.[3] of the International". None of these so-called "federations" can be shown to have existed. How then were the councils set up? I have no idea. I have kept no papers and can remember nothing about it, but there is no doubt that such councils existed . . .' It appears necessary to point out here the weaknesses of an organisation that was perfect in theory but whose principal working parts were missing in practice.

The Union of Rural Workers was founded during a Congress held at Barcelona in May 1872. Apart from the initiative shown by the agricultural workers at Olot, no trace of the preparatory work that led up to its foundation can be found and it is only due to the efforts of Lorenzo[4] that the following principal resolutions are known:

> In the fight against capital, all sections shall pay the subscription levied for the formation of resistance funds. These will always be available to the local grouping concerned.
>
> The subscription shall be twelve-and-a-half centimes of a *peseta* per week per member. Strikes shall be subject to the approval of the Council so that they be supported by all members.

As for the circumstances under which and following which strikes were to take place, the Congress decided that no 'scientific' strike[5] should take place for a year and that the sections were to discuss the matter thoroughly and submit a detailed report to the delegates representing them.

Circumstances led to the cancelling of the agreement adopted by the

[1] Cf. the ten unions mentioned in the report of the Cordova Congress.
[2] A. Lorenzo, *El proletariado militante*, vol. 1 ch. v p. 292.
[3] S.R.F. = Spanish Regional Federation.
[4] A. Lorenzo, op. cit., vol. 1 ch. v p. 294.
[5] The scientific strike involved concerted action by all workers, who regarded it as the only means of getting their claims met. This is opposed to the dignity strike which represented defensive action by workers against action taken by their employers.

U.R.W. Congress not to use strike action during the first year of the Union's existence. One cause was the effort of businessmen to lower wages and increase hours of work for the vegetable growers in Málaga, who had organised themselves into an agricultural section.[1] As a result, the Union was forced to enter the fray under the form of 'dignity strike' in spite of its desire to postpone claims to a later period. The most important strikes in addition to that of the 158 vegetable growers of Málaga were the strike of the agricultural workers of Carmona in the spring of 1873, the strike at Sanlúcar de Barrameda starting on 4 June 1873 and the strike of the agricultural workers of the Llobregat district of Catalonia.

IV. THE AIMS OF THE PEASANTRY

From the point of view of this chapter, what is of most interest is to define the aims of the peasantry in 1871-2, the areas in which they grouped together in organisations, became aware of their class problems and became deliberately involved in the ranks of the Internationalist movement in May 1873, after the Second Congress of the U.R.W.[2]

As there was no organ of the press that was both rural and international, all that can be done is to go through the workers' press of the time. This reproduced, often *in extenso*, the manifestos[3] drawn up by the most active agricultural sections and addressed to the farm workers of Spain. The most important passages of a few manifestos, and, some selections from U.R.W. circulars are given below and discussed, before the work of the second Congress of the Union, which declared itself an 'International unanimously less one vote'.[4] The manifestos are, in general, appeals designed to stimulate the move to form associations fostered by the International in rural areas. No reference is found to any definite agrarian programme. The point was rather to demonstrate the flagrant injustices suffered by the peasants.

The manifestos available for study are dated 1871. The propaganda campaign for setting up agricultural sections therefore began fairly soon after the Barcelona Congress. Several extracts are given below:

[1] U.R.W. Circular, Sans (Catalonia), 10 Nov 1872, in *Comunicaciones*.
[2] Barcelona, 18-22 May 1873.
[3] The extracts given are taken from *La Federación*.
[4] The delegate was personally in favour of joining the International but was bound by a categorical mandate. Neither the name of the delegate nor the section from which the mandate was issued is known.

*Manifesto of the Sabadell agricultural workers' section
to the farm workers of Spain (15 January 1871)*

The true harmony that exists among all useful workers, the only ones who will have any civil rights after society has been humanised by the liberation of all the slaves it harbours today, will result from exchanges made in a spirit of mutual solidarity and brotherhood.

Let us all unite under the banner of the I.W.A. Its guiding principles will lead us to the goal we seek.

This goal was the ending of all injustices, and these injustices are listed in another appeal made by the Sabadell section to the agricultural workers of the region.[1]

Society as it exists today condemns us to work like slaves for the support of a large number of people who do not work at all such as kings, priests, soldiers, lawyers, bourgeois and other parasites. We produce, and they consume the greater part of what we produce without doing any work themselves. As a return for all the good we do them, they keep us in the depths of ignorance, and in dire poverty. Our children too suffer the same fate, and seem to have come into the world only to become even more harshly exploited slaves than ourselves.

The same recriminations appear in the manifesto drawn up by the Andalusian sections, but couched in a rougher and more evocative style:

*Manifesto of the agricultural workers of Carmona
to the rural workers (October 1871)*

What is our aim? No more simple and natural a thing than to end the exploitation of man by man. That no man shall rob his fellows, that the product of labour shall go to the worker and not to an idler whose only hard labour has been the pursuit of pleasure and orgies.

Yet, understand this, Comrades, our taking up a revolutionary stand does not mean that we are to change the established order by throwing down those in power only to set up the weak and oppressed in their stead. Nor do we intend to form co-operative societies when the capital thus created might be used to exploit even a single one of our fellow men in the future. No, our aim is nobler and higher . . ., we wish all men to be workers and that all shall benefit from the fruit of their toil.

[1] 26 March 1871.

We consider that only direct personal labour gives any right to ownership of land and we condemn accumulation of capital as egoistical and against the interests of humanity as it is always obtained by somebody else's sweated labour.

We believe that we who cultivate the land have a right to its fruits, yet today as always we see these pass into hands which have never held a spade, a pick or a plough.

These few lines are typical of the thinking that lay behind the Spanish International and show the rejection of any dictatorship of the proletariat on the one hand and, on the other, a principle that was to become a rallying cry: 'The land to those who work it!' Yet the manifestos did not merely extol labour, they also did their best to put the peasantry on its guard against propaganda disseminated by the middle classes. This emerges from a reading of the manifesto drawn up by the federation (mainly agricultural) of Carmona and published by *La Federación* No. 119 (26 November 1871).

They offer you sops to keep you quiescent and in a state of precarious dependence by telling you fairy tales about co-operative societies and the federal republic. But these societies and republics will still contain your employers and masters, who will go on consuming everything you produce. We repeat that all this is only designed to dazzle you and make you believe that your lords and masters take an interest in your fate.

Lastly, a few lines are given from a manifesto drawn up by the agricultural workers of Seville (29 November 1871), which turns up practically word for word, in more literary style it is true, in V. Blasco Ibáñez's novel *La Bodega*, which is set in Andalusia among the most exploited section of the peasantry:

Nobody has a better view of social inequality than we have. As we make our way back from the fields to our wretched hovels, reeling with exhaustion, we pass through the streets of this busy town and listen to the triumphal singing of our exploiters. We see their way of life, their palaces, and through their doors and windows we can see the orgies to which they give themselves up and prostitute themselves. We are nearly run down in the street by their carriages. The dresses of their mistresses are an insult to us, and our eyes fill with tears and our hearts with sorrow when we compare them to the rags worn by our exhausted wives. Friends, this must stop! Equality shall come. No longer shall it be our lot to die of hunger while others are overfed. Justice shall be done. By what means can this be achieved? Not with armies, nor machine guns, nor parliaments, but by our own just and reasoned determination alone. But this determination has to be as united, single-minded and undivided as that of one man . . . So, comrades, take courage. Let us make haste to join the International Workingmen's Association, which today stands for the truth. It is a true revolutionary movement both in its principles and in the means at its disposal and it will bring an end to monopoly and to arbitrary rule.

This was the spirit in which the first agricultural sections were founded in 1870–71. It was a spirit of resistance to the abuses of the middle class and of boundless confidence in the virtues of the Association.

Apart from this, however, none of the texts examined up to now justify the conclusion that any true agrarian programme existed at section level. Not once do any of the manifestos mention the word 'collectivism' even though the Spanish International, after the 1870 Barcelona Congress, itself accepted all the resolutions passed by preceding I.W.A. Congresses. Was this prudence, tactics or reticence? It is impossible to tell. The fact remains that in Spain questions of theory faded into the background before the practical problems of organising the forces of labour whose stratification into sections, federations and unions was to prepare the way for a future society based on the 'free federation of associations of free agricultural and industrial producers'. In short, collectivism, while remaining a basic principle, had no influence on the structure of the organisation itself but was supposed to rise out of it spontaneously when the social revolution came. In any case, Internationalist propaganda among the peasantry at section level was not carried out on the basis of such themes as collectivism, *reparto*, and so on, but dealt with much more concrete questions.

The U.R.W. circulars, for their part, do not go much deeper into the question of land tenure, restricting themselves to the successful organisation of strikes and to the mobilisation of all efforts in preparation for 'the massive struggle between labour and capital'. 'Workers unite – Don't allow yourselves to be hoodwinked – No quarter to

landowners and landlords! Fight exploitation of man by man!'[1]
—Such was the tenor of their proposals.

V. THE PEASANT MOVEMENT AND THE INTERNATIONAL

The U.R.W. Congress at Barcelona in May 1873 marked a turning point. During the Congress, the Union was to proclaim its membership of the International even though some agricultural sections were already affiliated to the Association on their own account. This point is worth emphasis. Assuming that the Spanish members of the International aimed at developing and perfecting their organisation along the lines of the model described in section III above and that apart from strike action their main weapon was propaganda, it is necessary to specify, in the case of the peasantry at least, which were the centres from which revolutionary ideas were disseminated. In theory the Federal Council was the most important centre until the foundation of the U.R.W., that is until mid-1872.

In this first stage, a certain number of agricultural sections were set up that turned out to be among the most firmly based and loyal (Sanlúcar, San Fernando, for example). From their foundation, these sections became centres for the dissemination of propaganda and set up travelling committees that made their way about the surrounding countryside. From May 1872 onwards, the relationship between the Federal Council and the agricultural sections was supplemented by the relationship between the U.R.W. Council[2] and the agricultural sections.

The second relationship should have supplanted the first as a matter of course but it never developed sufficiently to do so. One has the impression that although the U.R.W. Council took a hand in Andalusian affairs (the Málaga strike, for example), it did not play a decisive role in Catalonia except where its propaganda made an impact. What was the reason for this? Geographical distance? Perhaps. However, the writer considers that there is a deeper reason. It should be remembered that when Lorenzo talked of the existence of Unions of like trades and their respective Councils, he was not able to give any accurate account of how many Councils were appointed, seeing that

---

[1] U.R.W. circular, Sans, 3 June 1873, from *Comunicaciones*, vol. v.
[2] Based at Sans (Catalonia).

in the light of the regulations adopted by the Congress they should have consisted of trade federations' delegates and that these federations never in fact existed. Yet it is known that a Council of the U.R.W. was in session at Sans (Catalonia) although its influence was scarcely felt outside the local or regional area. Why? The answer is quite simple. Although the agricultural sections expanded tremendously in 1872 and 1873, the U.R.W., although benefiting from this development, was itself (as all other unions were) founded in breach of the law and had no official existence. As no agricultural trade federations had ever been formed, there was no regular way of constituting a council with delegates from the federations. As a result, the Council at Sans only represented itself and it was unable to set up the lines of communication with the agricultural sections that would have guaranteed the U.R.W. autonomy within the S.R.F. Furthermore, in this vague situation, the co-ordination of the peasant movement fell mainly, in spite of the organisation that had been set up, on the shoulders of Federal Commission[1] members, who had to bolster up the deficiencies of the system with their own energy and initiative. The U.R.W. Council had thus always worked in collaboration with the Federal Commission. This situation was plainly abnormal and it led to overlapping at the level of the agricultural sections. Most of the agricultural sections that had been founded before the U.R.W., were affiliated to the International and kept in constant touch with the Federal Council. Most of them joined the Union in 1872, although the U.R.W. did not itself join the I.W.A. until May 1873. However, this made no difference to the relations of the sections with the Federal Council, which thus acted as a liaison between the sections and their own Union Council. On the other hand, sections founded after the U.R.W. (in particular the Catalonia sections) became members of the Union automatically without necessarily joining the International. This was logical as the Union had not yet made up its mind on the question. In practice this meant that where such 'new' agricultural sections appeared they led a separate existence from the 'real' International sections for other trades. In other words, they did not join the local federations and there was therefore no solidarity between rural and urban workers. This again was mainly the case in Catalonia and was not remedied until the U.R.W. formally joined the International in 1873. The Cantonalist Revolution in the summer of that year pre-

[1] The Federal Council was renamed 'Commission' in a revision of the rules of the Federation at the end of 1872.

movement from sorting itself out properly and fitting smoothly into the S.R.F.

Two texts are presented by way of conclusion. One was from the Federal Council and was contained in a letter to the U.R.W. Council.[1] The other was from the Second Congress of the Union and addressed to the Republican Cortes.[2] These texts are of the highest importance, the first because of the concept of alliances between different classes of the peasantry that it sets out, and the second for its criticism of the disentailment process, whose influence on the peasant question in Spain was discussed above.

Letter from the Federal Council of the Spanish Regional Federation of the First International to the Council of the Union of Rural Workers, 1872

In certain regions, such as Catalonia, the land is very much divided up and the owners either cultivate their plots themselves or rent them out to other workers. This system leads to [the formation] in many villages of a minority of agricultural day labourers and a majority of small landowners or tenant farmers.

Both classes are weighed down by exploitation and tyranny and it often happens that the small landowner or tenant farmer lives in more dreadful conditions than the day labourers, because the situation is equivalent to that existing in those areas where land is monopolised on a large scale by the great landowners.

Here the day labourers, the small landowners who cultivate their land themselves, and the tenant farmers of land owned by wealthy landowners must band together in a single agricultural workers' section, prepared to fight both the great landowners and the great tenant farmers without quarter or relief.

Let the day labourers demand increased wages and the tenant farmers lower rents or to pay a quarter or fifth share of their harvest instead of half. The small farmers in their turn will benefit when the price of their produce goes up.

Once solidarity has been established between agricultural workers, the fight against the robbers may begin. These last will be the only ones to suffer the consequences, while all workers will obtain an

---

[1] Signed by Francisco Tomás, Valencia, 2 Oct 1872, *Comunicaciones*, vol. II.
[2] Contained in the extract of the report on the Second Congress of the U.R.W. published in *La Federación*, No. 198 (31 May 1873).

improvement in their living conditions. To attain this result, all must be fully aware of the situation, knowledge of the facts will help us reach our goal. The length of this letter will not allow this theme to be expanded on; this will be left to another occasion. None the less we await your opinions on the ideas we have put forward here.

Valencia, 2 October 1872

for the Federal Council

Francisco Tomás

Letter from the Second Congress of the Union of Rural Workers to the Republican Cortes

The delegates of the different agricultural sections of the Spanish Regional Federation, having met in Barcelona for the Congress of their Union, and having attentively examined the decree of the present Minister of Finance dated 9 May 1873 respecting the disentailment of landed property derived from *baldíos, proprios, realengos* and *concejiles*, which decree purports to satisfy the social claims of the agricultural working class of the Spanish region;

Considering:

That the disentailment of civil and church lands which has so far been carried out by the governments antedating the Republic has, far from being of any general benefit to the working classes, benefited one class only and deprived the rural working classes of the few resources it could obtain through the cultivation of the common land; that as soon as the class for whose benefit disentailment was carried out became owners of land it not only abandoned the relatively revolutionary principles to which it owed its change of status, but also changed over into the bitterest opponent of the support and dissemination of these same revolutionary principles; that such conduct in the middle classes that came into being as a result of the so-called liberal revolution is natural and logical according to the principle of individual land tenure to which it owes its existence, as this principle is a purely exclusivist one that inevitably changes yesterday's revolutionaries into today's conservatives; that the disentailment purporting to be a measure beneficial to the working classes will only lead to an increase in the holdings of those who own land already or to the creation of a number of small landowners who by the sole fact of their becoming such will abandon the revolutionary interests of their brothers the workers and become supporters of the conservative interests of the great landowners, who will end up by absorbing them as an inevitable result of the law of competition; that advances in economic science, based on observed fact in all so-called liberal countries, have recently shown that the only just (and thus revolutionary) principle of land tenure is collective ownership of the land, the means of production and the tools of work;

Unanimously deny the goodwill of a decree which claims to satisfy the socialist aspirations of agricultural workers in Spain, especially as it will only lead to the creation of small individual interests serving the interests of the ignoble middle classes who exploit us pitilessly and urge all workers who truly desire their own and their fellows' emancipation to take no part in the purchase of this so-called property.

VI. THE INTERNATIONAL AND THE CANTONALIST REVOLUTION

The events of the summer of 1873 form one of the fullest and at the same time one of the most controversial pages of modern Spanish history. From June to September the country was in the grip of revolutionary unrest leading to the proclamation of Cantons, particularly in Andalusia, Valencia and the south-east. Such was the tragic end to the struggle between the two rival factions of the Federal Republican party, the 'benevolent' wing dominated by the personality of Pi and the 'intransigent' wing springing out of provincial radicalism. After the proclamation of the Federal Republic by the Cortes on 7 June 1873, a crisis broke out immediately over the fundamental question of whether the Federation should be set up 'from above' as the president of the executive power, Pi y Margall, proposed, or 'from below' as the Intransigents wished, through the proclamation of indedepennt sovereign cantons.

At first sight, this obviously 'political' quarrel should have left the mass of workers affiliated to the International indifferent. Indeed, it is known that the Spanish Internationalists were, from the start, hostile to any form of political action. Yet the Cantonalist Revolution, although dominated by the Intransigent republicans, was also marked by the participation of members of the International. What did they hope to achieve, and how massive was it?

As a first step, some declarations by prominent Spanish anarchists should be noted, since, although later than the period under review, they none the less demonstrate the confusion existing between internationalism, anarchism and federalism. This confusion over revolutionary aims explains why the Internationalists took part in a political revolution.

Mella has said that 'in Spain, Proudhon's doctrines are an article of faith for the majority and [that] every Spaniard is by nature a federalist of some sort. What is so surprising', he adds, 'about every socialist being an anarchist?' Federico Urales considers anarchism to be a natural offshoot of Federal Republicans and attributes its widespread diffusion throughout this country to the individualist and rebel spirit that flourished among the Cordovan Arab philosophers, the mystics, artists, the great captains, and the great explorers.[1]

Díaz del Moral goes on to conclude, 'As happened among the Catalonian and Andalusian workers, here [in the province of Cordova] the followers of the new school [anarchism] came from the ranks of the Federalists'. The S.R.F., however, stood out consistently against this confusion and, although it occasionally showed some interest in the Federalist movement, it informed its members early on, particularly after the proclamation of the Republic, that the Republic was a bourgeois myth that was incapable of achieving the emancipation of the proletariat. Yet there was no doubt that the proletariat was not indifferent to the attraction of Federalism, the more so as the leaders of this movement claimed to be socialists.[2] More research is needed in this field to clarify the impact of federalist ideas on the Spanish worker.

In the context of this study, two contradictory ideas about Cantonalism are seen to exist. The first, which is the official and indeed the European view, was backed by the Spanish governments immediately succeeding Pi's fall. They were not unaware of the Intransigent character of the insurrection but they deliberately set out to make the Internationalist participation seem greater than it really was in order to discredit the I.W.A., whose subversive character had already been exposed in a circular from the Minister of the Interior, Sagasta, at the

---

[1] Díaz del Moral, op. cit.
[2] Pi y Margall in particular, who was very much attracted to Proudhon's theories.

beginning of 1872.[1] Many Spanish historians took up this theme on their own account, leading to an outpouring of tendentious literature comparable to that dealing with the events of the Paris Commune of 1871. The second idea was put forward by the leaders of the Spanish International and is found in certain letters and also in the reports presented by the S.R.F. to the Geneva Congress of 1873 and the Brussels Congress of 1874. To understand why these stands were taken, it must be noted that the Spanish workers' movement led a very precarious existence in spite of its spectacular expansion in 1872–3. Declared illegal by the Cortes of Amadeo's reign, it had to contend with government repression on a national scale and, after the prohibition was lifted, with arbitrary action on the local level taken by the municipal authorities (*caciquistes*), particularly in Andalusia, where municipal councils were generally[2] in the hands of the Federal Republicans. In this permanently unstable situation, the movement was at the mercy of a sudden counter-blow. This induced the Spanish Federal Council, from 1872 on, to issue directives on the action to be taken by local federations 'in emergencies'.

The manifesto containing these directives follows 'the situation created . . . by the Sagasta circular' but its influence was such that it may be considered as contemporary with the Cantonalist uprising, for it seems undeniable that if the Federal Commission had had the means[3] to take up a stand in time in June 1873, it would have acted along the lines of this text,[4] the main passages of which are given below:

> To the workers who suffer with us the results of social injustice:
>
> Events outside our control and contrary to our wishes may force us into a position that we have until now avoided, as our thoughts have been fully occupied with the working out of our primary objectives and we have been confident that justice was on our side. The revolution, armed revolution may be upon us. Carried away by our generous impulses, by our love of liberty, and by the consciousness of injured dignity, it is likely that we shall take part in the struggle. Yet it is imperative that we should not repeat the old, and

---

[1] The offensive launched at that time against the International all over Europe has been described by Georges Bourgin as a 'sort of Holy Alliance', *International Review of Social History* (Leiden, 1939) IV 39–138.

[2] Especially after the proclamation of the Republic.

[3] After the events at Alcoy (see below), the Federal Commission took refuge in Madrid. All communication between the centre of the peninsula and the periphery were cut off as a result of the Cantonalist rising.

[4] *Manifesto of the Spanish Federal Council to all sections of the Spanish Regional Federation.* 1872.

fatal mistakes. We should not, in our anxiety to obtain our liberty and to give justice an indestructible foundation, shed our blood . . . only to tighten still further the vise in which we are caught. Workers, it is imperative that liberty, whose name is on everyone's lips and which all claim to love, carries a guarantee, the only one that can render it lasting: the transformation of social conditions. It is imperative that if revolution breaks out and we take part in it, that we do not abandon the battlefield, that we do not lay down our arms until our great objective is realised, that is 'the social emancipation of the workers by the workers themselves'. . . . It is imperative that once the workers are victorious, they should call a general assembly of federated members in each area as part of the full exercise of their rights and pass a solemn resolution to put individually owned land under collective ownership and immediately put all tools of labour such as land, mines, railways, shipping, machinery etc., into use under the administration of the local Councils of their respective federations.

This document, however, remains ambiguous in the sense that the circumstances to which it refers (revolution, armed revolution) are not clearly explained. In all likelihood, this does not mean the great social revolution which was the goal of the I.W.A. On the other hand, it would appear to imply that a revolutionary situation in which the International might find itself 'spontaneously' engaged should be taken over by the International and might lead somehow to the 'true' revolution. This was exactly the situation in 1873. There was a *petit-bourgeois* revolution with a great number of Internationalist groups taking part in it, particularly in Andalusia and in Valencia, where the social claims of agricultural workers took precedence over the political aims of the 'intransigent' middle classes. Was this the sign for the International to take over leadership of the movement for its own ends, to achieve 'the social emancipation of the workers by the workers themselves'? The question is clearly stated. The reply, however, remains ambiguous. There were several different and even contradictory attitudes.

In Bakunin's opinion the time was ripe for passing, as he said, 'from the political federation of the *petit-bourgeois* type modelled on the Swiss Confederation' to full-scale revolution.

The demon of revolutionary socialism [he wrote] has once and for all taken possession of Spain. Peasants in Andalusia and

Estremadura have, without instruction or advice from outside, appropriated and continue every day to appropriate the lands of the former wealthy landowners. Catalonia, with Barcelona at its head, has proclaimed its sovereignty. The people of Madrid have proclaimed the Federal Republic and refuse to allow the revolution to be subject to the future decrees of the Constituent Assembly. In the provinces of the north, said to be in the hands of the Carlist reactionaries, the social revolution is manifestly on the march. The *fueros* have been proclaimed as well as the autonomy of provinces and communes, while legal and civil documents have been burned. All over Spain, the common soldier is fraternising with the people and getting rid of his officers. General bankruptcy, both public and private (the first condition for the social and economic revolution) is beginning.

In short, destruction and disintegration are complete and everything lies in ruins, either destroyed or decaying from within. There is no longer an Exchequer, no army, no courts, no police. There are no government troops, no state troops. Only the people are strong, cheerful, and ready for anything, and from now on their actions will be dictated by social revolutionary ardour alone. Under the joint leadership of the International and the Alliance of Revolutionary Socialists, the people are assembling and organising their forces and they are laying the foundations of the society of the emancipated working man on the ruins of State and the decay of the bourgeois world.[1]

The Spanish 'joint leadership', however, was itself more hesitant. At Alcoy, Málaga, Grenada, Seville and other centres, it was indeed the Internationalists who took over leadership of the movement. However, in spite of the enthusiasm of its local leaders and groups, the Federal Commission's reservations about the movement have been recorded. 'It is certain', affirms the report of the Spanish delegation to the Congress of the International at Geneva in 1873, 'that this [Cantonalist] movement has engaged the sympathies of many Internationalists, but it is also clear that victory would have opened their eyes, for the Cantonalists, once victorious, would have carried on the same persecutions as all bourgeois governments have used.' This is a qualified position, which is found again in many other texts, in particular in letters sent by the Spanish Federal Council to federations

[1] Michael Bakunin, *Etatisme et anarchie 1873*, trans. Marcel Body, Introduction and notes by Arthur Lehning (Leiden: J. Brill, 1967) pp. 224–5.

in other countries during the summer of 1873. They express great anxiety, and by way of example an extract is given below of the letter dated 18 August 1873 to the Italian Federation:

'. . . Our Regional Federation is going through a terrible crisis, perhaps the most serious it has known. Most of our federations in the south have been destroyed by brute force and our brothers are persecuted like wild beasts, since in the eyes of the Government and the bourgeoisie they have been the moving spirit behind the Cantonalist movement. If the Internationalists in many federations did in fact support this movement they did so to defend the rights they have been denied by the defenders of the current bourgeois republican Government.

'. . . The Cantonalist movement is a political movement made by politicians without prior agreement with the Internationalists . . .

Many other examples of this ambivalent attitude could be given and an explanation of it will be attempted by way of conclusion.

VII. CONCLUSIONS

The Spanish Federal Commission, as has been shown, gave a single explanation for its scepticism with regard to Cantonalism. This was the political and bourgeois character of the movement. These reservations, which were frequently expressed, were equivalent to a refusal, even if only a refusal based on the principle: to 'act according to local circumstances while not losing sight of the fact that our cause is not involved!' Friedrich Engels, happy to be able to prove how useless and helpless anarchism was, took care to emphasise the harmful consequences of this attitude. Look, he said, where the apolitical policies of Bakunin's supporters lead. First to confusion and then to disaster.

In fact, the ambivalent attitude of the International and the subsequent defeat of the movement appear to have sprung from more complex causes. The Spanish International's failure to bring forth the 'demon of revolutionary socialism' was the result of many factors, not all of which can be laid at the door of the tactics adopted by the Federal Commission. In 1873, in fact, three revolutions in one took place in Spain.

If the general geographical framework is limited to the outer regions of the peninsula (Andalusia, the province of Murcia, Valencia and

Catalonia), and the isolated outbreaks of violence in the interior (at Salamanca, for example) neglected, then it is possible to divide the Cantonalist movement into three categories: 'social', 'political' and lastly the special case of Barcelona.

The 'Social Cantonalism' of Andalusia and Valencia

In these two cases, the social element was not only manifested by the presence of the International but was also reflected in the fundamental aspirations of the population (regional autonomy, equal distribution of wealth, etc.) under Intransigent federalism. In the present state of research, the defeat of the revolutionary forces can only be attributed to the reluctance of the Intransigents to throw in their lot whole-heartedly with the Internationalists and vice versa, and secondly to the static nature of the revolt, which recalls the military aspect of the Paris Commune.

A final inescapable conclusion regarding the nature of the Cantonalist Revolution emerges. It should not be forgotten that regardless of whether the social aspect was dominant, as in Seville or Valencia, or was submerged by political preoccupations, the revolt began with the events at Alcoy on 9 and 10 July 1873.[1] These events (assassination of the *alcalde*, pitched battles in the streets of the town between workers and the forces of law and order, setting fire to buildings, and the creation of a public safety committee with the participation of organisers of the International) had their origin in a labour dispute that degenerated into a revolt via a general strike of all trades.

The Spanish International always put forward the workers' and Internationalist character of the Alcoy revolt as an answer to Cantonalism of a bourgeois or political nature.

The 'Political Cantonalism' of Cartagena

The Intransigent generals and deputies assembled in this town of the province of Murcia proclaimed the foundation of the Canton of Murcia and seized the warships (the greater part of the Spanish fleet) that were anchored in its port.

The military history of the Canton of Cartagena does not come within the scope of this study, and only the political and social aspects will be considered. These may be summed up under two headings:

---

[1] A small town in the province of Alicante. One of the strongholds of the International, where the Federal Commission had its headquarters after the Congress of Cordova (December 1872 – January 1873) until July 1873.

- The creation of a Cantonal Government with the different portfolios assigned among the main intransigent leaders. The primary concern of this Government was the defence of the area. The two personalities most representative of it (General Contreras and Roque Barcia) belonged to that section of the middle classes which had not yet attained the right to public office. Their personal ambitions and frustrations had a large influence on the Cantonalist movement in Cartagena.
- The absence of any programme of social reform. This becomes clear from a reading of the newspaper *El Cantón Murciano* which appeared during this period.

Thus the Canton of Cartagena, which was characterised by a strong Government with no interest in social reform, represented a typical political uprising and stands out in clear contrast to the revolutionary Cantonalism of Valencia or Andalusia.

The Missed Opportunity: Barcelona

During the First Republic, Barcelona was in a constant state of ferment that brought it, on 9 March, to the brink of a Cantonalist rising. This was the day when the State of Catalonia could have been declared, giving the signal for a Federation covering all Spain to be set up 'from below'. But the Government was given the chance of getting the situation under control. Disappointment then succeeded enthusiasm in the federalist camp. This disillusion was a psychological factor going some of the way to explaining why Cantonalism failed to appear in Catalonia, the traditional stronghold of Spanish federalism. According to José Termes Ardévol, the young Catalan historian of the First International, 'at no time [during the summer of 1873] did the workers' organisations of Barcelona urge the masses into the streets to take over power'.[1] According to James Guillaume,[2] 'the workers of Barcelona . . . under the influence of the friends of Castelar and Marx, refused to join a revolution on the grounds that they had the republic and that that was sufficient'. It is also interesting to note the situation of the peasantry in Catalonia (where there were more agricultural sections than in other parts of Spain). Catalonia, of course, was one of the main theatres of the Carlist War, so much so indeed that it was practically isolated from the rest of Spain. The Carlists were in general drawn from the rural population. It may therefore be suggested that

[1] Op. cit., p. 105.
[2] *L'Internationale, documents et souvenirs*, III 86.

the International was never sufficiently well established in the rural areas to wean the peasantry of this region away from the dominant Carlist influence. In addition to this factor, it should be remembered that, unlike the situation in the wine-growing areas of Andalusia, where the International sections were extremely enthusiastic, the '*rabassaire*' of Catalonia was at heart more in sympathy with Federal Republicanism.[1]

Another reason is the Carlist War which, having started under the First Republic, was at its height in the province and constantly diverted the attention of the proletariat away from revolutionary objectives. Be that as it may, Barcelona (and all Catalonia) remained extremely cool to the Cantonalist revolt, adding yet another variation to the gamut of social and political movements contemporary with the First Spanish Republic.

In the face of these three situations, the International could either have given a single directive (which would have had no chance of being followed) or adopted three different sets of tactics (which would have made confusion worse confounded). In any case, the only kind of rising that was at all likely to develop into the social revolution was that which took place in the south and in Valencia, which had the support of the rural masses. Was the International capable of taking over the 'leadership' of this revolt from the Intransigents without the active support of its Catalan 'stronghold'? This is the crux of the problem.

In contrast to the viewpoint generally found in histories on the subject, the Spanish Federation of the I.W.A. in fact not only had the support of the rural masses but had also organised them into a very complex structure, perhaps indeed too complex, which went as far as integrating the rural sections into the urban workers' organisations. A systematic document search has shown that 145 groups of agricultural workers were in contact with the International. This figure represents approximately a quarter of the total number of sections. The newspaper *El Condenado*[2] goes even further. It mentions 27,894 Andalusian members of the International out of a total of 45,633 members. Whatever the truth of the matter may be, it is undeniable that the peasant element formed a very high percentage of the International organisation, as can be seen from the participation of these rural elements in the Cantonalist rising. It is clear that the Andalusian peasants' or day labourers' rush to join the International in 1873 and the upsurge of

[1] The Federal republicans were pledged to defend the reforms the '*rabassaires*' wanted.
[2] Internationalist newspaper of Madrid, 2 Jan 1873.

revolt in the same area at the same time were not mere coincidence but the result of a single revolutionary impulse. The pattern of earlier revolts confirms this. The famous revolt of Loja in 1861, and the revolt of the peasants of Jerez in 1868 under the leadership of Paul y Angulo foreshadowed the appropriation of land and the local 'take-overs' of power in the 1873 revolution. As a result, when revolution broke out in 1873, co-operation between revolutionaries (whether anarchist or of anarchist leanings) and the mass of the peasantry was already sanctioned by long tradition. On the other hand, what was missing was an agrarian programme geared to the needs of the impoverished peasantry and the agricultural labourers, who were more receptive to the idea of a redistribution of land than to the idea of collectivism that had sprung from an urban workers' environment.

The International in Spain stands on the dividing line between two economies, two societies and two mentalities. This was the reason for its successes, but at the same time it was the main obstacle that prevented it from achieving final victory.

Chapter 6

THE PUGACHEV REVOLT:
THE LAST GREAT
COSSACK-PEASANT RISING

by

Philip Longworth

RURAL revolt was endemic in seventeenth- and eighteenth-century Russia.[1] There were four risings of considerable scale during the period, in each of which the peasant formed the mass base, the Cossacks of the borderlands provided the leadership and the experienced fighting core, and in which other categories (convicts, deserters, religious dissenters, tribesmen, etc.) also participated. They were the Bolotnikov movement of 1606–7, the revolt of Stenka Razin in 1670–1, the Bulavin rising of 1707–8, and that led by Pugachev (1773–5). The last is of particular interest in the study of peasant movements in that while exhibiting characteristics broadly similar to the others (as well as some intriguing divergencies) it is the best documented of all.

In addition to the reports and correspondence of military and administrative functionaries, there is a large number of manifestos, orders and messages emanating from the insurgents themselves (a less usual feature of an unsuccessful rebellion where rebels aim to destroy

---

[1] The term 'rural' seems more appropriate to the subject of this study than the expression 'peasant'. Defined as a rural cultivator (see Henry A. Landsberger, 'The Role of Peasant Movements and Revolts in Development', on whose analytical framework this study, with some inevitable divergencies, is largely based, and Eric R. Wolf, *Peasants*, p. 1), the term 'peasant' excludes other participating categories sharing broad identities of interest and whose condition may in many respects be similar – for instance the men engaged in stock-farming. Moreover, in the particular context of Russian rural movements, official status, occupation and condition overlap (see section II below). Many Yaik Cossacks, for example, were stock-raisers; most Don Cossacks were little differentiated from peasants in Pugachev's time in that they derived the bulk of their income as rural cultivators; and peasants themselves (as that term is generally used in the Russian context) followed a wide variety of occupations, and sometimes multi-occupations, were of differing legal status and economic condition. Just as Cossacks were part-time paid servicemen, seasonal fishermen, occasional traders, as well as stock-farmers or cultivators, peasants, though they were (as we shall see) predominantly rural cultivators, were also artisans, foresters and merchants, engaged in craft industries and were sent out, seasonally or permanently, as factory workers or taken into gentry households as servants.

incriminating evidence, and in general of many rural movements whose participants are commonly illiterate, if not inarticulate). There are also invaluable records of the interrogations of Pugachev and many of his lieutenants after capture and of various others implicated in the movement, besides the testimony of hostile eye-witnesses.[1]

In this brief study, I shall first outline (section I) the course of the rebellion, which falls into three main stages, and its aftermath; then proceed (section II) to the roots of the revolt, briefly defining the more important participating groups, the economic and social background as it had developed since the late sixteenth and especially since the beginning of the eighteenth century, and its effect on the gentry and the mass of the population, examining traditional forms of peasant reaction and some particular precipitating factors affecting the timing and character of the movement. I shall then describe and examine the goals of the insurrectionaries (section III), discuss the mass base of their support (section IV), the question of allies, including some more particular motivations of various participating (and non-participating) groups, the limits of loyalty and the constitution and methods of the movement's enemies (section V); discuss, in so far as it is discernible, the rebels' ideology (section VI), the means of action they employed (section VII), and their organisation (section VIII). Finally, I shall try to identify some specific factors of success and failure which have a bearing on this movement in particular and seventeenth- and eighteenth-century Cossack-peasant movements in general (section IX). It should be noted, however, that throughout this paper material interlinks to a very large extent, so that matter included under particular conceptual headings frequently has relevance to other sections. The cross-references are by no means exhaustive.

I. THE COURSE OF THE RISING

The Pugachev revolt may be said to fall approximately into three stages, each defined by period, by central area of operations and by the relative numbers and activities of various groups of participants.

Stage I (Autumn 1773 to Spring 1774)

Yemelyan Pugachev, a fugitive Cossack from the Don, proclaimed himself to be 'Tsar Peter III', the murdered husband of the reigning

[1] See Bibliographical Note at the end of this chapter.

Empress Catherine II ('the Great'), to a group of Yaik (Ural) Cossacks at a lonely farmhouse sixty miles from Yaitsk (Uralsk) in eastern Russia, south of the Urals. A group of local Cossacks swore loyalty to him and he issued them with a 'decree' granting the Yaik Cossacks 'the rivers from the mountains to the [Caspian] Sea, and the land and pastures, and pay of money and lead and powder and of food', that is, communal fishing and grazing rights and the regular disbursement of military supplies, pay and grain in return for their military services to the state – privileges the Yaik Cossacks had enjoyed and to a large extent lost within living memory.

Soon, about a hundred fully armed Cossacks gathered and rode off with Pugachev towards Yaitsk, many more Cossacks from the outback joining them on the way. The citadel was held fast by a government garrison, however, and Pugachev headed away north-eastwards towards the provincial capital of Orenburg, passing along a cordon of settlement forts built to contain the steppe tribesmen. Their garrisons, chiefly Cossacks on periods of state service, welcomed him; resistance, mainly on the part of regular officers, was swiftly overcome; prisoners who refused to recognise the 'Tsar' were killed; those who did were welcomed into the ranks of the rebel force.

By the time Pugachev reached Orenburg early in October he had over 2,500 men and several cannon. He set siege to Orenburg and thousands responded to his manifestos, joining him at his winter camp at nearby Berda. By now the manifestos, so far from being phrased specifically for the Cossack caste, were addressed to 'all ranks of people'. Neighbouring non-Russian ethnic groups were approached with the additional offer of 'faith and law', that is, freedom of religion and freedom to follow their own customs, soldiers were promised pay, promotion and higher hereditary status, while Pugachev's addresses promising liberty had a marked effect on the workers in the mines and factories of the south Urals industrial zone. 'When the [factory] peasants gathered' at one place, reported one of the rebels later,[1] and heard the manifesto read to them, they 'cried out "Glad to serve him, the Tsar" and 500 men gathered, volunteers to to serve Pugachev'.

The victory over an army detachment led by Major-General Ker, sent to relieve Orenburg, swelled the flow of recruits, spreading the news of Peter III's coming even further afield and bringing over mal-

---

[1] *Krasny Arkhiv*, 68 (1935) p. 165 (for details of this and other publications referred to in the footnotes see Bibliographical Note).

contents who had been sitting on the sidelines – men of 'various sorts' who brought provisions, arms and other supplies in with them. Government arsenals were occupied, official funds seized, granaries ransacked, and Pugachev's lieutenants sped out ever greater distances, brandishing the manifestos, which though 'foolishly written' received an ever wider circulation and had an ever increasing effect, especially in areas north of Orenburg, including the central and southern Urals and eastwards into western Siberia. But peasants to the west across the Volga were also affected and in many villages that December, according to an official report, 'the common people, already drunk with the venom, were almost crying out aloud that their time was coming when they would take the upper hand over the authorities and there would be nothing to fear whatever they did'.[1]

By Christmas 1773 the rebels based at Berda had 86 cannon and over 15,000 men, though most of them were badly armed, and ultimately perhaps as many as 25–30,000 men and over 100 cannon, with another 40,000 or so active rebels operating in adjacent areas, including 15,000 besieging Ufa. In January 1774 rebel forces took Chelyabinsk, the peasants of Tiumen rose and Pugachev's propaganda penetrated Siberia as far as Irkutsk. But as a frightened government rushed in more troops the tide of revolt began to ebb. Towns were reoccupied, outlying rebel forces dispersed, a net gradually closed in round the centre of the movement near Orenburg, and at the beginning of spring Pugachev's main force suffered two crushing defeats in quick succession at Tatishchev and Kargal. The Pretender escaped in the company of a handful of supporters. At this point the movement might well have ended. It did not.

Stage II (Spring to Summer 1774)

Pugachev with his remaining supporters moved into the industrial zone of the Urals and the hills of Bashkiria. He kept constantly on the move now, always one step ahead of the pursuing troops who were delayed by muddy roads, broken bridges, swollen rivers and the partisan activities of independent rebel bands. Some of the latter managed to link up with Pugachev, including 300 Yaik Cossacks, 4000 factory peasants led by an ex-bombardier called Beloborodov and 5000 warriors brought in by the Bashkir leader Kinzya Arslanov.

[1] Report dated May 1774, quoted by Ovchinnikov in Mavrodin, *Peasant War*, II 429. The people of Astrakhan expressed themselves in even more violent terms when Razin was near (see Longworth, p. 144).

Further manifestos promising 'freedom without any demands for soul [poll] tax and other duties or recruiting levies' and freedom of peasants from their lords' demands¹ kept recruits flowing in. But the rebels of the central force were still fugitives who lacked a base and had to follow tactics of high mobility. Supply was difficult, communications confused, government troops in hot pursuit, so that the rebel army was subject to fluctuations in size. In May the rebels, about 11,000 strong, had been dispersed at Troitski by General de Kolong and his men. But the survivors had regrouped and their guerrilla strategy of avoiding superior force and constantly changing direction (first north, then east, then back north-west across the Urals to the Kama river – cf. Mao's Long March) was successful in that Pugachev eluded his pursuers, increased his strength again and was ultimately able to turn to the offensive.

Reaching the river Kama in mid-June he had captured the fort of Osa, taking eight guns and over 1000 prisoners, most of whom deserted to his side. Pugachev's force now comprised about 20,000 men – fewer Cossacks now, but many tribesmen and factory peasants, some soldiers and a contingent of unarmed peasants. This force suddenly appeared unexpectedly near Kazan, defeated a cavalry force sent out against it, and stormed into the city, though not into its citadel, in which the local clergy, gentry, officials and officers, including members of a special commission sent out to investigate the revolt, and some loyalist troops, had sought shelter. But within a few days a pursuing contingent of only 800 well trained troops succeeded in dispersing the main rebel force again and in relieving the citadel.

Stage III (*Summer to Autumn 1774*)

After Kazan, most of the Bashkirs returned home, where they were to wage their own guerrilla war for many months. Then, with his surviving followers, including a few hundred Cossacks and some factory peasants, Pugachev crossed the Volga and headed into central Russia. The movement branched west towards Nizhni Novgorod and south to Alatyr. This more highly populated region was one of normative serfdom and the manifestos attracted an unprecedented number of adherents.

The gist of these manifestos now concerned not only freedom of religion, the free use of land and other natural resources and freedom from compulsory recruitment, but cheap salt, increased pay for

¹ See *ukaz* (official proclamation) of 19 June 1774, etc. in Golubtsov.

soldiers and the total abolition of the poll tax and of serf duties paid in money, kind, or in work. The movement's aims took on a yet more extreme character as Pugachev promised to 'catch, punish and hang' the landlords, the 'real disturbers of the peace and the ruiners of the peasants, the enemies of Our authority . . . rebels against the realm'.

They were to be treated 'just as they, these men without Christianity, used to behave to you peasants'.[1] But other local classes besides serfs and state peasants were attracted and the number of revenge killings markedly increased.

Arriving at Saransk, Pugachev was welcomed by the clergy and by merchants as well as peasants, and 300 members of the gentry class, including women and children, were hanged. At Pensa he was greeted by a procession of townsmen, bearing icons, bread and salt – the customary welcoming symbols for an important guest – and the governor was burned down in his house together with twenty land-lords who had sought refuge there. By the time Pugachev reached Saratov, early in August, he had about 10,000 supporters with him – local Chuvash, Mordvs and Tatars as well as Russians, soldiers as well as peasants, though only about 2000 were adequately armed and there were only thirteen guns. Bands of peasant guerrillas, sometimes thousands strong, were operating at great distances from his mobile headquarters, but he himself was moving south, further away from the Russian centre, into more sparsely inhabited territory.

One motive for this southwards turn was the hope of raising the Don Cossacks, of whom Pugachev was one, and so gaining a new cadre of experienced fighting men. His call warned them not to be 'darkened and blinded by the allurements of that cursed stock of gentry who, not content with [enslaving] Russia want to demean the native Cossack armies to peasant [status] and to destroy the Cossack stock'.[2]

But, mindful of the Don Cossacks' propensity to rebellion,[3] the authorities had taken strict precautions and few of the messages got through. However, many members of a supposedly loyalist Cossack–Kalmyk force sent out against him came over to him and there were some disturbances in the middle Don area.

---

[1] Manifesto to Volga peasants, July 1774 (Golubtsov, I, 40–1).

[2] Manifesto to Don Cossacks (Longworth, p. 216; Golubtsov).

[3] The Vladimir Us, Razin and Bulavin movements had all originated on the Don, and there had also been disturbances in the region recently over the Yefremov and Bogomolov affairs – see Longworth, pp. 191–3, and Pronshtein in Kuznetsov (ed.), *Istoriya Dona* (Rostov-on-Don, 1965).

At Salnikov, further south down the right bank of the Volga, regular detachments finally caught up with Pugachev. Two thousand rebels were killed, 8000 wounded or taken prisoner. The Pretender with 400 men escaped yet again, re-crossed the Volga and headed east across the desert steppe. But the number of followers steadily diminished and at last the handful of Yaik Cossacks still remaining overpowered him and handed him over to the garrison at Yaitsk in hope of amnesty for themselves.

The Aftermath

Confronted by authority, Pugachev hinted (rightly) that his capture did not mean the revolt was at an end.[1] Gangs of peasant partisans were still on the rampage between Nizhni Novgorod and Astrakhan and some early scenes of the revolt across the Volga. But without its leader the movement lost all hope, though order was not finally restored to all the affected provinces until the end of 1775. In January of that year Pugachev was executed in Moscow, together with some of his lieutenants.

As many as 10,000 rebels had lost their lives in the fighting; probably as many as 20,000[2] were killed, or executed, for their parts in the movement. The Kirghis (Kazakhs) were amnestied provided they returned captives they had taken and promised to carry out local service; the Bashkirs and other semi-nomadic groups suffered heavy fines payable in horses. The Volga Cossacks were resettled in the Caucasus and the Zaporozhian Cossacks, some of whom had joined Pugachev,[3] were dispersed as a pre-emptive security measure. The clamp came down heavily on the Yaik Cossack rank and file.

However, the rebellion did produce some marginal benefits other than hastening the end of the Turkish war. The Government betrayed clear signs of wishing to lighten the load, especially on the tribal minorities and factory peasants. The missionary activities of the established Church, which had been a factor motivating members of Muslim minorities to rebellion, were curbed. Working conditions in the Ural industries were marginally improved, the owners' powers of punishment being limited and wages ultimately being increased by decree to double the 1769 figure. Some restrictions on peasant trade were also lifted.

[1] Pushkin, I 162–3.
[1] Article on 'Peasant War' in *Bolshaya Sovetskaya Entsiklopediya*.
[3] See Longworth, p. 216.

From 1775 the Government made increased state loans available to the landowning gentry, which may indirectly have lightened the burden on the peasant serf to some extent. Fewer gentry now risked living on their estates, and Catherine's reforms of the provincial administration, creating new offices for them, served further to raise gentry status. But overall there was no immediate or substantial alleviation of the agrarian peasant's condition.

The Pugachev revolt was the last great peasant movement to emanate from Russia's borderlands. There were only twenty further peasant disturbances recorded before Catherine died in 1796, and though there were a further 278, affecting thirty-two provinces, in the four years of Tsar Paul's reign[1] and nearly 1500 in the sixty years prior to the emancipation of the serfs in 1861,[2] none of them was remotely on so considerable a scale as that of 1773–5, largely because of improvements in military and policing techniques at the Government's disposal and because the State succeeded in taming the Cossacks and other warlike elements in the borderlands. Nevertheless the revolt, like Razin's a century before, lingered long in peasant memory despite zealous attempts made to ban all mention of it, including the changing of place-names, and there is evidence that around Orenburg at least Pugachev was remembered decades later as 'the good Tsar'.[3]

But eventually it was not peasant action but the dissemination of liberal ideas among the gentry that was to procure the liberation of the serfs, and the rural conditions which gave rise to the Pugachev outbreak were not to be transformed in all their economic implications until 1917 and after, when there was a wholesale appropriation by peasants of the large estates.

II. THE ROOTS OF REVOLT

(1) *The Participants*

The legal status, occupation and economic and social condition of peasants and other participants are matters of some complexity. It is therefore desirable to attempt very broad, and rather simplified,

[1] Semevski, I 456; Lyashchenko, I, 425.   [2] Blum, p. 558.

[3] Mavrodin, *Peasant War*, I 318; See also N. N. Firsov, *The Razin Movement as a Sociological and Psychological Phenomenon of the People's Life* (in Russian) (3rd ed., 1920). Rebel Bashkirs among others expected his return in 1775 and 1776 (Andrushchenko, pp. 310–1). Razin too was expected to return from the dead to free the people. Such was the optimism (or the despair) of the oppressed.

definitions of these various, often overlapping categories sufficient to the purposes of this paper.

The serfs accounted for just over half the male population of Russia proper at the time of the revolt. Of the provinces affected, up to three-quarters of the population of Nizhni Novgorod[1] and over 50 per cent of those of Pensa, Saratov and Simbirsk were serfs. They were of universally low legal, and generally low economic, status. They could be transferred, sold or gambled away by their lords; they could be separated from their families, and were not allowed to move from their villages or even volunteer for the army without their lord's permission. The lord could inflict any punishment on his serfs, only excepting the death penalty (though in practice he could have a serf beaten to death). Once they lost their right to petition the monarch against their masters in 1767, serfs had no right whatsoever to contest their lords' actions.

Conversely the serf-owner owed no obligation of service to the Crown. Peter the Great had insisted on state service by the entire gentry class, but this obligation had been whittled away by his successors, and finally abolished in 1762 by the real Peter III, whose title Pugachev assumed. The lord certainly had no obligation to his serf; nor could a serf be sure of redress against another serf, and if one were murdered by another lord's man, the victim's lord might claim restitution, but not the victim's next-of-kin.

The serf owed a duty to his lord either in the form of *obrok* (payments in cash or kind fixed by the lord in commutation of labour), or in the form of *barshchina* (labour in the master's fields or household, or other work for the master's benefit – of a type and to an extent also defined by the lord). *Obrok*-payers were prevalent in the north of the country, *barshchina*-payers in the south-central lands where labour had tended to be scarcer. The serf also had to pay the state poll tax, was affected by indirect taxation and was subject to recruitments (see also below).

The smaller sub-group of court or crown peasants, whose burdens, though often lighter, also included *obrok* or *barshchina* (paid to the Empress or to some other member of the royal family) may also be grouped under this head.

The factory peasants included assigned state peasants, made to work a set number of days annually at the factories or mines, generally in winter, which often involved their having to spend weeks travelling in order to fulfil their obligations and not infrequently in their being

[1] Mavrodin, *Peasant War*, I 293, and Lyashchenko.

kept longer than the period fixed. They accounted for nearly 60 per cent of the labour force in the areas affected by the movement. There were also peasant serfs working *barshchina* and consequently receiving no wages, and some peasants (*possessionalnye*) who were tied to the factory rather than to its owner (together about 35 per cent). Finally there were some hired workers (5–6 per cent in the affected area).

The factory peasant suffered appalling conditions and enjoyed virtually no legal or political rights. It should further be noted that since many of them were closely connected with the agrarian communities from which they had come, and even the permanent factory cadres usually had allotments to which they were released in order to tend them for a few weeks in summer, factory peasants still lived a semi-rural existence and so hardly constituted an industrial proletariat in the generally accepted sense, though they did engage in strike actions which are usually associated with such a proletariat.

The state peasants constituted the second largest class in Russia after the serfs and were variously descended from the old 'black-ploughing', or free peasants, from the depressed class of serving people known as the *odnodvortsy*, and included non-Russian tribute payers to the Tsar (see also below), etc.[1] Though legally of higher status than serfs, they were virtually the property of the State.

They could therefore be granted, together with the land which they worked, to a private landlord as a reward for political or other services (see section II(2) below) or ascribed to state or private factories. In many areas some of them were also under pressure from neighbouring landlords who sought to take over their lands and ascribe them as their serfs. State peasants had generally to pay higher taxes in addition to carrying out local services such as road maintenance and were subject to regular recruitments and sometimes to militia service. About half the Kazan region's peasants, including tribute-paying Maris, Mordvs, Chuvash Tatars and Udmurts belonged to this category.

The tribesmen, or what might more correctly be termed non-Russian ethnic groups, were of varied, overlapping categories. Some Kalmyks, for instance, bore services on Cossack lines (see below); others were nomads. Some Bashkirs were settled tillers, others semi-nomads, and organised on a traditional tribal basis albeit under close governmental supervision. While tribesmen, notably the Bashkirs of the Ufa area, provided a high proportion of support in stage II of the revolt, Mordvs,

---

[1] See Mavrodin, *Class War*, Blum, etc.

Maris, Mishars, Votyaks and Chuvash, Udmurts and Tatar tribute-payers accounted for nearly a third of the population affected in stages II and III of the movement.

The Cossacks, locally autonomous, though subject directly to the Government, traditionally enjoyed higher status and various 'freedoms', including exemptions from state taxation. However, they had a universal obligation for military service, had to maintain local guard duties, carry the post, etc. Many Don Cossacks may be regarded as peasants in so far as they were rural cultivators (mostly sharing out communally held land periodically among themselves according to need), though on the Yaik fishing and stock-raising were the important income-earning occupations. There were, additionally, strong affinities between peasants of whatever status and Cossacks, since (a) most Cossacks were descended from Russian or Ukrainian peasant runaways, and peasant runaways still settled among them, albeit unofficially, as hired labourers, and (b) Cossack traditions of independence, their leadership of previous peasant movements, had long attracted Russian peasants who aspired to the democratic Cossack ideal and to the free Cossack status (see section VI).[1]

(2) *The Origins of Discontent*

The long-term background. The complex of economic and social developments forming the background and mainspring of the Pugachev rising cannot adequately be covered here. The chain of relevant events stretches back 200 years to Ivan the Terrible (if not to the era of Kievan Rus). Muscovy's economic decline in the late sixteenth century led to mass flights to the southern steppe zone and, as attempts were made to tie the peasant to the land, to a period of economic, political and military collapse known as the Time of Troubles. These circumstances formed the background to the Bolotnikov movement. A slow recovery was punctuated by periodic famine and accompanied by a tightening of the bonds holding the peasant, without whom the land could not be worked, to his place. But the lure of the border-lands grew ever stronger as the burdens of wars, made heavier by the insufficiencies of the fiscal system, increased the pressure on the peasant masses. Eventually the economic crisis and increasingly desperate governmental measures of repression, together with the confusion and widespread despair resulting from religious schism, gave rise to

---

[1] See Longworth, p. 112 *passim* for the Ukraine; p. 127 *passim* for the Don.

the revolt of Stenka Razin (which began among impoverished new-comer-Cossacks to the middle Don[1]).

The seventeenth century seems to have seen little overall rise in *barshchina* worked for landlords, which ran at a general level of about one-third of the peasants' time. However, in view of the lack of improvements in farming methods, agricultural production could develop only by incursion into forest and pasture-land, and soon only the borderlands could provide any sizable land reserve. Popular discontent deriving from increased taxation caused by Peter the Great's (d. 1725) wars, from his wholesale introduction of Western customs, the hounding of runaways and of religious dissenters, and, finally, from the extension of magnates' land-holdings into the southern steppe zone, thus threatening the Don Cossacks and the runaways who had joined them, found expression in the Bulavin revolt.[2]

Economic change in the eighteenth century. Peter the Great succeeded in giving impetus to the economy, encouraging the growth of industry and the expansion of internal and external trade. One result of this was an increasing use of money (in demand for the new poll-tax payments, quit-rents and other cash demands). The swift development of crafts and industry, the growth of population and the concomitant growth of towns further stimulated the internal market, demanding an expansion of agricultural production.

But the slow development of agricultural techniques meant that existing resources, exploited as they were, could not keep pace. The three-field fallow system, generally inefficiently worked in scattered strips periodically redistributed among the tillers, the absence of adequate fertilisation and of any substantial use of crop-rotation, the primitive nature of the implements employed and the poor quality of working animals, all resulted in main crop yields (rye, oats, barley, spelt, etc.) remaining low. Though there were signs of advance in the newly settled south-lands, significant increase in production depended chiefly on the extension of ploughland first southwards and then eastwards into the trans-Volga plain.

The general economic background, rising taxation and landlords' demands encouraged both state peasants and serfs to till more land. At the beginning of the century an average peasant household sowed about sixteen acres. The area was increased to a limited extent through

---

[1] For Razin's movement, see Longworth, pp. 124–52; also Firsov, op. cit. For Bolotnikov's movement see D. P. Makovski, *The First Peasant War in Russia* (in Russian) (Smolensk, 1967).

[2] For Bulavin's movement, see Longworth, pp. 161–4.

forest clearance and ploughing marginal land, and through the reduction of fallow, but the possibilities were severely limited and increasing population led to a discernible movement to the towns. Nevertheless, Russia remained a preponderantly agrarian country throughout the eighteenth century (about 95 per cent of the population residing outside towns), and land-holding remained basically in the hands of the autocrat and the gentry class, both of which reckoned their wealth in 'souls' (i.e., peasants) rather than in the extent of their estates, the demand for labour having in the past tended to outrun even the demand for land.

The economic development to which Peter's reforms gave impetus had a continuing influence during succeeding reigns – notably those of Anne (1730–40) and Elizabeth (1741–61) – and had a particularly profound effect on the two classes at the extremes of the social system during Catherine II's reign (1762–96): the serf-owning gentry, and peasantry.

The condition of the gentry. More luxuries were reaching the market and the social aspirations of the gentry were on the rise. Standards of extravagance at Catherine's Court exceeded even those of her profligate predecessor Elizabeth. Though the majority of the gentry never went to Court, they, too, were tempted by the example into more luxurious styles of living. Spending became an index of social status (in the popular contemporary sense) as many tried to live up to standards set by richer neighbours, not only at Court but in the larger towns. In fact the aspirations and the consumption of many serf-owners were galloping ahead of their incomes. Many spent first and then sought to gear their incomes to keep pace with rising debts, and the situation became especially acute from about 1750. The sale of serfs reached an unprecedented volume under Catherine, as did the mortgaging of estates, and borrowing at usurious rates was hardly checked by Elizabeth's foundation in 1754 of a bank for the purpose of lending to the gentry at reasonable interest rates, the demand being far greater than the bank's resources.

A Soviet student attributes the Pugachev movement in part to 'the weakening power of the ruling classes'.[1] This remark must be qualified. In terms of privilege and political influence the bigger landowners at least were on the rise. In fact, the rising political power of the gentry was seen not only in their increasing influence, as a class, at Court, but in their accumulation of local civic powers during the reign (most local

[1] Ovchinnikov in Mavrodin, *Peasant War*, II 413.

officials, magistrates, etc., came to be drawn from the local gentry) and their accumulation of further privileges (and their ability in practice to ignore prescribed limitations). Since 1760 they had been empowered to banish serfs to Siberia and receive an indemnity for them from the State, and from 1765 they were able to condemn serfs to hard labour.

On the other hand, from the economic point of view, it is true that many a poor lord was hard put to it and many a rich one tempted to spend beyond his means in order to satisfy his inflated social aspirations. Many of these gentlemen who spent beyond their means may have been notoriously careless about repaying their debts, but on the whole the gentry's need for more money did lead them to exploit their serfs to an unprecedented degree (*barshchina* being increased to three, four and sometimes even six days a week in season and demands for *obrok* also rising), and to try to filch neighbouring land and peasants.[1]

The economic position of a part of the gentry may thus have been in decline but in general the class's social and political status and especially its aspirations to greater spending-power were sharply on the rise.

The condition of the masses. If the status of the gentry had reached a peak, that of the peasants in general and the serfs in particular, was near its nadir. Their sentiments were painfully described in a rustic dirge composed in the 1760s, which evinces strong aspirations to the abolition of serfdom:

'Oh, woe to us serfs from lords and poverty,
'Surely we would find bread for ourselves without the lords.'

Serfs are treated like cattle, the composer complains, they 'dare not talk'; the landlords 'change the laws to their present benefit . . . Ah, if only we had freedom . . .'[2]

Yet, though the grip of lord over serf was absolute, something akin to a new village bourgeoisie was emerging even among serfs. Some, if very few, payers of *obrok* were men of wealth in trade and industry and a handful of peasants were even serf-owners themselves. And

---

[1] It was against this background that Catherine founded the Free Economic Society to encourage the implementation of modern ideas in agriculture. These included the tentative advocation (by foreign entrants for an essay competition) of the abolition of serfdom. The airing of such a revolutionary idea had no immediate effect. The gentry, hardpressed or ambitious, was adamant against, it and Catherine, as a usurper. dared not alienate the class on which her power was based, even though she appears to have recognised that the system was not only unjust and contrary to fashionable Western concepts of natural law, but one which would ultimately lead to violence on a wide scale (see also note 3, p. 220 below).

[2] 'The Serfs' Lamentation', N. S. Tikhonravov, *Sbornik Obshchestva Lyubitelei Rossiiskoi Slovesnosti* (Moscow, 1895) pp. 11–14.

though their rights were circumscribed, they might bribe officialdom to overlook their infringements of the law. Those peasants shaken loose from the tight parochial bonds of village life in particular were becoming increasingly aware of the possibilities presented by the growth of markets and consequently restless at the limitations placed on their activities. Indeed, thanks largely to the increasing appreciation of money values, peasant aspirations as a whole were beginning to rise above subsistence level and hope of relief from increasing burdens was widespread. However, despite the emergence of nascent capitalist relationships, these remained for the most part within a 'feudal' setting, which delayed the process of any conscious class-differentiation in the Marxist sense. Peasant serfs were most hostile in the first place to the landlords rather than to their richer peasant neighbours,[1] who often shared their sentiments to a large degree.

As a class, the state peasants were more favourably placed than serfs. As for the crown peasants, their status had actually improved, since from 1766 they acquired the privilege of owning land and serfs (since 1758 officially a gentry monopoly). But, for the most part, the difference in status often counted for little in practice. Though not tied to lords, they were to the State or to the Tsar[2] and while the land-lack became more acute, demands placed upon both state and crown peasants were becoming steadily heavier. The poll tax was increased from 1·10 rubles to 1·70 in the 1760s, the rise having an exaggerated effect in that members of peasant communities had collectively to find the contributions of recruits and runaways, the old, the young, the sick, and often the dead as well. And in 1769 taxation reached new heights thanks to the war. Moreover, many state peasants suffered from encroachments on to their lands by the gentry. Some were in increasing danger of (illegal) ascription to neighbouring gentry estates and (before they were taken over by the State) to the monasteries. Not a few *odnodvortsy* even (who owned their own land) were forced to abandon the countryside to seek work in the towns, or were reduced to hiring themselves out as labourers while at the same time remaining liable for militia service, maintaining roads, bridges, etc. Moreover, state peasants everywhere had good cause to fear lawful reduction to serf status. The sovereign made gifts of lands and peasants on a vast scale. Between 1740 and 1801 1·3 million adult males were thus signed away[3]

[1] Mavrodin, *Peasant War*, I 323 ff.
[2] See Alefirenko, pp. 215 ff.
[3] Blum, p. 356.

and during Catherine's reign no fewer than 400,000 revisional (or census-registered) souls were handed over to private landlords.

In the areas involved in the Pugachev revolt, in the twenty years up to 1765 the number of serf-owning gentry (*pomeshchiki*) in the mid-Volga area increased one and a half times, the number of tied peasants more than twice, indicating larger-scale ownership, often associated with worse treatment. By 1770 the latter's numbers already accounted for 46 per cent of the rural population of the mid-Volga area – though the proportion was still less than in central Russia. The proportion of serfs in the total population in the Nizhni Novgorod region had risen from about 48 per cent some two decades earlier to as much as 75 per cent by the time of the rising, and from about 42 per cent in the Kazan region (Simbirsk, etc.) and Voronezh to over 50 per cent. Further, the lower Volga area (Stage III) was by the beginning of the nineteenth century to have the second-highest proportion of mortgaged serfs (68·5 per cent) in Russia,[1] possibly indicating their lords had been squeezing them hard for some time. It seems that many serfs in the area had either been moved in from other districts or had recently been reduced from the status of state peasants. Fall in status and economic decline was certainly the case among the *odnodvortsy*, especially in the provinces of Tambov and Voronezh. Many of them were losing land to, and, in some cases, becoming the serfs of, neighbouring land-hungry gentry against whom they could generally obtain no redress.

Non-Russian ethnic minorities or tribal groups had also suffered from being squeezed off their traditional pasture or arable lands or incorporated into the Russian peasant system by the creeping encroachments of Russian landowners, monasteries and industrialists on both sides of the Volga, as well as from restrictions imposed on their trading activities, and the pressure had increased especially since, in 1765, the State began to sell land east of the Volga to Russian lords.[2]

The singular condition of the Yaik Cossacks will be dealt with under 'Precipitating Factors' below, but the specific condition of the factory peasants demands attention here. In their case the equivalent of the exploiting landowner was the rapacious factory-owner. This was a period of fast industrial expansion. The number of large factories in Russia increased from 201 in 1761 to 478 in 1776 and by 1773 the Urals, one of the scenes of the revolt, formed the largest industrial region in the world.[3] Much of the State's original stake in its mining and metal-

---

[1] See Blum, pp. 380–2.   [2] See Mavrodin, *Class War*, pp. 76 ff.
[3] Lyashchenko, I 450–1.

lurgical centres had already been transferred to private hands – to the nobility and to members of the small class of merchant industrialists who exploited their workers unmercifully. The service periods of seasonal workers was rising (from 2–2½ to 3 and more months a year) and the labour force as a whole, including women and children, commonly worked from dawn to sunset. Real incomes had fallen, food was bad and, in all, conditions bear comparison with those obtaining in England's Industrial Revolution: the knout, the whip and the stick-torture were widely used for purposes of factory discipline, and owners like the Demidovs were reported to have 'tortured the male sex and the female at work summer and winter without peace'. Sickness was rife, 'many died and . . . women miscarried'.[1] Soldiers were often employed to break strikes and there were cases of trouble-makers having their nostrils slit, their ears lopped off or even being thrown alive into blast furnaces.

Severe discontent was thus widespread among the mass of Russia's population. Yet the majority had no effective legal means of improving either their status or their economic condition. We shall now turn to the more common forms of reaction found in such circumstances.

Reactions

Lacking other means of redress, the common alternatives the Russian peasant traditionally resorted to in order to improve his position or avoid extra burdens (apart from simple refusals to fulfil the obligations demanded) were (i) flight from authority, (ii) armed brigandage and (iii) mass revolt. In addition I shall also examine (iv) religious factors which, in Russia, served not only as consolation, but were intimately connected with movements of active social protest.

Flight had long been a widespread response. The Cossack communities were largely the product of peasant runaways who had fled to the borderlands in the fifteenth, sixteenth and especially the seventeenth centuries, and the immigration continued well into the eighteenth century despite the State's efforts to stop it. Siberia was another favourite refuge. The State's desire to populate its vast expanses often gave runaways the prospect of free status as state peasants there. Similarly popular in Pugachev's time (and nearer) were the newly

---

[1] Mavrodin, *Peasant War*, I 327–8; see also P. A. Vagina, 'On the question of the conditions of the working force in the South Urals factories after the peasant war of 1773–5, *Uchennyye Zapiski* (Uralsk University), XXXIX, Pt I (Sverdlovsk, 1961).

settled lands in the lower and trans-Volga areas where runaways might eke out a living and few questions were asked about their papers. But peasants were often content to move shorter distances to other, hopefully more humane, lords.

Between 1719 and 1727 at least 200,000 peasants fled – by no means all of them far from home.[1] In the following fifteen years over 325,000 male serfs – 5 per cent of the total number of revisional (census-registered) souls[2] – fled, though this increase owes something to the famine years of 1733–5 when the Government relaxed the rules. In general, penalties for flight and the rigour of the chase became increasingly severe, as did punishments for those who sheltered runaways. Nevertheless flights continued, encouraged particularly by the labour shortage in the border areas, the willingness of employers to shelter them and, occasionally, even take up arms in their defence.

Flight was not always individual. Families, sometimes entire villages, escaped, loading their possessions on to carts and driving their livestock before them. Oppressed Cossacks also reacted by flight, usually individually or in small groups, though there were cases of mass emigration into lands under Turkish protection.[3] Occasional cases are also recorded of fugitive gangs being joined by impoverished gentry and renegade officers. Such bands frequently used violence in the course of their escapes or to avoid forcible return, and some turned to brigandage to support themselves in hiding. Finally, it should be noted that there were many fugitives in the Orenburg and Kazan regions which were affected by the Pugachev movement.

Brigandage was an endemic reaction, closely allied to flight (which outlawed a man and often forced him to brigandage as a means of subsistence). Between 1730 and 1760 bands of robber runaways are mentioned as operating in ten central and south Russian provinces including the Volga area, sometimes on a fairly considerable scale.[4] A gang of about seventy heavily-armed bandit guerrillas (chiefly runaway peasants but also including deserters, factory serfs and impoverished *odnodvortsy*) led by Ivan Kolpin was operating in the Simbirsk area from 1768.[5] Pitched battles involving the use of artillery on both sides were fought between such large gangs and the forces of law and

---

[1] Blum, p. 552.　　　　　[2] Mavrodin, *Class War*, p. 13.
[3] See Longworth, pp. 163–4.
[4] The Volga had been a traditional haunt of river pirates and in earlier times Cossacks were notorious as steppe predators and for mounting huge robber expeditions round the Caspian and Black Sea littorals and into the Russian interior.
[5] 1768 was also a year of intense *gaidamak* activity in the Ukraine (Longworth, pp. 175–177).

order, and at least one such robber gang (led by Roshchina, active along the river Oka since 1769) was to join Pugachev.

Personal gain was not an unmixed motive among such brigands. Some who preyed on landowners and their property considered themselves to be 'daring, good fine fellows', claiming 'we aren't thieves and robbers – we're Stenka Razin's workers'[1] – thus identifying themselves with the most celebrated Cossack bandit-revolutionary and hero of the peasants. Indeed, peasants often saw them in that image and sympathised with them, as they had with dissident robber groups from the time of the river pirate Yermak in the late sixteenth century to anti-Bolshevik characters like Dikun and Shmalko who operated on the Kuban in the 1920s.[2] And the example of such gangs sometimes stirred oppressed peasants to take action themselves. There are cases on record, not long before the Pugachev rising, of peasants disguising themselves as bandits in order to murder their landlord or burn down his property.[3]

Revolt. The full-scale reaction of revolt was closely allied to both flight and brigandage, and may be regarded as a fully escalated reaction to social conditions. The Russian, like other, authorities referred to rebels as 'robbers' and 'villains' rather than as 'revolutionaries', and indeed the differences between brigand bands and rebel forces is often impossible to define, except arbitrarily by size. Hence I would prefer to include all direct, communal violent actions on the part of peasants against lords, their property and representatives, and officials in general, under this head. Such manifestations became widespread particularly in the third quarter of the eighteenth century. In the 1750s there were twice as many such disturbances as in the previous decade, including risings in Tver, Yaroslav, the Urals, Voronezh, Simbirsk and elsewhere. Between 1762 and 1772 there were as many as forty quite large peasant disturbances in the provinces of Novgorod, Smolensk, Kazan, Vyatka, Tver and elsewhere, so violent that the military had to be called in to restore order,[4] and between 1764 and 1769 no fewer than thirty proprietors in the Moscow province alone were killed by their peasants.[5] These appear to have been desperate, poorly organised affairs in the main, whose objectives were restricted to particular cases

---

[1] See Mavrodin, *Class War.*

[2] On the Razin legend, see Longworth, pp. 151–2 *passim,* and pp. 5–6 for further comparisons. Also E. J. Hobsbawn, *Bandits* (London, 1969), for the 'bandit-popular myth' syndrome in other countries and ages.

[3] Mavrodin, *Peasant War,* I 364.

[4] Lyashchenko, I 424.   [5] Blum, p. 554.

and particular lords. As such most of them may be regarded as local acts of vengeance – 'expressive', or at least unarticulated, actions conforming to the pattern of local *jacqueries* (but see section III under 'Depth' below). Peasant protests of this type appear not to have been aimed directly against serfdom as an institution, though one is in any case intrinsically less likely to find clear evidence of goals in small-scale, short-term movements after such a passage of time than one is for major disturbances such as the Pugachev movement. However, there are at least some indications that serfs viewed their situation as a temporary one which must ultimately be abolished. The widespread rumours that Peter III was about to abolish serfdom following his abrogation of the gentry's service obligations testify to this.

Further, there were several larger-scale movements involving up to 3000 armed men in the immediate pre-Pugachev period and some of the growing number of serf disturbances in the 1760s were particularly significant in that they displayed quite specific goals. Peasant rebels of Voronezh in 1766, for instance, hoped to obtain recognition as members of free village associations registered for state service roughly on the Cossack pattern (as had their predecessors who followed Vasili Us in the 1660s).

There had also been a growing number of disturbances among non-Russian groups of various categories. Mordv serfs in Nizhni Novgorod province rose in 1743–5, and the pastoral Bashkirs had risen in wars of 'secession' to join the Turkish Empire (and their Muslim co-religionists) in 1705–11, 1735–40, and 1747 (when they had been joined by Tatars, Chuvash, Udmurts and other local non-Russian elements incensed by Orthodox missionary activities, including forced conversions).

Violent outbursts, though on a smaller scale, were particularly common among factory peasants.[1] In the Urals, in 1750, 500 men clashed with the military at one Demidov works and sharp pay reductions led to risings at the Lipeitsk mills. In 1760 there were disturbances at the Avzyano–Petrovsk mill, south of Ufa, upon news that the owner was selling out to the notorious task-masters, the Demidovs, and strikes and violent outbreaks became common among the factory peasants in the area. In November 1762, for example, there was armed resistance at N. Demidov's Nizhne–Tagil complex,[2] and almost con-

---

[1] See Semevski, pp. 295 ff.

[2] The monastery peasants (taken over by the State in the 1760s) were another particularly rebellious category, being involved in 32 recorded uprisings in the 1750s. Catherine noted soon after her succession that 'the factory and monastery peasants were almost all

214   *Peasant Revolts and Disintegration of 'Feudalism'*

tinuous disturbances at his mill at Kyshtyinsk. There was thus a strongly militant streak among Ural factory peasants which was to serve Pugachev well.

The religious element had a threefold significance: as an ethnic factor, as a means (like heavy drinking) of spiritual escape, and as an expression of dissent and protest. Religion has already been listed as a factor motivating Muslim minorities involved in the revolt. These were responsible for murders of priests of the established Orthodox Church and the desecration of churches during the rising. However, apart from this, religion had none of the ethnic significance that had been the mark, for instance, of the Ukrainian rising against Polish lords in 1648.

Religion as a road of spiritual escape was a favoured one in Russia as elsewhere. However, non-conformist movements outside the established Church (which was closely controlled by the State and associated with the social order) attracted a significantly large following among the oppressed. Extreme sects, notably the *khlysty*, or flagellants, had gained many converts in the disturbed latter part of the seventeenth century. More important was the much larger, conservative, movement of Old Belief, product of the schism following the Patriarch Nikon's reform of the liturgy in the middle of that century. However, though communal self-immolation had been a common response on the part of Old Believers to governmental oppression, and though Old Believer monasteries were notorious as shelters for peasant runaways, reactions were not always passive or escapist. Indeed they were often an integral factor in the mainstream of social protest.

Religious non-conformism in general and Old Belief in particular nurtured ideas of Christian justice which were to be reflected in some of the insurgents' manifestos. Further, by virtue of its position vis-à-vis the state-dominated orthodoxy it became an 'underground' and to some extent a subversive movement and was regarded as such by the authorities. Consequent state oppression of Old Believers often gave them common cause with other categories of the oppressed. Old Believers had played a significant role in the Razin and Bulavin movements, and Old Believers of the merchant class played a conspiratorial role in encouraging Pugachev to declare himself Tsar. Further, many

in open disobedience to the authorities and . . . the estate peasants [i.e., serfs.] began to join them'. About 50,000 peasants are estimated to have been in a state of rebellion at that time, nearly 50,000 factory peasants and no less than 100,000 monastery peasants (Mavrodin, *Class War*, pp. 398 ff. and Semevski, pp. 200–35).

Yaik as well as Don Cossacks were Old Believers, as were many inhabitants of the areas affected by the movements.

Sometimes a religious movement has principles amounting virtually to a political programme. Of particular interest here is the *bogokhulstvo* movement which had a strong influence from the 1730s among soldiers and smaller merchants, and continued into the 1760s involving hard-pressed *odnodvortsy* of Tambov and Voronezh. Its adherents not only rejected the established Church but the state establishment in general, opposing recruitments and favouring the idea of common property and brotherhood not unlike that of ideal Cossackdom. Thus non-conformism in religion was also an expression of social discontent which was often channelled into forms of violent social protest.[1]

Precipitating Factors

The Pugachev rising may thus be regarded as a culmination and a fusion of many separate smaller peasant movements motivated by increasing exploitation and oppression. However, in order to understand the process by which these elements coalesced into so great a movement it is necessary to examine certain specific factors which may be regarded as precipitating the revolt, affecting its timing and its character. These are: war, the recent rising of the Yaik Cossacks, the tradition of Pretenders, and Pugachev's own career and experience prior to the commencement of the rising.

War commonly imposes extra burdens sufficient to induce violent reaction from an oppressed peasantry. Wars formed the background to all four mass Cossack-peasant risings in Russia: the Bolotnikov movement was set in a context of civil war involving Polish and Swedish intervention; the Razin rebellion was helped on its way by a long and costly war with Poland; the Bulavin rising coincided with the great Russo-Swedish war; and the Pugachev movement with military action in Poland (1768–72) and, on a far larger scale, against the Turks (1768–74).

Increased recruitment and heavier taxation due to war put a heavier weight on the already burdened classes while the State's commitment against the Turkish armies led to the absence of the best troops and generals who otherwise might have been able to suppress the movement at a much earlier stage. Just as recruitment was a major grievance

---

[1] See also Kadson, 'The Pugachev Rising and the Schism,' *Yezhegodnik Muzeya Istorii Religii i Ateizma*, IV 222–38.

among the peasantry, for the Cossacks war meant long absences from home, imposed an increased financial strain (since they had to furnish their own uniforms, equipment and horses) and, finally, had a deleterious effect on their domestic economy since in their absence their farms had to be run substantially by old men, boys and women.

The Yaik Cossacks, detailed to contain the tribesmen of the south-east, mostly served near home, though prolonged absences at distant cordon-line posts created a large degree of discontent among them too. But far more important was a concomitance of social and political factors which accounted for their very turbulent recent history.[1] The eighteenth-century expansion of markets (see 'The Origins of Discontent' above) had had a profound effect on their once largely class-homogeneous community, giving rise, as I have shown elsewhere, to a class of oligarchs who, encouraged to side with the Government, began to exercise a monopoly of power (instead of sharing in a fairly primitive democracy) and who, aspiring to higher social standing in the Russian system, sought to increase their wealth not only by misappropriating communal funds and official pay but by encroaching on common lands and expanding their shares in communal fisheries and hay harvesting, which they let out inequitably for their own profit.

At odds with the central Government which exercised increasingly strict control of them–searching out the runaways some of them employed as hired labourers, refusing to allow them to replace their venal and corrupt atamans, and threatening them with forced transmigrations to new areas of strategic importance – the Yaik Cossacks had a record of unsuccessful protest going back to the beginning of the century. Even when investigatory commissions conceded the justice of their complaints, punishments were meted out for daring to contest authority. Rumours that they were to be put on a more regular military footing (and incidentally be made to shave their beards, which, as Old Believers, they regarded as 'sinful') caused further disturbances in 1770. There were mass refusals to serve and 2000 Yaik Cossacks were condemned to conscription, extended service, knouting or banishment for life to state factories.

Continuing protests and petitionings were not confined to the poorer sections of the community. Some Cossack officers and officials, men of comparatively ample means, also took an active, sometimes a leading,

[1] On the Yaik Cossacks in the years immediately preceding 1773, see Rozner, and Longworth, pp. 179–86.

part in calling for redress and for a return to their ancient form of self-government. But grounds for discontent continued to grow until in 1772 matters came to a head. A huge crowd of Cossack protesters gathered in Yaitsk, refusing to disperse until their demands were met. Regular troops opened fire, but the crowd overwhelmed them and tore the commanding general to pieces, along with several officers and senior officials of the Host. Having committed this outrage against officialdom they naively tried to make their peace with the Government. They failed, and prepared to defend themselves in what amounted to a minor war of secession. But they were overwhelmed by a superior invading force which also cut off a last-minute attempt by many of them to flee to the protection of the Turks.[1] The movement's leaders were sentenced to exile (some to Siberia, which had a bearing on the Pugachev movement there), hard labour, slit noses and thrashings, and a staggeringly large extra burden of duties amounting to 37,000 rubles was imposed, while the community as a whole was placed under harsh and immediate military government. But the Yaik Cossacks remained unrepentant. Many of them remained vigilant for some promising opportunity to rise again, when they might put a new and more successful strategy into operation (see below). They had not long to wait.

The tradition of Pretenders, or the legitimist factor, is closely connected with the history of Cossack-peasant movements (as indeed with peasant movements elsewhere). The monarchic idea commonly involved with the messianic religious idea of the 'King-Saviour' was one that had very great force among the ignorant and politically illiterate Russian peasant (see section VI). There had been false 'Dmitris' during the Time of Troubles as well as a 'Tsarevich Peter' provided by Terek Cossacks. Even the more republican Razin took a spurious 'Tsarevich' with him when he moved up the Volga to disseminate his brand of Cossack liberty, and Bulavin at least protested loyalty to the Tsar for a time.

The eighteenth century had produced a veritable spate of Pretenders. In 1732 a deserter claiming to be Peter, son of Peter I, appealed to the Don Cossacks and urged the poor to act against their lords. Then peasant fugitives, deserters and Cossacks gathered round a runaway

---

[1] The Don Cossacks were also restless in the period immediately preceeding the Pugachev rising – and for much the same reasons (length of service and its rigour, forced transmigrations, loss of rights, fear of conversation into regular soldiers, etc.). Here, the Ataman, Yefremov, sided with the Cossack rank and file, but was spirited away into exile at the first sign of real trouble and the movement collapsed.

peasant claiming to be Alexei, Peter I's deceased eldest son, and in 1738 another 'Alexei' (this time a worker called Menitski) declared himself. However, only three Pretenders arose in the subsequent twenty years in contrast to the five in the decade of Anne's unpopular reign.[1] Rumour that Peter III still lived dates back at least to the spring of 1763. It gained the more force since the recently deposed and murdered Peter had gained popularity by converting monastery serfs into state peasants, by his take-over of church lands, the temporary reversal of the anti-Old Believer policy and by reducing salt prices. Further, his removal of the gentry's obligation to serve encouraged a widespread (and unjustified) belief that he intended to grant corresponding freedom to the serfs. Peter thus became known as the 'people's defender' and the propagation of this image was assisted by the unpopularity of his usurping wife, Catherine, a foreigner, not of the royal blood, placed on the throne by representatives of the same gentry class so many Russians identified as the creators of their distress. There were several 'Peter III's before Pugachev – three in 1765 (including an *odnodvorets* called Kremnev who promised the *odnodvortsy* of Voronezh freedom from 'heavy duties and recruitments'), one in 1766 (a deserter), and, finally, in 1772, the more dangerous Bogomolov, a peasant runaway, inscribed in the Moscow Legion who, proclaimed 'Peter III' at Tsaritsyn (Volgograd), caused particular excitement among Cossacks of the middle Don and Yaik before the authorities got hold of him.

These and other manifestations indicate a widespread belief that Tsar Peter was really alive – a belief which both influenced Pugachev's decision to call himself Tsar and explains his easy acceptance as such by broad masses of people.

Pugachev's career was in many respects representative of the dissident classes. Born a Don Cossack, he was a family man who had served in the Seven Years' War and besides tending his acres had founded a small transport business when he was drafted again to serve against the Turks. A brave man (he was promoted to the rank of cornet for gallantry) he became increasingly disgruntled at the seemingly endless period of active service, and failing to be retired on medical grounds, became a fugitive, fleeing first to the Terek, then to the Ukraine, and finally to the Yaik. Several times arrested, he escaped on each occasion.[2]

---

[1] Alefirenko, p. 325.
[2] On Pugachev's career prior to the revolt, see Longworth, pp. 187–97; on mutinies, strikes, etc., by Cossack servicemen at this time, Ibid., p. 227.

It is likely that the idea of raising a rebellion was formed when Pugachev returned to Russian territory from the Polish Ukraine in 1772, posing as an Old Believer (Old Believers being allowed at that time to immigrate provided they spent a period in quarantine and settled in the undeveloped area of the Irgiz, near the Yaik). Pugachev spent his quarantine working for an Old Believer blacksmith and trader, who appears to have urged him to pose as Peter III and to rouse the Yaik Cossacks, of whose situation he had heard, to a movement offering a relief to Old Believers who would provide financial and other support. The blacksmith himself provided money and introductions to Old Believers along Pugachev's route eastwards. Of these, the Old Believer Abbot Filaret (an ex-merchant from Moscow) seems to have played a notable part, by giving Pugachev introductions to dissident Yaik Cossacks, suggesting an alias as a trader in fish products and various embellishments to the story he was to tell of being Peter III and accounting for his eleven-year absence from the scene – a tall story, one might add, involving details of travels as far as Egypt and Constantinople. It was Old Believers of this connection who managed Pugachev's third escape from goal in Kazan, where he had been imprisoned as a suspicious character.

Arriving at Yaitsk disguised as a merchant in August 1773 (just four months after the Government had confirmed the sentences on the Yaik rebels), Pugachev sounded out his contacts, hinted that he was the real Tsar, and was sheltered in the Yaik outback until the rebellion began in September 1773, being moved from farm to farm for reasons of security since the Yaitsk authorities seem to have got wind of trouble.

Pugachev's pretence provided the last necessary element to launch the movement. The Yaik Cossack conspirators, as one of them confessed afterwards, 'noticed a quickness and an ability in him, so thought of taking him under our protection and making him lord over us' so that he might restore their ancient democratic and egalitarian 'customs, which the government has long been trying to change by introducing some new military-based order' which the Yaik Cossacks 'were never willing to accept . . . The spark of bitterness for such injustice,' he added, had remained 'concealed among us until some convenient occurance and time [for revolt] should be contrived. And so . . . we decided to call . . . Pugachev the late Tsar Peter Federovich, so that he might restore all [our] previous customs, and to destroy the boyars . . . hoping that our undertaking would be reinforced and our

220   *Peasant Revolts and Disintegration of 'Feudalism'*

power increased by the common people' [or peasants] 'who are also oppressed by the lords and in the end ruined.'[1]

It seems then that at least some Yaik Cossacks did not believe Pugachev's royal claims, but regarded them simply as a convenient 'front', a necessary expedient to attract allies to the cause. As to Pugachev himself, he seems to have been doubtful at times if he would act as Tsar if the rebellion should succeed. But his pretence was vital. His personal attributes, his knowledge of the rebellious Cossack past, his military experience, and, above all, his broad awareness of the plight of the Cossacks, of hounded Old Believers and of exploited peasants, gained in his extensive travels ('everywhere', he once said, 'I have seen that the people are ruined') qualified him to be a leader. But in the Russia of his time something else was needed. Only as 'Peter III' was he finally equipped to set the spark to the explosive situation already prepared in Russia by 1773.

III. GOALS

As a recent student of the Pugachev movement has pointed out,[2] the Russian peasant never proved capable of working out a clear and economically viable programme on which to base a new social order. He ascribes this inability to their lack of political organisation of a class nature, and to the lack of reliable allies among other, presumably literate and educated, sections of society, who might have given a movement political articulation.[3] It is true that the Pugachev movement lacked a revolutionary programme in the sense of a fully articulated, positive and coherent set of goals and a revolutionary organisation in the Marxist sense. But, however inadequate, the Pugachev movement did present a programme comprising reasonably well-defined goals.

[1] Gorshkov, quoted in Mavrodin, *Peasant Wars*, II 416; also Andrushchenko, p. 31.
[2] Ovchinnikov on the rebels' ideology, in Mavrodin, *Peasant War*, II.
[3] Interest in the peasant question was not extensive among the restricted educated class in eighteenth-century Russia. Pososhkov had written his thesis *On Poverty and Riches* in Peter's reign, and Tatishchev, Kantemir and Volynski later evinced some interest in the peasant question, though only to defend the *status quo*, and only Lomonosov appears to have betrayed leanings towards more advanced ideas (See Alefirenko's final chapter). Interest broadened under Catherine, but was for the most part restricted to discussing ways in which the peasants' agrarian activities might be diversified – without affecting lord-serf relationships. Only in the nineteenth century with the growth of the intelligentsia did the abolition of serfdom become a real issue for the educated classes. By then some members of the gentry were prepared to assume the role of peasant allies but the advance of military techniques and the taming of the Cossacks (see Longworth, esp. pp. 224–5, 233–4, 243, 248–50; also section IX below) made any large-scale, violent, peasant movement impossible.

These may be deduced from the rebels' actions, from the statements made by several of them after capture, and from the 'charters' and manifestos they issued. From this evidence it is possible to reach conclusions about the breadth, depth and clarity of goals, and their variations between participating groups and over time.

(1) *Breadth*

From the testimony of two of Pugachev's closest collaborators given in near retrospect – the Cossacks Podurov and Chika (also known as Zarubin[1]) – we can assess the breadth of the goals as declared by Pugachev himself. The main points in his programme during the first stage of the revolt may be summarised as follows. Firstly, to send Catherine into a nunnery (i.e., displace the present head of the social order though not to abolish the office). Secondly, to 'strive to put everything in order so that the people are not burdened', and thirdly, and more specifically, to take the land 'from the gentry who will be given a good reward' (i.e., an economic redistribution in favour of the peasant apparently combined with the vague idea, later dropped, of compensating the gentry out of the public purse). Fourthly, to repay 'the boyars' for 'their hospitality' (i.e., to exact personal vengeance on the larger magnates and officials who had oppressed Pugachev and, by extension, to punish all who had acted in a like way to others). Fifthly, according to Podurov, Pugachev wanted to make all Christians follow 'the old faith' (Old Belief), that is to restore the liturgy and church arrangements to what they had been in the early part of the seventeenth century, to have everyone wear 'Russian clothes' and beards (so banning foreign styles of dress which were offensive to traditionalists as symbols of foreign and especially German influence in Russia – a point which was later confirmed in Pugachev's message to the Cossack village of Berezov,[2] which inveighed against 'evil . . . German [foreign] customs'). Finally, to have everyone cut their hair in the 'Cossack style', implying the introduction of Cossack liberty to all who supported the movement (see section VI, 'The Cossack Ideal').

The movements' goals are, however, probably more reliably expressed in the manifestos rather than by remarks attributed at second-hand in retrospect. The first manifestos, dated 17/28 September 1773 (see section I), though specifically addressed to the Yaik Cossacks, in many respects provided a model for the expression of goals which was

---

[1] Podurov's evidence in Golubtsov, II 187–9; Zarubin-Chika's, ibid., pp. 128–36.
[2] Golubtsov, I 40–2.

reflected in other appeals addressed to other, and wider, audiences. It was, incidentally, prepared in consultation with the Cossack conspirators and written by one of them, Pugachev himself being an illiterate. The document appeals not only to status and morale ('Cossack glory'), but is specific about the possession of their means of livelihood, though in a form that is entirely traditional. The grant of 'the rivers from the mountains to the sea' refers to the Yaik river and its tributaries and implies a reversion to the communal and egalitarian forms of earlier times in the exploitation of their fishing resources. Similarly, the offer of 'land and pastures' should be interpreted as implying a more traditional share-out of grazing and hay harvest, of which the oligarchs had also been appropriating inequitably large shares. Finally, the promise of 'pay of money and lead and powder and food' refers to the traditional rewards given by the Tsar to the Cossacks in return for military service, which rewards the Cossacks had long considered insufficient for the whole community especially since the bulk of it tended to be sloughed off into the pockets of the atamans and their intimates.

This 'charter', therefore, besides serving the function of declaring a claim to the throne (see also section VI) by simulating actions by Tsars in the past, reflected Cossack goals in terms of better pay and supplies, long not received, and fairer distribution of their own communal resources according to ancient custom. It should also be noted that a different short-term goal had already been achieved through the replacement of hostile or unpopular atamans and officers (who were hanged) with insurgent Cossacks (usually democratically elected according to Cossack custom).

The manifesto issued at Rassypnaya on 24 September 1773 bears distinct similarities to the original manifesto, while broadening the appeal to 'all ranks of people'. It promises to reward all who would 'serve [Pugachev] truly and faithfully' with 'everlasting freedom', with 'rivers, seas, all benefits, pay provisions, powder, lead, rank and honour, and they will receive liberty for ever'.[1] The proclamation issued to the people of Krasnogorsk and Sakmara also offered 'river and land pastures and seas and more pay and grain, provender and lead and powder and everlasting freedom', though it is additionally specific in its promise of 'cross and beard' – freedom of Old Belief. In this Pugachev was both repaying a debt to his earlier protectors[2] and

---

[1] Golubtsov; Dubrovin, II 18.
[2] Golubtsov, I 32. Pugachev was well aware of Old Believer feeling (see Ovchinnikov, *Vop. ist.* no. 5, 1966).

bidding for the support of the wide schismatic section of the population which counted freedom of Old Belief as a major goal.

(2) Depth

In basic terms, the movement's goals can be reduced to the removal of disabilities and obligations (political, economic, social and religious) suffered by the various participants. They were predominantly negative, being aimed against the gentry, the representatives of state power who were seen as having changed an earlier and more satisfactory order of things and, of course, against all who proved hostile to the movement.

However, the murder of the gentry and the looting and arson of their property, which reached a climax during stage III of the revolt, cannot in this case safely be characterised as a mere non-goal-oriented *jacquerie*. There was an element of forward thinking in such acts of sweet revenge; the behaviour, though destructive, implied goals of some depth. The call issued to 'all ranks of people in the town of Chelyabinsk' at the beginning of 1774, for instance, displays at once an awareness of the social roots of discontent ('the whole world knows to what state of exhaustion Russia has been led . . . The lords own the peasants, but though it is written in God's law that they should treat peasants like children, they . . . treat them worse than the dogs with which they course hares'[1]) and offers the remedy – the destruction of the oppressors.

A similar line to that followed in the industrial Urals was pursued in areas of normative serfdom. There were also, incidentally, cases of rebels forcing their goals on the populations of some areas. Cossacks riding round farms near the village of Mikhailov in the autumn of 1773 told peasants they had been sent 'to destroy the landowners' houses and to give freedom to the peasants', and warned them 'not to do any sort of work for the landlord and pay him no dues. If we find you doing the landlord's work again we'll thrust you all through'.[2] But mostly there was small need to threaten peasants into acceptance.

The murder of the lord's family in addition to the lord himself, and the attempts to ensure, through the burning down of houses, that landowners should never return (partly successful in that after the revolt there was an increased tendency among the gentry to become absentee

---

[1] Golubtsov, I 75–6, (call of 'Ataman' I.N. Gryaznov, the factory peasant leader). See also section III below.
[2] Report of serf's interrogation, 18 Dec 177, Golubtsov, III 8–9.

landlords), seen particularly in stage III, represented more than an avenging of past wrongs suffered, more even than eliminating elements dedicated to the movement's destruction; it aimed at the elimination of the gentry, who had been defined (accurately) as a class central to the oppressive system. It is relevant to note in this connection that though the 3000 people who fell victim to the rebels included priests, loyalist soldiers, officials, merchants and even peasants and their wives, over half of them (796 men, 474 women and 304 children) belonged to the gentry class.[1] This sort of violence seems to have been a product of despair (if the movement were successful, expulsion would have been enough), but none the less goal-oriented, for though the leadership as a whole was not demonstrably less violent than the followers at this stage, a completely 'expressive' movement would not have required the remark attributed to Pugachev about the burning down of the gentry's houses.

Thus, though such actions may seem to result merely from the mob's pent-up resentments, excitement for vengeance, or from greed, they must not, especially in cases of largely inarticulate peasant elements such as were active in Russian movements, be taken necessarily to exclude the presence of widely shared goals of considerable depth as well as breadth. Indeed, they may well imply aspirations to a complete social transformation. *Jacquerie* actions of this kind, commonplace in Russia, were a particular characteristic of the Razin and Bolotnikov movements too (though the latter's promise to share out not only the gentry's land and property but their womenfolk as well may have aroused enthusiasms beyond those engendered by oppression). More positively, whether or not peasants were to continue paying state taxes or tribute, as was implied in some manifestos, it is clear that private serf-ownership as an institution was to be abolished.

The manifesto of July 1774 proclaimed that 'those who have been peasants subject to the gentry' were henceforth to be 'true subjects, the slaves of Our Crown', i.e., state peasants. The manifesto went further, however, in implying that peasants were to bear no recruitments, no taxation in the ordinary way and, in fact, were to own their own land, in that they were granted liberty 'to be Cossacks for ever.'[2] The freedom from all money and service obligations to the State that this implied (if universally applied) was radical – in fact so radical as to

---

[1] Semevski, I 381.   Unlike Razin, Pugachev seems to have harboured no animus against 'rich gentlemen' as a whole.   Merchants and rich peasants were protected so long as they were loyal.

[2] Manifesto to Volga peasants, July 1774, Golubtsov, I 40–1.

cease to bear credence as a programme of public reform, involving, as it did, the abolition of institutions necessary to the exercise of state power. However accurate the diagnosis of Russia's ills, then, the prescribed cure would, in all probability, have killed the patient.

(3) *Clarity*

The manifestos were apparently vague in promising 'liberty for ever'. Yet however unclear the programme may have been as an expression of workable policy by a prospective government, it was certainly unambiguous enough in its appeal. A report by General Reinsdorp, Governor-General of Orenburg, for instance, confirms the success of Pugachev's proclamations, inciting the Bashkirs 'to plunder mills and landowners', promising peasants (at that stage) to levy a 'soul tax of only three kopeks a soul', offering equal 'freedom to [all] those inhabiting the province of Orenburg . . . men of various religions'.[1] Eventually, in fact, the central Government came to view the appeal of the manifestos so seriously that General Potemkin felt bound to answer them publicly, referring, incidentally, to the Empress's virtues and her care for justice.

Like Razin and Bolotnikov before him, Pugachev was a leader who had travelled widely. He had experienced as well as observed many forms of oppression, and had the ability to translate the people's largely inarticulate aspirations back to them in articulate (if sometimes, as one suspects, deliberately unspecific) form. It is certainly true that in at least some attested instances the manifestos were composed, sometimes by members of the groups to which they were directed, in such a way as to reflect the more particular aspirations of the groups concerned.

(4) *Variations between Participating Groups*

Despite the multiplicity of categories of differing legal status and economic condition involved in the movement, there was a fairly high common factor of aims. However, there were marked variations in detail (i.e., sub-goals). The 'charters' and orders issued in Pugachev's name and directed to various groups reflect the more specific aspirations of each group as well as constituting inducements to recognise him as the Tsar. To quote some specific examples, the Kirghiz-Kaisaks were promised lands which had been encroached upon by the Russian expansion, arms supplies and religious freedom. Further, the

[1] Quoted in Mavrodin, *Peasant War*, ii 426.

tone of the missive, which addressed the chieftain Abdul Khairov as 'my friend and brother', may imply recognition of a tribal leader's status as one almost of equality with that of the Russian monarch, though, in fact, the Kirghis were not to be the most active participants.[1] More successful were the appeals to the Bashkirs promising the over-throw of oppressive Russian administration, the expulsion of intruding Russian industrialists, and the security of their tribal customs and religion ('faith and law') – plus the generous, all-embracing, promise of 'all that you wish in all your life'.[2] The factory peasants were roused in particular by the promise to free them from harsh discipline and forced labour in the factory colonies, which, as a government report confirmed, 'they hate because of the burdens of work and the distant journeys [so many of them had to make from their homes each year] on which account they zealously obeyed the orders [Pugachev] sent to them at the mills'.[3] However, the leadership attempted to keep the factories running in view of their value as potential suppliers of armaments, etc.

Incitements to the Volga peasantry to act against the gentry in addition to 'granting' of various 'freedoms' certainly reflected peasant opinion. According to one account, they believed that if 'it were possible to hang all *pomeshchiki*, then there would be freedom for all and . . . there would be no soul and other taxes, recruiting levies [or] state sales' (monopolies).[4]

Almost to the end, Pugachev continued to issue proclamations aimed at particular sub-groups. *Ukazes* were issued to the trans-Volga Kalmyks (14 August 1774), to the Volga Cossacks (18 August 1774)[5] and his own Don Cossacks,[6] though now with less success.

Throughout the rising there was a tendency for activists to transmit the specific aspirational variants of their own particular people back to them through the prism of Pugachev's addresses. However, some of

---

[1] Kirghiz raiders did mount a sizable kidnapping and cattle-rustling expedition during 1774, however, and a small group fought with Pugachev in Stage I; see Chuloshnikov, also N. Bekmakhanova, *Legend of the Invisible Ones* (in Russian) (Alma-Ata, 1968).

[2] Golubtsov, I 27.

[3] Quoted in Mavrodin, *Peasant War*, II 427.

[4] Golubtsov, II 223. Distinct parallels may be drawn between the goals of the Pugachev movement and of its predecessors, especially Stenka Razin's. The latter was also out 'to thrash the boyars and the rich gentlemen' (Longworth, p. 132), claiming to come 'by order of the Great Czar to put to death all the Bojars, Nobles, Senators, and other great ones . . . as Enemies and Traytors of their Countrey' (ibid., pp. 147–8), and people far distant from the scene of revolt also thought that Razin 'sought the publick good and the liberty of the people' (ibid., p. 148).

[5] Ovchinnikov and Slobodskikh, p. 138.

[6] See section I ('Stage 3') (manifesto to the Don Cossacks).

them, like I. N. Gryaznov, a factory peasant who became 'ataman' of rebels operating in the neighbourhood of Chelyabinsk in the first four months of 1774, apparently issued their own manifestos, though whether with or without the leadership's approval it is difficult to tell.

However this might be, the changes in emphasis contained in the manifestos addressed to specific sub-groups throw light on Pugachev as a shrewd politician, responding to the varying pressures exercised by actual and potential supporters at various moments in time. Primary 'sub-goals' did vary. Cossacks wanted their old 'freedom', while non-Russian ethnic groups wanted to chase out Russian colonisers and officials. Ascribed peasants wanted an end of factory duties, while permanent factory cadres wanted improvements in pay and conditions. State peasants wanted sharp reductions in taxation and obligatory services, while serfs aimed primarily at the abolition of serfdom. However, with one exception (explained in section VII) the differing aims expressed were not mutually exclusive. Given the identification of the common enemy and an increasing sense of group interdependence and solidarity, they appear as variations and extensions of the broad common theme rather than as divergencies.

(5) *Variations over Time*

Nevertheless Pugachev appears to have broadened his initial programme in response to political need at various times and in various areas. In order to clamp the Yaik community the more firmly to his side, for instance, he went beyond the scope of their 'charter', making the verbal promise that when the final victory was won, 'the Yaik will be St Petersburg [i.e., the capital] and the Yaik Cossacks will be promoted to the highest quality for being the cause of raising him to the Kingdom'.[1]

Far more significant was the way that goals in respect of serfdom changed over the period of the revolt. A hint was given in the autumn of 1773 to the effect that serfs would be freed by the extension of state funds to buy them out, implying a sort of serf nationalisation with compensation for the owners (see section III (1) above). By January 1774 the movement already covered a huge area east of the Volga, but agitation had spread even to the peasant-serfs across the Volga. A Senate courier passing through Kazan reported that villagers between Saratov and Pensa were saying that Peter III had freed them from obligations 'on which account they will now give nothing [to the

[1] Golubtsov, II, 111–12.

landlords] . . . and they have his assurance that they will be free and independent of everyone'. 'The present government', the report continued, 'is unbearable to them since the great boyars are rewarded with villages and money, while they have no immunities but only greater burdens on account of the war, namely recruitments and various duties which they pay both to the Tsar and the landowner.' Rumours of Pugachev's successes had clearly encouraged them to the extent of thinking that any governmental military action against them 'would all be useless: that all the soldiers will serve him [Pugachev] as soon as they come since their life is no better than a peasant's'.[1]

This local feeling appears to have had an effect on the leadership as the revolt moved west into the more populous peasant areas. The goals became more extreme. Mention of compensation disappeared and cases of murders of members of the gentry class increased sharply. Such incitements seem originally to have been prescribed for those who opposed the movement rather than for the gentry as a class. From the manifesto of 1/12 December 1773 (see section VII below) one gathers that the gentry were not to be harmed, nor their chattels or homes taken, unless they resisted the redistribution of their estates. But according to one enthusiastic rebel serf, Pugachev was soon saying[2] that 'a man who kills a landlord and destroys his house should be rewarded with 100 coins. A man who destroys ten houses of the gentry should receive 1000 rubles and the rank of general.' And in stage III, after the defeat at Kazan, Pugachev's manifestos openly incite the Volga peasants to 'catch, punish and hang' the landlords – the real disturbers of the peace and the 'ruiners of the peasants' – and promised that when the gentry were destroyed everyone would 'enjoy peace, tranquillity and a quiet life which will last forever'.[3] This apparent change of position seems to have been a product both of intense local feeling against landlords, and of the fact that in this third stage of the movement the struggle was at its most critical and intense, producing goals and actions which were correspondingly more extreme.

The awareness in stages II and III that a critical point had been reached, produced a broadening of the programme on several specific points. A soul tax levied at a modest three kopeks, as promised at Kazan (together with a fixed salt price of five kopeks a pud [36 lbs] and triple pay to soldiers, with five-year recruitments), became an offer of ten-year exemptions from it, after which it would be levied at the

---

[1] Mavrodin, *Peasant War*, II 434–5.   [2] Longworth, p. 144.
[3] Manifesto to Volga peasants, July 1774, Golubtsov, I 40–1.

initial rate laid down by Peter the Great. Then, with the struggle at its height, total abolition was promised – first in an order issued in June 1774 ('if Almighty God will allow me to take the throne of all Russia then these my subjects will be excused soul monies, as shall the peasants be freed from the *pomeshchiki*'),[1] and later the same month in a manifesto to the Bashkirs ('freedom of demands for soul and other taxes or recruiting levies').[2] Thus, it seems that the leadership became increasingly ready to promise almost anything to anybody, and the movement became one of all-out war against all members of the gentry class.

To sum up, then, the goals of the movement were broad in that they related to political, economic, social and religious status. The goals may also be categorised as deep in that in centring on the abolition of the gentry as a class they aimed at the chief pillar of the politico-economic system, together with that of the Orthodox primacy which had been closely identified with that system and until recently with serfdom itself. In its place the rebels appear to have sought to introduce a form of Cossack-peasant democracy (see section VI) and a system of co-operative utilisation of land resources in the areas where they took control. (Only in the case of the Bashkirs and some other tribal groups was a traditional form of patriarchal tribal leadership to remain.)

The goals were expressed in terms such as to suit specific circumstances and permit flexible interpretation capable of satisfying the aspirations of other classes, or sub-groups, besides the Cossacks. The goals appear to have become more radical as the movement progressed to some extent in response to the growing need for mass support and the increasingly effective opposition.

In the end, the final programme was not so much evolved from a pursuit of ideas but broadened in opportunistic response to the feelings of sub-groups who had to be attracted, and the need to muster all available support to cope with toughening opposition. The goals, incidentally, also expressed elements of xenophobia, foreigners being identified with some justification with the oppressive system.

In all, the manifestos and the rebels' statements and actions reflect an absence of revolutionary sophistication and theory. However, the rebels were able to define a common enemy, and the leader's success in rousing such considerable support is an index of his political astuteness in touching to the quick just those points of oppression each participa-

---

[1] *Ukaz* of 5 June 1774, Golubtsov, I.   [2] *Ukaz* of 19 June 1774, Golubtsov.

ting category felt the most. Goals eventually became so extreme as to imply the sweeping away (by the abrogation of taxation income, etc.) of those institutions on which any viable form of government could be based. The objectives were radical and immediate, but there is no clear evidence indicating the ways in which, should the movement have succeeded, its leadership might have been able to run the Russian state effectively, nor how it might have solved the contradictions in the exercise of state functions implicit in the various social and economic changes promised.

Pugachev may have thought in terms of a broad-based Cossack-type army of volunteers paid out of captured official funds, but his later promises to abolish taxation altogether (at least for some groups) would seem to be incompatible with the exercise of governmental functions in maintaining security and defending the borders of the State – a point which was made in the Government's counter-propaganda. Thus though the rebel leadership displayed some idea of their ideal Russia the actions and promises involved in the extension of their programme must be viewed, at least to some extent, as *ad hoc*, opportunist devices, dictated by immediate military needs in the struggle to gain power.

IV. MASS BASE

The Pugachev movement affected an area of some 400,000 square miles situated in eastern, east-central and south-eastern Russia: on both sides of the Volga, in the Urals and in western Siberia, though not all areas took flame at the same time. According to one estimate,[1] it involved about four and a half million people, and perhaps up to a fifth of the Empire's population.

The Extent of the Response

The response to the manifestos during the first stages was almost universally strong and favourable. A report by Governor-General Reinsdorp confirms that 'the low people, immersed in ignorance, certainly believe [Pugachev] and join his crowd in response to the . . . lying orders the villain sends out throughout the province'.[2] The Yaik Cossack Pochitalin testified that 'about 5000 men of various sorts' came to Pugachev's base camp at Berda in October 1773 alone. Supporters

---

[1] Tkhorzhevski, p. 212.   [2] Quoted Mavrodin, *Peasant War*, II 426.

continued to teem in, and by the summer of 1774 Pugachev's adherents might be counted in millions. Apart from the agrarian serfs, the men of the Ural factory colonies were among the most enthusiastic. According to a report by the secret investigatory commission, they were the most 'zealous of all the rest of the peasants for the Pretender'.[1] Certainly they were among the worst oppressed.

Further, there is every reason to suppose that, had the rebels been able to continue their march west from Kazan, support would have been forthcoming in central Russia too. Pugachev himself was certainly confident from an early stage that the poor would welcome him everywhere. The record of recent peasant disturbances in provinces such as Smolensk, Vyatka and Moscow (see section II, 'Reactions') helps to justify this view, as of course do reports from the Volga provinces and elsewhere indicating that the mood of large sections of the population were openly favourable to Pugachev even when he was far distant, and the fact that peasants did not always wait for his approach before taking action. In fact, there is evidence to suppose that even in distant St Petersburg itself, the common people talked in bated breath of Pugachev's coming,[2] just as the people of Moscow had done in Razin's time.

By the spring of 1774, Pugachev was able to tell one colleague:[3] 'I have people like sand', and in retrospect, under interrogation, he reckoned that sufficient manpower had been accreted to accomplish his purpose, and that he failed simply because his troops were 'irregulars'.[4]

Participating Groups and Sub-Groups

Not all groups to whom Pugachev addressed his calls actively participated in the movement. Nurali, shrewd Khan of the Kirghiz-Kaisaks, remained aloof, probably trying to play each side off against the other until such time as it should be apparent who would win, and over a third of the factory peasants in the affected zones failed to join the movement (see section V). On the other hand the Bashkirs, 42,000 strong, were almost solid in his support as were most of the factory and state peasants encountered (including tribute-paying ethnic minorities), and the vast majority of peasant serfs in the Volga provinces (an area whose peasants had risen fairly solidly for Razin too). Agrarian peasants as well as *odnodvortsy* provided the greatest numbers of insurgents, though the deaths of some 300 peasants at rebel hands is

[1] Ibid. [2] *Russkaya Starina*, XVI.
[3] Ovchinnikov in Mavrodin, *Peasant War*, II 429.
[4] Ovchinnikov, *Voprosy istorii*, no. 3, 1966.

an indication that by no means all were supporters of the movement.

Soldiers also participated in so far as they were conscripted peasants whose strict discipline and indoctrination had not completely weaned them from identification with their origins. However, the part of regular troops on the rebel side was small, except from prisoners. Substantial sections of the clergy, probably including a high proportion of more or less covert Old Believers, welcomed the rebels. However, about 300 members of the clerical class were killed by them, which may either indicate a substantial number of established clergy opposed to the movement or else reflect an attitude of undiscriminating hostility among members of the Muslim contingents who had resented the activities of missionary priests. Some merchants and traders also seem to have supported the movement. But though some gentry had participated in the Bolotnikov movement, virtually none supported Pugachev (see section V, 'Enemies of the Movement').

Since the mass base of the movement lay among the oppressed categories the Pugachev rising may be described as a 'class war'. However, within these broad divisions (oppressing and oppressed), class division, economic category or status did not exclusively define those who participated and those who did not. Many of the Cossack leaders had held rank (centurion, local ataman, etc.) and by no means all belonged to the poorer categories. Seventy-seven, the majority, of the Bashkir elders (beys, mursas, etc.) joined the rebel ranks, and, as we have seen, richer peasants (as in Pensa and Siberia),[1] some merchants, clergy and a few officers were to be counted among the insurgents, while a number of factory peasants, Orenburg Cossacks, etc., fought against Pugachev. (See also section V).

Degrees of Activity

The participants most active in the movement seem to have sprung from those groups who were not only oppressed but had a militant tradition of direct and violent action. Yaik Cossacks were always prominent in it, and men like Khlopusha (Sokolov) and Beloborodov, leaders of large groups of factory peasants, had an intimate knowledge of factory regimes and the possibilities of worker action. The question of leadership will be dealt with in section VIII. However, it would be useful at this point to discuss two factors which had a particular bearing on the formation of the movement's mass base – the population density and the structure of communities.

[1] Mavrodin, *Peasant War*, I 320–1.

The Population Density

In view of the extent of the area affected, the numbers participating may seem rather low as a proportion of Russia's total population. But apart from the end of stage II and beginning of stage III (when the movement operated in areas of normative serfdom) activities were confined to areas of low population density. However, the pattern of settlement (population distribution) in these areas were of a type favourable to the movement. Dense nodes of population may be generally conducive to mass participation, and prevalence in the mid-Volga area of village settlements of a much larger size than was usual in rural Russia as a whole was a significant factor. Similarly the factory peasants of the sparsely-settled Urals formed tight, near-homogeneous units (a product of the factory system) as did the Yaik Cossacks (in this case a product of the dangerous border environment). Such characteristics of the settlement pattern were conducive to militant organisation, as can be seen from the Cossacks' long-standing military organisation and the factory peasants' previous record of strikes and disturbances.

Community Structure

The basic social unit among agrarian peasant and Cossack communities was the family household ranging over three generations, and containing about three able-bodied men or youths. The social structure, however, was not in this case conducive to that form of conservatism which operated, for instance, against the Bolsheviks after 1917. In fact patriarchal traditionalism tended to operate in favour of the movement. Folk tradition, as manifested in song and legend, kept alive aspirations to a Cossack type of freedom, casting the rebel Stenka Razin as a popular hero; the sixteenth-century Cossack river pirate, Yermak, as a Russian Robin Hood; and propagated a vision of an ideal past when Russians were free from the present oppressive order with its strange modernities and foreign influences (see section VI).

Another factor which tends to affect the mass character of movements of this type is the role of women. Among the Cossacks, the able-bodied woman was often an important factor of the household's survival during the menfolk's absence on campaign or on some mission of rebellion. Don Cossack women had fought beside their menfolk at the siege of Azov in the seventeenth century and on other occasions when their homes were threatened. Further, during the Razin revolt,

234 Peasant Revolts and Disintegration of 'Feudalism'

a formidable peasant woman 'ataman', called Alena, had made an appearance, leading a large and violent rebel group in the neighbourhood of Alatyr. Apart from the fact that nearly 500 women were listed among the 4287 rebellious factory peasants killed in the rising, there is little direct evidence on the role of the Cossack or peasant woman in the Pugachev movement, but generalised evidence over a long period suggests that at the very least they were unlikely to have exercised any considerable restraining influence.

Sense of community had a significant bearing on the mass reaction. Cossack communal institutions both of an economic and political kind are well known; and tribal communal institutions require no special comment here. However, it is important to note that peasant behaviour was not as fissiparous or isolated as might have been expected.[1] The Russian peasant was by no means a stranger to co-operation with his neighbours. The *mir* or village association, for instance, though not a community of labour, bore many communal responsibilities, and serfs commonly arranged their landholdings and allotted dues imposed by their lords communally among themselves. True, peasants competed among themselves for available resources (and the avoidance of the group taxation burden), but the limitations of these resources were commonly attributed to outsiders and tended to unite the peasants, despite their differences, against the landlord and official.

Community structure and, notably, institutional communal or collective forms of settling village affairs were thus a contributory factor to the high degree of solidarity apparent not only among the Cossacks but among peasants of the factory colonies and agrarian peasants during the revolt.

To sum up then, the Pugachev movement attracted adherents on a massive scale from all sections of the population except the gentry, the officer class which was largely staffed by the gentry, the higher echelons of the merchant class, those Orthodox clergy loyal to the established Church, and serving regular soldiers. Further, its militancy was to some extent a product (a) of frontier conditions which bred

---

[1] See Eric R. Wolf, 'On Peasant Rebellions', *New Society*, 4 Sep 1969. The 'tyranny of work', the annual peasant routine, which Wolf also cites as a factor unconducive to peasant action, seems also to be limited in application. There are cases of peasant frustration building up to a point at which even the risk of rebellion seem preferable to the toil necessary to obtain a minimal and uncertain subsistence. Russian peasants were commonly near subsistence and not infrequently passed below it, whereupon cases of flight and brigandage became common and not infrequently, disturbances on a scale indistinguishable from rebellion. See also n. 1, p. 253.

distinct military characteristics among Cossacks and some tribesmen, and (b) of conditions in the Ural mines and factory colonies which produced informal but militant associations in some respects reminiscent of those of an industrial proletariat. Finally, traditional values, patriarchal forms and community structure among Cossacks, agrarian and factory peasants alike, so far from acting as brakes, tended to accelerate the movement.

V. ALLIES AND ENEMIES

It is not intended in this section to give an exhaustive account of the movement's allies and enemies (which would involve some rather tedious repetition), but rather to attempt to characterise some of the movement's major features in this connection, to comment on some motivations and to indicate some apparent syndromes, chiefly concerning the loyalty of participants which seem characteristic of Cossack-peasant risings in general.

The Yaik Cossack-Peasant Alliance

It is perhaps inexact to term the Yaik Cossacks allies in a movement which they largely originated and for which they provided the majority of leaders under Pugachev. However, their numbers were comparatively small (probably never much more than about 3000) and diminished, chiefly through casualties, as the movement progressed. The general link between Cossacks and peasants, the roots of their mutual sympathy, have already been outlined (see section II, 'The Participants'). What is significant is the Yaik Cossacks' appreciation of the necessity of an offensive strategy (after their disastrous defensive posture of 1772). This encouraged their alliance with other, much more numerous and predominantly peasant categories, whose condition, and, to a certain extent, goals were not identical with their own – an alliance which required 'Peter III' as a common legitimist symbol and universal rallying point.

The 'Urban Middle Class'

The 'urban middle class' which often provides literate and managerially competent allies for peasant movements, was as yet poorly developed in Pugachev's Russia. The strongest part of it was situated in the chief cities (Moscow and St Petersburg) and in the ports, more especially the Baltic ports – that is in areas distant from the scene of the revolt. In any case much of what might be termed 'middle' or 'artisan' classes, namely people making the bulk of their livings through entrepreneurial activities in trade and industry (including cottage industry) is more conveniently classifiable according to the more particular Russian categories which cut across class definitions often used for the analysis of Western movements of the period. A section of the gentry, especially gentry-magnates, was very much involved in industry and trade, and the populations of towns were made up to a significant extent by peasant serfs paying *obrok* to a distant lord – by people motivated to a large extent by disabilities suffered from the institution of serfdom, etc. Since the 'lower middle class' of tradesmen and artisans in both country and town cut across 'feudal' categorisations, definition becomes difficult (to quote but one example, Beloborodov may be classed as an ascribed peasant, as a retired soldier, or as a trader in honey and wax) and allegiances become easier to categorise in terms of gentry-peasant classifications rather than under what were often only part-time, economic functions. It is true that serfs with urban occupations, peasants of more than average wealth (like 'Ataman' Novgorodin in Siberia) and Old Believer merchant-tradesmen did join in the revolt, though the significance of their adherence lies perhaps more in their legal and political disabilities than in their relative wealth, just as non-Russian ethnic elements in the Volga area, properly classified as peasants, were additionally motivated by religious disability. This said, it seems that though merchants as a whole were opposed to the rebels, some were not, and there are several instances in stage III of 'burghers' actually welcoming Pugachev, though one suspects that their chief motivation may have been to secure their possessions.

Sectional Aspirations to Autonomy

Some ethnic groups, in particular pastoral tribesmen, most significantly the Bashkirs, joined the movement in considerable numbers, aspiring to a greater degree of communal autonomy (as indeed did the Cossacks). In this sense even the tied peasant – whether belonging to the State, landlord or factory – also hoped for an autonomous system of village government in which they would be free of landlord interference and central government action (the levying of taxes, the exercise of monopolies in necessity goods, and the compulsory raising of recruits). It should be noted, however, that though there were strong separatist trends among the allied groups, the common need engendered a large degree of solidarity. Thus, the Yaik Cossacks for all their strong separatist leanings in the past were content to remain within the Russian State (albeit as a favoured élite under Pugachev), and even Bashkir leaders who had good reason for anti-Russian sentiment could declare of the insurgents: 'There's no malice in our hearts against the Russians. We Bashkirs and Russians shouldn't quarrel and fight each other.'[1]

Other Motivations

It is especially difficult to evaluate the motivations accounting for the movement's support in towns for though many townsfolk, including 'bourgeois' elements and priests, greeted Pugachev when he approached (stage III), many of them may only have been seeking to guarantee their lives and the safety of their families and property. On the other hand there are recorded cases of obviously pro-Pugachev elements withholding from violent action in the presence of even small numbers of government troops, and sometimes until the actual arrival of rebel forces, if not of the 'Tsar' himself. As an eye-witness reported when the rebels were near Yekaterinburg, 'knots of people gathered on all the streets and one had to expect an outburst . . . at any moment',[2] but there was no spontaneous rising. Again, at the Shaitinski mill, early in January, with rebel forces still distant, though a ferment began as soon as news of the rebellion was confirmed, action was limited to a strike at the pig-iron works and the dispatch of messages asking Beloborodov to hurry with rebel support. In all, only twenty-two of the factory colonies in the affected areas rose spontaneously; a further forty-two in response to rebel approaches, while the populations of a further twenty-eight were isolated from the rebels and mobilised to defend the settlements by the authorities and the owners. However, several factory colonies outside the affected area sent contingents to the rebels' aid.

It is worth remarking in this connection that the threat of extreme punishment for refusing to recognise Pugachev as Tsar was a factor tending towards unanimity in areas the rebels occupied and that, conversely, the threat of draconian and enforcible measures dissuaded malcontents in areas under government control from action. Hence (i) the many cases of transferred allegiance among all sections of participants as the Government lost and regained a hold of various areas,

---

[1] Quoted by Andrushchenko, p. 299.   [2] See Limonov, p. 71.

and (ii) the frequent difficulty of estimating with any accuracy the extent to which various participants were motivated by an identification with the movement's objectives, rather than by the fear of punishment.[1] On the other hand, it is clear that some elements of the Volga population (stage III) responded to doles and the distribution of liquor, while the prospect of plunder was an additional incentive (see section VIII, 'Security and Discipline'). However, with these qualifications made at the margin, the factors inducing the mass of both peasants and non-peasants to revolt can be reduced to oppression, mainly of an economic kind, which increasing political disabilities allowed no opportunity to redress.

The Limits of Loyalty (or the Betrayal Syndrome)

As we have seen, the limits of loyalty to the movement were largely determined by factors of self-preservation. Though some 'neutralist' groups such as the Kirghiz–Kaisaks adopted a cautious approach towards Pugachev (also for fear of governmental retaliation should he not succeed), most groups stayed the course in so far as the military situation allowed them to. However, even in these cases, the prognosis of failure and the consequent attempt to escape apparently inevitable punishment led to desertions and betrayal (a common syndrome in movements of this type and one applying both to the leadership and the following).

The abandonment of the peasant masses by Pugachev and his Cossack cadre after unsuccessful battles (e.g. that at Kazan) seem to be repetitions of numerous other instances in Cossack-peasant risings when the Cossack fighting core left the peasant mass to its fate. This was the case at the battle of Berestechko in the Ukraine during the Khmelnitski rising, and of Razin at the battle of Simbirsk. In each case the circumstance was a hopeless tactical situation in which the leadership's motive may be interpreted not merely as a desire to escape, but to save the hard core of fighting men in the knowledge that further cadres of untrained, poorly armed, or unarmed, peasants could always be gathered again later. In Pugachev's case the separation of the leadership from the mass may also be attributed to the random scatter-

---

[1] To cite but one instance, Lt. Gen. Prince Shcherbatov recorded that following the rebel defeats in stage I, virtually the whole of Ufa province became obedient to the government, but when Pugachev moved into the Urals, 'everywhere' inhabitants 'unanimously and zealously' began 'to give [him] support' (Andrushchenko, p. 149). See 'The Enemies of the Movement' (above) and section VII (below), and generally on the factory peasants during the rising, Andrushchenko, pp. 274 ff.

ing of the rebel forces, and amounted to a separation of mounted from unmounted groups rather than of allied social groups from another. The separation of Cossack and peasant after an unsuccessful battle does not necessarily imply any difference, therefore, in the degree of fervour or the identification of immediate aims.

However, such cases represent only one form of the 'betrayal syndrome'. Another is seen in the Bulavin revolt, when elements of the Cossack elder-oligarch party which had joined him deserted after military defeat and tried to make their peace with the Government (conversely in Razin's time the more prosperous Cossacks of the lower Don remained aloof from the revolt and took firm measures against it only when the final outcome was clear). While there is no evidence in the Pugachev movement to indicate that richer Cossack supporters deserted him before others, it contained two extreme instances of that version of the syndrome in which the following betrayed the leadership: (i) after the defeat at Tatishchev two of Pugachev's aides were handed over to the authorities in Yaitsk by a mob of fellow Cossacks; (ii) Pugachev was himself betrayed by his last comrades – men who had played leading parts in the movement since its inception. These were both attempts on the part of rebels who saw their situation and their cause as absolutely hopeless, to save their own skins. They acted in hope of promised amnesty if not in hope also of the generous reward put on Pugachev's head by the Government (which had no apparent effect, however, until the very end). Conversely the leader showed little taste for martyrdom. The captured Pugachev cut an abject figure trying to convince his interrogators and judges that he was repentant and 'ready to serve in any way'.[1] However, in virtually all cases betrayals were made at virtually the last possible moment, which indicates a high degree of solidarity so long as there was the slightest hope of success.

The Enemies of the Movement

Besides the monarch herself, the enemies of the movement comprised the agricultural and industrial magnates and the serf-owning gentry, the officer corps and the governing and official classes generally. They could rely on the regular troops, who, though substantially of peasant origin, were effectively cut off from the outside world, kept

[1] Ovchinnikov, *op. cit.*, *loc. cit.* It is true that immediately after capture his attitude was bolder and that torture subsequently undermined him. Nevertheless, he presented a contrast to Razin's brave bearing to the end, and Bulavin's suicide.

substantially loyal through harsh discipline and by propaganda which in so far as it mentioned Pugachev at all cast him in the role of a godless traitor and rebel. However, it will be remembered, some troops (notably after Colonel Chernyshev's defeat and the victory at Osa) joined after capture, as did some irregular troops (Cossacks and Kalmyks) sent against the rebels, though the substantial part of the Don Cossacks remained aloof, partly through stringent security measures enforced with the co-operation of the elder-oligarch class which allowed little of the rebel propaganda to seep through[1] and partly through the absence of a substantial proportion of the younger Cossacks on the Turkish front. Further, about 500 Yaik Cossack householders, mostly belonging to the oligarch party, and most of the merchant class encountered in the first stages, over half the Orenburg Cossack force, including the more privileged sections, and many townsfolk east of the Volga refused to join the rebels (see 'Other Motivations' above), while the mill-owners succeeded in mobilising a large number of factory peasants in defence of some industrial colonies.

Methods

The methods employed in dealing with the movement involved no compromise. This was exemplified earlier during the Bulavin rising, and during Razin's main campaign. Bulavin did address explanations to the authorities at one stage, but in vain, just as the Yaik Cossacks had done in their previous rising (see section II, 'Precipitating Factors'). But amnesties offered by the Government to the men of Astrakhan, who had held out many months after Razin's execution, were characteristically forgotten by the authorities when the rebels agreed to surrender. In the Pugachev movement, too, methods tended to become absolute in the Clausewitzian sense. Government troops often slaughtered rebel prisoners and, even though a general amnesty was proclaimed by the Government for rank and file rebels as part of the pacification programme during the aftermath (just as Pugachev offered free pardons for the surrender to opposing forces), the movement may be characterised as one of all-out war with no compromise as to goals, and often no quarter expected on either side.

[1] See Pugachev's reference to 'forced obedience' to their 'disloyal commanders who corrupt you and deprive you along with themselves of my great favour' (Dubrovin, II 18.)

VI. IDEOLOGY

However ideologically innocent Pugachev and his followers may have been, the movement betrays the presence of a widely-shared view – however vague and impractical – of the sort of society the rebels wanted to form, and reasonably clear indications of the values and aspirations underlying its goals (discussed in section III above).

Broadly speaking, the most important element in their programme can be summed up under the slogan 'land and freedom' – the exploitation of resources for the benefit of their users, albeit communally, the reduction, if not the total abolition, of taxation, etc. However, two particular features of interest stand out, which may be termed ideological, and which were characteristic not only of the Pugachev rising, but of Cossack and peasant risings generally in Russia (and to some extent elsewhere in Slavic Europe). These were the concept of the just Tsar, and the Cossack ideal.

The Concept of the Just Tsar

This may be characterised merely as a form of naïve monarchism. The institution, as we have seen, had a wide currency in peasant revolt both inside and outside Russia (see section II, 'Precipitating Factors') but it was a concept almost universally accepted in Russia, and one of great appeal. A contemporary commentator (probably Catherine herself)[1] was undoubtedly right in commenting that 'there is not a nation in Europe more firmly and affectionately attached to their sovereign than ours'. But the sentiment attached to the institution rather than the incumbent; it was not naïvely passive. When an action was regarded as just, it was the Tsar's; when a monarch was unjust he could not be the rightful Tsar, or at least the action was attributed not to the monarchy but to ministers. And in this case the movement aimed not only at eliminating the monarch's 'evil' advisers, but to replace Catherine with the supposedly 'good' Tsar Peter Fedorovich.

Pugachev's claim gave him the means of mustering mass support and of maintaining broad control of the movement's disparate elements. It is interesting to note that many Yaik Cossacks did not believe the

---

[1] *The Antidote* (Retort to the Abbé Chappe d'Auteroche's account of Russia) (London, 1772) p. 127.

pretence. They supported him nevertheless as a means of gaining allies and securing their demands. There was also a significant departure from traditional Russian monarchism in that, unlike a true autocrat, Pugachev was prepared to enter into a social contract. On the first day of the revolt, not only do the Yaik Cossacks promise to serve 'Peter III' 'to the last drop of blood', but he promises them 'before God to love and reward the Yaik Host as the Tsars did of old'.[1] The movement thus betrays some signs of a monarchist ideology based not on heredity or 'legitimacy' in the formal sense, but on the idea of a monarchy which is responsive to the general will of the people.

The Cossack Ideal

The Cossack ideal had long been a powerful image in Russia. Peasant rebels in the Slav south-west had called themselves Cossacks as early as the fifteenth century.[2] Later they had 'gone Cossack' by their tens of thousands, following Bolotnikov, Khmelnitski and other leaders thrown up from the Cossack ranks. There had been a continuous flow of peasants to the borderlands to become Cossacks and the Razin revolt stemmed, like numerous other smaller movements, from peasants who, aspiring to Cossack status, fled (in that case to the middle Don), found themselves short of subsistence, turned to brigandage and, when state action cut off this source of supply, to open rebellion.

The ideal of Cossack social organisation, had been a particularly strong feature of the Razin revolt when inhabitants of town after town were encouraged to elect their own leaders Cossack-style.[3] In the Pugachev movement, as a sign of their true allegiance to 'Tsar Peter', captured soldiers were made not only to make the sign of the cross in Old Believer fashion, with two fingers, but to have their heads shaved in Cossack style, and even when Cossack custom was not imposed, oppressed non-Cossack classes instinctively reacted by favouring democratic Cossack forms, displaying their aspirations to free Cossack status by adopting Cossack terminology and organisation. The manifestos were carried about the country by tribesmen and peasants who called themselves Cossacks. Peasants under the blacksmith Volkov were known as 'factory and village Cossacks' and 'Ataman' Alishev, for instance, who brought the good news to Rozhdestvensk

[1] Longworth, p. 198.
[2] Galician peasants had been calling themselves Cossacks as early as 1491. (See Longworth, pp. 92 and 352-3.)
[3] Longworth, p. 146.

factory village was not a Cossack by origin. The peasant leader Beloborodov was given the title 'centurion' (*sotnik*), a recognised Cossack rank (though it also had wider connotations). Old and new Cossack ranks competed for popularity, especially among the tribesmen who had their 'regimental elders', their 'colonels' and their '*esauls*'.

More important than terminology, however, was Cossack practice. Beloborodov was one of several leaders elected Cossack-style, and elsewhere, 'craftsmen and peasants' held elections at village or factory-settlement level (and voted on important issues such as whether or not to recognise 'Peter III', i.e., join the movement). Such elections were often carried out for Cossack-style groupings of hundreds and tens. And if the powers of such elected leaders was dictatorial, this merely conformed to Cossack practice in time of war.

Further, there are indications that Pugachev himself thought of a Russia that would be a one-caste state ruled by a 'good peasants' Tsar', in which all surviving citizens would rule themselves in their localities but do service for the Tsar. As Pochitalin bears witness, Pugachev was of opinion that people throughout the empire of whatever rank should be made Cossacks[1] and this was publicly confirmed in the manifesto of 31 July 1774. However rudimentary it may have been, the ideology of the Pugachev movement was not anarchistic. Elements of authority were preserved, albeit exercised through elected leaders, and stress was laid on loyalty and service to 'the good Tsar'.

Thus the monarchic idea was allied to a general urge among oppressed classes to become Cossacks. Despite Catherine's conviction that outside interference was responsible for the revolt,[2] the zealous investigatory commission was only able to confirm that this was an entirely indigenous, grass-roots movement with a vision based on the participants' instinctive idea of natural justice, aimed at the oppressing gentry class, and aspiring to egalitarian institutions on the Cossack model. It was quite innocent of ideas imported from either the educated gentry or by articulate foreigners.

VII. THE MEANS OF ACTION

Previous movements both by Cossacks and peasants cover the whole range of protest action – strikes, petitions, flight and the threat and use

[1] Golubtsov, I 111.
[2] See W. Reddaway, *Documents of Catherine the Great* Cambridge 1931

of force. The Pugachev revolt belongs to the latter type. Indeed, it was characterised by extremities of violence, including the use of all arms, including artillery, on both sides on a scale amounting to war.

However, force was only the secondary means which was reserved by the rebels (at least at first) only for those who refused to recognise Pugachev as Tsar and submit to his will. The first means of action was the use of persuasion by propaganda, and here the manifesto played a highly important role. Pugachev himself reckoned on its power in sending them out 'to all places whence I hoped to receive help',[1] and the widespread broadcasting of the news helped significantly in rousing support. Rebel detachments and individual agitators, sometimes disguised, carried the manifestos far and wide. To a large extent, however, the news appears to have travelled spontaneously – and amazingly swiftly – over vast distances chiefly by being passed on from mouth to mouth. Yaik Cossack exiles were a factor in the revolt's taking root in Siberia and ascribed factory peasants working their seasonal stints in the Urals were given passes and encouraged to carry news of the movement and of its aims back to their villages.

Even when verbal persuasion failed, violence was used only as an extension of it. The leadership, at any rate in the first stage, seems to have set strict limits on its use. Instructions issued to Zarubin-Chika, commanding insurgents in the Ufa area in stage I, tell him to avoid bloodshed. He was to 'strive to reason' with those who held out against him. However, if they persisted in refusing 'to obey his imperial authority and to carry out his paternal orders', he must be severe. 'Their dwellings should be set on fire, the better to frighten them. Perhaps they would then . . . show their readiness' to obey. If they did, 'then efforts should be made to put out the fires'.[2] Similarly, the 'charter' of 1/12 December 1773[3] in promising 'land, fisheries, forests . . . beaver runs and other appendages of landed property, and also freedom', also contained an enforcement order: 'If this . . . is not obeyed by any *pomeshchik* [gentry holding land by reason of state service] or *votchinnik* [holder of land by outright grant in perpetuity] the latter . . . criminals against the law and the general peace, villains and enemies against my imperial will must all be deprived of life, that is executed, and their houses and all their property se-

---

[1] *Vop. ist.*, no. 4, 1966, p. 17.
[2] 'War College' decree to 'Count Chernyshev' (Zarubin-Chika) dated 29 Dec 1773, Golubtsov, I 46. This device was used successfully on more than one occasion (Andrushchenko, p. 144).
[3] 'Charter' of 1/12 December 1773, Golubtsov, I.

questered to yourselves as a reward' – a threat which, it will be noted, was to apply only to those landlords who opposed re-distribution. However, the threat of terror inevitably became an actuality. The people of an affected area, whatever their inclinations, were faced with an unenviable choice between two conflicting authorities, each using the sanction of terror in order to gain obedience and restrict its enemy's support (see also section V above).

Nevertheless only at a relatively late stage does violence seem to have been widely and spontaneously used, other than as a sanction, in order to eliminate the gentry as a class (hence the murder of children as well as adults and the burning down of manor houses). Though methods varied among different groups at various stages according to circumstances there seems little to choose between those approved of by the leadership and those employed by the generality of their supporters (though see section VIII, 'Security and Discipline').

VIII. ORGANISATION

No adequate form of organisation existed even in embryo among the conspirators on the eve of the Pugachev rising. Yet the movement's organisation was to become more sophisticated than any of its predecessors except the Khmelnitski movement, which was led by a class of Cossack gentry. Having started with only a leader, a few dozen men constituting a 'Cossack brotherhood', and a rudimentary *ad hoc* division of labour capable of producing the first manifestos, within three months Pugachev's forces, some 15,000 strong, were operating over a wide area centring on Orenburg. So considerable an army demanded some more complex and effective form of administration. One was provided. Arriving at Berda in mid-October, Pugachev ordered an office to be set up for 'written affairs'. This was soon functioning as the central directorate of the movement. It was known as 'The College of War'.[1]

'The College of War'

'The College of War' was the movement's central co-ordinating and executive organ. It is significant that in creating such an authority capable of administering Pugachev's numerous adherents, it should

---

[1] See *Krasny Archiv* (1935) p. 200. Generally on the organisation see Spirkov on 'The College of War' in Mavrodin, *Peasant War*, II 458–60.

have taken as a model an existing governmental institution, the real College of War, and one which *inter alia* administered the Cossack districts. Unfortunately, after defeat in March 1774 Pugachev ordered all 'War College' papers to be burnt. However, enough evidence remains to provide some picture of its composition and activities. The 'College' had its own hierarchy of 'Secretary of State' (*dumny dyak*), 'Heads of Chancery' (*povytchiki*), 'Chief Treasurer' and 'Commissionary', 'Chief Secretary' and 'Judges' besides a number of scribes and other lesser functionaries. Most of the top posts were occupied by Yaik Cossacks (many of whom, like Pugachev himself, were illiterate), but the 'College' also included representatives of other participating groups – notably the renegade Lieutenant Shvanovich, re-ranked '*esaul*', and members of tribal minorities.[1] However rudimentary, it dealt with written work, including the production of orders, manifestos, etc., in various languages (including Tatar, Arabic, Persian and Turkic) and the issuing of passports or *laissez-passers*, which were often dignified with the use of seals. It maintained communications with rebel bands operating at a distance, encouraged the introduction of self-government into territory under rebel control, organised supplies (which though irregular appear to have been adequate to maintain the considerable central force during the first winter), appointed commanders, dealt with promotions and awards, supervised the appropriation and disbursement of funds (including pay and the provision of clothing for the rebel troops) maintained discipline and became largely responsible for the administration of justice. Attempts were also made during the winter of 1773-4 to maintain the economy in regions under rebel control. Grants were made to factory peasants to obtain raw materials and repair the industrial equipment needed to maintain war supplies, and considerable efforts were made to manufacture gunpowder, ammunition and cannon in the Ural industrial zone, though for the most part the rebels had to rely on captured weapons and ready stocks. No special coinage was ever issued and, in all, defeat came too quickly for firm evaluation to be made about the effectiveness of this nascent administrative system or how it might have developed.

'The College of War' reached the peak of its effectiveness towards the end of stage I. Up to March 1774 it appears to have coped with a

---

[1] See *Russkaya Starina*, 1876; Dubrovin, p. 135. The various offices in the 'College' seem to have varied in relative importance over time, largely reflecting the personalities of the incumbents.

variety of considerable problems with remarkable success. However, the defeats in stage I and the consequent flight from Orenburg lost the movement many of its leaders, its records and artillery – in sum, put their organisation back almost to square one – and the 'College' as later reconstituted in the Urals was much weaker due to the loss of experienced personnel and to the constant movement consequent on a necessary guerrilla strategy. By the summer of 1774 its activities were for the most part reduced to attempting (inadequately) to maintain food and forage supplies for the mobile core of the movement and to establish and maintain contact with other groups, though manifestos continued to be manufactured in some quantity.

The Inner Council

From the beginning there was a less formal group of favourites surrounding the Pretender which in the rebel mind may have corresponded to Catherine's Senate. The members were largely but not exclusively identical with the chief members of the 'College'.[1] Mostly Yaik Cossacks, the most prominent members held differentiated offices. Tvorogov, for instance, was 'Judge' at the 'College,' 'Colonel' of the Iletsk Cossacks and later the College's 'Chief Secretary', while Ovchinnikov was head of Pugachev's personal bodyguard and 'Chief Ataman'. However, representatives of other elements, like Sokolov-Khlopusha, were also included. This inner group constituted Pugachev's informal 'secret' council and seems to have been primarily concerned with broad strategic policy. Its have been primarily concerned with broad strategic policy. Its importance appears to have increased relatively to that of the 'College' in course of time.

Hierarchies

There was also, at least until the Spring of 1774, a reasonably effective system of regional administration headed by middle-echelon leaders who generally maintained close contact with the high command at Berda. These were often local leaders whom Pugachev had encouraged to form their own units, and sometimes co-ordinators sent out from headquarters. The more important regional commanders

---

[1] This inner council may have corresponded to Catherine's Senate in the rebel mind. Some members certainly assumed aliases of personalities in Catherine's Government. Zarubin-Chika, for instance, became 'Count Chernyshev'. It might also be noted that Pugachev's mistress, Ustinya, was after some difficulty, recognised by rebel clergy as the 'Tsarina'.

were Zarubin-Chika, sent out to co-ordinate action around Ufa, I. S. Kuznetsov, sent to the Krasnoufimsk-Kungur district, Beloborodov sent to the Yekaterinburg mining area, 'Colonel' Gryaznov of the Isetsk-Chelyabinsk district and 'Brigadier' Salavat Yulayev in Bashkiriya. However, during stage I other large rebel formations were also operating under their own leaders (Derbetev's Kalmyks on the east-bank of the Volga, 'Ataman' Arapov of Stavropol, Cossacks of the lower Yaik, west Siberian peasants, etc.), some of them co-ordinating with regional commanders, some reporting directly to the 'College'. Various members of the central group were sent out on special missions from time to time – for instance 'Ataman' Sokolov-Khlopusha who was sent to the Avzyano-Petrovsk factory colony in stage I to organise artillery and ammunition supplies.

Various regional commanders made efforts to set up a rational recruiting system in 'occupied' areas. Zarubin-Chika called for 'suitable and worthy brave men, one man from each house' to report for duty with arms, 'good horses' and supplies.[1] Though primarily military leaders, regional commanders also concerned themselves with a whole range of administrative and even social problems, organised food supplies, coped with disorders, attempted to reduce unemployment.

Evidence of quite sophisticated organisation goes far down the chain of command. At least some commanders at middle and lower levels had their own chanceries or secretaries who issued written orders. (There is a document dated January 1774 signed by 'elected Corporal Adil Bigachev and Campaign Regimental Scribe Peter Lutokhin' pronouncing the 'retirement' of Esaul Grigori Ovchinnikov of the 'Krasnoufimsk Cossack forces'.)[2] Foraging detachments used written authorities to requisition supplies from those peasants considered hostile to the movement (and some who were not), and, when money was lacking, issued promissory notes instead of cash to other suppliers.

However, in the latter stages, hierarchies became much less effective and less complex, and the chain of command finally crumbled away. The various 'governors', 'atamans' and '*starostas*' Pugachev left behind him in various towns and villages as he passed south of Saransk, having turned off the Moscow road, represented only *ad hoc*, episodic attempts to set up some sort of new order. They did not survive long.

---

[1] Golubtsov, I 147; *passim* for other examples of recruitment on the bases of households or age-groups. Bulavin too tried to call up 20 armed men from each village.
[2] *Ukaz* dated 14 Jan 1774, Golubtsov, I. See Mavrodin, III 463–4 on administrative arrangements down to village level.

Though the number of insurgents multiplied in the final stages, co-ordination proved impossible. Huge rebel bands coalesced only to disintegrate again for lack of sustenance or through the actions of the military. Though many of the large and violent peasant gangs took a long time to disperse, their actions were unco-ordinated, the chain of command unclear.

Finally, it is worth recording that besides the 'vertical' command chain the movement's organisation showed signs of 'lateral' diversification of functions. This is seen in the various offices of the 'College' (see above), in unit chanceries and in specialised appointments such as the designation of the Cossack Chumakov as 'Colonel of Artillery'.

Security and Discipline

The fact that Pugachev and other leaders were able, after crushing defeats, to escape superior detachments of loyalist troops time and again without being betrayed by the local population suggests a climate of opinion favourable to their security. However, steps were taken to maintain security, especially in the earlier stages, beyond the customary administering of oaths of loyalty to 'Peter III'. Many of the peasants arriving at Berda were placed under the command of reliable Cossack leaders; most soldiers who joined were 'converted' into Cossacks and, when these were available, made to wear Cossack clothes. But even then they were not entirely trusted. Most were placed under the command of some member of the inner group, and their arms were often handed over to unarmed peasants who were evidently considered more reliable.[1] Further, Beloborodov is on record as having urged vigilance in 'Peter III's interests', warning against 'the flatterers' who offered their 'services with a view to betrayal'.[2] In all the degree of loyalty seems to have been very high until it cracked in the chaotic aftermath of severe defeat, when in conditions of low morale it tended to disintegrate entirely (see section V, 'The Limits of Loyalty').

Energetic attempts were made at all levels to maintain discipline. Regional commanders like Beloborodov arrested disturbers of the peace and took a stern attitude towards indiscriminate plunderers. Ataman Alishev, arriving at the Rozhdestvensk factory colony, commandeered the money found there but made it clear that this was not a

---

[1] Golubtsov, II 218. Razin also thought it prudent to place regular troops who came over to him in the middle of the marching order.

[2] Quoted by Andrushchenko, p. 194.

looting expedition, addressing the peasants as follows: 'All this money and chattels are taken for the Lord Peter Fedorovich. We are ordered to take away the chattels of gentlemen but not to enter peasant homes and to take nothing from your estates, and to seal all the factories.'[1] However, it was often extremely difficult to keep order, especially where the marauding Bashkirs were concerned. The 'College' at last ordered them 'to be obedient' and 'not dare to commit' any disorders on pain of 'corporal punishment'.[2] But since many Bashkirs wanted to clear their traditional pasture grounds of the intrusive factory colonies, the troubles continued, and since the factory colonies constituted the only means of livelihood and the homes of the permanently-based factory peasants, they defended themselves against Bashkir raiders. Peasants at the Satkinski Mill (February–April 1774), upbraided for their disorders, protested that they were not hostile to 'Peter III', but only taking precautions against Bashkir raiding parties. Again, in March 1774, came a report of disturbances at the Votkinski state factory. 'As you know', it ran, 'there is much confusion now among the people and . . . internecine and deadly fights and empty disagreements as there has already been in . . . other places.'[3] Both parties felt themselves betrayed and eventually this division of interest led some rebel factory peasants to change sides. Clashes between workers and tribesmen, between workers or peasants and groups of insurgents stationed on, or requisitioning from, them gave rise to discord and sometimes to bloodshed. However, most cases of disorder or disobedience seem to have arisen in conditions of shortages and usually when the military prospects of success were fading.

Executions were carried out to maintain discipline at least during stage I. The 'College' issued instructions for major offenders, including murderers, to be referred to it for judgement and regional commanders took measures to impose order and maintain it. There is, for instance, the case of a local commander sending a peasant to Berda for trial on a charge of executing a landowner, his fourteen-year-old son and a tribesman on his own initiative. But with the decline in the 'College's' capability and the general organisational decline in stage III, order could not be maintained from the centre and, ultimately, only very inadequately at local levels.

To sum up, at its most organised stage the movement disposed of a

[1] Ovchinnikov in Mavrodin, *Peasant War*, II 428; Golubtsov, I 48–9.
[2] Golubtsov, I 153–4.
[3] Message from Volkov of Rozhdestvensk, 16 Mar 1774, Golubtsov, I 118–9.

vertical hierarchy of authority under Pugachev – from the 'College of War' and the 'secret' council to village or tribal group headmen and detachment commanders often via regional commanders. Orders, advice, requests, etc., were transmitted up and down this scale by word of mouth, but also to a large extent in writing, cadres of literate adherents of many categories being employed for this purpose at all levels. There is also evidence of some horizontal form of organisation – functional differentiations, for instance in the command of artillery, while recruitment, supply, communications, etc., were subject to a certain degree of specialisation within the 'College'.

As in other massive peasant movements in Russia and the Ukraine, Cossacks provided most of the top-echelon leaders. However, each group of differentiated participants tended to find its own leaders – tribal elders, peasant workers, etc., some of whom became members of the inner controlling group. Very occasionally a regular officer, like Shigayev or Mineyev, commander of the 'Kazan Volunteers', would be given Cossack rank and responsibility, but inspiration or leadership by outside intellectual 'bourgeois' or clerical elements (other than the possible influence of Old Believer clergy) was notably absent. It was a quasi-military caste, the Cossacks, which assumed the leading role in the Pugachev movement as it did in all major peasant movements in seventeenth- and eighteenth-century Russia.

IX. SOURCES OF SUCCESS AND FAILURE

The Pugachev outbreak began in circumstances favourable to rebellion. Economic and political discontent among broad sections of the population was widespread and had reached a considerable degree of intensity. The Turkish War, in which the Russian army had gained no considerable success since 1770, placed additional burdens on the population and removed the best fighting troops from the countryside (Ker's men, for instance, were mainly over-age or inexperienced recruits) and, in order to cope, the Government had to withdraw a significant number of troops and competent generals from the front.

The presence in the south Ural borderlands of communities of Cossacks, of militant industrial workers, of recent runaways and war-like tribesmen provided elements necessary to the formation of militarily competent and dedicated cadres. Finally, Pugachev's pretence to legitimacy provided a focus for the discontented, and his political skill in touching to the quick the most sensitive nerve of each of the disparate elements among whom he sought support, together with the presence of an easily-identified common enemy, helped to a considerable degree to maintain a momentum of mass support.

The movement, like its predecessors, can be characterised as a war, and defeat when it came was military defeat. There was no lessening of discontent, no backsliding on goals. One may thus ascribe the defeat to the numerical inadequacy of the military cadre of Yaik Cossacks, to inadequate generalship, and to the failure to procure wholesale desertions by regular troops (as occurred with the *streltsy* in the Razin revolt).

However, deeper analysis reveals a complex of geo-strategic factors which go further to explain the failure. In fact in one respect it helps to account for the initial successes as well, for just as border areas tend to be the most difficult for governmental control and provide various conditions that favour the successful launching of rebellion, they also create serious problems for rebels. A co-ordinated series of movements operating on exterior lines from the periphery is intrinsically unlikely to be successful (as the powerful converging efforts of the White Armies failed in the Russian Civil War). On the other hand, if the movement arises from a single point on the periphery (as in the case of the Pugachev rising), it cannot tap potential support in other peripheral areas and areas distant from its line of advance. This is illustrated by the Bulavin revolt, which was immediately preceded by rebellion in Astrakhan and immediately succeeded by the revolt of Mazepa in the Ukraine and of the Zaporozhian Cossacks. Similarly, Pugachev was unable to co-ordinate his numerous, though scattered supporters in stage III, still less rouse obviously discontented elements (apart from a few Zaporozhians) in other, more distant, parts of the Empire. Thus, more specifically, the difficulty of the centralised state in controlling its distant borderlands has its corollary in the difficulties experienced by border rebels in communicating with others round the periphery.

The leader of a movement from the periphery is thus faced with the choice between a swift advance on the capital, and eliminating loyalist centres in the rear; he can either secure his base, or try to surprise the enemy's forces and catch them off balance by striking suddenly towards the centre. This choice was clearly recognised by Razin who took care to secure Astrakhan before proceeding up the Volga, though not by Bulavin, who suffered quick defeat by trying to do both at once, thus dividing his forces. Pugachev himself, despite the urgings of his Cossack advisers who had recently experienced the failure of a strategy of securing a base, insisted throughout the winter months on the capture of Yaitsk and Orenburg as a first objective before eventually moving on the capital. In the event his ultimate advance on a line Kazan–Moscow–St Petersburg was carried out without a secure base and though it preserved elements of surprise for a time, it soon petered out as a coherent movement, having lost the strategic initiative. Thus, when the movement's organisation was strongest, the base was static, operations confined to the periphery, and support, though militant, was restricted by low population densities. When support was most massive, the base was mobile, heading into the centre, but organisation was weak and the movement suffered from the lack of experienced warriors, poor communications and the lack of material.

Pugachev's revolt, like other Cossack-peasant movements, moved up from the periphery and failed near the centre – not because of reduced support, but because (i) lines of communications of the forces of 'law and order', working on interior lines, were conveniently shortened, and (ii) recruits gained in these more central areas lacked the military expertise possessed by farmer-warriors of the borderlands.[1]

One might therefore conclude that unless the movement accelerates extremely quickly to overwhelm the centre, it must secure a militarily tenable and economically viable base, form an adequate and permanent army, and an organisation capable of maintaining and co-ordinating the movement over a long period of time, as well as propounding, and in its own area implementing, as Mao did, goals which attract and maintain mass support. However, in view of the difficulty of adequate preparation and the impossibility, in conditions of the regime's efficiently repressive policing system, of maintaining a broadly enough based working conspiracy over a sufficient period prior to the revolt, his supporters' hatred of recruitments (though they were willing enough to fight in a hopefully short campaign) and other factors, Pugachev was able to pursue neither course successfully. In fact he and other leaders showed distinct signs of vacillating between the two.

[1] A further factor may be the peasant's unwillingness to fight far from home, especially near harvest time. This was certainly a feature of peasant revolt in Russia and most notably in the Cossack-peasant war led by Bogdan Khmelnitski in the Ukraine (see Longworth, pp. 97–120).

Finally, one might suggest some specific factors which apply to Russian peasant movements generally in the seventeenth and eighteenth centuries, which may also serve as hypotheses to be tested against examples of rural rebellion in other areas and periods:

(a) Such movements were more likely to succeed in time of war, which at the same time heightened discontent and created a situation in which repression by the State, preoccupied with external commitments, was less efficient than usual. This seems to have been the case in 1917 and appears valid for the Pugachev and other Russian movements under discussion.

(b) No peasant movement was likely to become massive without the help, if not the instigation, of a cadre of militarily competent Cossacks or *streltsy* (though peasants did not identify so closely with the latter since they were a group of law-enforcers with trading privileges, and not basically derived from the peasant classes).[1]

(c) In order to become massive, some programme had to be promulgated which combined Cossack-peasant (and other group) interests. (The movement of Vasili Us, prior to the Razin revolt, failed because, though many peasants joined it, the Cossacks would not identify their own more limited aims with theirs[2].)

(d) Such movements tended to become massive in proportion to the area the rebels occupied. Proximity tended to rouse peasants to action in neighbouring districts – in other words, success bred success (and failure, failure).

(e) A leader was required who was either charismatic, like the gay and dashing Stenka Razin, or who gained charisma by pretence to being Tsar. The presence of such a figure was often a strong psychological factor in swinging doubters to the rebel side (this was certainly the case on several occasions in the Pugachev and Razin risings). Moreover, he often had to be *seen* as charismatic by waverers at critical points. Thus the leader had to be mobile, so creating problems of a mobile base.

(f) A movement had quickly to overwhelm the major centres of state power or else suffer the strategic disadvantages of operating on the periphery.

[1] Rebellious *streltsy* (the soldier caste abolished by Peter I) had played parts in both the Razin and Bulavin movements.
[2] Longworth, p. 129.

(g) An organisation was required capable of administering both occupied areas and the rebel forces (as the 'College of War' came near to doing in stage I), but which was also able to be operated (in conditions of poor communications over wide tracts of territory) from a mobile base. It was this lack, together with the shortage of adequate cadres of trained soldiers and administrators, which probably contributed most to Pugachev's failure.

BIBLIOGRAPHICAL NOTE

For the primary material in printed form see Golubtsov (compiler) and Pokrovski (general editor), *Pugachevshchina*, 3 vols. (Moscow–Leningrad, 1926–1931); S. Piontkovski (ed.), 'Interrogation of Ye. Pugachev in Moscow in 1774–5', *Krasny Arkhiv*, vols. LIX–LX (1935) pp. 159–257; *Interrogations of Yemelyan Pugachev and the Letter about him by the Empress Catherine III to Count Panin* [Russian] (Moscow, 1858); Ya. V. Ovchinnikov (ed.), 'The Investigation and Trial of Ye. I. Pugachev', *Voprosy Istorii* (1966), no. 3 pp. 124–38, no. 5, pp. 107–21, and no. 7 pp. 92–109; M. Zhizhka, 'Interrogation of A. Khlopusha', *Krasny Archiv*, LXVIII (1935) pp. 162–72; 'Pugachev's Chief Helpers', *Russkaya Starina*, XVI (1876); Ya. K. Grot, 'Materials for the History of the Pugachev Revolt', *Sbornik Otdeleniya Russkogo Yazyka i Slovesnosti Imperatorskoi Akademii Nauk* (St Petersburg, 1876). See also *Russkaya Starina*, I–III (1883) pp. 167–70; *Russkoye Chteniye*, no. 1 (1848) pp. 118–32; and R. V. Ovchinnikov and L. N. Slobodskikh, 'New Documents on the Peasant War of 1773–5 in Russia', *Istoricheski Arkhiv*, no. 4 (1956).

For the most recent Soviet studies of the movement see V. V. Mavrodin (editor and chief contributor), *Peasant War in Russia in 1773–1775* [Russian], 3 vols. (1966–70); Yu. A. Limonov, V. V. Mavrodin and V. M. Paneyakh, *Pugachev and his Fellow Champions* [Russian], (Moscow–Leningrad, 1965), and A. I. Andrushchenko, *The Peasant War of 1773–1775* [in Russian] (Moscow, 1969). N. Dubrovin's *Pugachev and his Accomplices* [Russian], 3 vols. (St Petersburg, 1884), still has some value, as does A. S. Pushkin's *History of the Pugachev Revolt* [Russian], 3 vols. (1834) (which drew on material in Tsarist archives no longer extant). N. M. Firsov's 'psychological' study *Pugachevshchina* (St Petersburg, 1907), and the comparative study of M. Ya. Fenomenov *Razinovshchina and Pugachevshchina* (Moscow, 1923), as well as A. Gaisinovich's study translated into French (*La Révolte de Pougatchev*, 1938), should also be consulted.

More specialised studies include: S. Petrov, *Pugachev in the Pensa District* [Russian] (Moscow, 1930); A. P. Pronshtein (ed.), *The Don and the Lower Volga area during the Peasant War of 1773–1775* [Russian] (Rostov-on-Don,

1961); A. Chuloshnikov, 'The Kirghis-Kaisak Nomadic Hordes and the Pugachev Movement 1773-4', *Novy Vostok*, no. 25 (1926) pp. 201 ff.; N. I. Sergeyeva, *Peasants and Working People in the South Ural Mills during the Peasant War 1773-5*. Otherwise on the condition of the industrial peasant see R. Portal, *L'Oural au XVIIIe siècle* (Paris, 1950), and P. A. Vagina, 'The formation of worker cadres in the South Ural mills in the 50s and 60s of the 18th century'; *Istoricheskiya Zapiski Akademii Nauk SSSR* (Institut Istorii), vol. 47. On the religious aspect, I. Z. Kadson, 'The Pugachev Rising and the Schism', *Yezhegodnik Muzeya Istorii Religii i Ateizma*, IV (Moscow–Leningrad, 1960) pp. 222-238, and on pretenders, K. V. Sivkov, 'Pretenders in Russia in the last third of the 18th century', *Istoricheskiye Zapiski*, vol. 31. On the government's reaction, John T. Alexander, *Autocratic Politics in a National Crisis*, Indiana University Russian and East European series, vol. 38.

For the condition of peasants in general, see P. K. Alefirenko, *Peasant Movements and the Peasant Question in Russia in the 30s to the 50s of the 18th century* [Russian] (Moscow, 1958); V. I. Semevski's *The Peasantry in the Reign of Catherine II* [Russian], 2 vols. (1903); J. Blum, *Lord and Peasant in Russia from the 9th to the 19th century* (New York, 1965; paperback), and P. I. Lyashchenko, *History of the Economy of the USSR* [Russian, but an English translation is available], vol. I (1952); Lyashchenko's 'Russia's serf economy in the 18th century', *Istoricheskiye Zapiski*, vol. xv, various relevant contributions in *Ocherki Istorii SSSR* (Russia in the second half of the eighteenth century) (Moscow, 1956), and for contemporary thought about the peasant problem, V. V. Mavrodin, *Class War and Socio-Political Thought in Russia in the 18th century (1725-1773)* [Russian] (Leningrad, 1964). On developments among the Yaik Cossacks prior to the revolt, see I. G. Rozner, *The Yaik before the Storm* [Russian] (Moscow, 1966), and for a general description of this and other Cossack-peasant movements and the peculiarities and development of the Cossack communities in general, see Philip Longworth, *The Cossacks* (London, 1969; New York, 1970).

PART 2

THE PEASANT AND FORMAL POLITICS:
EASTERN EUROPE BETWEEN THE WARS

Chapter 7

PEASANT POLITICAL MOVEMENTS IN EASTERN EUROPE

by

George D. Jackson, Jr

THE first victim of industrialisation is the peasant. At least that is the conventional view. The peasant, it is said, is wrenched out of his parochial village life by the intrusion of the market and the money economy. His family swells in numbers out of all proportion to his income because of improved standards of health care and improved diet, and he is pushed off his land by some of his more efficient brethren, by non-peasant cultivators, and by landlords who have abandoned their *noblesse oblige* for the ethics of the market place. As taxes and money costs rise, some peasants are seduced into the production of cash crops or rural cottage production as a way of supplementing their meagre farm incomes. The former are in the end betrayed by the whims of the market and left stranded without either an adequate money income or a kitchen garden to fall back on. The latter become accustomed to their additional income, and then it is removed from them as industry shifts from the putting out system to the factory system. In the end almost all peasants must seek a place in the burgeoning cities and abandon farm work altogether, and with it the warm and intimate personal ties and satisfactions of village life. There are none to mourn the peasant's passing, for that is progress and the 'normal' pattern of modernisation. In Eastern Europe, however, before World War I a peasant political movement arose that claimed that this was not progress, that it was not inevitable, and that peasant society possessed some distinctive virtues that should be preserved at all costs.[1] It was a movement, then, evoked by modernisation against

---

[1] The two most sympathetic and most extensive treatments of East European peasant political ideology in English, by a Rumanian and a Croat respectively, are David Mitrany, *Marx against the Peasant: A Study in Social Dogmatism* (Chapel Hill, 1951) and Branko M. Peselj, 'Peasant Movements in Southeastern Europe, an Ideological, Economic and Political Opposition to Communist Dictatorship' (unpublished Ph.D. dissertation, Department of Political Science, Georgetown University, 1950). Neither one, however,

modernisation, or, at least against those aspects of modernisation that spelled the end of peasant society.

The peasant political movement in Eastern Europe deserves more attention than it normally receives in the West because its history, especially in the period between World War I and World War II, throws into sharp focus the most pressing problems of 'underdeveloped' and 'advanced' societies and at the same time provides a telling criticism of both the communist and capitalist paths of economic development and their social and cultural consequences. Moreover, the intensive study of East European populism could add one of the missing dimensions to the political history of Eastern Europe, which is too often cast in a purely Western mould. Populism, peasantism, or agrarianism, and the terms are used synonymously in this chapter, had a strong and often decisive influence on the pattern of change during the inter-war period, and, through its criticism of society and politics, laid the foundation for the communist era in the post-war period.[1]

In order to reassess the peasant political movement and bring it into sharper focus I would like to rely on the analytical framework provided by Henry Landsberger.[2] A new look at East European populism is long overdue. It should attempt to reconcile or account for the wide differences of opinion about such movements in Western studies.

---

deals with the evolution of peasant ideology, demonstrating the changes that took place from the formation of peasant political parties to 1947. I have provided a brief treatment in my book, George D. Jackson, Jr., *Comintern and Peasant in East Europe 1919–1930* (New York, 1966) pp. 40–48. There are two brief, personal interpretations of peasant ideology in Eastern Europe, by a Croat and a Bulgarian respectively, in Branko M. Peselj, 'The Concept and Sources of Peasant Ideology', International Peasant Union Monthly Bulletin, No. 9 (Sep 1951) pp. 9–12, and George M. Dimitrov, 'Agrarianism', in Felix Gross (ed.), *European Ideologies* (New York, 1949) pp. 391–452.

[1] It is only recently that scholars have begun to see the continuity between pre-World War II regimes and post-World War II communist governments. See, for example, Leonard Bushkoff, 'Marxism, Communism and the Revolutionary Tradition in the Balkans, 1878–1924; An Analysis and an Interpretation', *East European Quarterly*, I, no. 4 (Jan 1968) pp. 371–400; William E. Griffith (ed.), *Communism in Europe*, 2 vols. (Cambridge, 1966); and 'East Central Europe: Continuity and Change', *Journal of International Affairs*, xx no. 1 (1966). None of these have yet focused, however, on the role of populism in shaping the criticism of the old regimes, with the possible exception of Gati's unpublished doctoral dissertation (Charles W. Gati, 'The Populist Current in Hungarian Politics 1933–44', unpublished Ph.D. dissertation, Dept. of Government, Indiana University, 1965). The term 'Populism' is a source of some confusion, since it is habitually used in the United States as a label for 'the tradition of a strong liberal movement designed to protect the social and economic position of the small independent farmer or urban merchant': Seymour Martin Lipset, *Political Man, The Social Bases of Politics* (New York, 1963) p. 169. In its East European context the term is a label applied only to the political movements of farmers and peasants.

[2] Henry A. Landsberger, 'The Role of Peasant Movements and Revolts in Development: An Analytical Framework', International Institute for Labour Studies *Bulletin*, no. 4 (Feb 1968) pp. 8–85.

Unfortunately, within the limitations of space imposed here such an effort can only be impressionistic. There are too many countries to encompass and an abundance of native research that can only be sampled here. First, I propose to categorise briefly the approaches that have been used in the past in treating East European peasant movements. Second, as a foundation for what follows I will examine briefly the historic roots of these differences and of the distinctive qualities of East European peasant life. Third, I would like to sort out the differences and similarities between the various movements and sketch briefly some of the important social and economic differences between the countries in which they appeared and the status of their peasantry after World War I. Fourth, I will turn to the ideology of the peasant political movement and the ways it changed as a result of the experience of political responsibility. Finally, I would like to pull the strands together and compare the results with those scholarly judgements that we used as a point of departure. Let me begin with some of the current Western views.

I. WESTERN VIEWS OF EAST EUROPEAN PEASANT POLITICAL MOVEMENTS

It is no simple task to distil the truth about East European populism from the studies that are now in print, most of which, including my own, display a profoundly anti-peasant bias. Most Liberal and Marxist scholars seem to take their cue from Karl Marx, who remarked with some relish:

> The bourgeoisie has subjected the country to the rule of the towns. It has created enormous cities, has greatly increased the urban population as compared with the rural, and has thus rescued a considerable part of the population from the idiocy of rural life.[1]

Like many of his contemporaries, Marx believed in the inherent superiority and ultimate predominance of large-scale units of production in every human endeavour, and therefore could only rejoice in the imminent disintegration of the peasant economy.

> In the sphere of agriculture, modern industry has a more revolutionary effect than elsewhere, for this reason, that it annihilates the

[1] Karl Marx and Friedrich Engels, *Manifesto of the Communist Party* (New York, 1932) p. 13.

peasant, that bulwark of the old society, and replaces him by the
wage laborer . . . The irrational, old-fashioned methods of agriculture are replaced by scientific ones.[1]

And, indeed, there is much truth in this point of view. When the
East European peasant turned to politics between World War I and
World War II, not only did he lack the qualities of an efficient producer
under a capitalist system, but also he seemed devoid of the qualities
most useful for responsible citizenship in a democratic system, such as
cosmopolitanism, urbanity, an awareness and concern for the whole
nation, and a high degree of literacy. In his excellent chapter on the
Bulgarian Agrarian Union, Joseph Rothschild observes that the peasant
was far more of an anarcho-syndicalist in politics than a natural
democrat, '. . . He prefers burning down a manor house to casting a
ballot, and looting a merchant's shop to conducting parliamentary
discussions'.[2] In one of the best studies of a modern East European
country, Henry Roberts writes:

> . . . a purely peasant movement is almost impossible to sustain, both
> because of the nature of its support and the limitations of its program.
> Because of their relative physical isolation and simple, often prim-
> itive, way of life, the peasants are exceptionally difficult to organize
> politically. A peasantist philosophy has proved to be uncertain
> and ambiguous in its aims: it can provide mood or feeling, and is a
> natural inspiration to poster art, but it becomes confused on the
> more practical level and for a very fundamental reason. Those
> elements which are celebrated in the peasant – the primordial
> qualities, the roots planted deep in the earth – represent everything
> which the modern world is not. Insofar as the peasant is defined in
> these terms, he provides no clues to the solution of the manifold
> problems confronting contemporary society.[3]

Today communist historians tend to emphasise the shortcomings of
peasant ideology. According to them the fatal ambiguity of agrarianism was the assumption that there was a single, identifiable peasant
class. From the Marxist point of view rural society, like urban society,
had a bourgeoisie and proletariat, and would follow the same pattern
of development as the cities, i.e., through class warfare to capitalism

[1] Karl Marx, *Capital*, ed. by F. Engels (New York, 1906) 1 554.
[2] Joseph Rothschild, *The Communist Party of Bulgaria: Origins and Development 1883–1936* (New York, 1959) p. 86.
[3] Henry L. Roberts, *Rumania: Political Problems of an Agrarian State* (New Haven, 1951) p. 166.

and finally socialism. Peasant politicians who set out to defend the whole peasant class, so say the Marxists, ended up as agents of the rural bourgeoisie (the rich peasant). Their propaganda prevented the poorer peasant from seeing the goals he had in common with the industrial worker.

> . . . The leaders of rightist orientation tried to use theses about a 'single class of peasantry' and the 'community' of interests of the agricultural population in order to subject the movement of toilers to bourgeois leadership, and leaning on this movement, to strengthen the alliance of the exploiting classes of the country with the great bourgeoisie in order to strengthen their economic and political domination . . .[1]

Contrast these rather sour views with those of a partisan political leader of that period, Milan Hodža, leader of the Czechoslovak Agrarian Party in the 1930s.

> In the ten states of Eastern Europe, the most bloodless, quiet, and yet most profound, social revolution in world history took place after World War I. The strongest social class of all time, the landed aristocracy, was destroyed at one blow and replaced with agrarian democracy. The land reforms destroyed the great estates and now the small peasant economy predominates . . . The most important result of the World War is the appearance of new men in state and society. One can simply say that the role played by the bourgeoisie in revolutionary France will be played in contemporary Central Europe by post-war agrarian democracy.[2]

Hodža was right about one thing. Whatever its philosophical shortcomings or tactical errors, the peasant political movement in Eastern Europe was more than a fleeting phenomenon. Even today it probably represents more faithfully the aspirations and values of the East European people, than either liberalism or communism. As one scholar recently put it:

> Politically, the East European peasantry, which before the war had its parties and its governments, tends unmistakably to recon- stitute its own social representation and organized pressure groups,

[1] M. M. Goranovich, *Krakh zelenogo internatsionala 1921–38* (Moscow, 1967) p. 251. As far as I know this is the first Marxist work to deal with the inter-war agrarian move- ments as a whole, though since Stalin's death there has been much research in each East European country on their own indigenous movements.

[2] As quoted in S. Maslov, *Milan Godzha i novaia sila v Evrope* (Prague, 1938) p. 93.

and ultimately its own parties.[1] In cases of possible political pluralization in Eastern Europe, in this decade, it is more than probable that agrarian parties will reappear in one form or another.[1]

This probability was borne out in at least one instance, the Hungarian Revolution of 1956, in which one of the first acts of the revolutionary Government was to reinstate the two popular peasant political parties, the Independent Smallholders' Party and the National Peasant Party.[2]

Some Western scholars also assign a more positive role to the peasant political movement. For example, David Mitrany's views pose a challenge to Rothschild's notion that the peasant was no more than an anarcho-syndicalist. Mitrany points out that the peasant political movement should not be dismissed because it could not hold on to political power, since, by those standards, few East European political parties were successful. And Mitrany suggests other criteria:

> . . . what they lost as parties they apparently gained as a movement. Socialism had been a movement in the West long before it could organize in parties; the eastern peasantries found themselves called upon to act as parties before they had been educated politically and philosophically as a movement. Their discomfiture at the seat of government gave them the opportunity to make good that lack. It threw them back upon themselves and produced an intense, an almost introspective interest in the nature of their class and problems. Shut off from power and government they set out on a voyage of self-discovery and self-education, to give body to a movement which through historical circumstances had started with more form than content . . .
>
> Defeat in political action led them towards a new strategy, to an intense effort to develop the social consciousness of their peasant followers and to consolidate them as a class.[3]

One powerful expression of their success in achieving these other goals was the dynamic rural youth movement of the 1930s.[4]

In a more recent study Charles Gati pays tribute to both the short run and long run influence of the Hungarian populist movement.

> In the 1930's the populists raised incisive and important questions about Hungarian society and presented a vivid picture of what was wrong and who was to blame.[5]

[1] Ghita Ionescu, *The Politics of the European Communist States* (New York, 1967) p. 144.
[2] Paul W. Zinner, *Revolution in Hungary* (New York, 1962) pp. 304–10.
[3] Mitrany, p. 130.   [4] Ibid., p. 133.   [5] Gati, p. 257.

. . . the populists' ideas were read and discussed with growing interest, influencing, not only the young intellectual elite – part of which was to govern Hungary in the post-war era – and the peasantry, but also effecting uneasiness and thus causing concern to the government.[1]

Gati also quotes a communist writer, who describes the populist movement as 'the most important intellectual current of the last two decades in Hungary'.[2]

Nor is peasant ideology always dismissed as no more than an 'inspiration to poster art'. Nicholas Georgescu-Roegen concludes:

. . . Agrarians were the first to feel intuitively that the economic forms compatible with optimum welfare are not identical for all geo-historical conditions *even if the technological horizon is the same* . . . neither Barone nor others after him seem to have been aware of one important restriction, namely that marginal productivity principles presuppose the existence of a well-advanced economy in order to achieve optimum welfare. And thus numerous writers have felt secure in using in their arguments the converse proposition: Capitalism and controlled Socialism provide the best systems for developing an underdeveloped economy. Yet this proposition is patently false, at least for an overpopulated economy.

In this fight, the intuition that led the Agrarians to their double negative – not Capitalism, not Socialism – proves to have been surprisingly correct . . . [3]

These are some of the wide differences of opinion. The critics of the peasant political movement, on the whole, see it as a futile effort to hold back the inexorable tide of modernisation because of a romantic nostalgia for the past. In short, they feel to a large extent that Eastern Europe had to follow the same pattern of economic development as Western Europe (or Russia in the Marxist view). Yet the central thesis of peasant ideology was that because Eastern Europe's past was different, her future must also be different. Therefore, it would be useful to explore this claim about the East European past before going on to the peasant political movements themselves.

[1] Ibid., p. iv.
[1] Ibid., p. viii.
[3] Nicholas Georgescu-Roegen, 'Economic Theory and Agrarian Economics', in his *Analytical Economics, Issues and Problems* (Cambridge, 1966) p. 392.

II. THE HISTORICAL ROOTS OF THE PEASANT
PROBLEM IN EASTERN EUROPE

Before turning to the historical differences between Eastern and Western Europe, I must revise, at least in part, the conventional picture of peasant history I presented in the first paragraph of this chapter. The thesis presented there cannot be contested. Modernisation is inevitable and it probably does mean the eventual destruction of peasant society as a separate sub-culture within the larger community. But for the society in question, the process may be long drawn out, as in the case of modern France,[1] and the path chosen may be of more consequence than the final goal.[2] Far from being an immutable society, frozen in its customs and rituals since Neolithic times, the peasant sub-culture has always been remarkably dynamic, responding, not only to the wider culture of which it is a part, but also to internal innovation, social and technological.[3] Throughout history the peasant also supplied recruits to become the new aristocrats, artisans, merchants, and finally industrial workers. And it is precisely in these terms, that is, internal changes in character and status of the peasantry, that one must examine the differences between Eastern and Western Europe. Those differences begin with the so-called medieval time-lag.[4]

It is by now a well-known historical cliché that colonisation came later to Eastern Europe than to Western Europe. It is probably for this reason that their paths of development diverge in the Middle Ages. Because Eastern Europe was settled later than Western Europe, it did not fully develop its agricultural resources before the opportunity slipped away. Before Eastern European peasants had applied those

[1] See, for example, Wright's fascinating account of the gradual transformation of the French peasants in the twentieth century, in Gorden Wright, *Rural Revolution in France: The Peasantry in the Twentieth Century* (Stanford, 1964).
[2] For a sampling of the wide range of alternatives see Barrington Moore, J., *Social Origins of Dictatorship and Democracy: Lord and Peasant in the Making of the Modern World* (Boston, 1966).
[3] See Warriner's discussion of this in Doreen Warriner, *Economics of Peasant Farming* (London, 1939) pp. 8–12. The ground-breaking essay by Robert Redfield, 'The Peasant Society and Culture', in his *The Little Community and Peasant Society and Culture* (Chicago, 1967), has been criticised for overemphasising the stability and isolation of peasant society. Wolf's brief essay, Eric R. Wolf, *Peasants* (Englewood Cliffs, New Jersey, 1966), gives more recognition to diversity and change within the peasantry.
[4] Doreen Warriner, 'Some Controversial Issues in the History of Agrarian Europe' *Slavonic and East European Review*, xxxii (Dec 1953) p. 174.

technological innovations that gave Western Europe the agricultural surplus for a leap to the next level of economic development with expanding trade, growing towns, and a stronger central government, market conditions turned against her. The crucial period was the years between 1300 and 1600. Trade shifted from the East to the Atlantic perimeter in the fifteenth century, and at the same time, in the fourteenth and fifteenth centuries there was a European-wide depression that led to a long swing downward in grain prices.[1] Caught in a comparatively primitive level of political and economic development by comparison to the West, Eastern Europe was condemned very early in her history to 'the vicious circle in which countries are poor because they are poor'.[2]

One devastating consequence was that the bonds of serfdom continued to be tightened in Eastern Europe at the same time that they were being loosened in the West, in both cases as a way of retaining the diminishing supply of labour.[3] Paradoxically, at the same time that techniques of production were at a relatively low level, that cities and towns in Eastern Europe were in decline, the East European nobility became producers for the market and tied their peasants more closely to the soil.[4] The relatively greater power of the East European nobility made it possible for them to take these steps, and this too was a result of the medieval time lag. The restraints on aristocratic power that developed in the West in conjunction with the rise of towns and a stronger central government had no counterpart in the East. Although serfdom also increased in Russia during these years, in many other respects Russia was an exception, for in Muscovy the cities were growing and provided the new markets for agricultural products, and serfdom was a privilege granted by a strong central government as compensation for state service and for a rather dependent status.

When the European economy began to turn upwards in the sixteenth century, it was already too late. The pattern had been fixed. East European towns continued to stagnate, with some notable exceptions on the Baltic and Black Sea, and the bonds of serfdom were further tightened down to the eighteenth century, as the rural nobility now gleaned the profits from rising grain prices and frustrated every native

[1] Ibid., pp. 175–6.   [2] Ibid., p. 170.
[3] Ibid., p. 178. This theme is treated more extensively for the whole of Europe in Leopold Genicot, 'Crises: From the Middle Ages to Modern Times', in M. M. Postan (ed.), *The Cambridge Economic History of Europe*, 2nd rev. ed. (Cambridge, 1966) I 660–742, especially pp. 707–9 and pp. 739–41.
[4] Jerome Blum, 'The Rise of Serfdom in Eastern Europe', *American Historical Review*, LXII no. 4 (July 1957) 821.

attempt to break the pattern and move on to new frontiers of economic development.[1] Eastern Europe had become an agrarian hinterland, totally dependent on European markets and West European capital, with only the rural aristocracy profiting from the situation. In the Balkans the change was effected by the move from the *timar* system of land tenure to the *chiflik* system.[2] Under the former system absentee ownership was the rule and the powers of the landowner over the peasant were kept within definite legal limits. In the latter case, 'Rural adventurers, brigands, homeless vagabonds who belonged neither to town nor country, wage earners seeking to augment meager revenues from a stagnating trade or craft, and ambitious men of all social conditions made periodic forays into the country, seizing land and other properties, offering protection to the terrified peasantry in return for a stipulated portion of their crop.'[3] In Russia, grain was not an important item in her expanding foreign trade in the fifteenth and sixteenth centuries, but did play an important role in the continued expansion of her internal trade.[4] The results were the same in Russia as in the rest of Eastern Europe. The burdens of the serf increased as landlords tried to exact more from them and bind them more tightly to the soil.[5]

Although the imposition of serfdom may have seemed under prevailing circumstances to be the most expedient method for expanding production during a period of scarce labour and plentiful land, it made little sense in the eighteenth and nineteenth centuries when labour became abundant and land scarce. By shoring up the political power of the least progressive social class in Eastern Europe, the landed aristocracy, and by condemning the remainder of society to a demoralising and enervating round of rural drudgery, the state in Eastern Europe guaranteed the subsequent economic stagnation of the area.

Neither the emancipation nor the post-World War I agrarian

[1] Ibid., p. 828. See also C. H. Wilson, 'Trade, Society, and the State', in E. E. Rich and C. H. Wilson, *The Cambridge Economic History* (Cambridge. 1967) IV p. 554. Wilson speaks of 'potentiality frustrated by politics'. For an excellent over view of developments in Poland, see Marian Malowist, 'Le Commerce de la Baltique et le probleme des luttes sociales en Pologne aux XVe et XVIe siècles', in *La Pologne au Xe congrès international des sciences historiques à Rome* (Warsaw, 1955) pp. 125–66.

[2] L. S. Stavrianos, *The Balkans Since 1453* (New York, 1963) p. 138. Stoianovich calls the *chiflik* regime 'the second serfdom': Traian Stoianovich, *A Study in Balkan Civilization* (New York, 1967) pp. 161–2.

[3] Traian Stoianovich, 'Factors in the Decline of Ottoman Society in the Balkans', *Slavic Review*, XXI no. 4 (1962) 629.

[4] Jerome Blum, *Lord and Peasant in Russia from the Ninth to the Nineteenth Century* (New York, 1964) pp. 127–8.

[5] Ibid., p. 205.

reforms stimulated industrialisation or improved the techniques of cultivation. Emancipation, having been made by the landlords, rather than the peasants, not only did not solve the peasant problem, but may have made things worse. The famous Hungarian populist writer, Gyula Illyés, described the lot of the Hungarian peasants after emancipation as follows:

... Meanwhile even the peasants began to realize that freedom had dangerous side effects – free competition was sprung upon them. For decades it was they who had ploughed the estate lands, they who had reaped and they who had threshed in the huge threshing barns right up to Christmas in most places. Now steam plows began to turn the land. The peasant plots were divided into even smaller portions, and more and more of their children were forced to become landless or work in the pusztas. The number of estate laborers grew, and the more they grew the more the earth cracked and broke beneath them, like thin ice under the weight of a crowd. They tried to struggle, they tried to save each other, sometimes with heroic devotion and self-sacrifice, but all in vain. History again betrayed them, they sank inevitably to where they had been at the beginning of the eighteenth century. In the 1900's the total income of a family under all possible heads came to 200 forints. They recalled the good old days with sighs and did not realize that they had been but a brief glimpse of the sun.[1]

In Rumania, a Social Democratic theorist, C. Dobrogeanu-Gherea, christened the period after emancipation the era of 'neo-serfdom'. He pointed out that the combination of inadequate allocations of land, a burgeoning peasant population, and legislation that tied the peasant to the land created a new kind of bondage between peasant and landlord.[2] A recent communist treatment calls this kind of emancipation a second edition of serfdom, though it points out that it did not come in Serbia and Bulgaria, where the former landlords were foreigners who were expelled at the time of national liberation.[3] The post-World War I agrarian reforms did little to improve the situation, and often only increased the numbers of dwarf peasants.

[1] As quoted in Doreen Warriner (ed.), *Contrasts in Emerging Societies: Readings in the Social and Economic History of South-Eastern Europe in the Nineteenth Century* (Bloomington, 1965) pp. 106–7.
[2] Roberts, p. 276.
[3] Emil Niederhauser, 'Klassovaia bor'ba krest'ianstva v vostochnoi Evrope vo vtoroi polovine XIX – nachale XX v.', Acta Universitas Debreciensis, *Studia Historica*, no. 2 (1963) pp. 61–3.

There was, then, a built-in tendency for these countries to experience rural overpopulation and increasing rural poverty. The most obvious solution to the problem would have been industrialisation, which would have drained off the surplus population for industrial labour and thereby raised the per capita income and per capita product in agriculture correspondingly. Industrialisation would presumably benefit agriculture also in providing agricultural machinery for further raising per capita productivity and probably disseminating the spirit of rationalisation and efficiency that flourished in industry. But such industrialisation took place in Eastern Europe only in Bohemia, Russian Poland, and parts of Russia. The failure to industrialise cannot be explained wholly by the dead weight of the past, which included the prolonged survival of serfdom, the accompanying aristocratic mono-poly of political power and the absence of any internal sources of capital accumulation. The political and economic domination of East Europe by outsiders, the reigning kings and Western capitalists, also played a role. Russia and the Hapsburg monarchy were erratic in their use of state power to develop one area and stifle another, and, on the whole, the Ottoman Empire did nothing to encourage economic development. Western investment was rather meagre and rarely provided the quality or quantity of change needed to solve the problems of East European society. For most of Eastern Europe, then, foreign control accounted to a large extent for economic backwardness, except in Bohemia and Russian Poland, where it accounted for their industrial-isation. In the Balkan states Stoianovich blames both outsiders and the indigenous middle class for the slow progress to industrialisation, saying that the latter were timid in dealing with foreign investors and fearful that a dangerous industrial working class might arise if economic change came too quickly.[1]

The first path to modernisation, the liberal path of capitalist indust-rialisation was simply not available to East European countries. Once the lag between East and West had been established, it threatened to become permanent, for, as Rosenstein-Rodan and Alexander Gerschen-kron have pointed out, the latecomers cannot industrialise according to the same pattern as their West European predecessors, because, among other things, the cost of borrowing capital has soared and the capital available is less likely to be drawn to those areas, like Eastern Europe, that are most in need of it.[2] Liberation from foreign political

[1] Stoianovich, *A Study* . . . , p. 100.

[2] P. N. Rosenstein-Rodan, 'Problems of Industrialization of Eastern and South-Eastern Europe', *Economic Journal*, LIII (1943) p. 204. Gerschenkron explores some of the

control, emancipation from serfdom, and even the benefits of democratic institutions seemed to offer no escape from the dilemma. Despite the liberation of Rumania, Bulgaria, Serbia and Greece from foreign political control before World War I, they were no more successful than their neighbours in providing for their expanding rural population,

The second path, the Russian communist model of state controlled industrialisation and rural collectivisation, was not attractive to peasants with property, for it meant the surrender of that last symbol of independence and status, property, and probably the liquidation of the whole peasant way of life. The impossibility of the first path and the unattractiveness of the second path gave weight to populist arguments in favour of limited industrialisation and improvement, rather than the elimination, of peasant farming.[4] Peasant political parties were a direct response to this dilemma.

III. THE CLASSIFICATION OF PEASANT POLITICAL PARTIES IN EASTERN EUROPE

Peasant political parties were also a result of the medieval time lag, which kept most East European citizens within peasant society until democratic institutions were imposed from above, giving the peasant a political weight through the vote that he would not have enjoyed if democracy had come at a later stage of economic development. The decisive catalytic agents in bringing the peasant political movement to life were World War I and the Russian Revolution. They mark the beginning of the Green Revolution. World War I led, not only to the formation of a democratic political system in most of the countries of Eastern Europe, but also, through its apocalyptic character, to a questioning of all the old orthodoxies, making all changes seem possible.[1] Through conscription the war also tore the peasant from his daily routine, and gave him a vivid experience in the modernised non-peasant world, by which he could judge village life when he returned to it. The crises in food, price, deaths also made everyone less tolerant of old inequities.

---

implications of these factors on the pattern of development in underdeveloped countries in Alexander Gerschenkron, *Economic Backwardness in Historical Perspective: A Book o j Essays* (New York, 1965), Ch. 1.

[1] See, for example, Rudolf Herceg, *Die Ideologie der kroatischen Bauernbewegung* (Zagreb, 1923), p. 42, or A. Švehla, 'L'Homme et la terre', Mézinárodní Agrární Bureau, *Bulletin*, No. 1 (1923), p. 13.

The major peasant political parties in Eastern Europe arose in three waves, the first surge appearing in the late 1890s.

Group I – Founded before World War I
    The Bulgarian National Agrarian Union – 1899 (political party – 1901)
    Czech Agrarian Party – 1899
    Peasant Party of Greater Hungary – 1906
       (becomes Hungarian Smallholders' Party – 1909)
    Croatian Peasant Party – 1904
    Serbian Peasant Unity Party – 1903
       (becomes Serbian Peasant Union – 1919)
    Polish Peasant Party – 1895
       (becomes Polish Peasant Party 'Piast' – 1913)
    Russian Socialist Revolutionary Party – 1901

Group II – Founded during the Crisis of World War I
    Slovenian People's Party – 1920
    Rumanian Peasant Party – 1918
       (becomes the Rumanian National Peasant Party – 1926)
    Polish Peasant Party 'Wyzwolenie' – 1915
       (merges with 'Piast' to become Polish Peasant Party in 1931)
    Christian Slovak People's Party – 1918
    National Party of Slovakia – 1918
       (merges with Czech Agrarian Party to become the Czechoslovak Republican Peasant Party in 1919)

Group III – Founded during the Inter-War Period
    Independent Peasant Party of Poland – 1924
    Belorussian Workers' and Peasants' Hramada (Poland) – 1925
    Ukrainian Peasants' and Workers Socialist Union or 'Selrob' (Poland) – 1927
    Polish Peasant Party (split from Piast in 1926, merges with 'Piast' and 'Wyzwolenie' in 1931 to form Polish Peasant Party – 1931)
    Ploughmen's Front (Rumania) – 1933
    Hungarian Independent Smallholders' Party – 1930
    Hungarian National Peasant Party – 1944 (first formed 1939)
    Rumanian National Peasant Party – 1926

On the whole, the older parties in Group I proved to have greater staying power and were better able to build a distinct identity on the basis of their past traditions. The parties in Group II proved to be more unstable, perhaps because they were more eclectic in origin. They include the first two peasant parties to be organised according to the principles of Catholic social thought, which were also the first to be hospitable towards religion, and to include priests in their leadership. The third group consists of new parties and old parties that merged with other groups. The new parties were, on the whole, relatively small and ineffectual, and were created as alternatives to the older and more moderate peasant political parties. Among these new parties only the Independent Smallholders' Party represented a peasant political party of the traditional type. The Hungarian National Peasant Party remained a small intellectual movement, rather than a peasant political party until 1944. The three new Polish parties at the top of the list were communist 'front' organisations, with a strong peasant following from the hitherto unrepresented landless and dwarf peasantry. One of these, the Independent Peasant Party, would prove very useful to the communists in post-World War II Poland because it would serve, like the Ploughmen's Front in Rumania and the National Peasant Party in Hungary, as a foil to the older agrarian movements.

Even more important than timing in determining the character of peasant political movements was the nature of the economy in which they appeared. First of all, Eastern Europe after World War I, like many economically underdeveloped countries around the world after World War II, retained its rural character up to the point where democratic political institutions gave the country-dwellers an unprecedented opportunity to translate their force of numbers into political power.[1] And by even the narrowest definition most of the rural population in Eastern Europe during the inter-war period was peasants. Though there is a wide range of differences in status and outlook among the peasantry, peasants differ chiefly from farmers in that they have their own distinctive 'part culture' or sub-culture and regard agriculture as a way of life rather than a business. Other distinctive qualities setting the peasants apart from the farmer was that they live in areas where those who cultivate the soil was generally low in social and economic status, involved in a family household with close ties to their local community, relegated to a subordinate position in society with most of their produce appropriated by others, and living in a society where their social class predominated.[2] To this one might

[1] See Landsberger, pp. 31, 56.
[2] Ibid., pp. 13–14. I have taken Landsberger's narrower definition of the peasantry as a guide in order to demonstrate how perfectly and unambiguously Eastern Europe fits the model. On the term 'part culture' see Redfield p. 24.

add that peasants generally are self-sufficient. In all these respects most East Europeans were peasants and the populists were therefore right. Their circumstances were different from those in Western Europe, where industrialisation preceded the fullest development of democratic institutions and therefore the weight of social classes other than the peasantry could be felt in politics in elections under universal manhood suffrage. In Eastern Europe, by way of contrast, the peasantry dwarfed all other social classes in numbers and it seemed logical to identify the State and nation with the peasant class and to create parties to 'legitimise' the State by capturing it in the name of its peasants. This was the need and opportunity as perceived by the populists.

TABLE 1
PERCENTAGE OF TOTAL POPULATION
DEPENDENT ON AGRICULTURE – 1930[a]

Albania	80·0	Poland	62·8
Yugoslavia	76·5	Hungary	51·8
Bulgaria	73·2	Greece	46·0
Rumania	72·4	Czechoslovakia	34·5

[a] Jozo Tomasevich, *Peasants, Politics and Economic Change in Yugoslavia* (Stanford, 1955), p. 309. Figure for Greece from Wilbert E. Moore, *Economic Demography of Eastern and Southern Europe* (Geneva, 1945), p. 26 and is for the year 1928.

Opportunity is, of course, the operative word, for the creation of democratic institutions in peasant societies does not in itself guarantee the formation of strong peasant political parties. In Greece and Serbia peasant political parties never achieved much momentum.[1] The roots of 'peasantism' are nourished by a whole complex of economic and historical circumstances. In 1919 Eastern Europe exemplified the now familiar features of a peasant society in transition, that is, one suffering erosion from the intrusive forces of modernisation. Judging from the East European example, peasant political movements appear neither in stable and stagnant agrarian societies, nor in dynamic industrialised

[1] Sanders, in his study of the Greek peasantry, concludes that the Greek peasant was indifferent to politics because he felt that he had no influence. Irwin Sanders, *Rainbow in the Rock, The People of Rural Greece* (Cambridge, 1962) p. 240. Stoianovich argues that the peasant ideology never gained a strong foothold in Greece because the proportion of the peasantry in the total population was less than in the other countries and because the *mystique* of 'the people' was mixed up with the *mystique* of the Hellenic idea. Traian Stoianovich 'The Soviet Foundations of Balkan Politics, 1750–1941', in Charles and Barbara Jelavich, *The Balkans in Transition* (Berkeley, 1943), p. 334. Tomasevich attributes the weakness of the Serbian Peasant Union to internal factionalism, the competition of the Radical Party and the conditions created by the royal dictatorship after 1929. Jozo Tomasevich, *Peasants, Politics, and Economic Change in Yugoslavia* (Stanford, 1955) p. 252.

societies. Rather, they appear in 'peasant societies in transition', that is, peasant societies that are beginning to feel the corrosive effects of modernisation,[1] and when peasant political movements appear they are defensive and conservative movements, endeavouring to preserve the 'best' features of peasant society from being destroyed by the process of industrialisation.

The greatest single problem in 'peasant societies in transition' is rural overpopulation, or the presence on the land of more peasants than the land could support (see Table 2). When accompanied by backward agricultural techniques, rural overpopulation led Eastern Europe to very low farm incomes (see Table 3), and to an increase in the number of peasant households with inadequate land (see Table 4). It has been estimated that in 1943 the national income of the whole area was forty per cent that of Great Britain.[2] In 1939 annual per capita income in the Balkans, the most poverty-striken area in Eastern Europe, fluctuated between seventy-five dollars in Greece and 125 dollars in Bulgaria.[3] However too much emphasis should not be placed on a low cash income in a peasant economy because it represents only a portion of the peasants' real income, and is, therefore, not a very accurate measure of peasant welfare.

The results can be dramatised by a comparison with Western Europe. According to Doreen Warriner, who was referring to the inter-war period, '. . . roughly speaking, the farms of Western Europe are twice as large, carry twice as much capital to the acre, produce twice as much corn to the acre and employ only half as many people to the acre as the farms of Eastern Europe'.[4]

It is not enough, however, to define peasant problems for Eastern Europe as a whole, for, despite their common problems, the separate regions of Eastern Europe differ greatly from one another, and these differences were reflected in the character of each peasant political movement. One can experiment with various ways of categorising

---

[1] Landsberger puts it somewhat differently: 'Peasant movements are most likely to occur in societies where (i) objective economic changes in the place and structure of agriculture and/or (ii) objective political changes, such as war, have caused the traditional élites to lose ground vis-à-vis newer élites'. Landsberger, p. 31.

[2] P. N. Rosenstein-Rodan, *Economic Journal*, LIII (1943), 203.

[3] Stavrianos, p. 681. Such calculations are always suspect. Pepelasis gives a higher estimate of per capita income, between seventy-five and ninety dollars. A. Pepelasis, 'Greece', in A. Pepelasis, L. Mears and I. Adelman, *Economic Development: Analysis and Case Studies* (New York, 1961) p. 516, n. 30. Spulber estimates that in 1939 per capita income in the Balkans fluctuated between 100 and 130 dollars. Nicholas Spulber, *The State and Economic Development in Eastern Europe* (New York, 1966) p. 75.

[4] Warriner, *Economics of Peasant Farming*, p. 19.

TABLE 2

RURAL OVERPOPULATION

(around 1930)

Percentage of Population Considered Surplus

	Warriner[a]	Moore[b]
Bulgaria –	28·0	35·7
Czechoslovakia		11·7
Slovakia	49·5	
Ruthenia	86·0	
Greece	24·3	29·3
Hungary	18·0	2·9
Poland	24·0	29·4
Rumania	20·0	23·1
Yugoslavia	35·0	38·8

[a] Doreen Warriner, *Revolution in Eastern Europe* (London, 1950) p. 176.
[b] Moore, pp. 71–2.

TABLE 3

GROSS RETURNS AND FAMILY EARNINGS 1934–35[a]

(in gold francs per hectare)

	Gross Returns	Family Farm Earnings
Switzerland	1,061	177
Denmark	397	143
Germany	489	68
Hungary	194	48
Poland	123	52

[a] Doreen Warriner, *Economics of Peasant Farming* (New York, 1939 p. 80. These figures are a sampling, rather than reliable income figures, because they are drawn from farm accountancy figures published by the Institute of Agriculture at Rome that are based on a small number of farms in each country. Also the figures only have value for purposes of comparison, since the unit of currency is not easily convertible into meaningful modern, and familiar units.

the countries of Eastern Europe, but it remains true, as Burks points out, that the area is generally more highly developed in the north-western corner, and it becomes more and more backward as one moves to the south and east.[1] In Russia modernisation was more diffused.

[1] R. V. Burks, *The Dynamics of Communism in Eastern Europe* (Princeton, 1961) pp. 71–2.

TABLE 4

SOME EFFECTS OF THE LAND REFORM IN EASTERN EUROPE

	Percentage of all holdings that are five ha. or below in size		Average size of plot around 1930[a]	Agricultural wage labour[b] around 1930 (as percentage of total pop. dep. on agr.)
	Before Reform	After Reform		
Bulgaria	50·8[c]	62·1[c]	·4	1·06
Czechoslovakia	21·1[d]	22·9[d]	·3	14·6
Hungary			1·4	29·09[g]
Poland				14·8
Rumania	71·0[e]	75·0[e]	·9	16·7
Yugoslavia				1·4
Serbia	52·8[f]	62·1[f]		
Croatia	71·5[f]	74·4[f]		

[a] Folke Dovring, *Land and Labor in Europe in the Twentieth Century*, 3rd rev. ed. (The Hague, 1965) p. 40.
[b] Moore, pp. 226–52.
[c] Janaki Mollof, *Die sozialoekonomische Struktur der bulgarischen Landwirtschaft* (Berlin, 1936) p. 90. The figures are for 1908 and 1934.
[d] Vladislav Brdlík, 'Czechoslovakia', in O. S. Morgan (ed.), *Agricultural Systems of Middle Europe* (New York, 1933) p. 101.
[e] Henry Roberts, *Rumania, Political Problems of an Agrarian State* (New Haven, 1951) pp. 363, 370. The first figure is for the Old Kingdom only in 1913. The second figure is for 1930.
[f] Tomasevich, p. 389. The figures are for 1897 and 1931 for Serbia and for 1895 and 1931 for Croatia.
[g] Gyula Varga, 'Changes in the Social and Economic Status of Hungary's Peasantry', *New Hungarian Quarterly*, VI no. 26 (1965) pp. 28–9.

The area around St Petersburg was the most advanced technologically, the north central industrial region was already a significant industrial area, and the newer Donets Basin to the south was more important before 1914. But the peasant political movement in Russia had its base in Saratov Province, a relatively underdeveloped district that had remarkably low yields for the black earth region.[2]

In Eastern Europe there is a rough negative correlation between the degree of modernisation, as measured by per capita product in industry, and indices of backwardness and rural stagnation, like per capita product in agriculture, rate of literacy, and the proportion of population engaged in agricultural production (see Table 5). There does not seem,

[2] Oliver H. Radkey, *The Agrarian Foes of Bolshevism* (New York, 1958) pp. 53–4.

however, to be any strong correlation between these factors and the proportion of the population who are dwarf holders or landless labourers (see Table 4 above).

TABLE 5

CORRELATIONS BETWEEN INDICES OF ECONOMIC BACKWARDNESS[a]

(1930s)

Per capita product in industry – largest to smallest[b] 1938	Per capita product in agric. – largest to smallest	Rate of literacy – highest to lowest	Proportion of pop. in agric. – lowest to highest
Czechoslovakia	Czechoslovakia	Czechoslovakia	Czechoslovakia
Poland	Hungary	Hungary	Hungary
Hungary	Poland	Poland	Poland
Rumania	Rumania	Rumania	Bulgaria
Bulgaria	Bulgaria	Bulgaria	Rumania
	Yugoslavia	Yugoslavia	Yugoslavia

[a] Dudley Kirk, *Europe's Population in the Interwar Years* (Geneva, 1946) pp. 263–76.
[b] Nicholas Spulber, *The Economics of Communist Eastern Europe* (New York, 1957) p. 17.

It is striking that the most radical peasant political movements should occur in Bulgaria, Serbia and Croatia, three of the most economically backward areas in Eastern Europe, and that in Poland the more radical of the two major peasant political parties took shape in the economically more backward eastern provinces, while the Polish Peasant Party 'Piast' drew its support from the rest of Poland. But this is consistent with Landsberger's thesis that 'radicalization of goals will take place when originally narrow and shallow goals are frustrated'.[1]

However, it would be too hasty to conclude that there is always some direct correlation between the degree of economic and political frustration and the degree of radicalism in the peasant political parties. For example, two of the most moderate peasant political parties, the Polish Peasant Party 'Piast' and the Rumanian National Peasant Party, originated in those parts of their country where rural overpopulation and political frustration were both intense. In these two cases the political environment was probably more influential than the other factors. Moderate peasant political parties, such as the Czech, the Polish Peasant Party 'Piast', the Rumanian National Party (that later united with the Rumanian Peasant Party to form the Rumanian

[3] Landsberger, p. 51.

National Peasant Party), and the Hungarian Smallholders' Party owe their character, at least in part, to the experience of parliamentary activity. Where the revolutionary political tradition was closer to the surface, as in Russia, and in Yugoslavia and in Bulgaria, the peasant political parties tended to follow suit. This is consistent with another Landsberger hypothesis that 'changes in the degree of radicalization of goals will occur in accordance with general changes in social ideology. If radicalization is occuring in social sectors of relevance to the peasant movement e.g., the intellectual sector', then the goals of peasant movements may be expected to follow suit and vice versa'.[1]

Two other factors shape peasant political movements in Eastern Europe and sometimes even dominated them to the exclusion of other considerations. The first, the national question, often took precedence over economic programmes in peasant political movements, as for example, in the case of the Croatian Peasant Party. Some of the peasant political parties in Group III formed with communist help during the inter-war years among smaller national minorities, like the Belorussian Hramada and the Ukrainian Selrob in Poland, tended to be more concerned with the national question than with social and economic reform. Some peasant political movements had no agrarian reform programme to speak of, despite the fact that they drew their support almost exclusively from peasants, like the Slovak People's Party, the Internal Macedonian Revolutionary Organisation in Bulgaria (I.M.R.O.) and the League of Archangel Michael (better known in the West as the Iron Guard) in Rumania.

Religion was also a contributing factor. In particular, those movements where the influence of the Church was strong, like the Slovak People's Party and the Slovene People's Party, tended to be rather moderate on questions of social reform.

Finally, there is the role of status consciousness in stimulating the development of peasant political movements. Although a low income and inadequate land undoubtedly made the peasant conscious of his low status, cultural traditions also seem to be of crucial importance. Status is, after all, a state of mind, though it may be reinforced by physical circumstances. The traditions that seemed to assign the peasant a low status in society were probably strongest in those countries where a native aristocratic tradition persisted into the twentieth century, as in Poland, Hungary, Croatia and Russia. For example, the Polish sociologist, Iwanska, comments:

[1] Ibid.

All social classes in Poland looked down upon the peasants and inter-war Polish peasants had very little of their own class elite which could assist their self-respect, which could call attention to and clarify their own values, and which could help them to fight for better economic, social, cultural, and political opportunities for the village.[1]

There is, however, some doubt whether the peasants were always aware of the low status assigned to them by outsiders. Few of the anthropological or sociological studies of the area reveal much evidence of a sense of inferiority on the part of peasants living wholly within the village, though it was keenly felt by some of those who had already risen from the ranks of the peasantry.[2] In Poland schooling taught the peasant to be ashamed of his profession. As one young Polish peasant put it:

> I started thinking [in school] that one can't possibly be happy in the village. The village now was a dark cave for me from which there was no way out. School did not know how to awaken in me the love for my native village as it knew how to awaken patriotism in my soul. But I lost completely a love for working the land, and even more, I thought now that it was a very contemptible sort of work.[3]

In Serbia and Bulgaria, perhaps because of the absence of a native aristocracy and a relatively egalitarian society, the peasant does not seem to have felt inferior even after schooling. Tomasic, for example, writes about Serbia, '*zadruga* ploughmen feel neither superior nor inferior to others, but respect the right of each group to its own way of life'.[4] Halpern in his study of the Serbian village of Orasac cites peasant biographies that indicate that school was seen as a path to other careers, but that there was no great sense of inferiority on the part of those who remained in the village.[5] Similarly, Irwin Sanders, in his study of the Bulgarian village of Dragálevtsy, found that school was the crucial factor in changing people's áttitude towards farming as an occupation by making alternative occupations seem attractive and

[1] Alicja Iwanska (ed.), *Contemporary Poland: Society, Politics, Economy*, Human Relations Area Files, Subcontractor's Monograph No. 22 (Chicago, 1955) p. 127.
[2] Ibid., p. 129.
[3] Ibid., pp. 127–8.
[4] Dinka A. Tomasic, *Personality and Culture in Eastern European Politics* (New York, 1948) p. 183.
[5] Joel Martin Halpern, *A Serbian Village* (New York, 1958) pp. 257–9.

attainable.[1] But he observed that those who stayed behind seemed to take pride in their status:

> ... I had learned the importance of trying to view the world through the eyes of others before I passed judgement upon them. I knew that merely being different did not mean being inferior, and that physical appearance and material possessions were not the more important indices of contentment and security. I also knew that in the Balkans, the term peasant carried a connotation much more dignified than that usually ascribed to it. Bulgarian farmers were neither serfs nor dispossessed day laborers, but for the most part were proprietors of their land and home, and were respected by their families and associates.[2]

Despite these views there are some grounds for doubting the solidity of peasant pride especially in some of the northern countries of Eastern Europe, like Poland and Hungary, where many peasants had no land and a landed aristocracy persisted to perpetuate the tone of the old status system. Though no field study of Eastern Europe published in the West has clearly focused on the peasant's perception of his own status, there is some evidence that peasant ideology was most attractive to those who had given up any hope of rising beyond the peasant class, and, therefore, that it was an expression of futility rather than pride. In Poland, for example, the peasant whose social mobility was cut off was defensive in his effort to idealise the 'old ways' of the peasantry, to stress the spiritual superiority of the village over the town, and to forget useless acquired skills, like book learning and sometimes even the ability to read.[3]

It is even more difficult to link up peasant status seekings with peasant political action, for there is no clear correlation. Irwin Sanders, in his studies of Greek and Bulgarian peasants, both of whom live in similar economic and social circumstances and are inclined to seek reforms through personal influence or family relations, rather than political actions, found the Greek peasant indifferent to politics and the Bulgarian wedded to the Agrarian Party[4]. Similarly, the Polish and Hungarian peasants suffered very similar social humiliations, but only

[1] Irwin T. Sanders, *Balkan Village* (Lexington, Kentucky, 1949) p. 72. In Bulgaria Sanders demonstrated the attitude of the village schoolteachers towards village life by citing their behaviour on week-ends. The teachers all left the village as soon as possible for the comforts of the city of Sofia. Ibid., p. 12.

[2] Ibid., p. 274.

[3] Iwanska, p. 129.

[4] Sanders, *Balkan Village*, p. 217, and Sanders, *Rainbow in the Rock*, p. 240.

the Polish peasants mobilised behind a strong peasant political movement.

It is probably impossible to ascertain whether the ideological image
of the peasant embodied in the peasant political movement is a reflection of the peasant's self-confidence and assurance or an attempt to
recover a sense of dignity and pride that has been lost. It may have
served both functions, depending on the status of the peasant audience
to whom it was addressed.

And so, we return to the point from which we started. The peasant
saw the solution to all his problems of survival and status in land reform,
despite the fact that there was not enough land anywhere to satisfy
the needs of the growing rural population. But the 'land hunger' of
the East European peasant was a political myth that prospective peasant
political leaders could use to garner peasant support at the polls, while
at the same time, if they wished, educating the peasant to alternative
solutions. So land reform was the corner-stone of every peasant
political programme before 1917.

IV. THE THEORY AND PRACTICE OF PEASANT
POLITICAL MOVEMENTS

There were two major trends in the early peasant political movements.
The first trend was evident in the three movements created before
1900, the Bohemian (Czech – 1899), Galician (Polish – 1895), and the
Bulgarian (1899), which may all be regarded as optimistic reform
movements. They all appear in countries where an expanded franchise
offered the hope of improvement through legal channels. In this
respect they differed sharply from the second, or revolutionary trend,
best represented by the Russian Socialist Revolutionary Party formed
in Saratov Province in 1901.[1]

I would like to begin, however, with the second, or Russian, model
and then turn to its East European counterparts. The East European
peasant political parties will be treated in the order of their 'purity',
that is, those remaining closest to the original tenets of East European
populism will be treated first. Despite the differences between the
Russian movement and its East European counterparts, Russia is the
logical place to begin in any analysis of East European peasant political

[1] In this respect only Russia exemplifies Landberger's thesis number 3, where violence
becomes the major instrument in politics. Landsberger, p. 48.

movements, for the Russian *narodniki*, or populists, were clearly the most important model for all the others. The history of the Russian movements go back further than any others and their dramatic successes inspired imitation everywhere. The description of the Russian movement provided by Oliver Radkey could serve as an apt description of any of the other East European peasant political movements:

> . . . it must be admitted that the [Russian] Populists never succeeded in working out a doctrine as precise or watertight as that of their rivals. But Populism was less an ideology than a state of mind which brought men together in the absence of concrete formulas and held them together despite divergencies over program and tactics. The state of mind was induced by a desire to make a revolution quickly in an agrarian country where the regime of private property did not rest upon a broad foundation, and where the existence of pre-capitalist forms afforded hope that the individualist order of the West could be circumvented in favour of an early approach to the collectivist society of the future.[1]

These are the chief characteristics of the creed that took shape in Russia during the nineteenth century, nourished by the writings of German romantic philosophers and French socialists.[2] The populist movements in Eastern Europe would also lack any well-defined theory, and even regard the unsystematic and inconsistent quality of their ideology as proof of its 'organic' quality, its authenticity as a direct reflection of the deepest instincts and needs of the peasants.[3] The East European populists would also, like the Russian, seek to preserve the peasant community against the threat of urban individualism, though such old collective peasant communities as the *zadruga* were disappearing in Eastern Europe just as fast as the village commune in Russia.[4]

---

[1] Radkey, *The Agrarian Foes of Bolshevism*, p. 3.

[2] Billington contends that Russian populism owes more to the French romanticism of Rousseau than to German romanticism. James H. Billington, *Mikhailovsky and Russian Populism* (London, 1958) p. 87. The most comprehensive study of Russian populism in the nineteenth century is Franco Venturi, *Roots of Revolution: A History o the Populist and Socialist Movements in Nineteenth Century Russia* (New York, 1966). For a brief, but useful overview, see Soloman M. Schwarz, 'Populism and Early Russian Marxism on Ways of Economic Development of Russia', in Ernest J. Simmons (ed.) , *Continuity and Change in Russian and Soviet Thought* (Cambridge, 1955).

[3] See, for example, Petre P. Suciu, 'La Scission dans le Parti National Paysan Roumain' Mezinárodní Agrární Bureau Bulletin No. 2 (1927), 71.

[4] On the decline of the *zadruga* see Philip E. Mosely, 'The Peasant Family: The Zadruga or Communal Joint Family in the Balkans and its Recent Evolution', in Caroline F. Ware (ed.), *The Cultural Approach to History* (New York, 1940) pp. 95–108.

In Russian populism, like the East European populism that followed it, the people, and especially the peasants, were regarded as the ultimate source of virtue because they had preserved their simplicity and humanity in a communal organisation instead of suffering the atomisation and alienation that afflicted the individualistic urban dwellers. The virtues of the peasant were said to be his self-sufficiency, his diligence, his sense of loyalty to his community, his strong instinct for justice. The peasant's primary loyalties were to a collective community as opposed to the rampant individualism of the city – the peasant was instinctively peaceful as opposed to the competitive and aggressive city dweller – the peasant was a natural democrat, as opposed to the oligarchical power-seekers in the city.[1] The peasant political movement was stimulated by a wide variety of Russian writers, including the famous novelist, Leo Tolstoy, demonstrating once again the critical importance of the intelligentsia and the whole intellectual climate in bringing about a populist movement.[2]

Regeneration of the country would be achieved by unleashing peasant virtues, or at least by providing the proper institutional soil for those virtues to reach full flower and shed beauty upon the whole of society. In the Socialist Revolutionary Party that goal would be reached, according to its programme, by a redistribution of land. In the populist party formed at the turn of the century, Victor Chernov refurbished populist ideology with a Marxist vocabulary and orientation and abandoned much of the old romantic adulation of the village commune and the peasant way of life. But it was still the peasantry who were the chosen people of history, destined to lead humanity to a promised land of bliss. All cultivable land would become as free as air when the revolution came. It would be available to whomsoever needed it and could cultivate it with his own hands and the labour power of his family.[3] It was the pious hope of Socialist Revolutionaries that the peasants would come to realise the inherent advantages of a collective form of ownership and drift in that direction.

[1] Billington points out that the Russian populist movement, like its successors in Eastern Europe, became more critical of the notion of peasant virtue. Billington, p. 95.

[2] See Donald Fanger, 'The Peasant in Literature', in Wayne S. Vucinich, *The Peasant in Nineteenth Century Russia* (Stanford, 1968) pp. 231–62.

[3] For a complete English translation of the programme of the Socialist Revolutionary Party see Basil Dmytryshyn (ed.), *Imperial Russia: A Source Book, 1700–1917* (New York, 1967) pp. 331–7. For an analysis of that programme see Radkey, *The Agrarian Foes of Bolshevism*, ch. 2. Radkey's venomous hostility to the populists often warps his judgement, however, and for a corrective see M. V. Vishnyak, 'The Role of the Socialist Revolutionaries in 1917', *Studies on the Soviet Union*, III no. 3 (1964) 172–82.

The Russian populists predicted that this apocalyptic change would come about as a result, not of class warfare, that is, of war between the three Marxist categories of society, the industrial workers, the middle class and the aristocracy, but of war between toilers and their oppressors. The word 'toilers' embraced more people than either the words 'peasantry' or 'proletariat', since it included anyone who worked for wages. The populists wanted to see Russia industrialise, but slowly and without endangering the peasant society or the values it bred. It would be possible, they said, for Russia to strike out on a new path precisely because she was economically backward and her people but never developed a strong sense of property values or of class-consciousness.

The Russian neo-populists were hostile towards forced collectivisation, despite their own preference for this form of tenure, and they favoured a highly decentralised governmental structure and all of the standard democratic rights of man. Like their successors in Eastern Europe, the Russian Socialist Revolutionaries sought the widest possible use of the techniques of direct democracy, initiative, referendum and recall.

The last item in the legacy that the Socialist Revolutionaries bequeathed to their East European counterparts was the lesson provided by the October Revolution itself. That lesson was both positive and negative. Positive in that the Socialist Revolutionaries gave a dramatic demonstration of the power of populist sentiment among the Russian peasantry. Negative in that it showed the fatal dangers of factionalism and collaboration with the Bolsheviks. In the course of the revolution the Socialist Revolutionaries split and part of their left wing allied itself to the Bolsheviks and later acquired token representation in the Soviet Government. The split helped their more ruthless and efficient ally to wrest power from them despite their obviously greater popularity. In the only free elections in the history of Russia, the Socialist Revolutionaries garnered 53 per cent of the popular vote, but by then popular votes no longer counted.[1]

Nineteenth-century Russian populist writers and twentieth-century Russian populist experience undoubtedly influenced all other peasant political movements in Eastern Europe: some, like the Polish, Bulgarian, Russian, Croatian, Serbian and Rumanian, more than others. The successes of the Russian Constituent Assembly in 1917 encouraged

---

[1] Oliver Radkey, *The Sickle Under the Hammer: The Russian Socialist Revolutionaries in the Early Months of Soviet Rule* (New York, 1963) p. 281.

imitation elsewhere. The failure to meet the Bolshevik challenge was duly noted and inspired wariness, if not hostility, on the part of East European peasant politicians towards their own communist parties. Moreover, the Red danger was widely used as a reason for other political parties to support agrarian parties, which were portrayed as the strongest barriers to Bolshevik penetration. The Russian emphasis on terror as a political weapon, however, was jettisoned. After 1919 the presence of genuine parliamentary systems in every East European country except Hungary and Russia seemed to open new vistas to peasant politicians that had not been visible to the Socialist Revolutionaries[1] (see Table 6).

TABLE 6
POST-WAR ELECTORAL VICTORIES OF PEASANT POLITICAL PARTIES

Deputies	1919 Bulgaria	1920 Czechoslovakia	1920 Hungary	1922 Poland	1919 Rumania	1920 Yugoslavia
Peasant	85	42	90	70	130	50 & 39
Communist	47	—	—	2	—	
All deputies	236	300	164	444	568	419
% pop. vote	31%	18·6%	40%	13·1%		14·4% plus 9·4%

The Russian influence was directly evident in the development of the ideology of at least five of the other East European political parties, although, of course, each adapted its programme to local circumstances and borrowed from other non-Western philosophical sources. According to his own testimony, Ante Radić, the man who formulated the ideology of the Croatian Peasant Party, was a devoted student of Russian literature and especially Russian populist writers like Lavrov. 'As he became increasingly acquainted with the thinking of the Russian *Narodniki*, Radić came to share many of their values and to identify the peasantry as the "people" par excellence (an essential belief of the Russian Slavophils and *narodniki*) and to see in them the only stable element in society'.[2] The founder of the Polish Peasant Party in Galicia, Bolesław Wysłouch, while studying at the Institute

[1] Although there was an elected representative assembly in Tsarist Russia after the 1905 revolution, the Duma, a method of weighting votes by social classes kept down the number of Socialist Revolutionary deputies. See Alfred Levin, 'The Russian Voter in the Elections to the Third Duma', *Slavic Review*, XXI no. 4 (Dec 1962), 661-7.
[2] Robert G. Livingston, 'Stjepan Radić and the Croatian Peasant Party 1904-1929' (unpublished Ph.D. dissertation, Department of History, Harvard University, 1959), p. 59.

of Technology in St Petersburg in 1875, was drawn into the Russian populist movement, learning lessons he would later apply in his own country.[1] One of the founders of the Rumanian populist movement, Constantin Stere, had also taken part in the Russian populist movement, and had been banished for a time to Siberia because of that involvement.[2] One can only infer a connection between the Russian movement and the Bulgarian Agrarian Union and the Serbian Union of Peasants. The Serbian was clearly patterned on the Bulgarian,[3] and the Bulgarian owed its character in 1920 to its leader, Alexander Stamboliiski. Although Stamboliiski, who studied at universities in Halle and Munich between 1900 and 1902, paid special tribute to German influences,[4] his programme bears a marked resemblance to Chernov's in its definition of social classes, his desire to keep capitalism and class warfare out of the village and his faith in the efficacy of land distribution and the techniques of direct democracy.[5] It is not surprising, therefore, that his programme won the attention of at least one prominent member of the Russian Socialist Revolutionary Party, who went to Bulgaria to study the compulsory labour system there, and devote a book to Stamboliiski.[6]

All of the East European peasant parties after World War I, including the Bulgarian party, found themselves on somewhat different terrain from that occupied by the Russians before World War I. All of the East European states after World War I, except Hungary, had at least for a short time functioning democratic institutions and major redistributions of land. All of the peasant political parties garnered much popularity at the polls for their role in bringing about land reform. But the reforms did not usher in the millennium and the populist parties had to re-examine the premisses implicit in their ideology. Eastern European land redistribution lost its place as the centrepiece in the party programme. In Bulgaria and Croatia it was

[1] Peter Brock, 'Bolesław Wysłouch, Founder of the Polish Peasant Party', *Slavonic and East European Review*, xxx, no. 74 (Dec 1951), 140, and Peter Brock, 'The Early Years of the Polish Peasant Party', *Journal of Central European Affairs*, xiv no. 4 (Oct 1954) 219.

[2] Roberts, pp. 144–53.

[3] See the praise heaped upon the Bulgarian Agrarian Union in Kosta Krajšumović, 'Les buts et les succès du Savez Zemljoradnika', in Mezinárodní Agrární Bureau *Bulletin*, no. 3 (1926) 58–62.

[4] Petko Petkov (ed.), *Aleksandr Stamboliiski, lichnost' i idei* (Sofia, 1930) p. 140.

[5] A critical but frequently sympathetic account of Bulgaria under Stamboliiski by the French correspondent of *Le Temps*, who was living in Bulgaria during these years, gives a great deal of credit to the Bolshevik example. Paul Gentizon, *Le Drame bulgare* (Paris, 1924) pp. 78, 86, 94, 99.

[6] V. I. Lebedev, *Novym putem*(Prague, 1923).

gradually supplanted by the myth of the peasant State. In Rumania, Czechoslovakia and Poland to a large extent the parties lost their peasant character and became indistinguishable from the other bourgeois parties. Hungary belongs in a class by itself.

The Bulgarian Agrarian Union was the strongest and most successful of the peasant political parties in Eastern Europe in the period immediately after World War I, and in this way, as in so many others, the party's leader, Alexander Stamboliiski, put his mark on the whole post-war agrarian movement. It was the only peasant political party during the inter-war period, other than the Rumanian National Peasant Party, to form a one-party government in its own country. In Bulgaria this took place in 1919, and by 1922 the Bulgarian Agrarian Union had 120,000 members and threatened to establish a peasant dictatorship in Bulgaria.[1] Success did not temper Stamboliiski's radicalism.

It is difficult to account for the startling success of the Bulgarian Agrarian Union after World War I, though Stamboliiski's role as the most outspoken opponent of an unpopular war undoubtedly had something to do with it. Also, as Landsberger suggests, the experience of war did much to awaken those peasants who participated or were affected, and mobilised their hostility to the State.[2] Another factor may have been the unusually high rate of literacy in Bulgaria (for the Balkans). The Bulgarian Agrarian Union, like the Czech Agrarian Party, may have owed its success in part to the fact that it started primarily as a social, educational and economic self-help organisation in an intimate relationship with the Bulgarian co-operative system, and only later in 1901, capitalising on that organisational framework and experience, became a political party.[3] Finally, it is quite apparent that much of the direction of the Bulgarian agrarian movement, including its similarity to the Russian movement, probably came from the influence of other Bulgarian parties, especially the Bulgarian Social Democratic Party, which had very close ties to its Russian counterpart. In 1919 the Bulgarians were unique, not only in having one of the strongest agrarian parties in Eastern Europe, but also one of the strongest Social Democratic movements, the latter antedating the former by more than a decade.[4] Socialism of the Russian stamp was

[1] J. Swire, *Bulgarian Conspiracy* (London, 1939) p. 156.
[2] Landsberger, p. 31.
[3] I. N. Chastukhin, 'Krest'ianskoe dvizhenie v Bolgarii i vozniknovenie Bulgarskogo Zemledelcheskogo Narodnogo Soiuza', *Voprosy istorii*, no. 9 (Sep 1956) p. 95.
[4] Rothschild, pp. 2–20. The actual formation of political parties was much closer in time. The Bulgarian Social Democratic Party was formed in 1894, the Bulgarian Agrarian Union in 1899.

already one of the major intellectual currents in Bulgarian political life when the Bulgarian Agrarian Union appeared on the scene, and the peasant party reflects that influence in its programme.

Unlike the Russian Socialist Revolutionaries, Stamboliiski had profound hostility towards urban life and urban people:

> The village and the town are inhabited by two peoples, different in their appearances and needs. They differ from one another, not only in concentration of numbers, and in their standard of living, but also in the character of the ideas and interests that animate them. The town and the village are centres of two different world views, two different cultures . . . In the villages live a people who work, fight, and earn their living at the caprice of nature. In the towns live a people who earn their living not by exploiting nature, but by exploiting the labour of others. That is a rule to which there is no exception. These two basic principles are the primary cause of the unique and different interests, ideas, and world views that move society in these two areas. The way of life in the village is uniform, its members hold the same ideas in common. That accounts for the superiority of the village over the city. The city people live by deceit, by idleness, by parasitism, by perversion.[1]

He also drew a sharp distinction between traditional political parties and the Bulgarian Agrarian Union. The latter, he said, represented a *suslovie*, rather than a social class.[2] The word *suslovie*, like its Russian equivalent *soslovie*, means an estate in the medieval sense of the word, or a corporate group united in a common profession. In his major theoretical work, *Political Parties or Suslovie Organizations*, Stamboliiski contended, in what has been called 'biological materialism', that men gravitate towards professions that satisfy their deepest instincts and with which they can personally identify. Thus, the basic social groups in society are not the three Marxist social classes, bourgeois, aristocrat and proletariat, but rather such occupational categories as peasant, artisan, industrial worker, bureaucrat, trader, etc.[3] By way of contrast Marxists did not regard the peasantry as a single social group animated by any common interests. They divided rural society in the same tripartite fashion as urban society, a division that would, they said, gradually disappear as class warfare in the village progressed and the rural proletariat overwhelmed the rural aristocracy and the rural

[1] Petkov, p. 226.   [2] Ibid., p. 182.   [3] Ibid., p. 253.

bourgeoisie.[1] Liberals recognised the peasantry as a coherent social group, but called for their elimination in the name of progress. But Stamboliiski saw the peasantry as a corporate group whose common interests must be vigorously defended by the Bulgarian Agrarian Union against all other occupational groups, a view which apparently did reflect the surprising degree of class consciousness or self-identification that existed among the Bulgarian peasants.[2] Therefore, in order to enter the Bulgarian Agrarian Union one had to prove either one's peasant origin or one's vital interest in the welfare of the village.[3] Unlike the Russian Socialist Revolutionaries, Stamboliiski regarded private property and democratic institutions as a basic instrument for the development of the individual and society, though he encouraged the development of co-operatives to satisfy the credit and marketing needs of the peasants.[4]

From October 1919 to June 1923, Stamboliiski was Prime Minister and virtual dictator of Bulgaria and had his chance to demonstrate his 'third path' towards the modern world. Apparently he retained the support of the small peasants throughout. In 1921 about 65 per cent of the peasants in Bulgaria had less than five hectares of land, but three-quarters of the members of the Bulgarian Agrarian Union had less than five hectares of land.[5] As Premier, Stamboliiski tried to strengthen the peasant economy by improving technical education, developing the co-operative system, and land redistribution. His object was to make Bulgaria a land of prosperous middle peasants,[6] but there was not enough land to bring the peasant holdings up to the desired minimum of five hectares.[7] Through the co-operative system, most of which was originally created by the Bulgarian Union, the Stamboliiski Government did improve the quality of seeds and agricultural implements, and reduce the cost of marketing.[8] One of his most controversial pieces of legislation was the Compulsory Labour Law, which called for all citizens of both sexes between the ages of twenty

[1] Mitrany, p. 44. For a Marxist critique of Stamboliiski's theories see I. N. Chastukhin, 'Ideologicheskie i politicheskie vzgliady Aleksandra Stamboliiskogo', *Novaia i noveishaia istoriia*, no. 6 (1959) pp. 37–53.

[2] Sanders, *Balkan Village*, pp. 179–81. Sanders not only points out a surprising sense of solidarity among the peasants of Dragalevtsy, but also unanimous enthusiasm for the Bulgarian Agrarian Union, ibid., p. 150.

[3] Petkov, p. 182.

[4] Ibid., pp. 184–7, 189–90.

[5] [Gavril Genov] G. Tsonev and A. Vladimirov, *Sentiabr'skoe vosstanie v Bolgarii 1923 goda* (Moscow, 1934) p. 49.

[6] Petkov, pp. 187–8.

[7] Warriner, *Economics of Peasant Farming*, p. 72.

[8] Leon Pasvolsky, *Bulgaria's Economic Position* (Washington, 1930) p. 237.

and forty to be conscripted for eighteen months' service in manual labour in public works.[1] Stamboliiski believed that some exposure to manual labour would be beneficial for all Bulgarian citizens. The period of compulsory education was extended from four to seven years and a progressive income tax was introduced.

In keeping with his view of lawyers as social parasites, he passed a law limiting their use in courts and created special rural courts where peasants might plead their own cases.[2] He also forbade lawyers from practising their professions while serving in public office.[3] This law also provided a convenient excuse for replacing many public officials with trusted members of his own party. In Bulgaria there was a tendency on the part of the lower classes to aspire for status as an intellectual or professional person rather than as a worker or business-man, resulting in a supply of intellectuals beyond the country's needs.[4] Stamboliiski diminished the oversupply of intellectuals by curtailing instruction at Sofia University, and, at one point, even closing it down for six months, while at the same time building 1000 new primary schools in the villages.[5]

Stamboliiski was in many ways the victim of his own success. He mistook mass support for genuine political power, a common mistake among the leaders of the peasant political movement, and in the spring of 1923 Stamboliiski threatened to rewrite the Bulgarian constitution in order to create a peasant republic (or dictatorship).[6] The annual congress of the Bulgarian Agrarian Union had in fact already become the real legislature of the country, reviewing the activities of the Government during the preceding year and voicing its approval or disapproval.[7] By October 1923 Stamboliiski had antagonised every powerful urban pressure group in Bulgaria, the leaders of all the other political parties, some of the more moderate leaders of his own party, the savage leaders of the Macedonian national minority movement (I.M.R.O. or the Internal Macedonian Revolu-tionary Organisation), the entrenched bureaucracy, the officers of the army, and even his most promising potential ally, the strong Bulgarian Communist Party. He was overthrown by a *coup d'état* and replaced by a dictator. The Stamboliiski tradition would be perpetuated in the left wing of the Bulgarian Agrarian Union (the Pladne group), which

[1] Max Lazard, 'Compulsory Labour Service in Bulgaria', Series B, No. 12, *Studies and Reports* (Geneva, 1922) pp. 105–26 and Gentizon, pp. 94–7.
[2] Gentizon, p. 27.   [3] Ibid., p. 78, Rothschild, p. 88.
[4] Rothschild, p. 8.   [5] Ibid., p. 89.
[6] Swire, p. 186.   [7] Gentizon, p. 107.

lingered on until World War II, probably with the same mass support as before, but never recovering even a fraction of the political power it had enjoyed under Stamboliiski. The Bulgarian communists would overshadow the Agrarian Union in the resistance movement and in the post-war coalition Government.

The myth of a peasant republic also played a large role in the history of the Croatian Peasant Party. The plight of the Croatian peasants was similar to that of the Bulgarian, except that the Croats ended up after World War I as a national minority in a multi-national Yugoslavia. Like the Bulgarian party, the Croatian recruited its leaders from the peasantry or from intellectuals born among the peasantry. The Radić brothers, Ante and Stjepan, were born in a large and poor peasant family in the swampy Posavina district. The family was raised on a diet of corn meal mush, dried beans and noodles and Stjepan attributed his short stature and myopia to a poor childhood diet.[1] Both brothers became intellectuals and revolutionaries. Ante Radić, the father of Croatian peasant ideology, stressed the gap between the city and the country, also, like Stamboliiski, referring to them as two different cultures. The city culture was said to be Western or Greco-Roman, the rural culture was said to be Slavic and superior.[2] But, unlike Stamboliiski, and more like his Russian models, Ante Radić welcomed the intellectuals into his movement, for it was their assigned task to heal the breach between city and country by awakening the peasant. The 'peasantry must be educated to an awareness of its values and at the same time to a knowledge of the outside world'.[3] Like the Bulgarian party, however, the Croatian party put a great deal of emphasis upon peaceful methods of achieving its objectives and advocated the widest possible use of the techniques of direct democracy (especially initiative, referendum and recall) inside and outside the party. Up to World War I the theme of 'all power for the peasantry', and opposition to the forthcoming war came to dominate all others in party agitation.[4] There was less emphasis than in the Bulgarian party on the importance of private property and more emphasis on self-help. The Croats called for the creation of self-governing communes, which would get the first crack at state lands that were confiscated for non-payment of taxes and subsequently sold.[5] But the cry for land reform was muted in the programme of the Croatian Peasant Party by comparison to the demand for national self-determination. Before

---

[1] Livingston, pp. 55–6.   [2] Ibid., p. 61.
[3] Ibid., p. 62.   [4] Ibid., p. 103.   [5] Ibid., p. 107.

World War I the Peasant Party called for the creation of a Croatian State as a self-governing unit within a federal monarchy.[1] The mission of national independence was inextricably bound up with the mission of class liberation. There were, said Ante Radić, five estates (the same term used by Stamboliiski), which were destined to succeed one another in history, the aristocracy, the clergy, the bourgeoisie, the workers, and finally the peasantry (or the real people).[2]

Before World War I the Croatian Peasant Party was almost exclusively peasant in membership, like its Bulgarian counterpart.[3] Stjepan Radić and his disciples built up the party by their own strenuous efforts, especially by developing a style of rural recruitment that was different from the other political parties. Instead of the beer and goulash parties held at the local level only during election times, the Croatian Peasant Party held meetings in private peasant cottages and invited only thirty or forty potential recruits at a time.[4] Stjepan Radić took special pains to recruit as village leaders intellectuals who were proud, not ashamed, of their peasant origin.[5] However, the evidence confirms Landsberger's thesis that those peasants who were better off were more likely to organise.[6] The Croatian Peasant Party was strongest in those areas where the literacy rate was highest and there was a strong peasant middle class, with no wide differences in wealth.[7]

After World War I, when Croatia became part of the Kingdom of Serbs, Croats and Slovenes (Yugoslavia), there was a gradual but steady decline in the emphasis on social reform and a decline in recruitment among the peasantry. Ante Radić's role as a party ideologist was taken by Rudolf Herceg, who announced that the time had come for the fifth estate (in the German text *Stand*) to seize political power and create a peasant republic.[8] He also confirms Landsberger's thesis that peasant groups who have had their traditional values modified through such experiences as military service or war are most likely to participate in a peasant political movement.[9] Like the myth of the proletarian State, the myth of the peasant State rested on the presumption of deterministic forces in history and on idealisation of one social class as a unique repository of virtue. Herceg argued that the fourth estate, the workers, had fulfilled their historic role by winning universal suffrage and using it to the disadvantage of the peasants, which in turn

[1] Ibid., p. 111.   [2] Ibid., p. 108.
[3] In 1912 83 per cent of party members were peasants. Ibid., p. 178.
[4] Ibid., p. 120.   [5] Ibid., p. 129.
[6] Landsberger, p. 53.   [7] Livingston, p. 176.
[8] Herceg, p. 44.   [9] Landsberger, p. 56.

awakened the peasants.[1]   Once having passed through this 'mental revolution', the peasant would be ready to use the ballot box for winning power for himself.[2]   But, because of their way of life, peasants would use their numerical superiority at the polls, not for class domination, but as a means of expressing their innate sense of justice, charity, and humanity.[3]   War would be abolished in the peasant republic and the nation would become a homeland (*domovina*), rather than a State (*država*).[4]   Unlike the Bulgarian Agrarian Party, the Croatian Peasant Party also called for public ownership of industry.[5]

The fate of the Croatian Peasant Party is an illustration of one typical hazard facing peasant political movements that rest upon a national minority base.   Like the Slovak People's Party, which faced a similar problem, the Croatian Peasant Party, because of its position as the most outspoken opponent of a centralised Yugoslav State, became the party of the whole national minority, instead of the party of the whole Yugoslav peasant class.   In the 1923 elections the Croatian Peasant Party got 12·8 per cent of the popular votes and 70 seats out of 312, becoming the largest opposition party in Yugoslavia.   This marked the high point in the history of the Croatian Peasant Party, for it received almost all of the Croat vote.   This meant that the party for the first time got support from the city and the Croatian middle class, and the industrial working class.[6]   The result was:

> Although the Croatian Peasant Party leadership, particularly Radić himself, made constant efforts to keep in contact with the Croat peasants, and although lip service was still given to the party's social program, by 1937 the Croatian Peasant Party was more or less a nationalist party run by the urban bourgeoisie.   But its prestige in the Croat villages was as great as ever.[7]

Only one-half of its deputies from 1923 to 1925 were peasants, none of Radić's lieutenants was a peasant, and most of the original leaders of peasant origin had left the party by 1927.[8]   When Stjepan Radić was shot in Parliament in 1938, he was replaced by Vladko Maček, the son of a civil engineer, and himself a professional, a lawyer.[9]

It was in this guise, as a party representing the desire of a national

---

[1] Herceg, p. 43.   [2] Ibid., p. 44.   [3] Ibid., p. 79.
[4] Livingston, p. 352.   [5] Ibid., p. 353.   [6] Ibid., pp. 412–4.
[7] Ibid., p. 558.
[8] Ibid., p. 557.   Stjepan Radić's successor, Vladko Maček, confirms the changing social composition of the party after World War I.   Vladko Maček, *In the Struggle for Freedom* (New York, 1957) pp. 80–81.   [9] Maček, p. 36.

minority for greater self-government, rather than as a party defending the social and economic needs of the Yugoslav peasants, that the Croatian Peasant Party retained its popular support and in 1938 with the Serbian Agrarian Union and some other political parties became the nucleus of the opposition bloc to the Yugoslav central Government and won 41 per cent of the popular vote. In this sense the Croatian Peasant Party, by educating the Croatian people to see the national question as the key to all problems, paved the way for the creation of the Croat fascist State of Ante Pavelić during World War II, a State in which many Croatian Peasant Party leaders participated.[1]

The Serbian peasant's interests were defended by the Serbian Agrarian Union, and it proved unequal to the task. The Serbian Agrarian Union had a programme similar to that of the Bulgarian Agrarian Union, calling for a greater share of political power for the peasantry, the techniques of direct democracy, significant reforms and investment in agriculture, and expansion of the co-operative system. The party was severely handicapped by internal dissension, by competition from the old Serbian Radical Party (which had a devoted peasant following), and by competition from the Croatian Peasant Party.[2] Also, it was outlawed after 1925 and had to operate behind other façades at election time.

There was a tendency for the other peasant political parties in Eastern Europe to become indistinguishable from other bourgeois liberal parties, though all of them started as radical peasant organisations. The Rumanian Peasant Party is a case in point. Like most of the peasant parties formed during or after World War I it was more eclectic in its ideology and programmes from the outset than the older peasant parties, and far less of a class party than its Bulgarian and Croatian counterparts. The Russian populist influence was at first strong in the ideas of one Rumanian populist leader, Constantin Stere. Stere was a Bessarabian nobleman, a professor at the University of Iaşi. His province had been part of Russia before World War I and he had participated in the Russian populist movement.[3] He followed their thesis that the peasantry was a coherent social group which, moreover, represented the 'national genius' of the Rumanian people. He hoped to avoid the evils of industrialisation by strengthening the

---

[1] Hugh Seton-Watson, *The East European Revolution* (London, 1950) p. 79. As Seton-Watson points out, there were few Croats in the resistance movements before the end of 1943, since most of them felt that Croatia's destiny had been realised in the creation of the Croatian national State. Ibid., p. 130, n. 3.

[2] Tomasevich, pp. 252–3, and Stavrianos, p. 623.　　　　　　　[3] Roberts, pp. 144–7.

peasant co-operative movement and applying the techniques of direct democracy. A second influence in the party, Ion Mihalche, was a schoolteacher of peasant origin. He focused more exclusively on the urgent question of land redistribution, but without exploring the relationship of the peasant household to the whole economy.[1] But the strongest influence on the subsequent development of the Rumanian Peasant Party was that of the economist Virgil Madgearu, of middle class origin, who argued, contrary to Stere, that the peasant would profit from the free and untrammelled development of heavy industry in Rumania and the abolition of all tariff protection, trusts and cartels.[2]

A powerful impetus away from its narrowly peasantist orientation was given to the Rumanian peasant party when it fused with the National Party of Transylvania in 1926. As Roberts put it:

> The National Party was the defender of the Rumanian peasants against the Magyar overlords and advocated extensive agrarian reform, but it was more national than peasantist in its outlook, and its leaders were from the middle class. It was a vertical, rather than a horizontal organisation, and while it had great support among the Transylvanian peasants, it was also representative of the Rumanian intellectuals, professional men, and small tradesmen.[3]

Thus it is not surprising that when the National Peasant Party came to power from 1928 to 1930 its economic policies were not very different from those of previous governments, except with regard to tariff protection and foreign investment. On these last two items, the National Peasant Party lowered the tariff walls and opened the floodgates to foreign capital, thereby reversing the policies of its predecessor, the Liberal Party.[4] With regard to its supporters, the Rumanian peasantry, the National Peasant Party affirmed its support of the middle peasant, possessing land of approximately twenty-five hectares in size. The 1929 law on alienation of allotments was supposed to create prosperous middle-sized holdings by a process of 'superior competitive efficiency', but, in fact, increased the holdings of the wealthier peasants at the expense of the poorer, regardless of their relative efficiency.[5] In the Rumanian case the peasant political party gradually evolved into a multi-class party, like the Croatian Peasant Party, but also into a non-peasant party. As Roberts puts it, '. . . the Peasant Party's absorption of non-peasant principles was the beginning

---

[1] Ibid., p. 149.
[2] Ibid., p. 151.
[3] Ibid., p. 140.
[4] Ibid., p. 160, 180.
[5] Ibid., pp. 157–8.

of its actual alienation from the peasantry. Indeed in the 1930s and 1940s the National Peasants, as a party, became increasingly removed from their rural origins'.[1]

The failure of the Rumanian National Peasant Party to pursue a genuine peasant programme inspired the formation of an alternative radical peasant movement in 1933 in the form of the Ploughmen's Front of Transylvania. Although sponsored by a prosperous land-owner, Petru Groza, the programme of this movement harked back to Mihalache's radicalism in the 1920s, calling for renewed land re-distribution, cancellation of peasant debts, etc.[2] After World War II it would become a rural 'front' party for the communists.

More effective than the Ploughmen's Front in capitalising on the peasant's disillusionment with the National Peasant Party was the Rumanian fascist movement, the League of Archangel Michael, better known in the West as the Iron Guard. Eugene Weber described this movement as follows:

> Far from being a petty-bourgeois movement in the sense such words suggest, the Legion was a popular and populist movement, with a program which the masses (in the Rumanian context of peasants and workers) recognized as radical enough for them, and which the representatives of the established order, from Cuza to the king, recognised as revolutionary. It may be significant in this connection, that the only other party with populist velleities, the Peasant Party, was very weak in those Northeastern provinces where Codreanu started out, or else lost the peasants' trust (as happened in Muntenia and Oltenia after 1933) by abandoning its more reformist activities. Equally interesting: the only region where the Legion did not implant itself as a protest movement, Maramures in the North and Northwest, was also the only region where the small Social-Democratic Party showed some activity, which suggests once again that the Legion prospered where it filled a need some other movement failed to fill, where it found an available public.[3]

The Iron Guard rivalled the chief victor at the polls in 1937, the National Peasant Party.[4] Weber estimates that four-fifths of the members of the movement were peasants.[5] It was not that the Iron Guard had a more persuasive programme than any other political

---

[1] Ibid., p. 167.   [2] Ibid., p. 260–61.
[3] Eugen Weber, 'The Men of Archangel', *Journal of Contemporary History*, I pt I (1956) p. 212.   [4] Ibid., p. 103.   [5] Ibid., p. 107.

party, but that it was the only political movement in Rumania to seek out the poorest peasants and promise them some kind of regeneration.

The Polish Peasant movement began under different circumstances from all of those discussed above. Although Poland, like Rumania and Hungary, continued to have a native aristocracy and large landed estates, she differed from the Balkan countries in having achieved a generally higher level of industrialisation. As a nation formerly separated by more than a century of partition, she faced the unique task of reconciling three rather disparate political traditions and economic circumstances, the German, Hapsburg and Russian. Yet the new nation was already united by a stronger and deeper historical and cultural heritage than any ofthe Balkan countries.

The three major peasant parties examined thus far had evolved at least in part from peasant or rural intellectual leadership to middle class leadership, but before World War I the Polish peasant movement seemed to develop in the opposite direction, i.e., from middle class leadership towards peasant leadership.[1] It started in Galicia in 1895. The founder of the party, Bolesław Wysłouch, was a member of the Polish gentry, who had picked up most of his populist notions in Russia, while studying at the Institute of Technology in St Petersburg.[2] Going against the mainstream of the Polish political tradition, Wysłouch found Polish national identity in the character of the Polish peasant, rather than that of the Polish gentry, and foresaw national regeneration only in a programme that focused first on the regeneration of the peasantry.[3] As a beginning he proposed full political, economic and social rights for the peasant, and launched a movement to stimulate political consciousness among the peasants. Like the Bulgarian movement, then, the Galician populist movement started as an effort in self-help, focusing chiefly on lectures, reading rooms, libraries and newspapers for the peasants. That provided the organisational base for the Polish Peasant Party founded in 1895. In 1903 the Polish Peasant Party adopted a programme, or more correctly, a set of general principles, written for it by Wysłouch. It called for specific legislation to give the peasants a share of political power proportionate to their

[1] Landsberger, p. 79. Landsberger seems to argue that the pattern which is evident in the Polish movements is the more normal one, with leadership being recruited from the peasantry only when society has undergone considerable modernisation.

[2] Peter Brock, 'Bolesław Wysłouch, Founder of the Polish Peasant Party', *Slavonic and East European Review*, xxx no. 74 (Dec 1951) 140. Recent Polish research on the history of the Polish peasant movement is summarised in Jan Borkowski, 'Les Recherches sur l'histoire du mouvement paysan polonais', *Acta Poloniae Historica*, no. 13 (1966) 103–13.

[3] Brock, *Slavonic and East European Review*, xxx no. 74 (Dec 1951) 143.

numbers, and called for Polish national independence.[1]   Although affirming support for the peasant smallholder, the programme proposed no radical economic or land reforms.[2]

In 1913 the bulk of the party broke away to form the Polish Peasant Party 'Piast', which, under two leaders of peasant origin, Wincenty Witos and Jakub Bojko, proposed to carry on Wysłouch's belief that the Peasant Party should embrace the whole community, rather than the peasantry alone.   Like the Croatian, Czech, and Rumanian parties, 'Piast' became a multi-class party.   Both of the new leaders, significantly, had served their apprenticeship, not at the feet of Russian populist terrorists, but as Peasant Party deputies in Vienna.[3]   As in the Czech case, this experience would give the party an inclination towards parliamentary solutions involving bargaining and compromise, rather than inflammatory proclamations, and radical programmes. Also by the end of the 1890s 'Piast' had in fact come to represent the rich peasantry and the peasants with middle-sized holdings, rather than the landless peasant or smallholder.[4]   These two factors must be stressed in order to explain the party's moderate character in the decade after World War I.   For, having already achieved national independence, the party was freed of the obsession that diverted the Croatian Peasant Party from needed economic reforms, but 'Piast' did not, as might have been expected, seek radical changes.

In the post-war Polish Republic radical land reforms were espoused by a second peasant movement, the Polish Peasant Party 'Wyzwolenie' founded in 1915 in the Congress Kingdom (that portion of Poland occupied by Russia before 1915) and nourished on a diet of Russian populism.[5]   As one of 'Wyzwolenie's' leaders put it:

Nowhere as much as in politics is the question so vital as to whether someone began his political activity under the Russians or under the Austrians, that is to say, whether in the tradition of the insurrectionary struggles and underground conspiratorial work or in an atmosphere of petty skirmishes for the attainment of very secondary ends.[6]

[1] Ibid., p. 160.

[2] Ibid., p. 160, n. 62.

[3] Peter Brock, 'The Early Years of the Polish Peasant Party 1895–1907', *Journal o, Central European Affairs*, XIV no. 3 (Oct 1954) 221, 230.

[4] Ibid., p. 225.

[5] Peter Brock, 'The Politics of the Polish Peasant', *International Review of Social History*, I pt I (1956) 213.

[6] As quoted in ibid., p. 215.

Strangely enough, though 'Wyzwolenie' was the Peasant Party of the left, its leadership was drawn primarily from the middle class intelligentsia, and 'Piast', the Peasant Party of the right, drew much of its leadership from those born in peasant homes, and much of its support from the poorest peasants in Poland.[1] But the role of the middle-class intelligentsia in the leadership of both parties increased during the inter-war years.

When the Polish democratic system ceased to function towards the end of the 1920s, the two parties united with a third, splinter peasant party to form a single, united Polish Peasant Party. Faced with persecution, an increasingly authoritarian Government, and a growing sense of frustration, the new united party drifted slowly towards the left during the thirties. It called for a return to democratic procedures, the expropriation of large estates without compensation and a stronger co-operative movement.[2] Taking a leaf from the radical workers' movements, the Peasant Party organised strikes during which the peasants refused to market their produce or buy from the towns during a specific period of time. In the vanguard of the new radicalism was *Wici*, an association of young intellectuals of peasant origin who devoted themselves to the formation of a new synthetic political philosophy for the agrarian movement. Its goal was a peasant democracy in Poland dedicated to the strengthening of the independent smallholder and opposition to both capitalism and communism. Participants in this movement gradually moved into positions of leadership in the Peasant Party and in 1935 some leaders of the Peasant Party adopted a programme calling for collaboration with the workers' radical movement, the nationalisation of industry, mines and banks, and the expropriation of large estates without compensation.[3]

The effect of this rejuvenation is hard to measure, since there were no elections during the 1930s. Certainly, during their moderate phase the peasant parties of the twenties did not do especially well at the polls. From 1919 to 1926 the peasant parties never received more than one-third of the vote and were in power (and then only as junior partners in coalition governments) for only two-and-a-half out of seven-and-a-half years of democratic government.[4] The explanation for these earlier failures seems to lie in the constituencies of the peasant parties. The peasants of the western provinces tended to vote for the National

[1] Ibid., pp. 215, 217.   [2] Ibid., p. 219.
[3] Ibid., pp. 220–1 and Andrzej Korbonski, *Politics of Socialist Agriculture in Poland 1945–69* (New York, 1965) pp. 5–8.
[4] Brock, *International Review of Social History*, I pt I (1956) 218.

Democrats, the party that had led the struggle for Polish national independence, and the landless farm labourers and the national minorities gravitated towards their own national minority parties or communist worker-peasant parties.[1]

The Czechoslovak Agrarian Party was the peasant political movement that strayed farthest from its rural origins, even further than the Croatian Peasant Party or the Rumanian National Peasant Party. And in many ways the Czech party was the victim of its own success.[2] The Czechoslovak State was unique among East European states in two significant ways. It was not an economically underdeveloped country, at least in its western regions, and it was the only East European government to preserve functioning democratic institutions during the whole inter-war period. It was also a society in which the status of the peasant was quite high, in which there was a large middle class and the differences between social classes were rather narrow.[3]

Among Czechs, excessive wealth and excessive poverty have been very rare and differences in social status have been rather small . . . Czechoslovakia – and this is primarily true for Bohemia and Moravia – has been frequently described as the classic country of the 'little man', i.e., a country of hard-working, labour-loving, thrifty individuals who love their families and privacy and take pride in craftsmanship. At the time of the *coup d'etat* in 1948, a majority of Czechs were eminently middle-class in their style of life, aspirations and expectations. The transition between the upper, middle and lower classes was very gradual; the borderline between the latter two was especially fluctuating and relatively arbitrary.[4]

Unlike any other state in Eastern Europe, Czechoslovakia had, at least in its western provinces, no surplus agricultural population. In 1930 only 35 per cent of the population earned their living in agriculture, and Bohemia and Moravia actually experienced a shortage of agricultural labour.[5] In many ways the history of the Czechoslovak peasant movement illustrates Landsberger's thesis that a peasant movement

[1] See Jackson, *passim.*
[2] For some of the more recent studies of the Czech peasant political movement in Czech see the notes to Jaroslav César and Bohumíl Černý, 'O ideologii československého agrarismu', *Ceskoslovenský časopis historický*, no. 2 (1959) 263–85.
[3] Jan Hajda (ed.), *A Study of Contemporary Czechoslovakia*, Human Relations Area Files, Subcontractor's Monograph No. 15 (Chicago, n.d.) p. 62.
[4] Ibid., p. 86.
[5] H. Böker and F. W. von Bülow, *The Rural Exodus in Czechoslovakia*, International Labour Office, Studies and Reports, series K, no. 13 (Geneva, 1933) pp. 88, 155.

is most likely to succeed 'in those societies in which status differential has in any case already been reduced and where there is considerable institutional differentiation and specialization', and that where such a peasant movement succeeds its goal will become more narrow and more shallow.[1] To which I would only add that such a party also loses its peasant character in its programme, leadership and membership.

The Czechoslovak peasant political movement regarded Alfons Šťastný as the 'father of agrarianism'.[2] He was a south Bohemian farmer, who formulated and published a agrarian Czech programme in 1891 and disseminated his ideas through his *Farmers' Newspaper*. In 1896 the first all-Czech farmers' organisations took shape, and in 1899 the Czech Agrarian Party was founded, to be followed in 1904 with the formation of agrarian parties in Moravia and Silesia.[3] At first the movements were concerned chiefly with the development of peasant co-operation, organisations for peasant youths (like the famous Czech Sokol), mutual benefit societies, cattle insurance association, etc. But in 1905 a young Czech peasant leader, Antonín Švehla, forced the party leaders to support the movement for universal suffrage in Austria and to become a party with a mass base.[4] Švehla urged the party to seek, not only mass support among the Czechs, but also among neighbouring nationalities, with the effect of persuading the party to change its name to the United Czechoslovak Agrarian Party in 1905.[5] In 1906 he began to publish an agrarian daily, *Venkov* (Countryside).[6] Through new co-operatives, 'educational' branches in rural villages, and student groups, the agrarian message was spread.[7] They also organised the annual all-national party congress into a grand fair, advertising party ideology in conjunction with a number of other events calculated to bring out a large number of farmers.[8] In 1907 and 1911 in the last two elections in the Austrian half of the Hapsburg monarchy, the Czech Agrarian Party became the strongest Czech party in Vienna.[9] In 1909 Švehla became the head of the party. As in the case of the Polish Piast leader, Wincenty Witos, parliamentary experience explains much about the subsequent character of his leadership. Although Švehla is almost unknown in the West, because of his strange determination to

[1] Landsberger, pp. 43, 83.   [2] César and Černý, p. 265.
[3] Ibid., p. 268.
[4] Anthony Palaček, 'Antonín Švehla: Czech Peasant Statesman', *Slavic Review*, xxi no. 4 (Dec 1962) p. 700 and César and Černý, pp. 263, 271.
[5] César and Černý, p. 268.   [6] Ibid., p. 269.   [7] Ibid., pp. 269–70.
[8] Ibid., p. 270.   [9] Palaček, p. 700.

avoid publicity and even historical acclaim, Švehla was the man who most decisively shaped both the Czech Agrarian Party and the new Czechoslovak Republic.[1] He was Premier of Czechoslovakia from 1922 to 1929, and agrarian premiers succeeded him until 1938. In particular it was his genius for compromise that made the successive coalition governments work.

Švehla regarded the spirit of opposition as something in the nature of a sin and led his party into every coalition. Thus the Agrarian Party gradually became the centre around which the other Czechoslovak parties grouped themselves in order to form government coalitions. The special nature of the party, its consolidation and true conservatism predestined it for this task, but in order that a heterogenous group of parties forming the government coalition might be held together, here was need for the skill of Švehla, who had a unique gift for reconciling opposing points of view.[2]

In his political philosophy Švehla sounded very much like Ante Radić, with the latter's emphasis on peasant mystique and the need for peasant influence in politics.[3] The phase coined by Švehla which best expressed his belief that peasant society has a distinct identity was, 'All the countryside is one family'.[4] Švehla's efforts were reinforced by an outpouring of literary and sociological works extolling the countryside as a unique repository of virtue and national character.[5].

Like the other agrarian parties the Czech agrarians owed some of their popularity to their outspoken hostility to World War I. They were especially critical of those wartime policies, like requisitioning and conscription, that placed heavy burdens on the shoulders of the peasants.[6] After uniting with a Slovak agrarian movement (representing chiefly the Protestant Slovak intellectuals), the Czech Agrarian Party became staunch supporters of Czechoslovak unity, putting special emphasis on the democratic and republican character of the agrarian movement.[7]

[1] Ibid., pp. 700–701. Palaček makes some modest effort to right the balance. Švehla's aversion to publicity seems in retrospect almost pathological. For example, at Švehla's request Masaryk omitted all reference to him in his autobiographical *The Making of a State*.
[2] Josef Borovička, *Ten Years of Czechoslovak Politics* (Prague, 1927) p. 185.
[3] See, for example, Antonín Švehla, 'L'Homme et la terre', Mezinárodní Agrární Bureau *Bulletin*, no. 1 (1923) pp. 8–15; Antonín Švehla, 'Le Sol et la paix', Mezinárodní Agrární Bureau *Bulletin*, no. 1 (1924) pp. 3–9; and Antonín Švehla, 'Le Sol et l'état' , Mezinárodní Agrární Bureau *Bulletin*, no. 7 (1925) pp. 3–7.
[4] César and Černý, p. 272.
[5] Ibid., p. 273.   [6] Ibid., p. 275.   [7] Ibid., p. 277.

In practice, however, Švehla tended to favour the interests of the relatively prosperous Czech peasants and ignore the plight of the more typically impoverished Slovak and Ruthenian peasants in the eastern half of the Republic. In formulating a land reform, for example, the agrarians proved to be more conservative than the socialists, asking that former landowners be allowed to keep relatively large holdings.[1] Later on, Švehla's successor, the Slovak intellectual, Milan Hodža, would virtually suspend the operation of the reform, although 16 per cent of all Slovak land was still in the hands of large estates.[2] Even where the land reform was applied, it seems to have had the usual effect of increasing the number of dwarf holders.[3] But the Agrarian Party appears to have retained support from the small and middle peasants. In 1923 95 per cent of its members were peasants and 70 per cent of its members held five hectares of land or less.[4]

Because of its central position in the Government, the Czech Agrarian Party served as a lodestone for other non-peasant interest groups, and in order to participate in every coalition Government Švehla was forced to cut back his more extreme reform proposals. By 1925 Švehla found himself in coalition with Catholic, conservative, and national minority parties (the Green-Black Coalition). The coalition was a signal achievement for the Czechoslovak State, a victory for democracy and the democratic system, for Švehla had co-opted some of the stoutest opponents of the Czech State. From the point of view of the Czecholovak peasants it marked the abandonment of much of the original agrarian programme, for the new cabinet had 'the characteristics of a bourgeois conservative government'.[5]

Although Švehla had wisely co-opted some of the leading Slovak Protestant intelligentsia by merging his party with the Slovak National and Agrarian Party, he did not succeed in forestalling the movement for Slovak national independence, which was carried on by the Catholic Slovak intelligentsia through the Christian Slovak People's Party, or the Ludaks, founded in 1918. Thriving on some real and some imagined discriminatory acts of the Czech Government, the Ludaks, along with the Croatian Ustaše movement and the Iron Guard in Rumania, serve as an excellent example of the ease with which

---

[1] Lucy Textor, *Land Reform in Czechoslovakia* (London, 1923) pp. 30–2.
[2] Maslov, p. 91.
[3] See Vladislaw Brdlík, *Die sozialoekonomische Struktur der Landwirtschaft in der Tchecoslowakei* (Berlin, 1938) p. 6. The number of small holdings (2–5 ha.) increased by 1930 by 31 per cent, medium holdings (5–20 ha.) by 5·5 per cent, while the number of all other size holdings diminished.
[4] Goranovich, p. 75.   [5] Borovička, p. 185.

agrarianism, virulent nationalism and fascism could be blended in Eastern Europe. Strictly speaking, the Ludaks were not a peasant movement, despite the fact that they 'drew significant support from the village and paid much attention to it'.[1] But they resembled the Croatian Peasant Party in their focus on the myth of a people's or peasant State (People's Slovakia), and their notion that national virtue was best represented in the Slovak peasant.[2] Their populism looked towards Vienna or Rome for inspiration, rather than towards Moscow. They strongly supported the rights of property, opposed communism and socialism and called for social peace ('Christ, not Lenin').[3] Their model for a society was an idealised version of medieval corporate society. The leading social groups in the new society would be the middle class and the rich peasantry.[4] Among the East European peasant parties it most closely resembled the Slovenian Peasant Party, which also combined Catholic social theory with a leadership drawn chiefly from priests, but among political parties bearing the populist label, only the Ludaks tried and succeeded in creating a genuine fascist State.

The last, and perhaps, most unusual populist movement was the Hungarian. In its own way Hungary was as distinctive in inter-war Eastern Europe as Czechoslovakia. Although Hungary resembled Poland and pre-revolutionary Russia in its tolerance of large estates and persistence of a large landless peasantry, it differed from both of them in its political structure and in its attitude towards politics as a means of social reform. The traumatic experience of the unsuccessful Hungarian Communist Revolution of 1919 set in motion a deep antipathy to any significant social and economic reform and strengthened the conservative right in Hungarian politics. One consequence was that in Eastern Europe Hungary was the only country where the aristocracy continued to play an important role in politics.[5] It was somewhat paradoxical, but Hungary experienced an industrial revolution of sorts between 1867–1914, while at the same time preserving a quasi-feudal system in agriculture until 1944.[6] On the surface the political system was parliamentary, but the conservative right dominated the political scene through the government Party of Unity.[7]

[1] Yeshayahu Andrew Jelinek, 'Hlinka's Slovak People's Party 1939–49', (unpublished Ph.D. dissertation, Department of History, Indiana University, 1966) p. 191.
[2] Ibid., p. 171, 187, 191.   [3] Ibid., p. 176.   [4] Ibid., p. 179.
[5] Deák refers to the new counter-revolutionary regimes established in 1919 as 'the last political triumph of Hungary's historic classes', István Deák, 'Hungary', in Hans Rogger and Eugen Weber (eds.) *The European Right: A Historical Profile* (Berkeley, 1966) p. 366. See also pp. 370–7.   [6] Ibid., p. 367.   [7] Ibid., p. 376.

Efforts were made before 1919 to organise the dispossessed peasants. In 1906 a Peasant Party of Greater Hungary was created by Andreas Achim, and it soon transformed itself into the Independent Socialist Peasant Party of Hungary.[1] Like other peasant political organisations in Eastern Europe, this one arose out of a narrower economic organisation, the Federation of Agricultural Workers, originated by the Hungarian Social Democratic Party in Budapest.[2] But the modest programme of the Independent Socialist Peasant Party had only limited political success and almost no effect on the subsequent peasant political movement. The first genuine peasant political party was created by Stephen Szabó in 1909 and it was called the Hungarian Smallholders' Party. It stood for a major redistribution of land and the introduction of the secret ballot.[3] In the first post-war election in 1920, this party received ninety deputies, making it the second strongest political party in Hungary. But its leaders allowed themselves to be neutralised and absorbed in the government Party of Unity It was not until 1930 that the party was resurrected under the name, Independent Smallholders' Party and the leadership of Ferenc Nagy, Gaszton Gaál and Tibor Eckhardt. In 1931 the Independent Smallholders' Party elected fourteen deputies out of 245 entering the new parliament. Despite the radical orientation of some of its leaders, like Ferenc Nagy, the Independent Smallholders' Party became, in the hands of Tibor Eckhardt, a pawn in the game of power politics.[4] The programme they advocated was relatively moderate.[5] It became a centrist party, led chiefly by middle class urban politicians and representing the interests of the middle peasants.[6]

The case for radical rural reform in Hungary, which seemed especially urgent in a country where 40 per cent of the agricultural population had no land, and 52 per cent had less than three hectares of land,[7] was pressed from 1930 to 1943, not by any political party, but rather by a small band of intellectuals, known collectively in the West as the Village Explorers. These writers devoted themselves to what one of their number, Gyula Illyés, called the third road, a programme that seemed to consist chiefly of double negatives: 'neither capitalism nor communism, neither Germany nor Russia, neither West nor East,

[1] Niederhauser, pp. 75–6.
[2] Peselj, pp. 496–500.
[3] Ibid., p. 497.
[4] Carlile A. Macartney, *October Fifteenth: A History of Modern Hungary 1919–45* (Edinburgh, 1957) I 92.
[5] See Ferenc Nagy, *The Struggle Behind the Iron Curtain*.
[6] Macartney, I 122.　　　　　[7] Varga, p. 29.

neither political passivity nor direct engagement'.[1]   There was a positive side to the movement, however.   The Village Explorers felt they could best serve the poorest peasants in Hungary by studying rural conditions at first-hand and confronting the rest of the Hungarian people with this stark reality, artistically presented in books and articles.[2]   They created a new genre, partly literature, partly sociology.

Given the traumatic fear of reform, or even of change, that dominated Hungarian politics after the Hungarian Communist Revolution, the Village Explorers may have been right in trying to avoid direct political action.   Inspired by the first preliminary forays into rural sociology, several small groups of intellectuals took up the mission of 'going to the people' as early as the mid-1920s, such as the Miklós Bartha Society, the Movement of Agrarian Settlement, the Artistic Colloquium of Szeged and the Slovakian Sarlo.   Out of these small groups came such major Hungarian writers as Lázló Németh and Gyula Illyés.   The former saw the advent of capitalism as the beginning of men's dehumanisation, and hoped to avoid its consequences by a 'new politics' in which small collective rural communities would establish 'co-ordinate relations' with one another and limit the influence of industry and the State.[3]   Illyés saw no specific solution to the problem of rural poverty, but in his studies of the rural poor, such as his famous *People of the Puszta*, he painted a haunting picture of desperation in the countryside.   Among other things he focused on *egyko* and *egyse*, limitation of families to one child or none because of hopelessness, poverty and misery.[4]

There were three flurries of activity in which the Village Explorers tried to move beyond mere intellectual efforts.   They were the New Intellectual Front of 1935, the March Front of 1937–8, and the formation of the radical National Peasant Party in 1939.   All failed.   The

---

[1] This section is based almost entirely on Gati's excellent study, which should be published.   Gati, p. 150.

[2] The role of sociology in mobilising social reform in Czechoslovakia, Poland, Hungary, and Rumania deserves more detailed study.   In Czechoslovakia the trend was launched by Arnošt Bláha in his book, *The Sociology of the Farmer and Worker*, published in 1926. Bláha was the founder of the sociological school of Brno, and Hodža said, 'It was really Bláha who discovered the peasant for us'.   In Poland an important pioneering work was the multi-volumed study by W. I. Thomas and Florian Znaniecki, *The Polish Peasant in Europe and America*, published in the United States in 1919 and 1920.   After World War I Znaniecki went back to Poland and occupied the chair of sociology at Poznań.   In Rumania and Poland field studies of villages were subsided by the State.   One product of these investigations in Poland was Chałasinski's *The Young Generation of Peasants*, published in 1938 under the auspices of the State Institute of Rural Culture.   In Rumania the semi-official Institute of Social Sciences of Rumania published a series of such field studies under the guidance of D. Gusti.

[3] Gati, p. 85.   [4] Ibid., pp. 93–4.

first of these, the New Intellectual Front, was invoked in June 1935 when Lajos Zilahy, the editor of the daily newspaper *Magyaroszág*, called upon the populist writers to rally round the new Hungarian premier, Gömbös, and try to persuade him to follow the example of Franklin Roosevelt.[1] Zilahy said it was time to put an end to the invisible triumvirate that ruled the country, the Church, the landlords and the big capitalists. Gömbös gave them some encouragement, but not for long. The second foray owed something to the disillusionment inspired by the first. As one populist writer put it,

> the lessons of the past year have made many of us conclude that squeaking and toddling reforms cannot any longer help the present condition of the Hungarian people. Drastic reorganisation is needed, which can be achieved only by the conscientious Hungarian masses and by the seizure of political power.[2]

In 1937 the March Front was inaugurated by a speech delivered by Imre Kovács in Budapest on the anniversary of the revolution of 1848. He called for genuine democratic institutions in Hungary and a new dramatic land reform.[3] Intense political agitation and public discussion lasted for about a year, during which the whole editorial staff of the populist daily, *Valasz*, met with small groups of peasants around the country.[4] It was during this period that some Village Explorers, including Imre Kovács, began to plan the creation of a genuine radical peasant party. One of the foremost populist leaders, Peter Veres, argued against the new project, citing the history of the other radical East European peasant political parties, all of whom, he said, had been absorbed by the petty bourgeoisie.[5] Veres contended that only Stamboliiski's programme and example interested him, but he hastened to point out that Stamboliiski had been assassinated. The March Front had dissolved by the beginning of 1938, but in June 1939 a new radical peasant political party was formed under the name of the National Peasant Party.[6] The National Peasant Party was stillborn, however; the war swept all other considerations before it.

When, after the war, the first and last free elections in the history of Hungary were held, the Independent Smallholders' Party won 58 per cent of the popular vote and the National Peasant Party, 7 per cent, to the communist 17 per cent.[7] It was a clear expression of peasant

[1] Ibid., p. 99. [2] Ibid., p. 112. [3] Ibid., p. 120.
[4] Ibid., p. 129. [5] Ibid., p. 137. [6] Ibid., p. 190.
[7] Nagy, p. 152.

sentiment. But the circumstances were strikingly similar to those in Russia twenty-eight years before, when the Russian populists had finally won their popular mandate and the shadow of political power. In both instances another political movement, the communist, had seized the substance of political power and would continue to strengthen their grip by building upon the radical populist legacy and using it against those parties that had abandoned it. This is probably more than a curious historical coincidence. It is, perhaps, a pattern for 'peasant societies in transition'. For the communists, though building upon a radical populist heritage of criticism and projected reform, brought into the political arena a more single-minded pursuit of political power than the populists ever possessed, perhaps because they were not handicapped by a belief in democratic political processes.

CONCLUSIONS

In conclusion, it seems to me that the foregoing indicates that peasant political movements in Eastern Europe were a natural and welcome phenomenon, and that most Western studies dismiss them too easily as quixotic and naïve attempts to resurrect a dead or imaginary past. They were natural in that they were brought into being by indigenous historical forces, forces that make the history of modern Eastern Europe more like that of the colonial countries of Africa and Asia than of Western Europe. For in Eastern Europe during the inter-war years there was the combination of preponderantly peasant societies and democratic institutions, the dependent and somewhat stagnant semi-colonial character of their economies, limited experience in self-government and self-study, and the inexorable pressure of over-population on the land. It is significant, however, that the peasant political movement was not brought into being by peasants who were aware of these problems and their degrading consequences, but rather by those who were themselves the product of modernisation and wished to lend a helping hand to their less fortunate brethren, that is, by middle class intellectuals, by peasants who had risen from their social class, and by peasants returning from the army. In a word, peasant political movements are a natural phenomenon of the transitional period between agrarian and industrialised societies, because, though in many ways directed against modernisation, they are themselves impossible without some degree of modernisation. This brings me to the second point above. Peasant political movements were a welcome phenomenon because, despite their hostility to urbanisation and many features of modernisation, they offered a path to modernisation uniquely suited to their needs, since it proposed to provide many of the missing ingredients for successfully negotiating the trip, namely self-reliant, productive peasant households, a mass market for consumer goods, capital accumulation through taxation and private savings, co-operative organisations for pooling the limited capital resources available, and a wider political experience for the ordinary peasant. Peasant political organisations should be judged, then, as politics of transition, and this is where, in my opinion, many Western studies lead the reader astray, by praising such movements only where they resemble Western political models. Thus, although I have subscribed to Landsberger's excellent analytical framework throughout, I would argue that his hypothesis that 'only in modernised societies will peasant organisations be successful' does not apply to Eastern Europe. In Eastern Europe this is most relevant to the Czech case. Yet in Czechoslovakia the Czech Agrarian party 'succeeded' by abandoning, bargaining away, or compromising many of the ideals that Švehla professed.

I think that probably this hypothesis cannot be tested without a clearer definition of 'success'. But in Eastern Europe it was evident that success for the peasant political movement meant solving the problems of the peasantry by finding a path to the modern world that did not have such high costs in human welfare as capitalism and communism.

Western and Marxist studies have taken a dim view of the efforts of peasant political parties because they see no merit in the agrarian myth of the peasant as a noble savage, though this myth is probably no less deserving of respect than the myth of the common man or the myth of the proletariat. Their stance, however, often leads such studies to harsher judgements of peasant political movements that is warranted by the evidence. For example, most studies view the political failures of the peasant movement as irrefutable proof of its intrinsic weakness. If so, of course, then the more conventional political parties in Eastern Europe were also intrinsically weak, for they also failed in most instances to hold political power, once they had won it. Given the limited experience in non-revolutionary politics, the almost insoluble economic problems of East European countries, the impact of the Great Depression, and Germany's subsequent domination of the whole area, few genuine political parties survived, except in Czechoslovakia.

Other studies say that the peasant movement failed because it did not develop a comprehensive and internally consistent world view.[1] Yet the communist parties in Eastern Europe have such a world view, and their political performance before 1939 was even less successful than the agrarians. There is, of course, some reason to question whether the peasant political movement failed politically since their popularity endured, at least into the 1950s. Most Western studies have ignored or slighted the profound influence of the populists' publications and research on their country's history. Much remains to be done in exploring the impact of populist sociological research, populist literary work, and populist political criticism in shaping the post-World War II generation in Eastern Europe.

Moreover, many of the negative judgements cited above rest on unwarranted assumptions about peasant society. We need to peel away the clichés in which the subject has been wrapped for decades. We should discard such old 'chestnuts' as the natural antipathy between peasant societies and modernisation, the peasant as a natural anarcho-syndicalist and the assumption that modern peasant societies are no more than vestigial neolithic communities.

Change, for example, has always gone on in the village, though perhaps at a slower pace than in the towns. While preserving the family farm as the basic producing unit and the near-subsistence standard of living, peasant society has always been, as Redfield points out, a part society, depending on the larger society of which it is a part,[2] and adapting to changes in the larger society as they took place. Although these changes filtered down through the interstices of peasant values and customs, in the end they were probably as profound in their impact among the peasantry as elsewhere. This is one of the strengths of the Marxist approach, which, in its emphasis on class differentiation and alliances between the peasants and their urban counterparts, has presented a truer picture of the evolution of the village. It is also one of the strengths of Landsberger's analytical framework, because he focuses upon the inter-relationship between the whole society and its peasant component, rather than upon the latter alone.

Nor is the peasant as difficult to organise as is commonly believed. There is nothing inherent in the peasant way of life to make him act politically on his own initiative, except in the form of a *jacquerie*. But

[1] See, for example, Felix Gross, 'The Mechanics of European Politics', in Felix Gross (ed.) *European Ideologies* (New York, 1943) p. 16.
[2] Redfield, p. 20.

the same could be said of workers' movements in the nineteenth century. And, like the workers' movements, those peasant political movements that were the most rational and the most successful were first led by intellectuals from the outside, and those intellectuals tended to organise the well-to-do peasant first, rather than the poor. Once the effort was made, however, given modern conditions of communication, it was not much more difficult to organise the peasant than it had been to organise the industrial worker. It was, however, as Landsberger indicates, easier to organise peasant movements where there were traditions of co-operative organisation, a fund of sympathetic village intellectuals to draw upon, and an interpenetration of political and economic activities on the part of the State.[1]

Finally, the peasant political movement in Eastern Europe did have something to say about the problems they faced in their own societies. World War I had uprooted and galvanised a whole generation of young peasants and given them the vote. At that point in time most of the countries in Eastern Europe were experiencing the worst evils of industrialisation without any visible prospect of realising its benefits. In the absence of significant capital and markets for rapid industrialisation, which would, at least, have relieved demographic pressure, there seemed no other possible solution but to use the peasant vote to support 'the third path to the modern world', one that involved neither immediate extinction by forced industrialisation nor the gross inefficiencies of the Soviet collective farm.[2] How would the peasant politicians end rural poverty and rural overpopulation? By the creation of a society of self-sufficient independent peasant smallholders sustained by a network of producer and retailing co-operatives, while at the same time maximising educational opportunities and creating optimum conditions for marketing agricultural goods.

This was a formula that sought to make maximum possible use of existing resources at the existing technical level of production. It has been justly criticised on the grounds that, if implemented, it would violate the principles of marginal productivity and would not end

---

[1] Landsberger, p. 59.

[2] Dovring makes the important point that, 'The logical solution to the problems of East European agriculture should have been intensifying the pattern of land use first, followed by as much farm exodus as the rest of the economy would absorb, before mechanization were introduced on a larger scale at a much later stage . . . The collective farm, by its very constitution, tends to retain all the least desirable members, those for whom its function as poor pension is their best chance in life. That this cannot but lower the apparent productivity of agricultural labor is clear enough'. Folke Dovring, *Land and Labor in Europe in the Twentieth Century*, 3rd rev. ed. (The Hague, 1965) p. 150.

rural overpopulation. Georgescu-Roegen argues convincingly that, although this position is correct, it is irrelevant, since, if one wants to provide optimum welfare in a transitional economy, those other goals are not attainable.[1] He calls the agrarian solution a feudal solution, in that it calls for a maximum use of labour with a tithing system (state taxation) as the chief source of capital accumulation, and contends that it is eminently suited to the needs of a transitional economy.[2] For tithing may be the only source of capital in an overpopulated peasant economy, and this solution spreads the limited resources about more equitably. More important, it provides a more normal gateway to modernisation, which will ultimately mean the liquidation of the peasantry as a social class and, therefore, a dwindling importance of the peasant political movement as well.

Though 'intuitively correct', the peasant political movement in Eastern Europe did lack one essential quality: patient self-study. Peasant leaders made no systematic effort to adapt their programme to their own realities. In fact, many of them made a virtue of their own ignorance and indifference, extolling their own 'gut response' to problems, and contrasting it to the abstract theorising of many middle class politicians. As Georgescu-Roegen puts it:

> . . . there is no more dramatic example of the disaster that awaits him who in formulating an economic policy disregards theoretical analysis, than the well-known fate of the agrarian parties of Eastern Europe.[3]

Here was the Achilles heel of the movement. Its goals could not be reached unless certain other conditions were met, conditions that were neither spelled out nor pursued relentlessly at the time.[4] In order to succeed in reaching their goals, peasant leaders would have had to bring all peasant holdings up to an optimum size, and agriculture could not be expected to operate according to the principles of marginal productivity, since by those standards it would still have more labour than was needed. Some sectors of the economy, especially industrial production, would have to be allowed to operate according to the capitalist criteria of maximising production and profit, in order to grow and absorb at least a large part of the surplus rural population. Lacking a firm understanding of the prerequisites in their own programme, the peasant political movement did not include them among

[1] Georgescu-Roegen, pp. 392–3.   [2] Ibid.
[3] Ibid., p. 369.   [4] Ibid., pp. 391–7.

their own minimum goals. Instead one found everywhere agrarian reforms that in most instances increased the number of dwarf holdings, economic policies that increased the number of landless labourers in agriculture, an underlying hostility to the operation of any sector of the economy according to capitalist principles, and consequently a decline in the standard of living of the peasantry.

Having failed through their own measures to fulfil the trust placed in them by their own peasantry immediately after World War I, the peasant political parties naturally gravitated towards those aspects of their own programme that had no bearing on peasant welfare, and that had an appeal beyond the peasant class, like the drive for national independence in the Croatian Peasant Party and the Slovak Peasant Party, or towards an essentially capitalist programme, as in the case of the Czech Agrarian Party and the Rumanian National Peasant Party. In their drift away from the seemingly insoluble problem of peasant poverty, the Hungarian, Croatian and Rumanian peasant parties lost several of their leaders to the new extremists, the facist movements.[1] The mass following of the peasant parties spilled over into fascist and communist front movements that promised to accomplish those tasks that the peasant parties had left undone, like the restoration of a sense of dignity and security for small and landless peasants. The League of the Archangel Michael in Rumania was a fascist movement with significant support from peasants, the Slovak Peasant Party became fascist, and the three communist front peasant parties in Poland made a remarkable showing in the elections of 1928.[2] The Bulgarian Agrarian Union, the Serbian Agrarian Union and the Polish Peasant Party were able to cling to a genuine peasantist or agrarian programme because they had no effective political power under their authoritarian governments, and, therefore, did not have to conduct a conclusive test of their programme by implementing them.

Of course, to say that the agrarian programme of the peasant political movement was possible, and probably even desirable, is not to say that its fulfilment was probable. In many ways they were victims of adverse historical forces over which they had no control, like the prevailing political conditions and traditions in Eastern Europe during the inter-war years. In this sense their failure to obtain and hold political power was probably inevitable. That failure left behind a

---

[1] On the Croats, see Hugh Seton Watson, *The East European Revolution* (London 1950) p. 78; on the Rumanians see Roberts, p. 225, and on the Hungarians see Gati, pp. 145–89.

[2] Jackson, pp. 210–12.

potentially explosive situation. The peasant political movements had raised the hopes of vast numbers of the rural poor and urban intellectuals and then dashed those hopes, laying the foundations for a revolution of rising expectations. This was the base on which the communists would attempt to build after 1945.

Chapter 8

THE POLISH PEASANT MOVEMENT IN POLITICS: 1895–1969

by

Dyzma Galaj

INTRODUCTION

SPONTANEOUS forms of peasant protest have marked Polish social history for many hundreds of years. Countless serfs have rejected their station by fleeing from their masters, and countless more have expressed their bitterness in acts of personal violence. Similarly, organised peasant protest has a long history in Poland. During the seventeenth century, for example, many serfs from the south-eastern region of the country escaped from their lords' control by fleeing across the river Dniepr to the so-called Wild Fields, where they joined the Cossacks in setting up armed detachments to plunder the estates of their former oppressors. The rebels were finally defeated by royal armies in the battle of Beresteczko (1651), and their leaders summarily sentenced to death. Over a hundred years later (in 1769), another peasant revolt sparked by the reimposition of villeinage in the Szawel region of Lithuania, at the time under Polish control, met the same fate. And the Kosciuszko uprising of 1794, although primarily concerned with the national liberation of Poland, was undoubtedly supported by peasants who hoped to bring about the abolition of serfdom.[1]

Examples of organised peasant protest in Poland during the nine-

[1] See A. Przybos, *Materialy do Powstania Napierskiego 1651* (Materials Related to the Kosta Napierski Uprising, 1651) (Wrocław, 1951); S. Szczotka, *Powstanie chlopskie pod wodza Kostki Napierskiego* (The Peasant Uprising Led by Kostka Napierski) (Warsaw, 1951); W. Tokarz, *Insurekcja Warszawska, 17 i 18 kwietnia 1794 r.* (Warsaw Insurrection of 17 and 18 April 1794) (Warsaw, 1950); W. Lukaszewicz, *Targowica i powstanie kosciuszkowskie* (Targowica and Kosciuszko Uprisings) (Warsaw, 1953); B. Lesnodorski, *Polscy jakobini* (Polish Jacobins) (Warsaw, 1960); and W. Tomkiewicz, *Kozaczyzna ukrainna* (Ukrainian Cossacks) (Lwow, 1949).

teenth century could also be given. In 1837, for example, an important peasant movement led by the Reverend Piotr Sciegienny took place in the central provinces; and nine years later, the Jakub Szela movement swept more than ten *powiats* (counties) in the south.[1] The purpose of this paper, however, is not to consider these earlier forms of rural unrest, but rather to concentrate on the analysis of a more recent phenomenon: the creation of modern peasant parties which have, since the end of the last century, served as the principal means through which the Polish peasantry have fought for an equal status within national society.[2] Discussion of the historical development of peasant parties will be divided into four periods: (1) the founding of the earliest organisation in partitioned Poland between 1870 and 1914; (2) factionalism and party unity in reunited Poland (1918–1939); (3) the role of peasant parties during the German occupation of 1939–45; and finally, (4) the organisation of the peasantry in post-war Poland. A more general analysis of the characteristics of the movement as a whole will form the concluding section of the paper.

I. THE ROOTS OF ORGANISATION: CONDITIONS IN PARTITIONED POLAND DURING THE LATE NINETEENTH AND EARLY TWENTIETH CENTURIES

Peasant movements are, like all attempts at extensive organisation, subject to serious divisive strain: disagreement among factions over the legitimacy of certain goals or methods, differing assessments of appropriate allies and enemies of the movement, and so on. In Poland, the forced partition of the nation during the period 1815–1914 added a special dimension to the problem of division within the movement. Not only were peasant organisations physically split during their earliest days into geographical areas separately controlled by Germany,

[1] See M. Tyrowicz, *Sprawa ks. Piotra Sciegiennego* (The Case of the Reverend Piotr Sciegienny) (Warsaw, 1948); Cz. Wycech, *Ksiadz Piotr Sciegienny, Zarys programu spolecznego i wybor pism* (The Reverend Piotr Sciegienny: Outline of his Social Programme and a Selection of his Writings) (Warsaw, 1953); S. Kieniewicz, *Ruch chlopski w Galicji w 1846 roku* (The Galician Peasant Movement of 1846) (Wrocław, 1951).

[2] The term 'peasantry' is here used in a broad sense, to include all men who earn their living by working the land themselves (at times with the help of labourers), who live within the framework of a rural community. Subsistence farmers and small and medium capitalist farmers fall within that definition. Large landowners, however, do not; they do not work the land themselves and their class interests are fundamentally different from small operators. As a rough guide, it may be supposed that 50 to 100 hectares in some regions is the upper limit of 'peasant holdings' discussed in this paper.

Russia and the Austro-Hungarian Empire,[1] but at the same time they were divided in a more subtle way by the necessity to respond to different socio-economic and political realities within each of the partitions. The effects of partition have been so lasting that even now, many years after the reintegration of the Polish nation, local differences in approaches to organization can still be found within the peasant sector. Therefore, a brief review of conditions within each of the occupied areas at the time when the earliest political parties were founded must be a necessary prerequisite to understanding the later course of the movement as a whole.

The Prussian Partition

Because Germany had the most highly developed capitalist economy of the three partitioning powers, large semi-feudal estates (the characteristic form of agrarian organisation in areas under Russian and Austrian control) were virtually non-existent in the Prussian Partition. Polish peasants within the German sector worked within a capitalist framework of private holdings. Roughly 55 per cent of these holdings contained five hectares or less; and they provided a reserve of ready labourers for neighbouring establishments which often contained from 100 to 300 hectares. Surplus population on the land was also drawn into urban centres of the occupying power, where the rapid expansion of German industry provided alternative possibilities for employment. Between 1815 and 1914, it is estimated that some 650,000 inhabitants of the Prussian Partition emigrated to Germany, many to become industrial workers.[2] This possibility of migration eased the economic problems of a countryside threatened with the division of many agricultural enterprises into units of uneconomic size.

The condition of the Polish peasantry in the Prussian Partition was nevertheless a difficult one, because it was the policy of the German Government severely to restrict Polish participation in both economic and political affairs. Bismarck introduced an intensive campaign of 'Germanisation', continued by his successors, which prohibited the use of the Polish language in offices, schools and churches; strictly limited self-government within the Polish territory; and encouraged

---

[1] During the century of partition, Russia controlled 462,000 square kilometres of Polish territory, including (by the end of the nineteenth century) 5·5 million inhabitants. Germany controlled 130,000 square kilometres containing 2·6 million inhabitants, and Austria controlled 135,000 square kilometres including 3·2 million inhabitants.

[2] J. Rutkowski, *Historia gospodarcza Polski*, t. II (Economic History of Poland, vol. II) (Poznan, 1950) pp. 234–9.

Germans to buy the land of Polish farmers.   A bill passed in 1886, for example, established a Colonising Commission and endowed it with 100 million marks to be used for strengthening the German presence within the Partition, primarily through the acquisition of land.   And in 1894, the Union for Support of Germanism in the Eastern Region was founded to conduct extensive 'Germanising' activities in the occupied Polish territories.

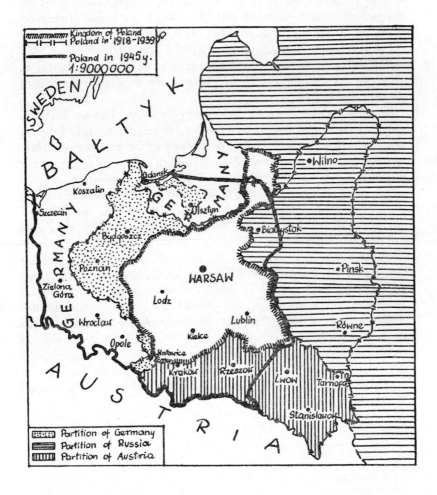

The Russian Partition and the Kingdom of Poland[1]

Capitalist development also occurred in the Russian Partition and the Kingdom of Poland during the period of occupation; but unlike the situation in German-occupied areas, that development was felt far more in urban than in rural areas. The industries of Warsaw, Lodz, Bialystok and other Polish cities in the Russian Partition were superior to those of the occupying power and therefore expanded to meet the demand of a new Russian market. Thus while the Polish population of the Prussian Partition migrated in order to join the ranks of industrial workers within Germany, a native Polish industrial bourgeoisie and working class developed within the boundaries of the Russian Partition. That fact was of considerable importance for the future shaping of political organisation.

Land tenure conditions in the countryside of the Russian Partition and the Kingdom of Poland were far less equitable than in the Prussian area. Although some land was distributed to the peasantry in 1864, many large properties of a semi-feudal nature continued to exist. For that reason, despite the rather small density of population and the high rate of emigration to the United States, the number of landless peasants increased during the period under discussion. In 1870, 3.5 per cent of the rural population did not own land; in 1891, the figure had risen to 13.5 per cent.[2]

Tsarist authorities controlled the political and cultural life of inhabitants of the Russian Partition in much the same way that German governments restricted the freedom of Polish residents in the Prussian Partition. The January Uprising of the Poles against Russian domination, crushed in 1864, brought on the prohibition of the Polish language in schools, state offices and courts, and the dissolution of Polish political, religious and cultural organisations. In contrast to the Germans, however, Russian authorities did not limit the initiative of the Polish population in the agricultural sector. Since the Russians had

[1] The Kingdom of Poland, or Congress Kingdom, was established by the Congress of Vienna in 1815 and united with Russia by a personal union. It included 128,500 square kilometres in the present voivodships (districts) of Warsaw, Lodz, Lublin, Kielce and part of Krakow, Poznan, Bydgoszcz and Bialystok. Those were purely Polish lands. The other areas of the Russian partition were Lithuania, White Russia, and the Ukraine. In this paper we deal primarily with the Kingdom of Poland.

[2] H. Brodowska, *Historia Polski drugiej polowy XIX wieku. Okres kapitalizmu przedmonopolistycznego* (Polish History of the Second Half of the Nineteenth Century. Period of Pre-monopoly Capitalism) (Warsaw: Polskie Wydawnictwo Naukowe [Polish Scientific Editions], 1961) pp. 129–43.

more than enough of their own land, they did not have to promote colonisation schemes in Poland.

The Austrian Partition

Economic conditions in the Austrian Partition were more difficult than in either of the other two occupied areas. This was in fact the time when the proverbial 'Galician squalor' came into being. Before partition, the area had contained flourishing industries, linked to world markets through Gdansk; but after 1815, access to the sea was no longer possible. The industrial products and handicrafts of the Austrian Partition were not able to compete within the Austro-Hungarian Empire with manufactures from the more highly developed regions of Czechoslovakia, nor could Polish farm products compete with more efficient Hungarian and Czech agriculture (which, by the way, were also much closer to the main markets for foodstuffs – Vienna, Budapest and Prague).

The lack of alternative possibilities of employment for the rural population of the Austrian Partition encouraged the continuing division of already small parcels of land. By the end of the nineteenth century, 79·8 per cent of all peasant homesteads in the region contained five hectares or less, while a comparable figure for the Prussian Partition was 55 per cent and for the Russian Partition 24·8 per cent.[1] At the same time, a large part of the land of the Austrian Partition remained in extensive holdings. Disputes between small peasants and estate owners over the rights of the former to use pastures and woodlands controlled by the latter were endemic – as they had been since the Middle Ages. And in most cases, those disputes were settled in favour of the estate. Thus of 32,000 cases of litigation reported between 1880 and 1900 in the Austrian Partition, only 2000 were not won by large landowners.[2]

Although poverty in the Austrian Partition was widespread, the cultural and political freedom of Polish inhabitants was greater there than in the other two partitions. It is true, of course, that as time passed, the occupying power gradually placed Austrians and Czechs in various key administrative positions. Nevertheless, the Polish population was granted relative local autonomy (including a regional Parliament), and sent representatives to the Parliament in Vienna. At

[1] J. Rutkowski, op. cit., p. 77.
[2] C. Wycech, *70 lat Ruchu Ludowego* (Seventy Years of the Peasant Movement) (Warsaw: LSW, 1965) p. 98.

the same time, a lively contact was maintained with the outer world through the letters and visits of peasants who had emigrated in search of work. Between 1891 and 1914 alone, some 770,000 residents of the Austrian Partition found their way to the United States, and their letters reflect concern with general social problems as well as particular local issues.[1]

Early Organisation

The earliest traces of what was later to become a large-scale political movement of the Polish peasantry are to be found during the last few decades of the nineteenth century, when progressive members of the national bourgeoisie and intelligentsia went to the countryside with programmes for the education and economic advancement of the peasantry. The motives of the bourgeoisie and intelligentsia varied, of course, from individual to individual. Nevertheless, their activity can in general be related to a stirring of nationalism, humanitarianism and the desire for economic development. A lethargic peasantry – despondent, illiterate and often still fettered by semi-feudal obligations – was considered an important obstacle to the construction of a newly liberated and economically progressive Poland.

Perhaps the most basic task undertaken by countryside activists during the late nineteenth century was that of making the individual peasant throw off his feeling of inferiority and recognise his own worth in society. As one outstanding Polish sociologist has noted, the literature of the period 'became the call to struggle for the internal, spiritual autonomy of the peasant, . . . a challenge to fight slave humbleness in the presence of the authority of lords and priests. The timeless . . . existence of the Polish peasant was coming to an end. The peasant began to shape his own and his nation's history'.[2]

Two Souls (Dwie Dusze), written by the peasant activist Jakub Bojko in 1904, is the most representative work of this phase. The author analyses peasant attitudes and points out that there is a struggle going on within every peasant: a soul shaped by the past – humble, shy, and frightened – is struggling against the soul of a man who is free, modern, equal to his former masters. 'The ghost of a hideous old hag who died in 1848 and who called herself "Serf Labour" still haunts us. That hag held the peasantry in captivity for four hundred years and succeeded

---

[1] H. Brodowska, op. cit., p. 77.

[2] Jozef Chałasinski, *Spoleczenstwo i wychowanie* (Society and Education) Nasza Ksiegarnia (Our Booksellers) (Warsaw, 1948) pp. 264–5.

in killing man within the peasant. She made of him a machine, to be operated according to her wishes.'[1] 'And you, peasant', Bojko continues, 'are your own master, even if it is only on a small piece of land – a master so great that even you yourself cannot understand it! In spite of your poverty, you are a greater lord on your little plot than a grave digger, a church-organ player, a vicar, a rector, a tavern keeper, a doorman, a cashier, a secretary, a commisar, a head of the *powiat* (county), or even some higher echelon.'[2]

Concrete organisational activity during this period took the form of promoting literacy, founding reading rooms and libraries, establishing agricultural circles and co-operatives, and encouraging Polish national pride. Thus, for example, the Association of Popular Education, founded in 1881–2 in Lwow and Krakow, had by 1890 provided the peasantry in the Austrian Partition with some three hundred libraries and reading rooms where books in the Polish language could be obtained. And in the German Partition, the Society for Popular Education (1872) fulfilled the same function. The Society lost its charter in 1878, but was replaced by the Society of Popular Reading Rooms, which set up over 1500 village libraries throughout the German Partition before 1914.[3]

Better agricultural practices were encouraged through such organisations as the Association of Agricultural Circles, founded in 1878 in the Austrian Partition. By 1890, the Association contained 23,000 members in 607 circles. Similar circles had existed within the German Partition since 1866, as well as an especially lively co-operative movement uniting the wealthier peasants with elements of the bourgeoisie. That movement was formally integrated into the Union of Polish Co-operative Societies in 1870, and by 1905 contained 19,354 members in 196 co-operatives.

In the Russian Partition and the Kingdom of Poland, organisations of even an educational nature were made difficult to establish by the rigorous opposition of the Tsarist Government. Therefore the Circle of Popular Education, organised in 1883 to distribute Polish books and set up village schools and educational centres, was a secret organisation. It is true that some educational activities, carried out by organisations under the supervision of large landowners, were allowed to exist

[1] Jakub Bojko, *Dwie Dusze* (Two Souls), Wydawnictwo Ludowe (Peasant Editions). (Warsaw, 1949), p. 16.
[2] Ibid., p. 18.
[3] *Zarys historii polskiego ruchu ludowego*, t. I (Historic Outlines of the Polish Peasant Movement, vol. I) (Warsaw: LSW, 1963) pp. 192–3.

openly, but they were carefully controlled. One example will illustrate the conflicting currents within such organisations. In 1900, the
Society of Apiculture and Horticulture, managed by estate owners,
began an agricultural school in Pszczelin, near Warsaw. Despite the
moderate intentions of its founders, an outstanding activist in the
nationalist peasant movement (Jadwiga Dziubińska) became the head
of the school and ran it on the model of Danish popular universities.
Students were encouraged to devote themselves to rural education and
to be active in promoting social and political reform. Such a development so frightened the wealthy sponsors of the school that Dziubińska
was eventually forced to resign.

The First Political Parties

The efforts of moderate reformers and nationalist leaders to gain the
support of the peasantry could not indefinitely be confined to the fields
of education and economic co-operation. By the last few years of the
nineteenth century, the first peasant political organisations began to
appear. And since relative freedom of participation in the electoral
process had long been allowed the Polish inhabitants of the Austrian
Partition, political organisation of the peasantry in that region most
nearly approached the classic model of the formation of parliamentary
political parties. Progressive members of the Polish intelligentsia
within the Austrian Partition, united in the Polish Democratic Society,
organised in 1895 a congress of peasant representatives to rural electoral
boards. Their intention was to establish a Central Electoral Committee
which would support the candidates recommended by the Democratic
Society. The Committee was in fact established, but at the same time
a formal political party, the Peasant Party, was also founded. That
organisation was the first of its kind in Poland.

Because one of the founders of the Peasant Party, Rev. S. Stojalowski,
had become deeply involved in the Christian Democratic movement
while studying in Belgium, the programme of the newly formed
Polish party was modelled closely on West European Christian
Democratic thought. Its programme declaration was not especially
radical; it demanded neither the redistribution of land nor immediate
national self-determination. It did, however, call for the disappearance
of remaining vestiges or feudalism, for the reform of highway, hunting
and church laws,[1] for the suppression of usury and the provision of

[5] There were the laws obliging peasants to construct and maintain public roads, provide
money and services to the Church and to the community office, and allow landowners
to hunt in their fields despite obvious harm to their crops.

cheap credit, etc. And it mobilised the peasantry to vote for candidates put forward by the Party – nine of whom were actually elected to the Austrian Parliament in 1895. Thus the ancient slogan 'Polish Peasants with the Polish Gentry' was replaced by a new theme: 'Vote for the Peasantry'.

In the Russian Partition and the Kingdom of Poland, the total absence of political freedom made organising activity among the peasantry far more revolutionary. Antagonism between peasants and estate owners over rights to the use of pastures and woodlands reached serious proportions during the first years of the twentieth century, at the same time that the Russo-Japanese War caused great hardship among the peasant and working classes. Therefore in 1904 the Popular Education Circle, whose nationalist educational activities have been noted above, took the lead in the founding of the Polish Peasant Union at Jaktorow. The purposes of the Union were insurrectionary: to bring about national liberation and at the same time to ensure the economic and political liberation of the peasantry from the estate system.

Specifically, the Polish Peasant Union asked for the autonomy of the Kingdom of Poland and the establishment of a national parliament in Warsaw. Both workers and peasants were to have full representation in Parliament, and at all levels of the political system. At the same time, after the division of the largest estates, a wide system of peasant co-operatives was to be established in order to 'stimulate the masses of the people to creative work for the common good'. The programme of the Party continued as follows: 'The transformation of the country as a whole into this type of a co-operative republic is the essential aim of the Peasant Party. This Party will pursue . . . that aim not by bureaucratic measures imposed from above but by self-reform of society, by the method of co-operation in all fields of culture and social economy'.[1] The influence of the Russian Social Democrats and Narodniks on the programme of the Polish Peasant Union is clear,[2] as is the much greater radicalism of the Union when compared with the Peasant Party of the Austrian Partition.

Political activity in the German Partition was minimal, perhaps

---

[1] *Zarys historii polskiego ruchu ludowego*, t. i (Historic Outlines of the Polish Peasant Movements, vol. i) (Warsaw: LSW [Peasant Editions Co-operative], 1963) p. 145.

[2] The Narodniks were peasant activists in Russia during the last thirty years of the nineteenth century. Their programmes included a rejection of both feudal and capitalism and an idealisation of the small farmer united with others through extensive co-operative systems. This programme strongly influenced some of the leaders of the peasant political movement in the Kingdom of Poland. An indirect influence (through Polish workers' movement) was also exercised by the Russian Social Democrats.

because Polish nationalists there had neither the hope of forming a parliamentary party such as the Peasant Party in the Austrian region nor the revolutionary example provided by Russian Narodniks and Social Democrats to Polish reformers in the Russian Partition and the Kingdom of Poland. Therefore efforts at organising the peasantry in the German Partition were limited to the short-lived Masurian Peasant Party, founded in 1896 and associated with the 'Peasants' Gazette' at Elk. The founders of the party never really understood the needs of the peasantry, and for that reason the organisation never developed a large membership. It was eventually dissolved by order of the German authorities.

Thus throughout this early phase of political awakening, organisations of the peasantry in each of the three occupied areas of Poland proceeded independently. There was a minimum of contact among peasant parties in different partitions; and only towards the end of World War I, when it became obvious that the day of Poland's liberation was at hand, was the necessity of common action in the interests of a national peasantry recognised. The socio-economic differences among partitioned areas proved so great, however, and the consequent agreement among political parties so infrequent, that the integration of peasant factions into a single united organisation could not be achieved for many years.

II. FACTIONALISM AND PARTY UNITY IN REUNITED POLAND (1938-39)

With the end of World War I and the reunification of the Polish nation, one of the original stimuli to early peasant protest – foreign domination – disappeared, and the attention of activists among the peasantry turned to a more careful analysis of socio-economic problems of the countryside. Those problems were great, and they increased in intensity and complexity throughout the inter-war period. The continuing impoverishment of the rural population as a whole, accompanied by a growing differentiation of various strata within the peasantry (medium and small capitalist farmers, subsistence farmers, wage labourers) and the eventual definition of clearly conflicting interests among them, form the background against which changes in the political organisation of the Polish peasantry during the inter-war period must be seen.

Socio-economic Conditions in the Countryside

The agricultural sector in Poland suffered from a number of serious problems after 1918. Perhaps the most basic of those was a sharp growth of population, which placed by 1939 an average of ninety people on the same square kilometre of land occupied in 1921 by seventy. One source estimated that in the 1930s there were between five and nine million 'superfluous inhabitants' in the Polish countryside.[1] At the same time, opportunities for alternative employment in industry were severely limited. The relatively late industrialisation of Poland fixed the largest part of the population on the land for many years after agriculture had ceased to absorb the majority of the work force in more highly developed capitalist nations. Thus as late as 1931, 72·6 per cent of the entire Polish population lived in rural areas and 61 per cent of it earned a living from agriculture.[2]

Overpopulation of the countryside encouraged the steady division of already small agricultural holdings. By 1931, 64·2 per cent of all farms in Poland contained five hectares or less, and only 4·5 per cent of all holdings were larger than fifteen hectares in size. These were, of course, geographical variations in land tenure figures: in the counties of Rzeszow and Krakow, for example, nearly 90 per cent of the farms contained less than five hectares and only 0·6 per cent over fifteen hectares; while in the Poznan and Pomerania areas comparable figures were 30 per cent and 20 per cent. Nevertheless, the majority of the peasantry throughout Poland may be said to have worked plots of an uneconomic size.[3]

The situation was made worse by the lack of credit and a general decline in agricultural productivity during the inter-war period. Thus the grain crop of 1929–33 was on the average about one hundredweight less per establishment than in the years 1909–13, and losses were in fact much greater on peasant plots than those figures (including the production of large estates) indicate.[4] By 1936, the average debt of a peasant household in Poland was equal to the value of 26 hundredweights of rye per hectare, when the total value of a hectare of land on the open market varied from about 55 hundredweights of rye in

---

[1] Various authors have given this figure. See H. Kolodziejski (ed.), *Mlodziez siega po prace* (Youth Searches for Work), (Warsaw: Wydawnictwo Instytutu Spraw Spolecznych [Editions of the Institute of Social Work], 1938) pp. 41–53.

[2] *Maly Rocznik Statystyczny 1939* (Concise Statistical Yearbook, 1939), (Warsaw: Main Statistical Office 1939), p. 29–30.

[3] Ibid., pp. 68–9.

[4] J. Rutkowski, op. cit., pp. 285–6 and *Maly Rocznik Statystyczny 1934* (Concise Statistical Yearbook, 1934) (Warsaw: Main Statistical Office, 1934) p. 29.

the Poznan region to about 93 hundredweights near Rzeszow.[1]

Continuing economic decline, combined with the experience of war and migration, affected the traditional social relations of the Polish countryside in various ways. It must be remembered that within most Polish villages, a client-patron relationship had existed for hundreds of years between richer and poorer elements of the peasantry. That relationship contained definite elements of exploitation: poorer peasants borrowed money, animals, land, and so on, from their better-off neighbours and repaid the loan with interest (often in labour). Nevertheless, the exploitative nature of the exchange was generally not emphasised; transactions were made in a way which softened group conflict and stressed the interdependence of all parties to the agreement.[2]

Potential conflict between richer and poorer peasants was delayed not only by an intricate system of reciprocal obligations, but also by the traditional isolation and local pride of Polish rural communities. Inhabitants of each village could be distinguished from others by slight differences in speech or clothing, social customs and working habits. Therefore, the wealthier and better-educated sectors of the peasantry were the pride of their villages, representing the particular culture of each community to the outside world. And localism was so strong that any resident of a given village could often count on the votes of his neighbours – even if the political platform of the candidate were not at all in the interests of the peasantry.

It was only with expanding communications, the experiences of war and migration, and the commercialisation of agriculture that these old patterns of behaviour changed and conflict among peasant strata became more frequent. There can be no doubt that a very important role in the breakdown of village isolation was played by Polish emigrants, forced by the scarcity of land and work in the countryside to travel in search of a livelihood. By 1939 almost three million people had left the nation to live abroad, and their new knowledge (transmitted through letters as well as personal visits) represented a challenge to traditional ways of life. Not only did the migrants question the relation of the peasantry to more privileged groups, but they questioned the patron-client ties within the villages as well.[3]

[1] *Wies w liczbach* (The Countryside in Figures) (Warsaw: Ksiazka i Wiedza [Book and Science], 1954) p. 11.

[2] See S. Czarnowski, *Spoleczenstwo-kultura* (Society-Culture) (Warsaw-Poznan: Polski Instytut Socjologiczny [Polish Institute of Sociology], 1939) pp. 298–420.

[3] On the basis of a number of letters written by peasants who emigrated to work in the United States, W. Thomas and F. Znaniecki wrote a five-volume work of rural sociology, *The Polish Peasant in Europe and America* (Boston, 1918).

An even greater challenge to village localism was the impact of war. Two world wars rolled over Polish territory, and a large part of the peasantry took part in them, either as combatants or as members of the resistance movement. Refugees from the cities lived in peasant homes; peasant men fought in foreign lands. The result of these confrontations with a wider world was a change in peasant values and an increasingly critical attitude towards existing social relationships.

Political Organisation during the Inter-War Period

In 1918, peasant political parties which had until then operated separately within each partition of Poland were presented for the first time with the necessity of co-ordinating their efforts in a reunified nation. Differences in organisation, allies and ideology among parties were so marked, however, that only sporadic co-operation took place during the early inter-war period. It was not until 1931 that all branches of the Polish peasant movement were forced to form a single united party in order to meet the twin challenges of economic depression and political persecution.

Immediately following the end of World War I, three important peasant parties existed in Poland. These were, in the former Russian Partition and Kingdom of Poland, the *Polish Peasant Party 'Wyzwolenie'* (created by the merger of the former Polish Peasant Union, described above, with two other groups in 1915); and in the former Austrian Partition, the *Polish Peasant Party 'Piast'* and the *Polish Peasant Party 'Lewica'* (both formed in 1913 when the original Polish Peasant Party of 1895, described above, split in two). In 1926 a fourth party which was to play a significant part in the inter-war period appeared: the *Party of the Peasants*

Differences in programmes and ideologies among parties within the same geographical region were much less important after reunification than the broad differences between regions created by differing socio-economic realities. Thus, for example, the leadership of the 'Piast' Party, by far the most important group within the region of the former Austrian Partition, was strongly influenced by landowners like Count Rej and Count Lasocki, and by businessmen like Angerman and Dlugosz. Consequently, the 'Piast' Party adopted a conservative programme emphasising co-operation with the traditional parties of the right and respect for private property. Similarly, the orientation of the 'Lewica' Party was generally conservative, despite the intermittent bandying of radical mottoes during contests with 'Piast'.

The Polish Peasant Party 'Wyzwolenie' of the Kingdom of Poland and the former Russian Partition, on the other hand, contained no landowners or businessmen in their leadership; and in keeping with their tradition of struggle against the Tsarist regime they put forward a programme similar to that of the Polish Socialist Party: equal opportunities for all Polish citizens, the division of large estates, and the socialisation and nationalisation of such sectors of the economy as the mining and armaments industries, banks, trade and forestry. Specific provisions of the Party of the Peasants and the 'Wyzwolenie' Party for agrarian reform included the forced sale of all land held in extensions greater than sixty to one-hundred-and-eighty hectares (depending on the quality of the land in question) and its division among landless peasants and smallholders, to be worked as individual family farms. Finally, a number of programme items dealt with the establishment of co-operatives, the provision of agricultural insurance and food-processing industries, agricultural education, and so on.

The first parliamentary alliances of the post-war Polish Parliament did not cut across old partition boundaries to unite the peasant class, but rather united the important peasant parties of each geographical region with non-peasant organisations of the same area. Regionalism and long-established ideological ties with non-peasant groups proved more important than class solidarity at that time. Thus during 1918, the 'Piast' Party formed an alliance with the rightist National Democracy of Galicia (the former Austrian Partition), and the 'Wyzwolenie' group co-operated closely with the Polish Socialist Party of the former Russian Partition and Kingdom of Poland. These alliances prevented the integration of the Polish peasant movement on a national level for more than ten years.

One example of the early lack of co-operation among factions within the movement is to be found in the refusal of the 'Piast' Party, led by W. Witos, to lend support to the first Polish Government, headed by a Prime Minister of the Polish Socialist Party. That Government contained representatives of the 'Wyzwolenie' Party; and one member of the party, Stanislaw Thugutt, was in fact its Minister of Internal Affairs. Nevertheless, Witos found co-operation impossible without the inclusion of more representatives from parties of the right.

Endless discussions among leaders of the major peasant parties of Poland ended in 1918 with no agreement on a common list of candidates for the parliamentary elections of January 1919. Therefore, the election success of the peasant sector was only partial, as the following results show:

TABLE 1

POLISH PARLIAMENTARY ELECTION RETURNS, JANUARY 1919:
FORMER RUSSIAN AND AUSTRIAN PARTITIONS AND THE KINGDOM OF POLAND

Parties	Seats (*Held by Peasant Delegates)
1. Territory of a part of the former Russian Partition and Kingdom of Poland:	
(a) Polish Peasant Party 'Wyzwolenie'	58*
(b) Polish Peasant Party 'Piast'	8*
(c) Polish Socialist Party	25
(d) United Right (Christian Democracy, National Democracy and other parties of the Right)	90
(e) Others (various minor political groups)	50
2. Territory of the former Austrian Partition (Galicia):	
(a) Polish Peasant Party 'Piast'	33*
(b) Polish Peasant Party 'Lewica'	12*
(c) Polish Socialist Party	17
(d) Others	7
Total	300

Source: A. Prochnik, *Pierwsze pietnastolecie Polski Niepodległej* (The First Fifteen Years of Independent Poland), Ksiazka i Wiedza (Book and Science) (Warsaw, 1957) pp. 50–3.

These delegates were later joined by two candidates of peasant parties elected in the German partition,[1] raising the total number of seats held by members of the peasant parties to 113 out of 413 in the entire Parliament.

[1] In January 1919 parliamentary elections took place only on the territory of the former Austrian Partition (Galicia) and the Kingdom of Poland. Other Polish territories were still occupied (such as Poznan and Pomerania, where the elections took place later in 1919), or did not yet have an organised political and administrative authority which could arrange parliamentary elections (such as Bialystok, Suwalki, and Vilna in the former Russian Partition).

The reader should note that in the former German Partition, no political parties existed at the time of the first parliamentary elections, although economic and socio-cultural organisations were operating among the peasantry. Therefore, political parties of the former Kingdom of Poland and Galicia gradually extended their influence into the former German Partition after independence and were eventually successful in winning some voters there. Among the peasants, the Polish Peasant Party 'Piast' was most favoured.

The total number of seats held by representatives of the peasant sector fluctuated between one-fourth and one-third of the entire Parliament during the period 1918–28, and for that reason, Cabinets constructed during those years often included a representative of the peasantry. Nevertheless, it is interesting to note that with the exception of the first Minister of Internal Affairs, mentioned above, who came from the radical 'Wyzwolenie' group, peasant leaders within the Cabinet came only from the conservative 'Piast' Party. W. Witos served three times as Prime Minister,[1] and Maciej Rataj, also of 'Piast', was elected Parliamentary Speaker in 1922.[2] That the programme of those leaders did not meet the demands of the peasantry at large is shown by the sharp decline in electoral support for their party after 1922, and a parallel growth in support for the more radical 'Wyzwolenie' Party, as well as smaller radical groups, illustrated in the following table.

TABLE 2

NUMBER OF VOTES RECEIVED BY VARIOUS POLISH PEASANT PARTIES IN THE PARLIAMENTARY ELECTIONS OF 1919, 1922, AND 1928

Parties	1919	1922	1928
Polish Peasant Party 'Piast'	432,000	1,153,000	480,000
Polish Peasant Party 'Wyzwolenie' and smaller radical parties	1,000,000	.	1,812,000

Source: A. Prochnik, op. cit., pp. 52, 133 and 281.

One outstanding accomplishment of the peasant sector in Parliament was nevertheless registered. In 1925 an agrarian reform law was passed which allowed, during the following fourteen years, the division of

[1] The years of Witos' service were 1920–21, 1923 and 1926.

[2] Some leaders of peasant political parties in Poland (like Boleslaw Wyslouch, Maksymilian Malinowski, Ilona Kosmowska, Wladyslaw Kiernik) came from families of intellectuals. Maciej Rataj, on the other hand, was one of a numerous group of leaders (including Jan Stapinski, Jan Dabski, Josef Grudzinski, Kazimierz Baginski, Stanislaw Osiecki, Ignacy Solarz, Wladyslaw Kowalski, Stefan Ignar, Czeslaw Wycech, Kazimierz Banach and Jozef Ozga-Michalski) who grew up in a peasant family but through education gained employment outside the peasant sector. A third group, including Wincenty Witos, Jabub Bojko, Tomasz Nocznicki, Blazej Stolarski, Teofil Kurczak, Piotr Koczara, Wincenty Baranowski and Boleslaw Podedworny continued to run their farms while engaging actively in politics. In most cases, these farms were larger than the average, but they could hardly be called capitalist enterprises. Their owners were likely to have attended a few years of primary school, and then to have trained themselves to become excellent speakers and essayists. Witos, for example, completed only three years of formal schooling, yet was undoubtedly one of the most outstanding politicians in interwar Poland.

some 2·6 million hectares of estate land and its delivery to approximately 734,000 peasants. All deputies of peasant political parties, the Polish Socialist Party, and minor political groups of the centre voted in favour of the law. Representation of the right and the communists, on the other hand, opposed it. The former found the land reform too radical, for it allowed landowners to keep only 60 to 700 hectares (depending upon the quality of the land). The latter held that the law was too mild, and that land should be confiscated and delivered without cost to agricultural workers and smallholders.

At the same time that peasant demands were becoming increasingly radical, the strong faith of peasant parties in their eventual ability to carry out reforms through parliamentary means was profoundly shaken by the Pilsudski coup of 1926. It should be noted that even the peasant organisations on the left had begun the post-war period with the certainty that the simple numerical strength of the peasant sector would assure its victory in a democratic system. But that possibility became remote indeed when Jozef Pilsudski (who came to power with the support of the Polish Socialist Party and the two major peasant parties of the former Russian Partition) betrayed his own supporters and brushed aside Polish democracy to institute a semi-fascist regime. It was that sudden challenge to the parliamentary system, combined with the increasing economic hardship associated with the world depression, which at last forced the integration of all peasant parties in Poland.

Formal co-operation among political parties opposed to Pilsudski began in the fall of 1929, when an agreement among six groups of the centre and left (including the only three remaining peasant parties at that time: 'Piast', 'Wyzwolenie', and the Party of the Peasants) created a coalition known as Centrolew ('Centre Left'). Activists within the coalition organisation anti-Pilsudski rallies which were countered by the Government with mass arrests. Thus W. Witos, K. Baginski, W. Kiernik, J. Putek, and A. Sawicki – all important members of Polish peasant parties – found their way to jail. The first three later emigrated to Czechoslovakia, from which they directed further activities against Pilsudski.[1]

The formal merger of all peasant parties came in 1931, when the Peasant Party was founded as an organisation of opposition to Pilsudski.

---

[1] Witos' memoirs of his days in exile were published by Ludowa Spoldzielnia Wdawynicza (People's Editorial Co-operative) in Warsaw in 1967 and are titled *Moja tulaczka* (My Homeless Wandering).

Expecting no success in the parliamentary elections of 1935 (given the ruthless methods used by the Government against dissent), the Party proclaimed an election boycott. Although a number of activists broke the boycott in order to register their dissent against Pilsudski, it is nevertheless significant that only 37 per cent of all the registered voters of the nation took part in those elections.

Simultaneously with the founding of the united Peasant Party, a new and important organisation of peasant youth appeared in Poland. The Union of Peasant Youth, or 'Wici', as it was called,[1] broke away from the Central Board of Agricultural Circles in 1928, when the latter subordinated it to the Pilsudski regime. From that time forward, although the Union was independent of the Peasant Party and emphasised educational and cultural matters more than political ones, it co-operated closely with the Party.

It was with the help of young activists affiliated with 'Wici' that the newly united peasant movement of Poland developed, for the first time in its history, a comprehensive agrarian ideology. That ideology could never, of course, satisfy all the conflicting factions and individuals within the movement; but it did nevertheless provide the framework for the common action of a very large group of people.

The starting-point of the agrarian ideology of the 1930s in Poland was the promise that the peasant population constituted a uniform social stratum. And that stratum, as the most numerous one in the country, was entitled to full participation in a democratic system of government. Dictatorship in any form – whether that of Pilsudski or the dictatorship of the proletariat contained in Marxist programmes – was rejected. In the economic realm, the agrarians proclaimed agriculture the basis of the national economy and relegated to industry only secondary importance. The agricultural sector itself was to undergo a thorough reform, including the division of large estates, the strengthening of individual family farms, and the creation of a wide system of production and marketing co-operatives.

Much stress was placed within the agrarian ideology on the essential wholesomeness of agricultural life, unspoiled by the negative features of industrialisation. The small family farmer, linked to the land and to nature in his daily work, was therefore the person most fitted to aid in the moral regeneration of the nation. This outlook was reflected in the work of 'Wici', which established people's universities modelled

---

[1] The name 'Wici', a sign announcing oncoming danger and warning people to prepare for defence, symbolised the opposition of the organisation to Pilsudski's dictatorship.

on the pattern of the Grundvig experiment in Denmark. There young peasants were taught industry, good administration and a love for nature and for each human being.

In reality, the future envisioned by the agrarian ideology was to be a democratic utopia. It would not be a continuation of the capitalist system, which had proved its weakness in the far-reaching economic crisis of 1929–32, as well as in the distorted political development of Nazi Germany, Fascist Italy, and Pilsudski's autocratic regime. Nor was the agrarian utopia to be an institution of the socialist system, which agrarians felt lacked appreciation of the value of the individual human being, and particularly, the moral value of personally performed agricultural labour. The new system would be a Co-operative People's Republic, born not so much out of political struggle as through a process of spiritual regeneration, beginning in the country-side. And that regeneration would spread to other countries through the International Slavonic Union of Peasant Youth, whose task was to extend the boundaries of the agrarian ideal.

Thus the agrarian ideology tried to find a middle road for the peasantry, an independent way somewhere between the workers and the bourgeoisie. It was a true reflection of the dilemma of the peasant stratum at the time, uniting both working people and property owners in a single movement. The tragedy of the ideology was, however, that it encouraged utopian dreams which did not count in the current struggle for power within Poland. The Peasant Party of the 1930s thus served merely to pacify revolutionary trends among the peasantry, and in so doing it posed no threat to an increasingly rightist Government. Members of the rank-and-file of the Party were forced to seek other outlets for the redress of their grievances.

The precarious position of the united Peasant Party as it balanced between the left and the right is well illustrated by its inability adequately to support important strikes of rural workers, whose frustration with the political immobilism of the thirties found expression in public protest. During the period 1932–36, numerous spontaneous demonstrations of the peasantry took place without the sanction of the Party. Finally in 1937, the Peasant Party Congress voted to support a nationwide strike; but when it could not be controlled and forty-nine peasants were killed by the police, the leadership of the Party became alarmed. An alliance with the Communist Party, which strongly supported the strike, was unacceptable to the leadership and to a part of the members of the Peasant Party (as was any formal co-operation with Polish parties of the right).[1] Therefore no further concrete stand on the question of strikes could be taken.

III. PEASANT POLITICS DURING THE GERMAN OCCUPATION (1939–45)

The German invasion of 1939 increased the pressure on groups of all ideological persuasions within the Polish peasant movement to forget their differences and to unite in a common effort to defeat the occupying power. In fact, the danger was so great that even an issue as fundamental as opposition to the Pilsudski legacy became lost to view among some groups within the Peasant Party. As the war progressed, however, the hardships it imposed on the population increased discontent with continuing bourgeois leadership to such an extent that the united Peasant Party eventually split in two. The Polish peasantry definitively left the 'middle road', and the largest number of them at last found a spokesman for their cause in the new Polish Workers' Party.

The immediate reaction of the Peasant Party to the German occupation of 1939 was to join with three other strong parliamentary parties (the Polish Socialist Party, the National Party, and the Labour Party) in the creation of a united front supporting the Polish Government in exile. Unfortunately, however, the military detachments of the Government in exile were led by Pilsudski's officers, thus precluding any change in government after the end of the Nazi occupation. The leadership of the Peasant Party could not at the time accept such an eventuality, and they therefore established in mid-1940 their own underground army. The Peasant Battalions, numbering some 160,000 men at the height of their strength, were not only to fight the German army, but to ensure that the defeat of the Nazis would mean the defeat of the Pilsudski legacy as well.

They accomplished the former task with distinction. Some 2400 battles and skirmishes were fought by the Peasant Battalions against

---

[1] The Polish Communist Party for many years did not consider peasants as class allies. In fact, only after the Second Congress of the Party in 1923 was the idea of an alliance between workers and peasants adopted as a basis for political action against the bourgeoisie; and only during the 1940s was a formal effort made to co-operate with the leadership of the central peasant movement by the Polish Workers' Party (successor of the Polish Communist Party). Nevertheless, during the thirties informal co-operation between the communists and local activists and organisations affiliated with the Peasant Party and 'Wici' did take place.

the Germans. In addition, a widespread nationalist conspiratorial movement sprang up among the peasantry, inspired by the slogan of an important underground periodical, 'Peasants Feed and Defend' (*Zywia i Bronia*). And a specialised resistance organisation for peasant women appeared as well.

The latter goal of the Peasant Battalions, the lessening of Pilsudski's power, proved more difficult to implement. Unfortunately, in the course of 1942, the leaders of the Peasant Party became increasingly linked with the London Government in exile, and thus with a centre-right political programme. The issue of national liberation was more and more emphasised, while that of social liberation receded into the background. It was thus proved once again that the 'middle road' of the Polish peasantry, the independent course between the workers and the bourgeoisie, was not practicable. As in the past, the Peasant Party was eventually controlled by the bourgeoisie.

A number of rank-and-file activists of the Peasant Battalions observed the shift of their leaders towards the right with dismay and began to search for allies within the leftist camp. The organisation which eventually offered them the programme they sought was the Polish Workers' Party, founded in early 1942 and led by the communists. In the further struggle against the Nazi occupiers, as well as the internal struggle among Polish political groups, that party became the mainstay of the left.

Thus by 1945, two opposing camps had emerged within the Polish peasant movement. One contained the leadership of the Peasant Party, allied with centre-rightist elements of the bourgeoisie and with the London Government in exile. The other was organised around the new peasant party 'Wola Ludu' ('the will of the people'), founded at the turn of 1944 to further a policy of alliance with the Polish working class, the Polish Workers' party and the Soviet Union. Between those two extremes oscillated numerous groups of peasant activists who tried to reconcile their interest in a radical social programme with their conviction that traditional leaders must be supported for the moment in order to maintain national unity and to defeat the German invader. It is safe to say that in many cases, local peasant groups simply made their own independent policy as the occasion dictated.

IV. POST-WAR PEASANT ORGANISATION IN POLAND

The end of the war brought the transformation of 'Wola Ludu' into a full-fledged socialist peasant party within liberated Poland. Changing its name to the 'Peasant Party' shortly after independence, 'Wola Ludu' put the concept of a workers' and peasants' alliance into practice by joining the Polish Workers' Party in initiating a revolutionary land reform. Nearly 500,000 peasant families received land expropriated from former estates, thus meeting one of the most ancient and fundamental demands of peasant politics.

During the first years of independence, the more conservative original Peasant Party, supported by the Prime Minister of the Polish Government in Exile, Stanisław Mikołajczyk, continued to exist and vigorously to oppose an alliance between workers and peasants. When Mikołajczyk arrived from England, he refused to co-operate with 'Wola Ludu' (now also known as the Peasant Party); and in so doing, he forced the original Peasant Party into a position of support for liberal-democratic adversaries of socialism in Poland. This policy was resisted by many leaders within the Party itself, who in 1947 abandoned Mikołajczyk and his allies to form the Polish Peasant Party 'Lewica', an organisation basically in sympathy with the ideas of the 'Wola Ludu' Peasant Party. Mikołajczyk eventually left Poland, and with his departure the remains of the original Peasant Party disintegrated; a part of its membership turned to the 'Lewica' group, while others simply discontinued political activity altogether. The process of reorganisation of the peasant sector in politics was completed several years later when members of the 'Lewica' merged in 1949 with 'Wola Ludu' thus founding the United Peasant Party. The aim of the newly united peasantry was clearly stated: to further the development of Poland through support for the main reforms of a people's State (land reform, the socialisation of industry, and political power for workers and peasants).

As these programmes were progressively implemented, they brought with them profound changes in the economy and society of Poland. Large and medium landowners disappeared, thus eliminating the most obvious class enemy of the peasantry. At the same time, the age-old question of national minorities was resolved. And finally, the economic policy of the State, which emphasised the development of industry as the key to national development, promoted a wave of migration from rural to urban areas, growing demand for agricultural products, and an improved supply of manufactured goods in the villages. In a country so devastated by war,[1] any other course would have been utopian and would simply have delayed a necessary improvement in the standard of living of both urban and rural dwellers.

The role of the United Peasant Party (Z.S.L.) in the post-war reconstruction of Poland was initially to work in partnership with the strongest political group of the nation, the Polish United Workers' Party. During the early 1950s, however, a crisis developed in this partnership; and because of certain tendencies in the management of the State, Z.S.L. was inhibited in its efforts to serve the peasant population. The situation changed for the better only in 1956, when new leaders who rejected dogmatism and bureaucratic procedures assumed control of the United Workers' Party. The speech of the Secretary of the Party's Central Committee, W. Gomulka, to the Plenary Session of the Central Committee on that occasion reflected the necessity for a reorientation of inter-party relations.

> Erasing the mistakes of the past, our Party will change its policy towards its ally, the ZSL. We recognise ZSL as an independent party and we will progressively confirm this attitude in practice. We do not want to and we will not encroach on its party sovereignty. We want [the ZSL] to develop and to unite in its ranks all radical members and activists of the peasant movement, regardless of their political past. We consider the ZSL's power as our allies' power and that is why we want it to grow in size. We want to enforce the workers' and peasants' alliance shoulder to shoulder with the ZSL; we want it to share with us the leadership of the state, the establishment of the people's authority, the building of socialism.

This reorientation was indeed carried out, thus restoring the vitality which had characterised the work of the United Peasant Party in the earliest post-war period. As the programme declaration of the Party stated in 1959:

> The United Peasant Party is a party of peasants which organises them to work for the development of People's Poland, maintaining

[1] Two hundred and twenty of every one thousand Polish citizens were killed as a result of the policy of extermination followed by the Nazis, and 38 per cent of the national wealth was destroyed.

the independence, power, and security of the nation through cogoverning the people's state and building a system of social justice, i.e., socialism. ZSL represents the interests of the village and links them with the needs of the working class and the whole Polish nation.

V. ALLIES AND ENEMIES OF THE MOVEMENT

It seems worthwhile at this point to step back from the details of the Polish peasant movement, presented above, and to view the development of the movement throughout the last eighty years as an historical process intimately related to the socio-economic development of the entire nation. Such an analysis must be based not only upon changing configurations of interests within the peasant stratum itself, but also upon the changing position of the peasant sector in relation to other major social groups in Poland.

It can be said at the outset that the allies and the enemies of the Polish peasant movement changed in accordance with changes in the entire social structure of the nation. Thus the beginning of the movement coincided (certainly not fortuitously) with the bourgeois-democratic attack on the remaining strongholds of feudalism in Poland. At that moment, therefore, the principal allies of the peasantry were progressive elements of the bourgeoisie: village teachers, intellectuals, some clergymen, industrialists, and modern agricultural entrepreneurs. On the other side were the semi-feudal landholding class and the high-ranking clergy, both of whom saw their traditional authority threatened by the development of new attitudes among the peasantry.

During this period of peasant organisation, programmes which would seem to later generations little short of reactionary were truly revolutionary. Thus at a time when the peasantry as a whole was considered by traditional elites to be hardly human – ignorant creatures fit for 'dung fork work' – the attempts of the Rev. Stojalowski and his co-workers in Galicia to draw the peasantry into the political system through the founding of a peasant Party (1895) was a serious blow to the established order. The point was not so much that the candidates for which the peasantry voted were members of the bourgeoisie, but rather that, for the first time in history, the small landowners and rural workers of Poland were a factor to be considered in national political life.

The different historical experience of that part of Poland under Russian control gave the early years of the movement there a slightly different configuration from the Galician example. Since the industrial sector of the Kingdom of Poland and the Russian Partition was highly developed by the 1890s and a strong workers' movement had come into being, the peasant movement in that area was from the beginning integrated into a more advanced socio-economic structure. Leaders of the movement, for example, had ties with industrial workers as well as with the teachers, intellectuals and professional men who made up the principal allies of the Galician peasantry. And the industrialists and agricultural entrepreneurs who played such an influential role in the Galician movement were more likely to be identified as enemies than as allies of the peasantry in the Russian-dominated areas, since they disliked the close ties between working-class and peasant activists.

During the inter-war period, the socio-economic pattern of the former Russian Partition became the rule for Poland as a whole. The growth of industry, the transition from feudal to capitalist agriculture and the integration of the landed bourgeoisie with industrial and financial capitalists made the organised peasantry a 'third force' between the expanding working class on the one hand and the bourgeoisie on the other. It was therefore not surprising that the bourgeoisie, which had earlier sought the support of the peasantry in the defeat of feudalism in the countryside, should in this period try to use the peasant movement as an ally against the working class. Nor was it unusual that the workers should in turn also seek an alliance with the peasantry.

The continuous splits within the parliamentary peasant parties of the 1920s, their short-lived alliances first with one political faction and then with another, illustrate the instability of a movement containing so many heterogeneous interests (small capitalist peasants, subsistence farmers, landless labourers) and desired as an ally by both the bourgeoisie and the workers. The process of social differentiation within the peasantry itself was only slowly progressing towards a stage in which the interests of each stratum within the movement would attain independent importance.

The dilemma of the Polish Peasant Party during the 1930s provides a graphic illustration of the conflicting currents tearing at the formally united movement. The impact of the world depression, combined with the repressive policies of the Pilsudski Government, had accelerated the process of pauperisation of a large segment of the Polish peasantry, thus dramatically differentiating it from the better-off elements within the movement. The poorer peasants therefore demanded radical action in concert with the revolutionary left, while the better-off segments of the peasantry opposed such an alliance. The Peasant Party, as the formal representative of both groups, was immobilised; it could take neither course without losing a large part of its membership, and found itself truly a 'third force' isolated from the rest of the nation. That such a course could not be maintained indefinitely was proved by the final split of the movement during the 1940s, and the alliance of the largest part of the Polish peasantry with the Communist Polish Workers' Party.

It should be noted that there was undoubtedly one outstanding reason why the Polish peasant movement had such an especially wide following (including many different rural interests) and was so unusually co-operative with the bourgeoisie throughout so many years of its history: the periodic appearance of serious foreign threats to national existence overcame internal division, interrupted developing social conflicts, and forced the temporary co-operation of most elements of Polish society in order to defeat a common enemy. That was certainly the case during the period before World War I, when nationalism spurred the first alliance of the peasantry and the progressive bourgeoisie to bring an end to partition. It was true of the period of the Nazi occupation. And it explained the existence of the united Peasant Party, which tried to save the nation from Pilsudski.

VI. METHODS OF PEASANT ORGANISATION

In general, the formal organisation structure of all peasant parties which functioned in Poland after 1895 was similar to that of the united Peasant Party of 1931–45. At the most local level, a *powiat* (county) board was elected. County boards in turn elected representatives to voivodeship (district) boards. Those intermediate organisations then chose representatives to the supreme authority of the Peasant Party, the National Congress, which convened every four years to draw up programmes and to elect a General Board which served as the continuing decision-making body of the Congress during periods when it was not in session. Finally, the General Board designated an Executive Committee of the Party which directed the day-to-day activities of the organisation and implemented resolutions passed by the Congress and General Board.

In practice, peasant parties always functioned with a minimum of formality and discipline, since their rank-and-file were not accustomed to follow regulations drawn up by the decision-making bodies of the Party. Although members were formally obliged to pay dues, attend meetings, and so on, there was no way to force them to do so. Therefore, peasant political parties were always short of funds and did not dispose of the full-time staff which is considered such an integral part of modern mass organisations. The Executive Committee of the United Peasant Party employed only two people on a full-time basis during the 1930s. One of those was the head of the Party as well as the editor-in-chief of its newspaper, the 'Green Flag' (*Zielony Sztandar*). Other activists performed their duties on a voluntary basis.

Great attention was paid by all parties to their local activities in village centres. The personal contact of activists with peasant masses was always of essential importance, and for that reason a special role in Polish peasant organisation was played by mass meetings. Those meetings were usually scheduled to coincide with a local or national holiday (the anniversary of the Kosciuszko Uprising, the November Uprising, or the death of the great poet Mickiewicz, for example), with religious pilgrimages and festivals, or with village agricultural exhibits and fairs. Assembled crowds were addressed by several speakers, often representing opposite political viewpoints. The audience expressed its approval or disapproval of each speaker with applause or angry shouts, and unpopular orators were at times forced to run for their lives.

These meetings offered an opportunity for dialogue and a possibility for gifted local leaders to make themselves known. The quality of personal contact between audience and speaker was far more important during such occasions than the concrete details of programme offered. The ability to run a discussion, personal appearance and charismatic qualities, number of promises made – all these elements determined the popularity of a particular speaker, and consequently fortunes of this party.

The Pilsudski dictatorship brought changes in the methods of peasant organisation in Poland, because the kind of large popular gathering described above was proscribed and repressed. Therefore, open meetings were gradually transformed into closed-door sessions, but, as in the past, attendance was not limited to the membership of any party. Throughout the history of the peasant movement, the number of 'followers' of various parties always greatly surpassed the number of their official members, and that was precisely the strength of the movement.

An extremely important role in the development of peasant organisation in Poland was played by newspapers. The work of writers associated with those publications was to deal with the everyday problems of the peasantry and to present large political issues in a simple way. The papers were not read by one subscriber alone, but by a group of listeners (often illiterate), who went regularly to the home of a subscriber-activist in order to have the papers read to them and then to discuss the contents.

The great influence of these peasant newspapers is illustrated by the case of the 'Zaranie movement'. The *Zaranie* ('Daybreak') was a newspaper published between 1907 and 1915 in the Kingdom of Poland. It was not sponsored by any specific political party, since parties in that partition had been proscribed by the Tsarist Government. Nevertheless, the columnists associated with the paper, country teachers and peasants, succeeded in stimulating such a strong current of interest in politics among the peasantry that this period of peasant history in the Kingdom of Poland has come to be called the 'Zaranie movement'. The newspaper had contributors in 412 villages, a subscription list of 8,000, and a still larger group of the peasantry closely linked to its activities.[1]

Dozens of other important peasant newspapers of the pre-World War I period could be mentioned at this point. Many of them attracted a very large number of subscribers. The 'Grudziadz Gazette' of the German Partition, for example, recorded before World War I a printing of approximately 100,000 copies. And during the Nazi occupation, illegal publications of the Polish peasant movement reached the height of their popularity and prestige, maintaining national spirit during a time of great difficulty.

The publication of books and pamphlets was another means used by peasant parties to communicate with the rural population. This form of activity was especially characteristic of the organisations in the Kingdom of Poland before World War I, and it served to supplement schoolwork, as well as to provide a rational and scientific counterweight to the vaguely theological view of the world presented in the textbooks issued by the Tsarist Government.

[1] See W. Piatkowski, *Dzieje Ruchu Zaraniarskiego* (A History of the Daybreak Movement) (Warsaw: LSW Editors, 1956).

In the years between the wars, one final organising tactic became popular: the celebration of a 'People's Holiday', coinciding with the religious observance of Whitsuntide. The holiday included mass meetings all over Poland, as well as many cultural events, and was designed to manifest the political power of the masses associated with the Peasant Party. It was not a form of organisation compatible with Pilsudski's dictatorship, and in 1932 the People's Holiday was ended by clashes with the police in which several peasants were killed and a number arrested.

VII. SUCCESS AND FAILURE: AN EVALUATION

As the preceding discussion suggests, the Polish peasant movement has made an invaluable contribution to the democratisation of the nation. At the time of writing, the most profound aspirations of many generations of peasant activists (political power, land and education) were well on their way to being met. In 1969, for example, the United Peasant Party (Z.S.L.) counted 117 of the total 460 deputies in the national Parliament, including the Parliamentary Speaker; the Deputy Chairman of the State Council; two Ministers; eight Deputy Ministers; the Deputy Chairman of the Planning Commission within the Ministers' Council; five of seventeen Chairmen of Voivodship People's Councils; and twelve Deputy Chairmen of Voivodship People's Councils. And the participation of representatives of the Z.S.L. in lower regional and local administrative bodies, agricultural organisations and institutions was still greater.

The United Peasant Party itself has functioned democratically. Its supreme authority is a national congress held every four years in order to elect a Board of approximately 100. That Board in turn elects a Praesidium of eleven, which is charged with the direction of the daily activities of the Party. Leaders are linked with the countryside through a hierarchy of organisations at the voivodship, county, community and neighbourhood levels.

Aside from political power, a second long-standing demand of the peasantry has largely been met; land was provided by the post-war land reform. That reform was, however, only the beginning of the economic transformation of the Polish countryside. A most significant success of the political leadership of Poland, heavily influenced by the Z.S.L., has been the reconstruction of the rural sector and the promotion of systematic growth in agricultural production since the war. This has been accomplished in Poland through programmes which differ considerably from those employed in other socialist countries. Reorganisation has proceeded rather slowly and has been carried out not against, but with the consent of the peasantry; their economic conditions and level of social consciousness have been taken into account in planning. The principles which have governed the re-organisation of agriculture, approved by the Polish United Workers' Party and the United Peasant Party, are as follows: freedom for the peasant to choose the kind of farming organisation he feels best; the provision of technical assistance and machinery through agricultural circles (a form of peasant self-government) and state machine centres; encouragement of the rational production of foodstuffs through a contract buying system; and promotion of a number of social institutions intended to make the farmer's work easier and more efficient at the village level. The satisfactory progress of Polish agriculture in the past years speaks well for the validity of this plan and the wisdom of the political leadership of the nation, including representatives of the Z.S.L. among its most prominent members.

The third basic goal of the Polish peasant movement, increased educational opportunities for the rural population, has been conscientiously pursued by the United Peasant Party with some notable results. In 1969 over 40,000 peasant youths were found to be in higher educational institutions; and although that figure represented only 17 per cent of all students in institutions of higher learning, it was still a large step forward from the past. Z.S.L. has carried out a continuous campaign to further the equal access of peasant youth to education above the primary level, thus persistently attacking one of the largest remaining problems of the peasantry. In addition, the Party has kept its members informed through the publication of a daily newspaper, a bi-weekly periodical, two weeklies, a theoretical monthly entitled 'Contemporary Countryside', and the Annals of the History of the Peasant Movement. The total circulation of these publications is more than 400,000 per issue. Through the Z.S.L. publishing co-operative, some two hundred books of fiction or popular science, usually dealing with village matters, are printed each year. And finally, the Party maintains its own centre for the investigation of agrarian history (the Centre for the History of the Peasant Movement).

Thus, through participation in peasant political parties, the rural population of Poland has progressively destroyed the ancient barriers which kept them so long at the margin of national life. Land, education and political power are within their reach, and the United Peasant Party defends their interests within the framework of a socialist State.

PART 3

PEASANTS, DEVELOPMENT AND NATIONALISM

Chapter 9

THE PEASANT MOVEMENTS OF DEVELOPING COUNTRIES IN ASIA AND NORTH AFRICA AFTER THE SECOND WORLD WAR

by
Yu. G. Alexandrov

INTRODUCTION

IT is impossible to discuss the dynamics of socio-economic and political change in the developing countries today without including a careful analysis of the history and progress of peasant movements. The peasantry constitutes, after all, the most numerous stratum of the population. It still provides the bulk of the labour force in developing economies, as it has for many centuries; and it is becoming an increasingly important element in the balance of political power in many cases as well. The prospects for economic and social progress in developing countries therefore depend to a considerable extent on the kinds of agrarian contradictions generated within each country and the nature of peasant movements growing out of those contradictions.

At the same time, however, an objective investigation of peasant movements in developing countries is not at all an easy matter. Reliable information on the social structures of rural communities, the economic status of different strata of the peasantry, and the social psychology of specific peasant groups is rather limited. And data on the dynamics of peasant movements themselves are even more difficult to obtain. This is true, first, because peasant discontent often takes the form of a vague murmur, not articulated through the establishment of formal organisations. And second, even when large regional or national peasant interest groups are founded, the majority of them have no clearly stated programmes of action, nor do they issue many publications. Their activities are unfortunately very sparingly covered by the Press.

This article will rely primarily on information gathered by Soviet scholars, and will attempt to discuss the principal stages through which peasant movements in North African and Asian countries have passed since the Second World War. It must be stressed that only the broadest trends in the development of these movements can be discussed here, and that many general statements made in the course of this article would require amendment if applied to individual cases.

I. THE PEASANTRY IN THE STRUGGLE FOR NATIONAL LIBERATION

During the Second World War and the years immediately following it, a movement for the national liberation of colonial peoples swept North Africa and Asia, enveloping not only officially recognised dependencies of colonial powers but also officially independent, but factually dependent, semi-colonial states. The role of the peasantry in that movement was important, both because of the direct participation of some elements of the rural population in liberation armies, and because even those segments of the peasantry not directly engaged in military activities were likely in one way or another to provide assistance to nationalist forces.

In part, the participation of the peasantry in national liberation movements was related to their growing consciousness of national identity, encouraged by the immediate necessity of expelling a foreign invader or repelling a threatened attack. It would be misleading, however, to discuss the growth of nationalist feeling in the abstract, without pointing out the concrete social grievances which formed the roots of peasant nationalism. Wartime devastation, forced requisitions and mobilisations, served only to increase the discontent which the peasantry had long felt towards colonial oppressors, whether associated with the Allies or the Axis powers. Thus, for example, many peasants who had taken part in guerrilla activities against the Japanese in South-East Asia joined the armed struggle for the attainment of new social goals in the post-war period. The goal of the rural poor in joining national liberation movements was not simply the expulsion of an occupying power, but more basically, the construction of a new and more equitable social, economic and political order.

It must be remembered that in many countries of North Africa and Asia, the most obvious forms of economic exploitation were associated in the peasants' minds with colonial rule. This was particularly true in areas where there was no strong indigenous feudal structure to oppose direct foreign domination in the countryside and where land ownership by foreigners was therefore widespread. It was precisely in countries where the national liberation struggle was most directly linked to the expulsion of foreign landholding interests that peasant participation in nationalist movements reached its highest point.

That was the case, for example, in Algeria, where in 1951, Europeans owned 6,750,000 acres of the most fertile land of the littoral region, or in other words, one-third of all the arable land of the nation. Under those circumstances, the poorest elements of the Algerian peasantry (*fellahs*) made up approximately 80 per cent of the National Liberation Army. As one of the leaders of the nationalist movement, Bashir Haj Ali, wrote, 'The cherished dream of the poor peasant is to come down one fine day into the fertile valleys and recover the land of his ancestors, stolen by the colonialists'.[1]

A similar situation could be found in Indonesia and Burma during and immediately following the Second World War. Over 750,000 acres of foreign-owned plantations in Sumatra and Java, as well as vast areas of state forests, were taken over by 'squatters' (representing some 150,000 peasant families) during those years.[2] And in Burma, 3,000,000 acres, 35 to 40 per cent of the best rice lands formerly owned by Indian money-lenders (Chettyars), were seized by the peasantry when the Chettyars fled the country on the eve of the Japanese invasion.[3]

In some colonial regions, local feudal interests as well as foreign landowners were challenged by the peasantry. Thus an anti-feudal 'social war' raged in Sumatra during 1945 and 1946, as well as in Iranian Azerbaijan during the same period. Parts of the Philippines and India witnessed similar attacks by the peasantry on the indigenous feudal system. These efforts were to become far more important, however, during the post-independence period, when the element of external oppression had been removed and internal relationships of dominance and subjection were more clearly visible.

[1] 'Agrarnyi vopros i natsional'no-osvoboditel'noe dvizhenie' (The Agrarian Problem and the National Liberation Movement), in A. M. Rumiantsev (ed.), *Materialy obmena mneniiami marksistov-agrarnikov* (Proceedings of the Conference of Marxist Agrarians), (Moscow: Sotsekgiz [Social Economics State Publishing House], 1963) p. 58.
[2] Yu. G. Alexandrov, *Politika Respubliki Indonezii v sel'skom khoziaistve* (The Policy of the Indonesian Republic in the Agricultural Sector) (Moscow: Izdatel'stvo 'Nauka' ['Science' Publishing House], 1964) p. 42.
[3] N. J. Lazarev, 'Birma' (Burma), in *Agrarnye otnosheniia v stranakh Vostoka* (Agrarian Relations in the Eastern Countries) (Moscow: Izdatel'stvo vostochnoi literatury [Eastern Literature Publishing House], 1958) pp. 232–3.

The ideological content and political programmes of peasant movements throughout North Africa and Asia during the struggle for national liberation were extraordinarily complex, precisely because they reflected the complexity of the economic and social structures of colonial dependencies at that time. New social groups such as the bourgeoisie, the proletariat, the middle classes and the intelligentsia, all characteristic of modern society, had begun to appear and had in fact supplied the majority of the principal leaders of national liberation movements. Similarly, a developing market economy had encouraged the increasing differentiation of the rural community into small capitalist producers, the rural bourgeoisie, and the landless proletariat. Nevertheless, this process was by no means complete; in most cases, modern social classes were still in a formative stage and constituted relatively small groups directly tied to various pre-capitalist social strata. Religious leaders, feudal lords and tribal chiefs continued to exert considerable influence over certain groups of the population, and at times led the peasantry in campaigns to resist the encroachment of capitalism and return to former traditional ways of life.

In general, it can be said that a large part of the peasantry, particularly in more developed countries like Syria, India and Turkey, were by the end of the war under the ideological influence of the national bourgeoisie, who were themselves often engaged in the promotion of Western middle class values. At the same time, however, various strata of the peasantry in many countries were in touch with petty-bourgeois or leftist revolutionary thought. Not infrequently, supporters of these last two currents turned to socialism; and it was under the leadership of such men that a few peasant movements and organisations of this period were able to overcome the limits set for them by less radical elements of the national liberation struggle and to demand profound changes in the relationship of the peasantry to the land.[1]

The growing social consciousness of the peasantry during the postwar nationalist upheaval, as well as the increasing interest of the

---

[1] A. M. Melnikov, 'Krest'ianskoe dvizhenie v stranakh Vostoka mezhdu dvumia mirovymi voinami' (The Peasant Movement in the Countries of the East between the Two World Wars), in *Krest'ianskoe dvizhenie v stranakh Vostoka* (The Peasant Movement in the Countries of the East) (Moscow: Izd-vo 'Nauka' ['Science' Publishing House], 1967) pp. 13, 20.

The Indonesian Sarecat Islam Party is a particularly good example of an organisation founded by the native bourgeoisie which gradually came to include more and more elements of the left. These elements put forward radical demands and organised a number of peasant clashes. See A. B. Belenky, *Natsional'noe probuzhdenie Indonezii* (National Awakening in Indonesia) (Moscow: Izdatel'stvo 'Nauka' 1965) pp. 187, 200, 274–6 et seq.

nationalist bourgeoisie in obtaining large-scale political support from the countryside, encouraged the formation of numerous national peasant organisations throughout Asia and Africa at this time. The All-Indian Kisan Sabha (Peasant Union) counted 825,000 members by 1945,[1] and a number of smaller district and state organisations sprang up throughout the country as well. Several large peasant organisations emerged in Indonesia following the proclamation of independence in 1945; and the All-Burma Peasants' Union, which joined the Anti-Fascist People's Freedom League, re-emerged during the same year. Other national peasant interest groups appeared in the Philippines, Korea and Malaya; and local peasant committees were formed in Pakistan and Syria.

II. PEASANT MOVEMENTS IN THE IMMEDIATE POST-INDEPENDENCE PERIOD

The attainment of political independence in former colonial states was generally followed by a marked decline in the vitality of their peasant movements. One reason for the decline was simply that part of the economic and social demands of the peasantry had been met during the last years of colonial rule, and another part had been won in the course of the national liberation struggle. Colonial powers had, for example, passed legislation granting some degree of protection to tenants in India, Burma and the Philippines, while regulating the activities of money-lenders in those countries as well.[2] In addition, Indonesian peasants benefited after independence from the elimination of the majority of the feudal principalities and privately-owned foreign land-holdings in their country, abolition of the practice of compulsorily leasing peasant land to sugar refineries, and a certain democratisation of rural community administration. And finally, in South Korea peasant pressure for land had by 1945-9 (still before the enactment of a formal reform programme) reduced the area of landlords' holdings by one-half.[3]

Aside from the fulfilment of the most outstanding demands of the rural poor in some Asian states, the peasantry was often quiescent after

[1] G. G. Kotovskii and P. P. Moiseyev (eds.), *Agrarnyi vopros v stranakh Azii i Severnoi Afriki* (The Agrarian Problem in the Countries of Asia and North Africa) (Moscow: Izd-vo 'Nauka' 1968) p. 102.

[2] Melnikov, op. cit., p. 8.

[3] I. S. Kazakevich, *Agrarnyi vopros v Iuzhnoi Koree* (The Agrarian Question in South Korea) (Moscow: Izd-vo 'Nauka' 1964) p. 25.

independence because the attainment of national sovereignty gave rise to an atmosphere of general expectation and hope. Now the long, ruinous wars had ended and social justice would be furthered by a new nationalist government. At the same time, a resurgence of religious controversies and local rivalries, partially suppressed during the fight against colonialism, diverted the attention of the peasantry from the pursuit of wider goals.

In these circumstances, only the poorest peasants in regions where oppression and lack of land were greatest (such as the central Luzon area of the Philippines, and parts of Vietnam, Indonesia, and Burma) continued to participate actively in protest movements.[1] These peasants were predominantly tenants and farm labourers with very small holdings who struggled against the most intolerable remnants of feudal exploitation, and who found themselves very much isolated from other, less militant, strata of the peasantry.[2] Thus a movement of the rural poor attempting to improve the terms of lease holding and to prevent the eviction of tenants by feudal landlords flared up in the *zamindari* areas of India immediately following independence. And in West Pakistan a strong movement of *hari* tenants appeared in Sind; while in West Punjab and the former North-West Frontier Province, where there were fewer tenants and more landed peasants, the movement was noticeably weaker.[3]

Numerous other examples of tenant unrest during the period under discussion could be given. In the great majority of cases, these peasant protests were spontaneous local actions, poorly planned if indeed they were planned at all, and not co-ordinated with activities of the peasantry in other communities or regions. They were usually reactions to concrete grievances, and only seldom involved wide social and political demands.

As time passed and the long-promised enactment of agrarian reform programmes by new nationalist governments was further and further delayed, the number of incidents of the kind described above increased markedly. In fact, it is possible to say that after a few years of relative quiet following the attainment of national independence, a clearly

[1] V. A. Popov, 'Nekotorye osobennosti krest'ianskogo dvizheniia v razvivaiushchikhsia stranakh, sviazannye s provedeniem agrarnykh reform' (Some Specific Features of the Peasant Movement in the Developing Countries Related to the Implementation of Land Reforms), in *Krest'ianskoe dvizhenie v stranakh Vostoka*, op. cit., p. 41.

[2] Ibid., pp. 41, 43.

[3] A. M. Melnikov, 'Agrarnoe dvizhenie v Indii posle dostizheniia nezavisimosti' (The Agrarian Movement in India after Independence), in *Krest'ianskoe dvizhenie v stranakh Vostoka*, op. cit., pp. 102–6.

distinguishable current of anti-feudal protest swept the East. As in former years, these protests were not part of a co-ordinated movement, but rather represented separate local reactions to specific grievances. Unlike the earlier protests, however, the new current of discontent was no longer the creation of the poorest elements of the peasantry alone; it united all strata of the peasantry, from the agricultural proletariat to relatively wealthy tenants and landholders, in opposition to the remaining feudal structure. As long as that unity could be maintained, noteworthy pressure was brought to bear on the new governments to effect anti-feudal reforms.

Unfortunately, however, the unity of the peasantry during the struggle for anti-feudal legislation proved only a temporary alliance, determined not so much by the coincidence of interests among various strata of the peasantry as by the fact that all groups faced, for the moment, a common enemy: the feudal landholding class. The well-to-do peasants participated actively in the agrarian movement of this period only as long as the struggle was carried out exclusively against remaining feudal strongholds, or for lighter taxation, better marketing conditions, credit, and so on. When the village poor eventually turned their attention to the fact that rich peasants often used the same exploitative methods as feudal landlords, only differing from the latter in their capitalist aspirations, the alliance could no longer be maintained and quickly degenerated into extreme hostility between rich and poor peasants.

An example of temporary peasant unity against feudalism, later evolving into antagonism between the upper and the lower strata of the peasantry itself, was the massive Telingana uprising of the late 1940s in the state of Hyderabad, India. (This uprising is, by the way, one of the few cases of extensive, well-organised protest, involving sweeping anti-feudal demands, which can be cited during a period marked in general by alliances for the redress of specific local grievances.) The most active elements in the uprising were the lowest segments of the agricultural population, but their initial demands were also supported by the rich peasants. Led by the Communist Party and the peasant organisation 'Andhra Mahasabha', tenants and landless labourers forcibly carried out reforms which in their first stages merely curtailed feudal privileges. When they went further, however, and championed a redefinition of the land tenure structure which affected properties of the richer peasants, the Telingana movement was irrevocably split.

III. PEASANT MOVEMENTS IN THE YEAR OF
AGRARIAN REFORMS

The First Reforms

During the late 1940s and early 1950s, the governments of many North African and Asian countries found it both politically and economically necessary to institute limited agrarian reform programmes.[1] Economic development required a transformation of the traditional rural structure and political stability was endangered by the explosive unrest of impoverished peasants. The ruling circles of these states could no longer afford to ignore either the numerous concrete demands of the peasantry, or the influence of revolutionary ideologies which threatened to unite disparate dissenters under a common banner. Therefore moderate agrarian legislation, combined in a number of countries (such as the Philippines and Burma) with military operations against peasant rebels, began to appear throughout the region.

This legislation aimed first of all at undermining the economic and political power of the traditional feudal landlords by limiting the extension of their lands and their privileges. It also provided for the strengthening of the landed peasantry and the encouragement of a rural capitalist sector through granting lease-holders definitive title to land. Finally, agrarian legislation of this period was often concerned with the protection of tenants, the introduction of rent ceilings, and so on. It should be noted that these measures, while challenging feudal prerogatives sufficiently to evoke fierce resistance from traditional elements in many regions, were in fact not of utility to all segments of the peasant population. The poorest peasants, very small holders and labourers, received little or no benefit from them.

Nevertheless, the initial effect of agrarian reform legislation on many peasant movements was to unite all strata of the peasantry, to strengthen already existing peasant organisations, and to encourage the formation of new peasant pressure groups. That was the case because public debate on the new legislation, often encouraged by national governments themselves, intensified the interest of all groups of the peasantry in change, while the dogged refusal of feudal landlords to comply with agrarian reform provisions heightened the sense of impatience and frustration in the countryside. Peasant movements therefore found

---

[1] Land reforms were carried out in Turkey (1945–9), the Philippines (1946), India (1948), Burma (1948, 1953), South Korea (1949), Pakistan (1950–2) and Egypt (1952), among others.

for the first time a rallying cry sufficiently broad to appeal to all the groups within them: the full and consistent implementation of existing national agrarian legislation. And from this time forward, extensive, well-organised peasant protest assumed an importance never before possible.

One example of increasing organising activity among the peasantry following the promulgation of agrarian reform laws can be found in India, where the All-Indian Kisan Sabha, led by the Communist Party, attracted the largest number of members in its history (1,100,000) at the height of the struggle for implementation of anti-*zamindari* legislation in 1955.[1] Also during the mid-fifties, a Socialist Party peasant organisation called Hind Kisan Panchayat (Indian Peasant Council) gained considerable influence in Uttar Pradesh and Kerala, and various caste organisations associated with the National Congress Party were strong among the rural population as well.

In the Philippines, there was no organised peasant movement for some years following the banning of the communist-led National Peasant Union. Nevertheless, after land reform was proclaimed, peasants faced with the need to defend their newly-won rights began to set up numerous small organisations (often within the boundaries of one neighbourhood). These were usually led by young lawyers, born in the same neighbourhood, who were paid to represent the peasants in confrontations with landlords. In 1953, the nation-wide Federation of Free Farmers, led by Catholic intellectuals and controlled by the Magsaysay Government, was founded. The Federation played an active part in pushing through the 'Magsaysay reforms' of the mid-1950s, and by 1959 its membership had reached 400,000.[2]

A number of peasant organisations of various political persuasions were also active in Indonesia during the 1950s. Among those were the Barisan Tani Indonesia (B.T.I.), closely linked to the Communist Party of Indonesia, whose membership in 1957 exceeded 3,500,000;[3] Petani, tied to the National Party of Indonesia; and Petanu, organised

[1] A. M. Melnikov, 'Bor'ba indiiskogo krest'ianstva za radikal'nye agrarnye reformy (1957–1962)' (The Struggle of the Indian Peasantry for Radical Land Reforms, 1957–62) in *Narody Azii i Afriki* (Peoples of Asia and Africa), a magazine edited by the Institute of the Peoples of Asia and the African Institute, Academy of Sciences of the U.S.S.R. Moscow, vol. 1964, no. 5, p. 85.
[2] S. D. Cater, *The Philipine Federation of Free Farmers*, Southeast Asia Program, Cornell University, Ithaca, New York, May 1959, N35, mimeograph, pp. 5–23, 103–6, 127.
[3] Yu. A. Sotnikov, 'Sel'skoe khoziaistvo i agrarnyi vopros' (Agriculture and the Agrarian Problem), in *Respublika Indoneziia, 1945–1960* (The Republic of Indonesia, 1945–1960) (Moscow: Izd-vo vostochnoi literatury (Eastern Literature Publishing House), 1961), p. 295.

by the Muslim Nahdutal Ulama Party. In addition, a national peasant organisation was founded in Pakistan in 1958 (the All-Pakistani Peasant Association, formed from already existing, and highly active, local interest groups), and in Iraq in 1959 (following the publication of the Land Reform Law of April 1959). The latter united 200,000 peasants from over 3000 local organisations.[1]

Despite the impetus given by early agrarian reform legislation to the wider organisation of the peasantry in many countries, it must nevertheless be admitted that the majority of the peasantry throughout North Africa and Asia were still unorganised during the 1950s. In Morocco, Yemen, Turkey, Iran, Nepal, Afghanistan and Thailand, for example, there seems to have been no peasant organisation at all during this period. And in Egypt and Ceylon only relatively small interest groups of agricultural labourers had made their appearance.[2] The social and economic backwardness of the peasantry in many regions contributed to such a state of affairs, as well as the survival of feudal institutions and religious and tribal strife, and the continued existence of obsolete political structures which denied even elemental political participation to the masses.

The lack of an organised peasant movement did not mean, of course, that the peasantry in these countries exercised no pressure on the ruling élite. It merely meant that peasant demands were expressed indirectly, as they had been for many years, through local conflicts and occasional violence, the representations of urban working groups, and so on.

Reforming the Reforms

During the years following the proclamation of moderate agrarian reforms of the kind described above, the peasantry of many countries became increasingly convinced that existing legislation was inadequate or insufficiently enforced. As a result, the further limitation of extensive landholdings and the delivery of new tracts of land to the peasantry were demanded by a large number of peasant organisations throughout Asia and North Africa during the late 1950s and early 1960s. This demand was supported by all strata of the peasantry, since all groups, from the wealthy peasants to agricultural workers, hoped to receive a part of the land in question.

In India, for example, the implementation of early anti-*zamindari*

[1] S. N. Alitovskii, *Agrarnyi vopros v sovremennom Irake* (The Agrarian Problem in Contemporary Iraq), (Moscow: Izd-vo 'Nauka', 1966) p. 147.
[2] 'Agrarnyi vopros i natsional'no-osvoboditel'noe dvizhenie', op. cit., p. 192.

legislation was immediately followed by agitation for an even stricter limitation on the maximum number of acres per landholding unit. The most dramatic challenge to the Government occurred in the state of Kerala, where an electoral victory for the Communist Party in April 1957 allowed the preparation of far-reaching agrarian legislation intended to benefit the poorer peasantry. A violent political struggle ensued, the state Government was dismissed, and the reform act suspended and further amended. Nevertheless, 700,000 acres of unused land were distributed to landless peasants, and rural labourers received wage increases. There can be little doubt that increasing peasant pressure of the kind illustrated in Kerala greatly influenced the agrarian policy of the Congress Party and allowed its left wing to push through the famous Nagpur Resolution of 1959, instructing state governments to elaborate legislation setting maximum limits for private holdings. Such legislation had been passed in most Indian states by 1962.[1]

Other examples of increasing peasant pressure for 'reforming the reforms' can be found in Pakistan and Iran. The growing impatience of the Pakistani peasantry played an important part in the passage of new agrarian legislation by the Ayub Khan Government in 1959.[2] And the stubborn struggle of Iranian peasants, including several mass demonstrations against large landlords and clergy, was undoubtedly instrumental in the eventual passage of the land reform law of 1962, essentially concerned with the limitation of landlords' holdings.[3] In Indonesia, an agrarian law limiting private landholdings had been passed in 1960 after increasing activity by various peasant organisations. And in the Philippines, existing agrarian legislation was radically revised in 1963 to provide for a noteworthy reduction in the legal landholding 'ceiling' and the redistribution of holdings in excess of the new limit to sharecroppers.

Peasant groups dissatisfied with the initial reform programmes of nationalist governments were not, of course, solely concerned with forcing further reductions in maximum limits for private holdings. They also sought guarantees that peasant representatives would be

[1] A. M. Melnikov, 'Bor'ba indiiskogo krest'ianstva za radikal'nye agrarnye reformy (1957–1962)', op. cit., p. 86.

[2] S. I. Tansykbaeva, 'Agrarnaia Reforma 1959g. v Pakistane' (''Agrarian Reform of 1959 in Pakistan''), in G. G. Kotovsky et al. (eds.), *Sotsial'no-ekonomicheskie posledstviia agrarnykh reform i sotsial'naia struktura derevni v razvivaiushchikhsia stranakh Azii i Afriki* (The Socio-Economic Consequences of Agrarian Reforms and the Social Structure of the Peasantry in Developing Countries of Asia and Africa) (Moscow: Izd-vo 'Nauka' 1966) pp. 69–70.

[3] A. I. Dzhomin, *Sel'skoe khozhiaistvo sovremennogo Irana* (The Agriculture of Contemporary Iran) (Moscow: Izd-vo 'Nauka' 1967) pp. 200–15.

allowed to participate in local reform programmes; they demanded lower rents and better terms for tenants, while fighting mass evictions; they protested against the practices of usurious traders and money-lenders; and they insisted on government assistance in the form of cheaper credit, better marketing facilities, encouragement of co-operatives, and so on. Obviously, each of these demands was especially appropriate to a particular sub-sector of the peasant movement as a whole.

Although the struggle of tenants against eviction had characterised earlier phases of the peasant movement in various countries, it was particularly important during the period under discussion, when capitalist relationships had begun to develop on a wide scale throughout the countryside. Threatened by agrarian reform legislation, large landlords began to set up modern agricultural enterprises in order to avoid confiscation of idle lands. Even the upper groups of the peasantry followed suit in part, and a wave of evictions swept the countryside.

In India, for example, tenants were evicted from large landholdings during the 1950s on a scale never before imagined. In Bihar alone, 1,200,000 peasants were thrown off their plots within five years.[1] Evictions on a mass scale also occurred in Pakistan, where 400,000 tenants were dispossessed from land in the western part of the country during 1956 alone and received no land in other regions to replace their loss.[2] In Turkey, landlords expelled more than 200,000 peasant families after 1950;[3] and in the Philippines, landlords used land reform provisions for consolidation of plots to bring pressure to bear on tenants who attempted to achieve more favourable terms for sharing crops.[4] Other examples of massive evictions could be given for Syria, Lebanon, Iran and Ceylon.

These actions against tenants were facilitated by land reform legislation which, in most cases, had not provided for the participation of

[1] V. G. Rastiannikov and M. A. Maximov, *Razvitie kapitalizma v sel'skom khoziaistve sovremennoi Indii* (The Development of Rural Capitalism in Contemporary India) (Moscow: Izd-vo 'Nauka', 1965) pp. 108–9.

[2] S. I. Tansykbaeva, 'Polozhenie krest'ianstva i krest'ianskoe dvizehnie v Pakistane v 1953–1964' (The Position of the Peasantry and the Peasant Movement in Pakistan in 1953–1954), in *Krest'ianskoe dvizhenie v stranakh Vostoka*, op. cit., pp. 187–8 and 197–8.

[3] P. Moiseyev and B. Karabayev, 'Krest'ianskoe dvizhenie v Turtsii posle vtoroi mirovoi voiny' (The Peasant Movement in Turkey after the Second World War) in A. M. Samsutdinov et al. (eds.), *Problemy sovremennoi Turtsii* (Problems of Contemporary Turkey) (Moscow: Izd-vo Vostochnoi Literatury, 1963) p. 100.

[4] N. Savelyev, *Filippiny: Ekonomicheskii ocherk* (The Philippines: A Description of the Economy) (Moscow: Izd-vo Sotsial'no-Ekonomicheskoi Literatury [Socio-Economic Literature Publishing House], 1960) pp. 37–8.

peasant representatives in reform programmes. In fact, landlords at times actually enjoyed the assistance of local government authorities and police in evicting tenants. The reaction of the peasantry in many areas was at first no more than spontaneous resistance to eviction, sometimes including armed clashes. Nevertheless, in areas where rural overpopulation and unemployment among the village proletariat were greatest, the struggle assumed a mass character and became the principal preoccupation of important regional or national peasant interest groups. These groups submitted frequent petitions to the courts, and in many cases organised protest demonstrations and direct action against landlords as well.

Despite a number of difficulties, including poor organisation, repression, and anti-tenant legislation, some notable gains were made during this period in protecting tenants from eviction. In Indonesia, a 1954 law prohibited the arbitrary eviction of squatters; and the dismissal of sharecroppers (*hari*) was prohibited in Pakistan four years later. The governments of several Indian states followed the same path, issuing decrees for resolving conflicts between landlords and tenants which were by 1957 operative over 12 per cent of the cultivated acreage of the country.[1]

The question of exploitative credit arrangements was another preoccupation of peasant movements in many countries following the first agrarian reform legislation, It was true that as capitalism gained strength throughout the countryside, rural traders and moneylenders were more and more likely to become the agents of large urban industrial and financial interests. Nevertheless, private landowners (including some upper strata of the peasantry) and professional moneylenders retained control over a significant proportion of the credit system. In India during the early 1960s, for example, 47·1 per cent of the debts of the agricultural population were owed to private landlords and 14·9 per cent to professional money-lenders.[2]

Unfortunately, the peasants' struggle against unreasonable terms of credit was not usually very effective. Without the creation of an extensive state credit and marketing system, the removal of the only available sources of credit within most villages (not only for production and marketing, but also for the most elementary kinds of

[1] G. G. Kotovskii, *Agrarnye reformy v Indii* (Land Reforms in India) (Moscow: Izd-vo Vostochnoi Literatury [Eastern Literature Publishing House], 1959) p. 101.

[2] R. P. Gurvich, 'Krest'ianstvo' (The Peasantry), in *Problemy ekonomicheskogo i sotsial'nogo razvitiia nezavisimoi Indii* (Problems of Economic and Social Development of Independent India) (Moscow: Izd-vo 'Nauka', 1967) p. 131.

consumption needs) was impossible. Some victory was apparently achieved only in areas where village traders and money-lenders happened to be either of an alien nationality or religion (such as the Indians in Burma, the Chinese in South-East Asia, the Muslims in India, or the Hindus in Pakistan), or spectacularly large landowners against whom not only the village poor but also well-to-do peasants could unite.

The fact that no group within any peasant movement found all its demands satisfied during these years gave a special resilience to the movement. Thus although concessions on certain issues might temporarily calm specific elements within the movement at a given moment, causing a brief decline in support for large peasant organisations, there were always so many other demands waiting to be met that the movement soon gained momentum once more. Wealthier peasants, for example, had no sooner received concessions on questions of credit and marketing facilities than they turned to other issues (the provision of modern farming equipment, improved seeds and ferti-lisers, better state purchasing prices for farm produce, policies of state-run processing plants, and so on). In that way, peasant movements of the period came to contain the nuclei of agricultural organisations of quite modern socio-political tendencies, while small landholders, share-croppers and squatters simultaneously continued the struggle for their rights. Nevertheless, it should be noted that contradictions between the upper and lower strata of the peasantry were increasingly evident, as disputes arose over such issues as the redistribution of confiscated landholdings. These contradictions weakened the movement as a whole and foreshadowed a definitive split between the richer and poorer strata within it.

IV. PEASANT MOVEMENTS AFTER THE REFORMS

The effect of the agrarian reforms on the socio-economic conditions of the countryside, as well as on the balance of social forces within national societies as a whole, has been far from uniform throughout North Africa and Asia. Nevertheless, if one always remembers that differences among many of these developing nations have grown greater rather than smaller during the past few years, it is possible to discuss post-reform developments in the peasant movement under two general headings: continuing impediments to reform in the relatively backward regions of North Africa and Asia; and the effects of socio-economic change in the more advanced areas.

The Backward Regions

Up to the present time, feudal and even pre-feudal social systems continue to dominate the rural sectors of certain countries of North Africa and Asia, including Saudi Arabia, Jordan, Yemen, Nepal, Laos and Cambodia (although there are, of course, regions within each of these countries characterised by more advanced social relations), as well as specific regions of other countries, especially in the Near East. Conditions prevailing in all these areas strongly impede the emergence of a well-organised, legal peasant movement.

In the first place, political power is, as a rule, in the hands of feudal lords, the sheiks of large tribes, and the high clergy, all of whom may in some cases share it with certain groups of the bourgeoisie (and most especially the trading bourgeoisie). The broad masses of the agricultural, semi-nomadic and nomadic population are denied all political expression, including the right to form legal interest groups and parties. Even their ideas remain very much under the control of their leaders, who impress their illiterate subjects with the majesty of the monarchy, the tribe and the Church.

Religion has played a particularly important role in preventing the appearance not only of an effective peasant movement, but in fact of any general democratic movement in these areas. There can be no doubt that the deep piety of the population makes it much easier for traditional leaders to retain their authority. For a long time, for example, the principal political slogan found in the Moroccan country-side was 'Allah and the King'.[1] And in the Arab East, the kind of fanatic faith so strikingly illustrated by Wahhabism in Saudi Arabia has been widely exploited by the ruling élites.[2] The majority of the mass movements which do arise under such circumstances are likely to be launched under religious slogans, led by feudal lords or tribal chiefs, and destined to restore some lost traditional territory or prerogative, rather than to bring real socio-economic change.

The strength of tribalism has made it difficult even for some of the more progressive governments of the region to carry out limited

---

[1] A. S. Solonitskii, *Sotsial'no-ekonomicheskoe razvitie sovremennogo Morokko* (The Socio-Economic Development of Contemporary Morocco) (Moscow: Izd-vo 'Nauka', 1965) p. 164.

[2] N. I. Prosin, *Saudovskaia Araviia: Istoriko-Ekonomicheskii ocherk* (Saudi Arabia: An Historico-Economic Essay) (Moscow: Izd-vo 'Nauka', 1964) p. 197.

reforms in the countryside. Recent events in Yemen provide a case in point. During the first days following the republican revolution in that country, the new Government tried to enlist the support of the nation's powerful tribal leaders by making them members of the Supreme Council of National Defence, set up in 1962 and later transformed into a legislative body.[1] Nevertheless, the relations of the central Government and Yemenite tribes have been far from satisfactory. As one republican said, 'Most of [the tribal] chiefs at present support the republican regime. But one cannot help seeing that this support is only temporary. In many of them, it is founded on personal hatred of the Hamid-ed-Din dynasty. . . . Yet the sheiks and the tribes . . . are a real, and perhaps the greatest, force in the Yemen of today.'[2]

Similarly, armed nomadic and semi-nomadic tribes constitute a source of political weakness in Afghanistan, limiting the ability of the central Government to implement its policies in the provinces.[3] In Iran, there have been armed clashes between tribesmen led by patriarchal chiefs and forces of the national Government engaged in promoting limited socio-economic reforms. And finally, in Burma, official programmes for many years had to make allowances for the wishes of feudal princes and tribal chiefs, whose rights and privileges were recognised by the Government immediately following independence and who long retained great influence over the peasant masses of minority groups.[4] These privileges have only recently been curbed. It is obvious that under such circumstances only a gradual process of weakening the economic and political power of tribal chieftains, and curtailing the separatist sentiments of local princes, can assure the eventual implementation of progressive reforms.

One peculiarly modern political element has at times been used by tribal or monarchical leaders to reinforce their already powerful positions, and that element is nationalism. In numerous cases, ruling groups have directed the discontent of the peasantry towards resident national minorities, thus diverting attention from the oppressive policies of the ruling élite itself; or, on the other hand, the grievances of national minorities have been manipulated to bolster the position of

[1] E. K. Golubovskaia, *Iemen* (The Yemen) (Moscow: Izdatel'stvo 'Mysl' ['Thought' Publishing House], 1965) p. 8.

[2] Quoted by E. Primakov in his article 'Yemen: problemy i nadezhdy' (The Yemen: Problems and Hopes), *Pravda*, 2 Feb 1966.

[3] R. T. Akhramovich, *Afganistan posle vtoroi mirovoi voiny* (Afghanistan after the Second World War) (Moscow: Izd-vo Vostochnoi Literatury, 1961) p. 151.

[4] See G. N. Klimko, *Agrarnye problemy nezavisimoi Birmy* (Agrarian Problems in Independent Burma), (Moscow: Izd-vo 'Nauka', 1964) pp. 198–207.

the élite. The former tactic was used in southern Thailand, where the Moslem clergy and feudal leaders encouraged peasant protest against the Siamese. And hatred of a foreign occupier has also served to strengthen threatened monarchical or tribal leaders. The struggle for Moroccan independence was, for example, carried out with the intention of restoring an exiled monarch, Sultan Muhammad V.[1]

For all of these reasons, then, it is not possible to talk of a well-organised peasant movement in any of the countries under discussion. The mass of the agricultural and nomadic population does not yet take an active part in the struggle to bring about socio-economic and political change. At times, of course, local protests against certain archaic forms of exploitation have spontaneously occurred; the peasantry has refused to countenance conscription, state levies of crops, or certain specific instances of arbitrariness and abuse by state authorities, feudal lords or tribal chieftains. But such protests have not yet grown into a broadly based peasant movement.

It should not be assumed, however, that there have been no changes of consequence for peasant organisation in the more backward areas since the war. On the contrary, all regions have been affected to a greater or lesser degree by socio-economic and political development within their boundaries, as well as by changes in the internal affairs of neighbouring states. For that reason, it is possible to talk briefly here about the prospects for the eventual formation of strong peasant movements in the least developed areas of North Africa and Asia.

There can be little doubt that, however slowly the process has taken place, modern social classes and groups are being formed within the national societies under discussion. With the development of more diversified market economies, the rural population is becoming increasingly differentiated, and contradictions among groups with conflicting interests are becoming more and more clearly visible. Thus, for example, differences in size of land holdings have become greater in Afghanistan, Nepal and the least developed part of Jordan (Transjordania) since the war.[2] And contradictions based on the changing economic status of different strata of the peasantry and the increasing exploitation of the peasantry by traders, money-lenders and landlords have also grown sharper in the backward regions of northern Malaysia

---

[1] Solonitskii, op. cit., pp. 142–50, 155, and 179.

[2] For more information on this subject, see L. N. Kotlov, *Iordania v noveishee vremia* (Jordan in Modern Times) (Moscow: Izd-vo Vostocnoi Literatury, 1961) p. 121; and A. D. Davydov, *Agrarnyi stroi Afganistana* (The Agrarian Structure of Afghanistan) (Moscow: Izd-vo 'Nauka', 1967) ch. iii.

and north-eastern and southern Thailand.[1] In such a process, the social consciousness of the peasant masses is increased.

A part of the peasantry has also been affected by the ideology of bourgeois democratic nationalism, to be distinguished from the kind of traditionally-led nationalist reaction discussed earlier. Developing democratic movements, originating in the cities and directed against the feudal or monarchical order, as well as against foreign domination, have influenced the ideas of the rural population in such countries as Afghanistan, Nepal and Laos.[2] When there has been at the same time a fierce struggle of opposing political camps within the educated élite over the adequacy of various roads to development, the awakening of the peasantry has been furthered even more. That is certainly the case in Laos. And finally, the social consciousness of the rural population of Saudi Arabia, Yemen and Jordan has been heightened by political changes outside their own borders, in the neighbouring countries of the United Arab Republic, Algeria and Syria.[3]

The presence of pressure for socio-economic change even in the relatively backward areas of North Africa and Asia is confirmed by the fact that many governments have proclaimed (if not necessarily implemented) limited agrarian reform measures in these countries.[4] As a rule, the reforms have been concerned with eliminating such archaic relationships as slavery (in Saudi Arabia) and certain forms of forced labour (in Nepal), as well as strengthening productive agriculture. The effect of most reforms seems generally to have been the preservation of the political initiative by ruling élites, and the discouragement of nascent peasant movements.

There can be no doubt, however, that as new class and political forces become stronger and social contradictions in the villages grow sharper, peasant movements will develop in these countries as a part of a wider national-democratic movement. At the same time, increasing

---

[1] Yu. A. Sotnikov, 'Zemel'nye otnosheniia v Malaie' (Agrarian Relations in Malaya) in *Agrarnye otnosheniia v stranakh iugo-vostochnoi Azii* (Agrarian Relations in the Southeast Asian Countries), (Moscow: Izd-vo 'Nauka', 1968) pp. 153–81; and V. I. Iskoldsky, 'K agrarnomu voprosu v Tailande' (On the Agrarian Problem in Thailand) in *Agrarnye otnosheniia v stranakh iugo-vostochnoi Azii*, op. cit., pp. 100–52.

[2] See for example, R. T. Akhramovich, op. cit. and I. B. Redko, *Nepal posle vtoroi mirovoi voiny* (Nepal after the Second World War), (Moscow: Izd-vo Vostocnoi Literatury, 1960).   [3] Prosin, op. cit., pp. 195–6.

[4] See 'The Agricultural and Land Situation in South Arabia', World Land Reform Conference, F.A.O. (Rome, 1966) Rhiad El Ghonemy, *Land Reform and Economic Development in the Near East*, World Land Reform Conference, F.A.O. (Rome, 1966); G. G. Kotovsky and P. P. Moiseyev (eds.), op. cit.; and M. I. Lukianova, R. A. Ulianovsky et al. (eds.), *Agrarnye reformy v stranakh Vostoka* (The Agrarian Reforms in the Eastern Countries) (Moscow: Izdatel'stvo Vostochnoi Literatury, 1958).

differentiation within the peasantry itself will eventually lead to independent organisation on the part of each of its strata, and thus to conflict within the peasant sector.

The More Advanced Areas

It is in the more advanced countries and regions of North Africa and Asia that the most notable changes in peasant movements have occurred during the past decade. Land reform programmes have accelerated socio-economic change in the countryside, altering the nature of agrarian contradictions and providing in the process a new background for peasant organisation. In fact, although reform measures have differed in content rather markedly from country to country, the social and economic consequences of their implementation seem to have been quite similar: the political and economic power of feudal landlords has been curtailed and the most archaic social relationships destroyed; the economic position of the upper elements of the peasantry, and to a lesser degree all smallholders, has been strengthened; and the evolution of a capitalist economy in the agricultural sector has been hastened.

It must, of course, be remembered that in some cases, land reform programmes have been either insufficiently radical or insufficiently well implemented to destroy all pre-capitalist forms of large land ownership. A high degree of concentration of land ownership can therefore still be found in a number of the more advanced North African and Asian countries. India is a dramatic case in point. According to national survey data, land was still almost as unequally distributed after the anti-*zamindari* agrarian legislation as it was before.[1] And even after the introduction in 1959 of maximum limits to holdings, only 2·2 per cent of the land estimated to exceed the new limits had by 1963 been distributed to poorer peasants.[2] Extensive landholdings are also still very important in parts of the agricultural sectors of Turkey, the Philippines and Iran. Nevertheless, a very large number of formerly landless peasants have, in the course of agrarian reform, become the owners of plots of varying sizes and thus assumed a new socio-economic role in their communities.

Equally as important as the continuing redistribution of land in influencing the programme and social composition of peasant movements

[1] During 1953–4, 5 per cent of the rural families possessed 41 per cent of the land, and 1 per cent had 17 per cent of the land; in 1959–60, the same 5 per cent of the families owned 40 per cent of the land, and 1 per cent owned 16 per cent. See V. G. Rastiannikov, 'Ekspluatatorskaia verkhushka derevni i formirovanie sel'skoi burzhuazii' (The Exploitative Upper Crust of the Village Community and the Emergence of a Rural Bourgiosie) in *Problemy ekonomicheskogo i sotsial'nogo razvitiia Indii*, op. cit., p. 175.   [2] Ibid.

in these areas has been the changing economic content of large land-ownership during post-reform years. Agrarian legislation has given strong impetus to the idea of farming for profit, and thus to the establishment of rational agricultural enterprises on estates and medium holdings not divided up by the new reform agencies.[1] The development of an important capitalist agricultural sector dominated by large enterprises has thus taken place in Turkey, India and the Philippines, among others.

At the same time, the social background of the entrepreneurial class which controls commercial agriculture has changed as a result of the reforms, and the integration of a uniform stratum of rural employers from disparate elements of the population has gradually occurred. In general, the original landed aristocracy, including feudal princes, has been weakened and a new rural élite formed from less noble ranks.[2] Members of the upper strata of the peasantry, whose economic position was considerably strengthened by the reforms, now constitute a significant part of that élite. It is, of course, not yet a completely uniform group; there are certainly still conflicting interests within it. But a common interest in presenting a united front against the village poor grows daily stronger.

As a result of such changes in the nature of the agrarian problem, more and more of the landholding peasantry have abandoned all demands for redistribution of land. That is the case not only for members of the new élite, but also for holders of medium-sized plots and a certain part of the smallholders as well. Since the reforms in most cases merely created landholders out of tenants by granting title to land, without at the same time attacking the extreme inequality of holdings found at the time of reform, it is difficult at first glance to understand why medium and small holders are not engaged in more active protest against the existing agrarian tenure structure. The answer must be found in the fact that in areas where rural overpopulation is great and the shortage of land acute, the demands of completely landless labourers constitute a threat to any landed peasant, no matter how small his plot. Therefore the latter have not infrequently been unwilling to support any movements for land redistribution which might easily be pushed to radical extremes by the rural proletariat.

[1] G. G. Kotovskii, P. P. Moiseyev, and V. A. Popov, *Sotsial'no-ekonomicheskie posledstviia agrarnykh reform i sotsial'naia struktura derevni v razvivaiushchikhsia stranakh Azii i Afriki*, op. cit., p. 22.
[2] N. I. Semionova, 'Bor'ba sel'skokhoziaistvennykh rabochikh Indii' (The Struggle of the Agricultural Laborers in India) in *Krest'ianskoe dvizhenie v stranakh Vostoka*, op. cit., p. 135.

On the other hand, a part of the landless village poor and agricultural labourers who at an earlier time actively participated in peasant movements also seem to have abandoned the struggle for land. The immediate needs of some of them have been satisfied to a certain degree by lower rents, the distribution of government lands, and so on. And in those countries where rural overpopulation rules out any eventual reform programme of sufficient scope to provide the majority of the poorest peasants with land, some of the latter apparently lost all hope of further benefits after the completion of the campaign against feudal estates. Others may have dropped out of the peasant movement for reasons related to the survival of traditional loyalties to caste or tribe.

Peasant movements have been affected not only by changing socio-economic relationships on the land, but also by increasing disagreement among various segments of the peasantry concerning the proper scope and direction of demands to be put forward by interest groups of the rural population. Although all may agree on the desirability of reducing the land tax or, in some countries, lessening the burden of forced sales of agricultural products to the State, for example, conflicts arise over which group should be helped first, and what proportion of the total tax burden should be borne by each segment of the peasantry. Similarly, landless peasants are likely to be especially interested in a reduction of the prices of consumer goods, while better-off elements of the rural population would rather assure higher prices for their crops.

In recent years, conflict among different strata of the peasantry over how to use state aid to co-operatives and community development projects has also become sharper. There is serious rivalry among groups for control over the administration of new organisations, in many cases precisely because each faction has its own view concerning the most important functions of the co-operative. The economically independent part of the peasantry is much more interested in marketing arrangements and cheap credit, while the landless workers struggle to secure consumers' co-operatives and to use the new organisations as instruments in defence of the poor.[1] Experience has shown that in fact, it is the village élite which in the long run has derived the greatest benefit from co-operatives.[2]

One final element of considerable importance in widening the area

[1] Kotovskii, Moiseyev and Popov, op. cit., p. 26.
[2] Rastiannikov and Maximov, op. cit., pp. 83–9; and also R. P. Gurvich, 'Sotsial'no-Ekonomicheskie rezul'taty deiatel'nosti obshchinnykh organizatsii' (The Socio-Economic Consequences of the Activities of Communal Organizations) in Kotovskii, Moiseyev, and Popov, op. cit., pp. 28–39.

of disagreement between the richer and poorer elements of the peasantry following the implementation of agrarian reforms has been the changing nature of trading and credit relationships in the countryside. After the elimination of the traditional estate owners, who with professional traders, money-lenders, and rich peasants had originally exercised monopolistic control over credit and marketing in their areas, the new rural bourgeoisie (including the upper segments of the peasantry) adopted money-lending and trade as methods of primary capital formation. Thus the latter have become the newly recognised exploiters of the poorer strata of the rural population, while ironically finding themselves at the same time absorbed more and more by urban industrial and financial interests who merely use them as the intermediaries between the city and the countryside.

Given this background of increasing division within the peasantry itself, it is not surprising that there has been, during the post-reform period, a general decline in the strength of peasant movements throughout the more advanced regions of North Africa and Asia. This decline has been manifested in various ways, including the division of some large peasant organisations and the complete disappearance of others; a lessening of demonstrations and protests; the predominance of limited economic demands, and so on. At times, such a trend has been officially stimulated through banning all peasant organisation (as in the case of Pakistan and South Korea) or conducting military campaigns against peasant insurgents (as in the Philippines and Burma). And at times, limited economic benefits have been held out to the peasantry by ruling élites in order to calm as many rural dwellers as possible.

A few examples will suffice to illustrate this point. In Iraq, after the transfer of a large amount of land to the peasantry during the reform years, the peasant movement declined. The Government then passed a law which placed all peasant societies under the control of the Home Ministry, and left-wing elements were by that means expelled from the leadership of the most important peasant unions. This measure was followed by further limited concessions to rural groups, including a reduction in land redemption payments.[1]

After land reform in South Korea, the nation-wide Peasant Union, supported by the poorer peasants, was banned and only the Peasant Society (uniting credit and marketing co-operatives) was allowed to continue in existence.[2] The peasant movement as a whole entered a period of virtual stagnation, broken only by occasional local clashes

[1] Alitovskii, op. cit., pp. 148–52.　　　　[2] Kazakevich, op. cit., pp. 122 and 150.

against particularly oppressive measures. A similar pattern was followed in Pakistan, where all political parties and organisations were outlawed following the coup of 1958, and an agrarian reform bill passed the following year. The combined effect of those two measures was for all intents and purposes to eliminate the Pakistanti peasant movement until 1962.[1]

Finally, it can be noted that throughout the post-reform period, the peasant movements of Indonesia, Turkey and India failed on the whole to present anything more than the most limited economic demands. The Turkish peasantry in fact disposed of no mass organisations, and were grouped exclusively in local co-operatives, dominated by the rural bourgeoisie.[2]

V. NEW TENDENCIES IN PEASANT MOVEMENTS

Recent events suggest that the decline in the strength of peasant movements in Asia and North Africa under the effects of agrarian reform legislation may be only temporary. In the first place, the anti-feudal, democratic tasks of these movements are far from completed. Many measures designed to transform the traditional agrarian structure have been inconsistently applied and have met stubborn resistance. Oppressive landlord-tenant relationships are still clearly visible in many regions, and broad sections of the peasantry continue to be bound in exploitative arrangements to money-lenders and traders.

Even more important for the future of the peasant movement than the continuation of these traditional land problems is the steady growth of new contradictions within an increasingly commercialised capitalist agricultural sector. It will be remembered that the lower strata of the peasantry constituted from the first days of the anti-feudal struggle one of the most active elements in the movement, for the simple reason that the poorest peasants suffered most from oppressive terms of tenancy, indebtedness, serfdom and personal dependence. At that stage, however, they were united with the rich peasantry against feudal landlords. That is no longer generally the case, and the future direction of the peasant movement will therefore most probably be towards the growing militancy of the rural proletariat and semi-proletariat in opposition not only to traditional inequalities but to modern capitalist exploitation as well.

[1] S. I. Tansykbaeva, 'Polozhenie krest'ianstva i krest'ianskoe dvizhenie v Pakistane v 1953–1964', op. cit., pp. 196–7.   [2] Moiseyev and Karabayev, op. cit., pp. 95, 98.

The uneven economic development often found within national boundaries makes it rather difficult to assess the scope of contradictions for any single country as a whole. For instance, within Turkey, capitalist economic relationships predominate in western and southern Anatolia: the rural proletariat and working small peasantry are pitted against the rural bourgeoisie in that case. But central and northern Anatolia, and to an even greater extent eastern Anatolia, are still characterised by an alliance among all sectors of the peasantry against large traditional landowners. Finally, the most important struggle in the Kurd regions is led by feudal princes.[1] Nevertheless, despite this motley pattern of socio-economic conditions, it is possible to say that the trend throughout the nation is towards an eventual solution of the agrarian problem through the resolution of conflicts related to the advance of capitalism.

One specially significant indication of new dimensions in the peasant movements of North Africa and Asia is the growing strength of agricultural workers' organisations during the past few years. These organisations are particularly strong in regions containing plantation systems (Algeria, Morocco, Tunisia, Turkey, Ceylon, Indonesia, the Philippines and Malaya), but they have also begun to be formed by field hands in local villages. Their demands are often quite similar to those of modern industrial workers, and little related to petitions for land. Thus in Malaya, for example, members of rural unions have gone on strike for better working conditions and higher wages.[2] Agricultural labourers in Morocco have demanded, and been granted, the signing of a collective contract, paid holidays and higher wages.[3] And in the United Arab Republic, the first National Conference of Agricultural Labourers, held in October 1963, drew up a programme to introduce social security benefits in the countryside, to assure adherence by employers to the minimum wage law, to introduce paid holidays, and so forth.[4] The same demands have preoccupied the powerful All-Turkey Trade Union of Agricultural Labourers, formed in late 1965 and having more than one million members.[5]

The Algerian case is perhaps the most vivid example of the potential

[1] P. Moiseyev, 'O dvukh sotsial'nykh voinakh v turetskoi derevne' (On the Two Social Wars in the Turkish Village), in *Krest'ianskoe dvizhenie v stranakh Vostoka*, op. cit., pp. 207–9.
[2] V. S. Rudnev, *Malaia, 1945–1963* pp. 130, 132.
[3] 'Agrarnyi vopros i natsional'no-osvoboditel'noe dvizhenie', op. cit., p. 100.
[4] From an unpublished manuscript by V. K. Ariskin, 'Krest'ianskie organizatsii v OAR' (Peasant Organizations in the UAR).
[5] P. Moiseyev, 'O dvukh sotsial'nykh voinakh v turetskoi derevne' op. cit., pp. 213–14.

role of agricultural labourers in many regions of North Africa and Asia. Since a rural proletariat, largely divorced from any ties to small individual holdings, had been created there even before independence, it was not in most cases necessary to satisfy demands for small plots of land following the expulsion of the French. Agricultural labourers accepted a more advanced form of economic organisation, electing executive committees to run large co-operative farms, and in that way took an important step towards involving working people in the direct management of modern agricultural industry.

Despite undoubted gains by some elements of the rural poor, however, the organisation of the agricultural proletariat has encountered enormous difficulties. In fact, the majority of all hired labourers remain unorganised, and in a number of countries the creation of agricultural trade unions is prevented by the existence of obsolete political structures which deny any form of political participation to the masses.

A part of the problem encountered in organising agricultural labourers in North Africa and Asia, even when there is no official opposition to peasant interest groups, stems from the fact that very few of those labourers are members of a modern agricultural proletariat (employed on a full-time basis by large agricultural enterprises). The great majority are merely day labourers, employed intermittently by a semi-capitalist landlord or by members of the upper, middle or even lower strata of the landholding peasantry. It has been estimated that approximately fifty to sixty million people in Asia and North Africa may be classified in that way.[1]

A further complication arises when it is remembered that many of these intermittent farm hands are also small holders themselves; in other words, they are landed labourers. Although from a purely economic standpoint these men should have more interests in common with the agricultural proletariat than with the upper strata of the peasantry, it is nevertheless obvious that social and psychological factors intervene to place them closer to the ranks of the small producers.[2] This controversial position of the bulk of the agricultural labourers is manifested in very wide-ranging demands. On the one hand, field hands may pose demands similar to those of a modern agricultural proletariat: higher wages, shorter hours, social security benefits, and

[1] L. Gordon and L. Fridman, 'Rabochii klass osvobodivshikhsia stran' (The Working Class in Liberated Countries) in *Mirovaia ekonomika i Mezhdunarodnye Otnosheniia* (World Economy and International Relations), 1966, No. 1, p. 27.

[2] G. G. Kotovskii, 'Sel'skokhoziaistvennyi proletariat i poluproletariat' (Agricultural Proletariat and Semi-Proletariat) in *Problemy ekonomicheskogo i sotsial'nogo razvitiia nezavisimoi Indii*, op. cit., p. 151.

so on. Yet, at the same time, great attention may also be given to requests for land, better credit facilities or less oppressive tenancy terms.

The survival of traditional class and caste divisions constitutes a final barrier to massive organisation of agricultural labourers. In many countries (most specifically the Arab East, India and Pakistan), a considerable part of all rural workers are members of, or descendants from, lower castes and classes. The dire economic plight of these agricultural labourers may therefore be further worsened by a complete lack of social respect. Feelings of inferiority based on caste are an impediment to the growth of social consciousness and make trade union organisation extraordinarily difficult. In India, for example, workers belonging to high castes refuse even to be united with lower-caste workers in the same organisation.[1]

Despite all these problems, however, it is safe to say that the peasant movements of many countries in North Africa and Asia are showing marked signs of revival and growth. This revitalisation is related quite directly to the acceleration of property and class differentiation in the rural sector, the pauperisation of great numbers of small producers, growing unemployment among the rural semi-proletariat and proletariat in the wake of the population explosion, and the threat in some regions of mass starvation. Under those conditions, renewed activity can be seen not only among the agricultural proletariat, as noted above, but also among small tenants still struggling against exploitative landlords. While the upper and middle peasants limit their demands mainly to such questions as improved production and marketing facilities, tax relief and technical assistance, the demands of the village poor are in a number of cases becoming notably more radical.

In India, for example, it is the proletarian and semi-proletarian elements of the peasantry who have swelled the membership of the All-Indian Peasant Union during the past few years. Many of these new members have been affected by a growing movement against the caste system in the countryside, and have carried original reformist demands in the religious sphere still further, to include attacks on all forms of discrimination against 'untouchables'.[2]

In Turkey, several important demonstrations of landless peasants and agricultural labourers have taken place during the 1960s, and the demands put forward on those occasions have been of a mixed peasant-proletarian nature. Progressive intellectuals began in 1962 to form

[1] Semionova, op. cit., pp. 133–4.   [2] Ibid., pp. 140–41.

'Committees of Struggle for Land Reform' in various parts of the country, and to encourage meetings and protests by landless labourers in favour of agrarian reform measures.[1] At the same time, increasing unrest among small producers was manifested in the main tobacco-growing regions of Turkey, where peasant demonstrations during 1965 supported the nationalisation of tobacco trading and a rise in purchasing prices for that product.[2]

Radicalisation of the peasant movement has also occurred in Indonesia during recent years. Led by the Communist Party of Indonesia, the Barisan Tani Indonesia (B.T.I.) peasant union reached a membership of over 10,000,000 by the middle of 1965 and posed wide-ranging demands even on such questions as foreign policy.[3] On a lesser scale, the demands of peasant organisations in Pakistan have become more radical as well. And since the repeal of former Emergency Legislation in 1963, a series of new peasant interest groups have appeared there, including a Peasant Committee for West Pakistan, a Peasant Council for East Pakistan, the National Peasant Party, the Association of Settlers of the Lower Sind, the Organisation of Ejected Tenants, and various associations of small producers.[4]

Finally, it should be noted that new organisations including substantial numbers of agricultural workers have appeared recently in the Philippines, Syria and Burma. These are the Philippine Association of Free Peasants and the Syrian General Federation of Peasant Associations, both founded in 1964, and the Central People's Peasant Council, established in Burma in 1967.

The existence of formal organisation is not, of course, the only measure of the growing importance of the peasantry in national affairs. It is becoming increasingly clear in fact that even in those countries where the peasantry cannot be said to constitute an independent political force, it is nevertheless a critical factor in national politics, a social class whose support is sought by many groups. For this reason as well as the objectively greater strength of many peasant organisations, it is possible to conclude that during the coming years the peasant movements of North Africa and Asia will progressively break the boundaries of traditional societies and come to represent new social forces, characteristic of modern societies.

[1] P. Moiseyev, 'O dvukh sotsial'nykh voinakh v turetskoi derevne', op. cit., p. 213.

[2] Ya. Demir and H. Okan, 'Turtsiia: puti razvitiia' (Turkey: Paths of Development), in *Problemy Mira i Sotsializma* (Problems of Peace and Socialism), 1965, no. 5, p. 75.

[3] An estimate by the former leaders of Barisan Tani Indonesia (B.T.I.).

[4] S. I. Tansykbaeva, 'Polozhenie krest'ianstva i krest'ianskoe dvizhenie v Pakistane v 1953–1964', op. cit., p. 197.

Chapter 10

PEASANT MOVEMENTS AND LAND REFORM IN LATIN AMERICA: MEXICO AND BOLIVIA[1]

by

Gerrit Huizer and Rodolfo Stavenhagen

I. THE GENERAL BACKGROUND

MOST of Latin America has traditionally been a continent of large landholdings and landless peasants. In areas where before the Spanish Conquest there existed a numerous Indian population, the Spaniards developed means to tie the Indian peasants to a small landed ruling class in a system of semi-feudal servitude. In other regions, where the Indian population was sparse or had been exterminated by the conquerors, the large plantations imported slave labour from Africa. In the course of three centuries of colonial rule, land became concentrated in either private or church hands, whereas a growing proportion of the agricultural population, with almost no rights in land, had to eke out a meagre subsistence on tiny plots, or work under oppressive conditions on the commercial plantations or the large haciendas belonging to a small, powerful rural élite. This system acquired great stability, for neither the struggle for independence in the early nineteenth century nor various political reform movements during the latter half of that century were able to change the basic characteristics of the agrarian structure. On the contrary, the Spanish or Portuguese overlords and the Church were soon replaced by a native oligarchy that derived its wealth, prestige and power from its possession of land and its control over the labour of an increasing number of landless, powerless and hungry peasants.

The same situation, with hardly any change, has stretched well into the twentieth century, despite efforts to modernise agriculture and massive rural-urban migrations in most countries. A recent study of land tenure conditions in seven Latin American countries by the Inter-

[1] This chapter covers events up to 1968, i.e. before the major land reforms of Chile and Peru, which it is as yet too early to evaluate.

American Committee for Agricultural Development (C.I.D.A.) shows to what extent the unequal distribution of land has been an obstacle to economic and social development in these countries. In all of them prevails the latifundia-minifundia complex, in which most of the farmland is concentrated in a relatively small number of large, multi-family-size farms, whereas, at the other end of the scale, the majority of farm units are sub-family sized, possessing only a small percentage of total farm land. The middle-class group of farm owners is unimportant in most of these countries. Holders of minifundia and landless farm workers constitute nearly nine-tenths of the farm population in Ecuador, Guatemala and Peru, and over two-thirds in all of the seven countries studied except Argentina. The great inequalities in land distribution are accompanied by a rural power structure based on traditional land tenure and labour institutions, variously known as *peonaje*, *pongueaje*, *inquilinaje*, etc., whereby rural labour is tied to the large farms through a variety of customary and very stable bonds. Wage labour, tenancy and share cropping are also common. These tenure institutions are generally considered to be the primary obstacle to economic and social development, and the only realistic alternative to the prevailing situation is land reform.[1]

Over the years, and long before land reform had become a political catchword, the peasants of Latin America had resisted and protested (often violently) the process whereby the expanding haciendas robbed them of their lands and turned them into oppressed peons. At the end of the eighteenth century, the Indian leader Tupac Amaru led a rebellion against the Spaniards in Peru, which threatened the whole Spanish Empire in the Andean region. The so-called 'Caste War' in Yucatán (south-eastern Mexico), waged by the Maya Indians against the local government and landowning aristocracy, began in 1844 and simmered on till the first years of the present century.

Particularly in the second half of the nineteenth century, as part of the process of economic expansion of the haciendas, in many Latin American countries legislation was adopted which was used by the rural élites to take over much of the village land of indigenous communities. Communal property was transformed into privately owned land and, since the indigenous communities were not able to defend

[1] Solon Barraclough and Arthur Domike, 'Agrarian Structure in Seven Latin American Countries', *Land Economics*, XLII 4, (Nov 1966); and Inter-American Committee for Agricultural Development (CIDA): *Land Tenure Conditions and Socio-Economic Development of the Agricultural Sector* (Argentina, Brazil, Colombia, Chile, Ecuador, Guatemala and Peru), 7 vols (Washington; Pan American Union, 1965–66).

themselves adequately within the framework of the new legislation, most of the communal lands fell into the hands of the large estate owners.[1] This process, which one author has called the 'rape of the *pueblos*', was often carried on with help from the armed forces. Since the use of judicial procedures by the indigenous population in defence of their legal rights proved unsuccessful, uprisings took place against the hacienda owners. Most of these peasant movements were spontaneous and localised and were repressed at great cost in peasant lives. In scattered areas of Mexico – in the states of Hidalgo, San Luis Potosí, Veracruz, Sonora, Yucatán – hundreds and sometimes thousands of peasants rose to reconquer their lands during the last decades of the nineteenth century. As will be described later, only during the Mexican Revolution of 1910, when many of these scattered movements were integrated into a large-scale peasant guerrilla force, did they become successful.[2]

In Bolivia, the reaction of the peasantry against the (often violent) usurpation of communal lands continued, in a more or less spontaneous way, till the Bolivian Revolution of 1952. Most of these movements were bloodily repressed. Some of them, however, took on such proportions that the political structure of the nation as a whole was threatened or even changed. In 1898–9, a peasant protest movement was organised on a large scale by Zárate Willca. This movement helped the liberal groups in the country to come to power by overthrowing the conservative Government. Once the liberals were well established, they saw in the strongly organised peasant movements a threat to their power, and they turned against their former supporters. Zárate Willca was assassinated and the movement violently repressed.[3]

In 1927 another uprising which had national impact started in the Bolivian province of Chayanta and spread mainly through the regions of Potosí, Chuquisaca and Oruro. Abuses by one hacienda owner against the peasants provoked a local movement in which the Indians' long suppressed feelings of vengeance found expression. The inter-

[1] A brief description of this process in Latin America can be found in International Labour Office: *Indigenous Peoples*, Studies and Reports, New Series, No. 35 (Geneva: 1953), pp. 292 ff.

[2] For an extensive bibliography on peasant movements and land reform in Bolivia and Mexico and Latin America as a whole, see Gerrit Huizer, *The Revolutionary Potential of Peasants in Latin America* (see p. 400), pp. 229 ff. See also Gerrit Huizer and Cynthia N. Hewitt, 'Bibliography on Latin American Peasant Organization' in Henry A. Landsberger (ed.), *Latin American Peasant Movements* (Ithaca: Cornell University Press, 1969), pp. 451 ff.

[3] Ramiro Condarco Morales, *Zárate, el 'terrible' Willka, historia de la rebelión indígena de 1899* (La Paz, Bolivia, 1966).

vention of the army triggered a reaction of the peasant over a wide area, involving, according to official estimates, as many as 50,000 men. After a month of struggle, the movement was suppressed.

The expansion of the haciendas at the cost of the communal lands of the indigenous peasants has continued in several Latin American countries to this day. It is part of a complex trend recognised as 'internal colonialism'.[1] As a result of this process, and in order to maintain it, a 'culture of repression', as Holmberg calls it, prevails in the rural areas of many countries.[2] Symptoms of this culture of repression are the apparent submissiveness, apathy and fearfulness of the peasantry. It nourishes considerable resentment, however, which may lead to reactions as described above, whenever abuses and frustration become unbearable.

Most recently, massive occupation of hacienda lands by thousands of peasants in the Peruvian highlands (1963–4) have sharpened agrarian conflicts and increased pressures for land reform in that country. In Brazil, Francisco Julião's Peasant Leagues and various rural syndicates exerted pressures for land reform, and the political reaction of the conservative forces against these movements was partly responsible for the downfall of the Goulart Government in 1964.

Up to 1967 only three countries in Latin America had carried out extensive land reform: Cuba (1959), Bolivia (1955) and Mexico (1915). In this chapter, only the Mexican and Bolivian land reforms will be studied; the Cuban land reform, being socialistic in character, deserves special analysis.

It should be noted, however, that in the Cuban revolution the peasantry of the Sierra Maestra played an important role. Most of these peasants were squatters who were frequently dislodged by armed force from the plots which they had cultivated for years, because landholders claimed them as theirs. It was among these peasants that the small guerrilla forces headed by Fidel Castro found increasing support for their movement. A provisional land reform giving land to those who tilled it was carried out in the areas controlled by the guerrilla movement, even before the revolution became victorious.[3]

[1] For a discussion of the concept 'internal colonialism', see Pablo Gonzáles Casanova, 'Internal Colonialism and National Development', *Studies in Comparative International Development*, 4 (1965); and Rodolfo Stavenhagen: 'Classes, Colonialism and Acculturation', *Studies in Comparative International Development*, 6 (1965).

[2] The concept 'culture of repression' is elaborated in Allan R. Holmberg, *Some Relationships between Psychobiological Deprivation and Culture Change in the Andes*. Paper presented at the Cornell Latin American Year Conference, 21–25 March 1966.

[3] Enrique González Pedrero, *La revolución cubana* (Mexico: Universidad Nacional Autónoma de México, 1959) pp. 75–9.

II. PEASANT MOVEMENTS AND LAND REFORM IN MEXICO

Mexico's agrarian structure before 1910 was typical of that of many other Latin American countries. Large haciendas dominated the countryside, many of them occupying hundreds of thousands of hectares. Many of the largest were owned by foreign companies. The landowning class (*hacendados*) were the economic, social and political élite of the country. The hacienda, as an economic unit, was inefficient by modern standards, being based on extensive agriculture, backward technology, low capital-intensity, the widespread use of cheap and servile labour and low productivity. Yet, for the absentee owners, the hacienda was not only good business but also a symbol of political power and social prestige. Under-utilisation of land and over-exploitation of labour were the two basic characteristics of hacienda economies. Indeed, the hacienda held virtual monopoly rights over land, and thus could control most of the employment opportunities of the peasant population. Over the years, the expanding hacienda, protected by legal privileges and government favours, invaded the communal landholdings of Indian villages and the independent freeholds of small agriculturists, thus creating for itself large pools of available labour.

When Francisco I. Madero raised the banner of political revolution against the Díaz dictatorship in 1910, the peasants in various parts of the country rallied to his side in the hope of obtaining restitution of their communal holdings and freedom from oppressive living and working conditions. The role of the organised peasant movement that was the life-blood of the revolution and which led to the adoption of land reform can best be illustrated by the story of the Zapata uprising.[1]

Emiliano Zapata was the son of a peasant who had farmed a small plot of communally held land before losing it to a neighbouring hacienda. It has been said that, while still a child, Emiliano Zapata tried to console his weeping father as he was being dispossessed, saying:

---

[1] Some outstanding biographies of Zapata are: Gildardo Magaña, *Emiliano Zapata y el agrarismo en México*, (Mexico: Editorial Ruta, 1951); and Jesús Sotelo Inclán: *Raíz y razón de Zapata, investigación histórica* (Mexico, Editorial Etnos, 1948); and, more recently, John Womack, *Zapata and the Mexican Revolution* (London: Thames & Hudson, 1969; New York: Knopf, 1968).

'I will take it back when I grow up'. From an early age, Zapata took part in local activities, the purpose of which was to recover legally what had been unjustly taken from the village. At the age of thirty, he was elected president of the village council of his birthplace, Anenecuilco in the state of Morelos. The council tried unsuccessfully to recover the lost lands. Previously, he had been forced into military service (due to his openly rebellious attitude against the hacienda owners) and had taken care of the horses of a well-to-do landowner in Mexico City. This period of absence from his community had given him contacts with the outside world and experience and insights which were to be useful in his role as village and peasant leader.

His ability as a mover of men enabled him to form a union between Anenecuilco and two other villages that had similar problems, and they hired a lawyer to plead their rights in court against the claims of the powerful haciendas. But after repeated failures the villagers were ready to try other means. Madero's call for revolution in 1910 fell on fertile soil. Zapata and his men joined the armed struggle which led to the fall of Díaz and the triumph of Madero. But when the new President gave only lip service to the solution of the agrarian problem, Zapata formulated in November 1911 his programme of radical land reform measures, known as the Plan de Ayala, and continued the struggle against Madero and his successors. In the areas that fell under the control of his guerrilla troops, Zapata redistributed land to the peasants according to this programme. On 6 January 1915, President Carranza, in order to weaken and win to his cause the rival revolutionary factions, including the peasant armies of Zapata, that were trying to gain control of the Government, published a decree which incorporated the main points of Zapata's programme and which is generally considered to be the formal starting-point of the Mexican land reform. At the same time, he armed the radical urban workers and sent them to quell the peasant revolt.[1] Zapata, still sceptical, retreated to the mountains south of Mexico City, where he continued to implement his own reform measures and, in alliance with Pancho Villa in the north, maintained his struggle against Carranza. After his assassination by one of Carranza's officers in 1919, the Zapatista rebellion petered out.

The decree of 1915 was later incorporated, as article 27, in the new Constitution of 1917, which is the constitutional basis for the extensive

---

[1] Frank Tannenbaum, *The Mexican Agrarian Revolution* (New York: Macmillan, 1929) pp. 165–71.

land reform that took place in later years. The law was applied only on a limited scale at first, and effective redistribution of lands took place mainly in those areas where the new revolutionary leaders were supported by the organised peasants. During the 1920s, a considerable amount of legislative activity on agrarian matters was carried out by the Government, but the process of land distribution continued to be slow. The landowners took advantage of the revolutionary lull to organise effective political and sometimes violent resistance to land reform. Armed bands in the pay of hacienda owners terrorised the peasant population, principally in the central states, and were able to block land reform in many cases. The peasants countered by armed self-defence and by organising local and regional agrarian committees and peasant leagues.[1] In the state of Veracruz, Úrsulo Galván, a local labour leader, was able to weld a number of these committees into a state-wide league, with the support of the state governor, against the opposition of the hacienda owners and the local military commander. The league was instrumental in supporting the federal Government against an attempted military uprising in 1925, and its members were given arms and formed into battalions.[2]

During the same period, in the state of Michoacán, in central Mexico, Primo Tapia, a peasant who had worked as a migrant labourer (*bracero*) in the United States, began to form a peasant union in his community and surrounding villages, in order to effectively petition for the restitution of communal lands, according to the law.[3] The landowners countered by forming their own 'white syndicates', and the clergy supported these by preaching against the 'agrarians' and counselling submission to the traditional power structure. Religious pressure was so effective that in many communities peasants who were entitled to land grants refused to receive them. Despite these obstacles, a state-wide league was formed in 1922, and by 1924 the land of a number of haciendas had in fact been redistributed. The struggle cost many lives, and in 1926 Primo Tapia himself was captured by a local military commander and shot. The armed counter-reform became particularly strong in the late 1920s when the church-supported 'cristero' rebellion broke out against the Government as a

[1] For examples, see Ernest Gruening, *Mexico and its Heritage* (New York, 1928); and Marjorie Ruth Clark, *Organized Labor in Mexico* (Chapel Hill: University of North Carolina Press, 1934).

[2] Liga de Comunidades Agrarias del Estado de Veracruz, *La cuestión agraria y el problema campesino* (Veracruz: Jalapa-Enríquez, 1924) especially p. 21.

[3] See Apolinar Martínez Mugica, *Primo Tapia. Semblanza de un revolucionario michoacano*, 2nd ed. (Mexico, 1946).

result of long-standing State-Church conflicts. The rebellion came to an end in 1929, after two years, but continued to flare up sporadically well into the 1930s.[1]

The peasant leagues of Veracruz, Michoacán and other states where similar movements had occurred joined together in 1926 to form the National Peasant League, which was supported by a few national political leaders. During this period, many local or regional peasant organisations were formed, directed by politicians who saw in peasant support a means to become important on the national political scene. Some land was distributed by state governors and many promises for more land distribution were made in order to win the peasants' vote or even their armed support in the political arena. At the 1934 Convention of the National Revolutionary Party, where Lázaro Cárdenas was nominated as presidential candidate, peasant representatives, led by Graciano Sánchez, were able to get their proposals incorporated in the party platform. These measures included: speeding up land reform; creation of an independent Agrarian Department in charge of the reform; participation of peasant representatives on the state agrarian commissions, which advised on petitions for land grants; provision that resident workers of haciendas could benefit from agrarian reform, etc. This form of peasant pressure, continued political unrest and the effects of the Great Depression, among other reasons, had again turned agrarian reform into a burning national issue when Lázaro Cárdenas won the presidency in 1934. By the end of his six-year term, land had been redistributed to the peasants on a massive scale, and the traditional land tenure system had been completely modified. Cárdenas needed peasant support in order to cope with the many forces opposing this and other reform programmes.

Under the Cárdenas regime, opposition against the execution of the agrarian reform law of 1915 continued to be so strong that the organised action of the peasants was needed in order to guarantee its implementation. Thus, the spectacular distribution in 1936 of 150,000 hectares of irrigated land to 35,000 peasants in the cotton-producing Laguna area, took place only after a strike of all the agricultural workers in the region which seriously affected the national economy. This strike was organised by the unions which had been created in 1935 with the help of urban labour leaders from nearby towns. The unions initially only demanded economic improvements under the National

[1] Nathaniel and Sylvia Weyl, *The Reconquest of Mexico. The Years of Lázaro Cárdenas* (Oxford University Press, 1939) pp. 78–9.

Labour Code, but the intransigence of the landowners (several of whom were foreign companies) resulted in the expropriation of the estates, as the only appropriate solution. President Cárdenas' promise that he would apply the land reform law to the cotton estates brought an end to the strikes. In about forty days land was distributed to over 300 villages. These were then organised into co-operative farms in order not to break up the plantations into uneconomic units.[1]

In the state of Michoacán, two haciendas comprising about 60,000 hectares owned by the heirs of an Italian immigrant were distributed in 1938 after similar events had taken place. When, in the 1930s, the 2000 workers of these estates began organising in order to defend their rights, guaranteed by the law, the owner struck back. The leader of the organisation was assassinated and several other peasants were killed or wounded. The struggle went on, however, and in 1938 the peasants took the land by force. This act was legalised a week later after urgent petitions had gone out to the central Government from the workers.

In many other areas, the execution of the agrarian reform legislation encountered violent opposition from the landowners. In order to cope with these forces, Cárdenas promoted the formation of rural defence units among the peasantry and distributed 60,000 rifles so that the beneficiaries of the reform could defend themselves against the so-called 'white guards' (armed bands in the landowners' pay).[2] In addition, and very importantly, President Cárdenas succeeded in bringing the different peasant organisations which existed in several states of Mexico all together in one national peasant federation (Confederación Nacional Campesina, C.N.C.) in 1938, whose main purpose was to support the Government politically. Indeed, this federation became one of the pillars of the official government party (later called the Party of Revolutionary Institutions, P.R.I.), which has been predominant in Mexico until today. When Cárdenas' successor took office in 1940, groups of armed peasant reserves stood on guard in the capital to prevent possible disorder.[3] Yet, after 1940, peasant influence diminished, while the middle class sector increased its strength considerably.

[1] Clarence Senior, *Land Reform and Democracy* (Gainesville: University of Florida Press, 1958), deals with the agrarian reform in the Laguna area. See also Salomon Eckstein, *El ejido colectivo en México* (Mexico: Fondo de Cultura Económica, 1966).

[2] *Seis años de gobierno al servicio de México, 1934–1940*, el Secretario de Gobernación, 30 Nov 1940 (Mexico: La Nacional Impresora) pp. 95–6.

[3] Paul Nathan, 'México en la época de Cárdenas', *Problemas agrícolas e industriales de México*, vii 3 (Mexico, 1955) pp. 171–2. For a journalistic account of these events, see Betty Kirk: *Covering the Mexican Front* (University of Oklahoma Press, 1942) pp. 84–5.

This is reflected in the ups and downs of the land distribution under the various administrations:

LAND REFORM BENEFICIARIES IN MEXICO, 1915–1966

Period	Total beneficiaries	Beneficiaries per year
1915–1920	46,400	7,733
1921–1934	736,930	52,600
1935–1940	811,160	135,000
1941–1958	487,115	27,000
1959–1966	352,170	44,000
Total	2,433,775	46,803

Source: Departemento de Asuntos Agrarios y Colonización (unpublished statistics).

The main principle of land redistribution had been set forth in the 1917 Constitution, but a large number of laws, decrees, rulings and statutes were necessary before an Agrarian Code was finally adopted in 1934, incorporating all previous legislation relating to land reform.

The reform's first objective was the restitution of communal lands to villages which had lost them to neighbouring haciendas, but which could prove a legal title to them. Very few communities in the country found themselves in such a favourable position, and the Constitution therefore stipulated in addition that communities which lacked sufficient land and water to satisfy the needs of their members – even if they were not able to prove that they had been dispossessed – were to receive such resources through the expropriation of hacienda properties, within a radius of seven kilometres. Most land grants to rural communities during the last fifty years have been made under this arrangement, which gave rise to a new system of land tenure, the *ejido*.

Under this system, the rural community receives a collective grant consisting of cropland, pastures and woods. The pastures and woodlands are destined only for communal use and cannot be divided. The arable land can either be distributed among the members of the community to be farmed individually or can be worked co-operatively by the *ejido* as a whole. In fact, the great majority of the *ejidos* have been divided up and farm plots are under individual management.

Though reform beneficiaries are not required to pay for the land, proceedings for obtaining land grants have to be initiated by the peasants and often turn out to be long and costly. *Ejido* lands are not full-fledged private properties, for they cannot legally be bought or sold, leased, mortgaged or otherwise disposed of. The individual member has usufruct rights over his plot of cultivable land only so long as he continues to farm it, and at best he can designate a person of his choice to inherit his rights after his death.

But if he fails for two consecutive years to farm his land without adequate justification, his plot reverts to the community to be allocated to someone else. *Ejido* cropland is distributed among individual farmers in units of equal size, established by law. The minimum amount of individual cropland per beneficiary has been raised over the years from two irrigated hectares to ten irrigated hectares (or their equivalent in other types of land). However, most of the existing *ejidos* received their land at a time when the individual unit was smaller than it is today; thus, the average plot of cultivable land per member was only 6·5 hectares in 1960.

According to the last agricultural census (1960), 1·5 million farmers have rights in *ejido* lands, and they control approximately 43 per cent of all cropland in the country. The other 57 per cent belongs to 1·3 million private farm units. About three-fourths of these can be classified as minifundia (sub-family farms), controlling not more than 5 per cent of all cropland. These small private farms are in themselves the indirect result of land reform, through the process of subdivision and fragmentation of larger holdings. At the other end of the scale, 1·6 per cent of all farm units still own 55 per cent of all cropland.

Land reform in Mexico has thus not abolished inequalities in land-holdings. Indeed, agrarian legislation specifically exempts from expropriation large farms up to 100 irrigated hectares (or even 300 hectares when certain kinds of specified cash crops are grown). Many large farm units, however, control much more than this, through the subterfuge of registering parts of large properties under different names.

Aside from *ejido* farmers and private operators, one half of the economically active population in agriculture has no permanent rights in land. Over three million peasants are landless labourers, migrant workers, sharecroppers or tenants. At the present rate of demographic growth (3·5 per cent per year for the overall population and 1·6 per cent for the agricultural labour force), this part of the peasant population will grow steadily for many years to come, before the non-agricultural sector will be able to absorb it. On the other hand, the rate of land distribution has necessarily tapered off as the amount of redistributable land has steadily decreased. Land for land-hungry peasants must increasingly be found in the sparsely settled tropical lowlands where settlement is slow and costly. While the Government has financed some model colonisation schemes in these areas, it appears that non-directed spontaneous settlement of the tropics is often as efficient and economically productive as anything that can be organised under the land reform programme.

However, the geographical redistribution of the peasant population, while constituting a long-range need in terms of the country's development, will not solve the immediate problems that the established land distribution programme is unable to overcome. Mexico's land and water resources are not bountiful, and the amount of arable land per agricultural worker is decreasing. While productivity per hectare has risen considerably in recent years, thanks to more intensive farming methods, better seeds, the use of pesticides and fertilisers, etc., the gravest problem facing agriculture is rural unemployment and under-employment. The rate of rural unemployment has been estimated at 40 per cent of the available labour force.

The great majority of farm operators (both on *ejidos* and private owners) are subsistence farmers, who work at low levels of capital intensity and generate meagre incomes for their families. These farmers are not, strictly speaking, inefficient producers, inasmuch as they make the best use of the poor resources at their command. But their limited financial and technical means, together with the small amount of land and the poor soils they possess, present them with almost insurmountable difficulties in their efforts to improve their standards of living.

In this new, post-reform situation, the role of peasant organisations has been changing, and new kinds of social movements have arisen.

The official National Peasant Confederation (C.N.C.) is by far the largest and most important peasant organisation in the country. It is composed mainly of *ejidatarios*, through the collective affiliation of *ejido* communities which are incorporated into regional committees and state leagues, thus forming a pyramidal structure through which the top leadership exercises control. An undetermined number of small private farmers are also members as well as a few unions of agricultural labourers. Several agricultural producers' unions (composed of *ejidatarios* and private farmers who produce certain cash crops such as coffee or sugar) are also affiliated with the C.N.C.

Since 1940, however, when the agrarian reform programme began to slow down, the C.N.C. has lost its role as a promotor of a dynamic agrarian policy. Aside from its political function of keeping the peasants within the fold of the official party (P.R.I.) and mobilising support, when needed, for the Government, the C.N.C. devotes much of its activities to help solve a number of legal, technical or administrative matters for its members, related to land tenure and agricultural development. Its officials, particularly on the regional and state levels, are the necessary intermediaries whom the peasants approach when they have become too entangled in the web of bureaucratic inefficiency, or when they need roads, schools, water supply and agricultural credit. For the C.N.C., the days when the organised peasants stood in armed defiance of the traditional power structure are over. Its national and local leaders, many of whom are not of peasant origin, are now careful brokers who sense peasant unrest when it arises and attempt to control or neutralise it. To that effect, they are able to delicately needle certain sectors and departments of the public administration into a more efficient performance but are careful not to upset the overall structure, of which they are one of the most important pillars.[1]

For many local leaders and political aspirants, the C.N.C. is only a vehicle for their personal social mobility. Since, in order to be successful, they conform to the standards set by the top leadership, who generally identify with middle-class interests, they often lose their effectiveness as defenders of peasant demands. Many complaints about graft and corruption of leaders at different levels are continually voiced by peasant groups.

Yet the post-reform situation, as was mentioned earlier, has brought a host of new problems that not even the C.N.C. has fully grasped, and which require not only small-scale technical adjustments but large-scale overall structural changes. The increasing marginalisation of large numbers of subsistence farmers, the growing population pressures on the limited resources of existing *ejidos*, the lack of employment opportunities for the younger generation for whom the struggle for the land does not have the same meaning as it had for their fathers; and, on the other hand, a renewed concentration of land, power and resources in the hands of a new, commercially oriented, regional bourgeoisie closely linked to the mainsprings of the political system – all of this, despite undeniable progress in recent years, is feeding new currents of frustration and discontent among the rural population. A

[1] For a historical account of the C.N.C., see Moisés González Navarro, *La Confederación Nacional Campesina, un grupo de presión en la reforma agraria mexicana* (Mexico: Costa-Amic Editor, 1968).

number of smaller independent, radical organisations have been successful in harnessing these forces into a more militant political framework.

In 1958 President López Mateos reactivated the land reform programme after an independent 'popular socialist' peasant movement had become strong in northern Mexico, under the leadership of Jacinto López.[1] At that time, local peasants who had exhausted all legal procedures to force the expropriation of the illegal, American-owned 400,000-hectare Cananea Cattle Company near the United States border, organised a massive, peaceful occupation of the estate. All the tactics that are usually employed against a peasant movement – intimidation, attempts at corruption, jail and even murder – were used against López and his followers. The movement, however, became more radical and extended to other areas of north-west Mexico. One of its consequences has been an intensification of government land reform activities since 1958.[2] As a result of peasant pressure, the Government bought the Cananea estate from its owners and created a number of *ejidos*, which are now modern co-operative cattle ranches. It is generally accepted that the growing problem of underemployment in the rural areas can at least be partly solved by increasing emphasis on co-operative or collective forms of agriculture, such as those that arose during the late 1930s. In the case of the Cananea experiment in co-operative cattle-ranching, it may well be that the experienced and cohesive leadership of the peasant organisations which were instrumental in effecting the land reform measures, will also be a key to the success of the collective experiments.

Summarising, it can be stated that organised peasant pressure was largely responsible for setting in motion the Mexican agrarian reform programme, and constituted its main support during the years of massive land redistribution (1934–40). Further, it can be hypothesized that the lack of efficient peasant mobilisation since the early 1940s (which, in turn is due to a number of complex historical and political causes) is partly responsible for the slowing down of the land redistribution programme since that time. Finally, though organised peasants participate in the political system, it cannot be said that they

[1] The influence of the peasant movements of 1957–1958 on the Government's reform policy was noted by Martin C. Needler, 'Mexico: Revolution as a Way of Life', in Martin C. Needler (ed.), *Political Systems of Latin America* (Princeton, N.J.: Van Nostrand Political Science Series, 1964), pp. 23–4; also by Karl M. Schmitt, *Communism in Mexico* (University of Texas Press, 1965), p. 14.

[2] See Gerrit Huizer, *La lucha campesina en Mexico*, Centro de Investigaciones Agrarias (Mexico, 1970), pp. 91–6.

wield political power in proportion to their demographic or economic importance in the country.

III. PEASANT MOVEMENTS AND LAND REFORM IN BOLIVIA

The agrarian structure of Bolivia up to 1952 was similar to that of Mexico before the revolution, but the exploitation of the Quechua- or Aymara-speaking peasants (a majority of the country's population) by the small, white, Spanish-speaking landowning aristocracy, allied with the 'tin barons', was perhaps even more intense. The Indian serfs (*colonos*) who lived on haciendas had the right to farm small subsistence plots (*sayañas*) for their own use, in return for which they had the obligation to provide free labour to the hacienda owner three or four days a week, either on the hacienda itself or at the owner's town residence. It was thus not uncommon for the peon to sharecrop his plot with another, even lowlier peasant, and to mobilise the members of his family in order to fulfil his labour obligations.

Besides Indian labourers on hacienda lands, a number of 'free' Indian communities (*communidades originarias*) maintained precarious control over communal lands, which in most cases were appropriated individually by the members. The communities had to provide a number of man-days of labour as tribute to local authorities.

The Chaco War against Paraguay (1933–5) accelerated the disintegration of the old political system. Thousands of Indian soldiers for the first time left the haciendas and came into contact with the outside world. Bolivia's defeat in the war left many frustrations and much political bitterness.

In the aftermath of the war, peasant unrest increased in many areas of Bolivia. In 1936 a rural syndicate was formed in Ucureña, in the temperate, fertile Cochabamba valley, which is one of the most prosperous agricultural regions in Bolivia.[1] In this area, a local monastery was leasing some of its land to local large landholders, and the lease included the right to the labour services of the resident

---

[1] Jorge Dandler Hanhart, *Local Group, Community and Nation: A Study of Changing Structure in Ucureña, Bolivia (1935–1952)*, M.A. Thesis, University of Wisconsin, 1967, mimeographed; Richard W. Patch, *Social Implications of the Bolivian Agrarian Reform*, Ph.D. Dissertation, 1956, and Richard W. Patch, 'Bolivia: U.S. Assistance in a Revolutionary Setting', in *Social Change in Latin America Today* (New York: Vintage Book, 1960).

colones. These decided to organise a union in order to rent the land themselves from the Santa Clara monastery and thus avoid the onerous labour obligations that were imposed upon them. Their efforts encountered strong opposition from various local landowners, who saw in it a direct threat to their customary rule. It was these in turn who bought the land from the monastery and evicted the peasant families who had been living and working there for years, destroying their homes and forcing them to leave the area or to revert to serfdom. A young radical peasant leader, José Rojas, whose father had been dispossessed in this fashion, had to escape to Argentina, where he worked as a labourer and acquired a political education. He returned secretly to Bolivia a few years later, and soon revived the peasant movement in Ucureña, of which he became the undisputed leader.

In the meantime, the urban middle sectors found the traditional oligarchical control based on landed and mining interests wanting. They initiated a number of political movements which culminated in the Revolution of 9 April 1952, under the leadership of Paz Estenssoro's M.N.R. (National Revolutionary Movement) with the widespread support of the urban and mining proletariat and the organised peasants.

The M.N.R. was founded in 1943 and participated in the Villarroel Government (1943–6). Several events took place during this period which contributed to the awakening and organisation of the indigenous peasantry. In August 1944 Paz Estenssoro and Walter Guevara proposed to the National Convention a moderate agrarian programme. Opposition from the majority in the Convention, oriented by the powerful organisation of large landholders, the *Sociedad Rural Boliviana*, was strong enough to block acceptance of the proposal. However, the M.N.R.'s defence of the programme made the peasants aware that they had political allies in their struggle for land.

In early 1945, the first Bolivian Indian Congress took place, which increased national consciousness about the peasant problem. Some time before, in 1944, an Indian leader, Luis Ramos Quevedo, had been able to interview President Villarroel in the National Palace about the possibility of organising an Indian Congress, and having received a vague promise from the President, he started a campaign to effectively bring together Indians from all parts of the country. A photograph of himself together with President Villarroel was sold all over rural Bolivia to collect contributions. Ramos Quevedo thus became the major Indian leader, and called people to come to La Paz in February 1945. When Indian peasants began coming into the capital, the

Government, which was not too enthusiastic, found itself obliged to support the meeting, in spite of opposition which had grown in the meantime. However, it prevailed upon Ramos Quevedo to agree to a postponement. This led to protest meetings of several thousands of peasants who had already gathered in Oruro, on their way to La Paz. President Villarroel intervened personally when more than a thousand delegates, already gathered in La Paz, requested attention.[2]

The main points of the agenda of the congress, which opened on 10 May 1945, were the following: abolition of compulsory services which peasants had to render to landlords (*pongueaje*); education; regulation of agricultural labour; formulation of general agrarian policy; other affairs. No particularly radical measures were proposed by the peasants' delegates. Rather, they emphasised adjustments which would improve their lot, directed against the most abusive forms of servitude and lack of educational facilities. Government decrees concerning the abolition of servitude and the obligation to establish schools in the large haciendas were issued a few days later. Land reform as such was not dealt with.

In August 1945 the large landholders organised a congress of their own, in Cochabamba, at which they spoke out against the new decrees, indicating that their execution would lead to 'indiscipline and disobedience' in the rural areas. Also, some of the important newspapers opposed the new measures and agitated against the restitution of private large landholdings to the indigenous communities which were its original owners. Such restitution was favoured by some of the members of the Villarroel Government, who belonged to the M.N.R. Party. Opposition became particularly strong during the parliamentary discussions of a bill prohibiting the eviction of peasants from haciendas. Peasants who, in accordance with the new decrees, refused to continue rendering compulsory labour services to the landlords were frequently evicted from their homes. During the debates, a peasant who had been whipped by a landowner was presented as proof of the abusiveness and cruelty of many landlords and of the repressive conditions under which the Bolivian peasantry laboured. Although the bill was passed, it was later vetoed by the Government under pressure from the landowners' association and their allies.

During this period, the many spontaneous peasant strikes and uprisings against the landholders, and also the struggles between

---

[2] Luis Antezana, *Resumen del proceso de un siglo de movimiento campesina boliviano,* manuscript (La Paz, Bolivia, 1967), from which most of the following data were taken.

indigenous communities over territorial boundaries, abated. But as a result of the negative reaction of the landlords after the Indian Congress, the sit-down strikes revived with more vigour, covering large areas of Tarija, Ururo and Potosí. By refusing to render the traditional compulsory services, the peasants were in fact complying with the decrees issued in May 1945. Indian peasant organisers, especially those who had experience as miners or who had been jailed occasionally for their political activity, travelled around in many areas, agitating among the peasantry. Political organisers of the M.N.R. also participated in this campaign. The press, however, spread fear of the indigenous movements among the urban middle class, exaggerating their importance in order to discredit the Government. The peasant movements were described as 'racial war', and dire predictions about a decrease of agricultural production and imminent hunger in the country were widely circulated. The reformist Government was finally overthrown on 21 July 1946, and President Villarroel was hanged from a lamp-post by an enraged mob. The reform measures were revoked, and the traditional order restored in the rural areas.

The peasant protest movements which occurred in subsequent years as a reaction to the change of Government in 1946 were not met by conciliation as before, but by armed force. Many peasant leaders, particularly those who had participated in the Indian Congress, were jailed. Revolts in protest against these repressive tendencies started at the end of 1946. In Ayopaya, Cochabamba, several thousand peasants invaded large landholdings and assassinated some of the landlords who had tried to reintroduce compulsory labour obligations. Soon many areas of the country were in turmoil. Most of the peasant movements now became violent, the peasants using arms, whereas before they had generally been non-violent. The rural estates and even some provincial capitals were threatened or effectively attacked. Dynamite, with which peasants who had worked in the mines were well acquainted, was frequently used as a weapon in the struggle. Miners and workers occupied important leadership functions in these movements.

Their goals at this stage went beyond mere changes in the peasants' working conditions to include radical changes in the political and social structure of the country. The intransigence of the rural élite had apparently provoked a strong awakening of the peasants as to where their real interests lay. Workers from La Paz, affiliated with the Federación Obrera Local, tied to the M.N.R., helped to organise the peasants' protest movements in the Altiplano. Several of the labour leaders who were active in this field were jailed.

In 1947 several movements in various parts of the country were repressed by large-scale army intervention and peasant concentrations were bombed by air force planes. A special rural police corps was created. In several parts of the country civil militias were formed. A concentration camp (*colonia fiscal*) was created in Ichilo, one of the isolated tropical areas of the country, where over two hundred peasant leaders were confined. This agrarian revolt, which involved several thousand soldiers and many thousands of peasants, was finally crushed by the end of 1947. The landlords, several of whom had fled to the towns, returned to their estates. After 1947, localised revolts against landowners continued to flare up sporadically in increasingly violent form. Sometimes as many as 100 policemen were needed to dominate these scattered uprisings, such as the one in Achacachi not far from La Paz in 1951. At the same time, efforts to organise peasants into unions, with help from miners and urban workers, continued in spite of repressive measures against the organisers. In 1951, the land-owners tried to organise their own 'yellow' unions in an attempt to neutralise the peasant movement. In March of 1952 they planned to hold an Indian Congress in Pacajes, department of La Paz. The serious agrarian reform issues would be carefully avoided at this congress, which was to concentrate its attention on minor problems. Shortly before, however, a National Congress of Indians took place in Azanaques, where the execution of the decrees of the Villarroel regime was requested. Because of increasing unrest, related to the elections in 1952 in which the M.N.R. was to gain considerable support, the Pacajes congress was forbidden. At the beginning of 1952, peasant unrest occasionally took the form of guerrilla movements. On 9 April 1952, the army and other defenders of the conservative Government who had tried to prevent the electoral victory of the M.N.R., were defeated by a short, bloody revolutionary movement, directed by the M.N.R. in La Paz and other towns. The power of the landholding élite, which depended on army support, came to an end.

In the power vacuum created in the rural areas by the disappearance of the forces which traditionally supported the landowners, new forms of exercise of power now arose. Peasant syndicates were organised all over Bolivia, which practically took over local government functions. New leaders were elected in massive peasant concentrations or community meetings. The newly formed Ministry of Peasant Affairs and organisers of the M.N.R. directed this drive. Many landowners fled to the cities. One of the strongest centres of organisation of this movement was Ucureña, department of Cochabamba. Here, a regional peasant federation was organised, headed by José Rojas. The movement grew rapidly when rumours circulated that conservative forces were trying to regain control. Many haciendas were invaded, and buildings burned down. The movement put strong pressure on the Government to take radical land reform measures. Partly as a reaction to the growing violence of the movement in the Cochabamba area, President Paz Estenssoro appointed a commission to study this question in January 1953, and asked it to deliver a report within four months. On 2 August 1953 the Bolivian agrarian reform was officially launched by presidential decree in a public ceremony, attended by thousands of peasants, in Ucureña. One of the main functions of the peasant syndicates, belonging to newly formed federations in all departments and united at the national level in the National Confederation of Peasant Workers of Bolivia (C.N.T.C.B.), was to petition for land for their members under the new land reform programme. An armed peasant militia was created to support the Government and the peasants against counter-revolutionary violence. Many landlords fled their estates, and the *de facto* distribution of hacienda lands by the organised peasants often took place well in advance of the slower legal proceedings.

The Bolivian land reform was partially inspired by the Mexican agrarian reform. As in the latter, the Bolivian reform affirmed the nation's original ownership of its natural resources, and established the right of landless peasants and Indian communities to ownership and restitution of land, respectively, through the expropriation of haciendas. Its principal achievement, however, which profoundly affected the Bolivian social and political structure, has been the abolition of the *colono* system, whereby the peasants have been freed from their forced labour obligations to the landowners.

As in Mexico, beneficiaries have had to petition for land, through their peasant syndicates. In some places, however, the landowners' traditional position of power and pre-eminence discouraged direct peasant action, and in these areas land reform has come slowly. The implementation of the reform was put in the hands of a national Agrarian Reform Service, and local proceedings and redistribution measures have been the direct responsibility of agrarian judges, aided by a small number of technical personnel. For reform purposes, estates were classified regionally by sizes into four categories: small properties, medium-sized properties, agricultural enterprises and latifundia. The first two categories were the direct beneficiaries of land redistribution measures. Estates that were farmed intensively and were commercially oriented, and on which labour was paid on a cash basis, were classified as 'agricultural enterprises' and were not expropriated, regardless of their size. Latifundia were defined as extensively farmed, inefficient and generally underutilised estates of the traditional type where compulsory labour by the Indians was the rule. These were outlawed by the reform, and their lands were to be wholly distributed among resident labourers. Thus, a number of procedures were established by the land reform law.

In most cases, the reform programme merely handed over legal ownership to the peasants of the subsistence plots to which they had access in the haciendas, thus in fact creating a large number of small owner-operators, whose farm size has not enabled them to appreciably improve their standard of living. But the abolition of servitude has certainly allowed them to dispose at will over their own labour and the produce of their farms. In other areas, where haciendas were legally classified as latifundia by the Agrarian Reform Service, hacienda lands were redistributed *in toto* among the resident peasants, thus adding land resources to their subsistence plots, and effecting considerable improvement in their standard of living. In some parts of the country, the landowners kept parts of their haciendas as legally protected 'small' or 'medium-sized' properties, the rest being used for reform purposes. In other cases, the traditional landowner, scared away by the agrarian reform and by peasant militancy, gladly sold his property to his ex-serfs. In still other cases, large estates were simply classified as 'agricultural enterprises', and in these areas, except for the abolition of compulsory labour and the transformation of the traditional peon into a wage-worker, there has hardly been any redistribution of land rights. In fact, in the tropical lowlands of the eastern regions of Bolivia, large, capital-intensive, cash crop plantations have developed since the land reform, legally organised as 'agricultural enterprises'.

Unlike Mexico, no attempt has been made in Bolivia to organise reform beneficiaries into communal forms of land tenure. The small and medium-sized private property is the corner-stone of the new land tenure system. The abolition of the *colono* system, and private landownership by peasants, has been the basis upon which agricultural development has taken place in recent years. A large part of the peasant population still lives at subsistence levels in a subsistence agriculture, but reform beneficiaries are increasingly engaged in the production of cash crops, and participate in the local and regional markets. Though the land reform law specifically establishes the desirability of agricultural co-operatives, very little progress has been made in this field.

On the other hand, the traditional free Indian communities with their collective lands have hardly been touched by the reform. The land reformers originally thought that the Indian communities could be transformed into co-operative and collective farm units, through a return to their original structure and spirit in combination with modern agricultural technology. But this utopian ideal has been completely frustrated. Inequalities in land tenure exist within the communities themselves, where usually a small group of traditional families hold local power and concentrate most of the resources. The small plots of arable land that most community members possess (*sayañas* and *aynocas*) are fragmented and dispersed. Many people in the communities lack land altogether, and have to work as peons or sharecroppers for their more fortunate brethren.

Although much more ex-hacienda land is possessed *de facto* by former peons, the Bolivian Government had by 1967 given land titles to 191,000 family heads, covering a total of six million hectares.[1] This includes not only outright land grants but also land consolidation titles handed out to legitimate (that is, non-expropriable) ex-hacienda owners, and collective titles given to pre-existing communities. Only about 10 per cent of all existing properties have been officially affected up to now, and approximately 30 per cent of all available land has come under the reform programme. Most of the new titles cover individual properties that have been classified as 'small' and 'medium'; only a fraction belong to 'agricultural enterprises', 'co-operatives' or 'communities'. The most intensive activity in land reform was carried out between 1961 and 1963, when more than 50 per cent of all those who have received land between 1955 and 1967 received their titles. Since 1963, and particularly after the counter-revolutionary military coup of 1964, the rhythm of land title distribution has decreased.

[1] Preliminary data from Comité Interamericano de Desarrollo Agrícola and the Land Tenure Center of the University of Wisconsin: *Estudio de la estructura agraria en Bolivia*, 1967, mimeographed.

IV. INFLUENCE OF PEASANT PRESSURE IN OTHER LATIN AMERICAN COUNTRIES[1]

Not only in Mexico and Bolivia, where large-scale agrarian reforms have taken place, but also in the rest of Latin America, the impact of organised peasant pressure has been crucial. In several other countries where more or less important agrarian reform efforts have been undertaken, these are generally a consequence of direct action on the part of the peasantry.

In Venezuela,[2] where the land reform law was passed in 1960, the majority of the peasantry is well organised in the Federación Campesina de Venezuela (F.C.V.). This organisation was created and directed by political leaders and became influential particularly after the fall of the regime of Pérez Jiménez in 1958. An estimated 500 cases of invasion by peasants of expropriable land took place at the beginning of the reform process. Some of them were organised by local unions of the F.C.V. on lands which could be legally claimed under the reform legislation. Cases are known where the police helped the peasant leaders to give the occupation of lands an orderly course. In later stages, the reform has been carried out under less radical pressures from the peasants, but the rhythm of land distribution in Venezuela is considerably slower than was the case in Bolivia and Mexico.

In Colombia, the lengthy internal upheaval, called *la Violencia*, which prevailed in the rural areas during the 1940s and 1950s and which took an estimated 200,000 to 300,000 lives, was one of the reasons for the acceptance of agrarian reform legislation in 1961. Actual distribution of lands has taken place very slowly. The Colombian Land Reform Institute (I.N.C.O.R.A.) has been helpful, however, in the legalisation of several invasions of publicly owned lands, the ownership of which was in dispute. In some areas, particularly along the Magdalena river on the Atlantic seaboard, several local priests and the Catholic Federación Agraria Nacional (F.A.N.A.L.) headed by Eugenio Colorado, helped to organise the peaceful occupation of

---

[1] For a comparative analysis of peasant movements and land reforms in Latin America, see Gerrit Huizer, *The Revolutionary Potential of Peasants in Latin America* (Lexington: Heath-Lexington Books, 1972).

[2] See John D. Powell, *Preliminary Report on the Federación Campesina de Venezuela: Origins, Organization, Leadership and Role in the Agrarian Reform Program*, Land Tenure Centre, University of Wisconsin, no. 9 (Sep 1964); and John D. Powell, *The Politics of Agrarian Reform in Venezuela: History, System and Process*, Ph.D. Dissertation, University of Wisconsin, 1966.

public land claimed by private estates. Later, I.N.C.O.R.A. was called in to initiate agrarian reform projects in those areas.[1]

In Peru up to 1968, agrarian reform has taken place only in regions which had suffered peasant unrest between 1960 and 1963. The most spectacular case was the Valle de la Convencion in the Department of Cuzco. Peasants in that area were mainly settlers on formerly virgin land. In return for the right to work a plot of their own, they had to perform labour services for the landlords. As the settlers were able to progress economically by growing coffee, a profitable cash crop, the semi-feudal obligations to the landowners became increasingly burdensome. They organised local unions to bargain with the landholders. The abusiveness and intransigence of the latter, however, resulted in a radicalisation of the movement. A federation of unions was formed for the whole valley with help of labour organisers and lawyers from the town of Cuzco. Under the leadership of a young Trotskyite agronomist, Hugo Blanco, who went to live among the peasants and soon became the secretary-general of the federation, radical forms of pressure were adopted. A general strike of all the peasants against the work obligations to the landholders, and the invasion of some of the estates where landowners were most abusive, led to a critical situation in the area. A special land reform decree for that area was promulgated by the Government in 1962 to appease the peasants. Together with a considerable show of military force and the imprisonment of many union leaders (including Hugo Blanco, who was captured later and sentenced to a long term in jail), these measures were intended to prevent the movement from spreading to other areas.[2]

In spite of these measures, and as a result of promises about land reform during the 1963 election campaign, in August of that year a wave of land occupations took place in the highlands in which about 300,000 Indian peasants participated.[3] They claimed that they 're-covered' the lands of which they had formerly been despoiled and

---

[1] For a case description of a land invasion which later became a land reform project, see Víctor Daniel Bonilla, 'De la lucha por la tierra al Atlántico 8; *Tierra*, no. 4, abril-junio 1967, Ediciones Tercer Mundo, Bogotá.

[2] See Wesley W. Craig, *The Peasant Movement of La Convención, Peru: Dynamics of Rural Labor Organization*, in Henry A. Landsberger (ed.), *Latin American Peasant Movements* (Ithaca: Cornell University Press, 1969); Eric J. E. Hobsbawm, 'Problèmes agraires à La Convención, Pérou', in *Problèmes agraires des Amériques Latines*, (Paris: C.N.R.S., 1967); Hugo Neira, *Cuzco: tierra y muerte* (Lima: Populibres peruanos, 1964); Victor Villanueva, *Hugo Blanco y la rebelión campesina* (Lima: Librería Editorial Juan Mejía Baca, 1967).

[3] Inter-American Committee for Agricultural Development (CIDA), *Peru: Tenencia de la tierra y desarrollo socio-economico del sector agricola* (Washington: Union Panamericana, 1966) p. 397.

which were promised them by the presidential candidate. The occupation of the huge Algolan estate took place after the owners prohibited indigenous communities from grazing their cattle, as they had been accustomed to do. Whole communities, including men, women, children and their cattle, passed through the newly built fences and constructed symbolic living quarters on the invaded lands, where they settled until the police came to throw them off. This act was repeated in various parts of the estate on such a large scale by a group of communities organised in a federation that there was no other solution than to make an arrangement. The estate was bought by the Government and became one of the first projects of the Peruvian land reform office, which was founded in 1964. Successful communal cattle enterprises were set up in the communities.

In Chile, one of the first projects of the land reform corporation set up in the mid-1960s concerned the Choapa valley. This was an estate owned by a government agency, where – exceptionally for Chile – peasant syndicates had gained considerable strength. When the Christian Democratic Government, on assuming office in 1964, announced its intention of pursuing land reform with greater vigour, demonstrations were staged in that area. The unions had been organised many years before by peasants who had gained experience as miners and had participated in the miners' unions, generally of Communist or Socialist orientation. The fact that the estates were government property and not privately owned perhaps explains why unions were tolerated. Before the recent land reform law, Chilean legislation was not favourable to the formation of agricultural workers' unions.

Various examples from different countries in Latin America confirm the Mexican and Bolivian experience: that opposition of vested interests against land reform is rarely overcome only by legal provisions or government programmes, but mainly by direct action and pressure by well-organised peasant groups.

V. COMPARISON OF MEXICAN AND BOLIVIAN EXPERIENCE

Because we are more concerned here with the role of peasant movements that lead up to agrarian reform than with peasant organisations in the process of land reform implementation, a more detailed comparison between Mexico and Bolivia will be useful.

The areas in both countries where the peasant movements took root originally and gained considerable strength have certain characteristics in common. In Mexico, the state of Morelos, where Zapata was active, is near Mexico City and had been an important producer of cash crops (mainly sugar cane) for many years; the state of Veracruz had several important industrial centres and Mexico's most important port; and the state of Michoacán was fairly densely populated and had good communications with the rest of the country. In Bolivia, the valley of Cochabamba had traditionally been considered the country's 'foodbasket', which had developed around an important urban centre (Bolivia's second city). These are examples of areas where the process of modernisation was under way even before the rise of the peasant movement. Peasants had frequent urban contacts and were increasingly exposed to, and experienced in, modern ways of life and work. Though poverty and oppression of peasants were common in all of the areas, these factors in themselves do not appear to have provoked automatically the formation of resistance or protest movements. It was rather the confrontation of their conditions with modernising influences which led to an awakening of political consciousness. Indeed, the areas where agrarian movements started appear to have been less poverty-stricken and isolated than the average, and more exposed to 'cultural contact'.

This awakening seemed to occur particularly under conditions of acute frustration. This is often a result of the conflict between the intransigence of the traditional rural élite and the rising expectations and aspirations of the peasants. It can also result from the increasing exactions of the rural élite, which needs more land for cash crops and despoils the indigenous population of its remaining communal lands, as happened in the state of Morelos around 1900. The frustration may also result from the fact that well intentioned legislation is not implemented or meets with strong opposition from vested interests, as occurred in the states of Veracruz and Michoacán in the 1920s. Able leaders can under such circumstances rally the people into a struggle for legitimate improvements which, if legal and orderly procedures are not successful or even meet with violence, become increasingly radical in their approach.

Some peasant movements have during their process of organisation drawn lessons from the fact that the less poor are more easily organisable. The spread of the Ligas Campesinas in the north-east of Brazil during the late 1950s and early 1960s was due not so much to the poor agricultural workers as to the sharecroppers and tenants. This category was economically a little less vulnerable and land reform appealed more to them than to the peons who were often migrant workers. This last category could give strength to the movement in mass demonstrations and similar activities once some kind of organisational structure existed.

Another important element which the twentieth-century movements in Mexico and Bolivia have in common is the fact that the main leaders, although of peasant origin, had some kind of urban or modernising experience (such as travel to foreign countries). Zapata had been in the army and had worked in Mexico City. Primo Tapia had been a migrant worker in the United States. Úrsulo Galván was a carpenter by profession and had worked in the United States and in the oilfields of Veracruz. In Bolivia, José Rojas, had spent various years in Argentina. Only Galván and Rojas, though, had previously had union experience in an urban environment before becoming leaders of their respective peasant movements. Jacinto López was a shoemaker with many years of experience as a labour organiser.

In addition to the proximity of modernising influences and urban experience of the principal leaders, it is noteworthy that the peasant organisations, particularly in their early stages, were in close contact with, and indeed under the influence of, certain individuals who were not peasants and who may be considered as agents of social change or modernisation. Zapata was supported by a rural schoolteacher working in his village, Otilio Montaño, who helped him draft the Plan de Ayala, and in the later stages of his movement, by the lawyer Antonio Díaz Soto y Gama, who became the national leader of the Agrarian Party in Mexico during the 1920s, as well as other urban intellectuals and political figures. Primo Tapia in Michoacán received help from Apolinar Martínez Múgica, a minor official in the local court who had previously been a petty industrialist. In Ucureña, the syndicate of José Rojas received counsel and active aid from Eduardo Arze Loureiro, son of a local landowner who had taken up the peasants' cause, and who after the Bolivian revolution became the first head of the National Agrarian Reform Council.

In the Laguna area in Mexico, the urban workers and their leaders played a crucial role in building a strong peasant organisation. In the north-west of Mexico, where the symbolical land invasions of 1958 took place, rural schoolteachers had been important allies of the peasant movements ever since the days of the presidency of Cárdenas. Several of them became top leaders in the regional federations.

There is a good deal of evidence to show that the intransigent resistance (often violent) of the class of large landowners had a stimulating and radicalising influence on the development of the movements, as their goals became clearer and their means more extreme. The landowners' opposition to the peasants' demands for legitimate restitution of the communal lands of which they had been illegally deprived, or for the proper execution of land reform legislation, provoked the more 'organisable' of these peasant groups into greater cohesiveness and towards more drastic action. Thus, in those cases in which peasant groups overstepped the bounds of order and due process, this was more often than not in reaction to the landowners' refusal to comply with land reform measures and their recourse to violence against the peasants themselves.

The organised opposition of the landed élite to the peasant movements in fact helped the latter in the long run by enabling them to unite and harness their forces. The case studies in Mexico and Bolivia show that, despite considerable opposition by the landowning class, the peasant movements were successful in reaching their goals, though in the later stages of land reform their roles and function have been changing. This has not always been the case, however. In many other Latin American countries in recent years, where movements similar to those of Mexico and Bolivia in their early stages have arisen, they failed to reach their objectives or achieved only limited and partial results. This has been the case of the peasant leagues in north-eastern Brazil (1955–64) and to some extent of the peasant movements in Cuzco and other highland areas in Peru (1952–64).

The success or failure of peasant movements depends very often on the nature of the opposing forces. The tactics that the opposing landowning classes have employed are of various kinds. Intimidation, isolation, corruption or physical elimination of leaders and potential leaders of peasant movements appear to be most frequently used. Emiliano Zapata was drafted into the army as soon as he became a 'trouble-maker', even before his efforts to rally the peasants of his area had become really effective. After his movement had gained strength and contributed significantly to the success of the Mexican revolution, he was offered an estate for his services, if he would give up further efforts to achieve genuine agrarian reform. He was assassinated in 1919 precisely because he refused to give up his struggle. The peasant movements in Veracruz and Michoacán suffered severe losses among their leaders before they were able to gain recognition and achieve regional and national impact. In Bolivia, José Rojas was persecuted for several years, and after the triumph of the 1952 revolution the more moderate leaders of the dominant M.N.R. party tried to replace him with a less radical leader. Rojas, however, was supported by a majority of the peasants in the Cochabamba valley and he went on to become Minister for Peasant Affairs in one of the M.N.R. governments.

In Mexico, strong opposition to land reform was also presented by the Catholic Church, which has traditionally been politically allied with the *hacendados*. Frequently, peasants were enjoined from taking land and joining the agrarian movement under threat of excommunication, and the agrarian reform was publicly decried by the church hierarchy as being no better than robbery. The church-instigated 'cristero' rebellion in 1927 represented an extreme form of opposition. However, there were exceptions to this tendency at the local level. A village priest was the first to make typewritten copies of Zapata's Plan de Ayala, in 1911. In Bolivia, there is little evidence to show that the church took a stand either way. In recent years, and in other countries, however, church dignitaries have made definitive commitments in favour of agrarian reform and have helped organise militant rural unions, such as in Brazil. And the Colombian priest and sociologist turned guerrilla, Camilo Torres, who was killed by the army in 1966, is already becoming a legendary figure in Latin America.

Whereas opposition to peasant movements is frequently an important stimulant for their development, political support from certain quarters may often become a hindrance. In many areas of Mexico, regional peasant movements, such as those described above, were used by local *caciques* (political strongmen), who were themselves often of revolutionary origin, to further their own personal political ends. Land distribution became a means to exert patronage and gain the peasant vote or armed support in critical moments. Corruptive influences appeared and the movements were neutralised or disintegrated.

It has already been mentioned that, in Mexico, at the height of the land distribution process, during the late 1930s, the government actively promoted the unification of various peasant organisations into a large National Peasant Confederation which became one of the principal supports of the official party. After 1940, the political influence of the peasantry within the party gradually diminished, while that of the smaller but economically more powerful middle sectors increased. Although less than in Mexico, official control of the peasant movement in Bolivia also weakened its political bargaining power.

Characteristics of Leaders

An important element in the development of peasant movements is the ideology and personal attitudes of the leaders. Emiliano Zapata did not have much of an explicit ideology, but his strongly charismatic personality kept his followers well together in situations of great hardship. However, after his assassination, no other leader of his stature was able to take his place, and the movement disintegrated. In the state of Veracruz, the Peasant League and its leader, Úrsulo Galván, were under communist influence; yet the movement rallied to the Government's side in 1929 when the constitutional order was threatened by an attempted military coup, despite the party's wish to stage a coup of its own. Galván was expelled from the party. It is difficult to assess to what extent such conflicts are due to personal rivalries or real ideological differences. In Michoacán, in turn, Primo Tapia was influenced by a brand of socialism of which a national revolutionary leader, General Mújica, was the spokesman.

In the movement which brought about the spectacular land distribution of the Laguna area in 1936, the 'popular front' ideas held by the Mexican Communist Party at that time were influential. In the peasant movement headed by Jacinto López in north-west Mexico, the orientation of the Popular Socialist Party (Partido Popular Socialista), inspired to a large extent by Vicente Lombardo Toledano, has had a strong influence.

In Mexico, the individual characteristics of the peasant leaders have always been extremely important, and each one of them had, to some extent, his own personal ideology. *Caciquismo* or *caudillismo*, that is, the personal domination of a leader based on charismatic qualities and patron-client relationships, is a common phenomenon in many Latin American countries. In Bolivia, José Rojas was at first influenced by an independent Marxist Party, the P.I.R. (Party of the Revolutionary Left), which had been founded by the sociologist José Antonio Arze, but he later moved closer to the moderate nationalist party, the M.N.R. 'Personalism' and charisma, rather than a clear-cut class ideology, have also been attributed to other leaders of peasant movements in Latin America.

Means Employed

There is a great variety of means used by peasant groups to express their demands. The formation and institutionalisation of an organisation is generally a first step. Meetings are held at the local or regional level, where peasants jointly discuss their needs and nominate a board or committee to present the demands to the landowners or the authorities. There is considerable evidence that such procedures only rarely meet with success. The economic and social power of the landowners with whom the local authorities are generally identified is so strong that demands presented in an orderly way can be ignored. Although in several instances this has led to apathy and resignation, the resentment created can easily lead to the use of forms of civil disobedience in order to pressure for the application of the law. One of the most frequently used methods is the peaceful occupation or invasion of the lands which are claimed. These may be lands which in earlier years have been usurped through legal manipulations but which the peasants continued to consider theirs. In many areas such occupations are called 'recoveries' of land. Elsewhere, squatters who have been working formerly idle lands, the legal ownership of which was not properly defined, are considered 'invaders' when a large landholder finds it convenient to extend his area of cultivation, and claims them as his own. In other cases, peasants who have petitioned in vain for certain plots of expropriable land symbolically occupy the lands in question in the hope that this will speed up the lagging legal procedures. This happened with the Cananea estate in north-western Mexico. Other means which have been used successfully by peasant organisations are caravans and sit-ins. When the peasants in the Laguna area in Mexico wanted to emphasise their demands for better credit and irrigation facilities, they organised a caravan to the national capital of twenty-five trucks with thirty representatives each from the villages of the area. They covered the 1000 kilometres to Mexico City slowly, organising demonstrations of solidarity in various towns along the road in order to draw public attention. By the time they reached the capital, they had received so much publicity and support that a delegation from among their midst was received almost immediately by the President of Mexico, to discuss their demands. Another tactic used to obtain due attention to demands are 'sit-ins' in, or in front of, the building of the agency to which the demand is directed. A large group of representatives just sits and waits and refuses to leave till negotiations are started.

Results of Peasant Pressure

There is considerable evidence that much of the agrarian reform in Latin America until today has come about as a result of such pressure tactics. The ups and downs of the fifty years of agrarian reform in Mexico are full of cases of this kind, and the sudden overall *de facto* land distribution in Bolivia is another case in point.

As was noted above, in several other Latin American countries where a beginning of agrarian reform has been made this frequently occurred in areas where the peasant had taken initiatives of this kind, supported by Catholic priests or politicians of various tendencies.

The relative success or failure of peasant movements has to be judged in terms of their changing goals and the new economic and political structures that arise in the course of time. In Mexico and Bolivia, extensive land redistribution has taken place in great measure as a result of peasant pressures. In Bolivia, in the course of ten years, a marked increase in welfare and decrease of unrest in the rural areas has occurred, principally due to the abolition of compulsory labour and *de facto* distribution of large landholdings. In Mexico, the picture is somewhat more complex. Land redistribution has been taking place now for fifty years and has not yet been concluded. Due to accelerated demographic growth, new generations of landless workers, who now represent more than half of the total agricultural labour force, are again exerting pressure on limited land resources with no realistic hope of ever receiving a land grant. After the integration of the national peasant movement into the political establishment in the 1930s, grass-roots pressures for land reform diminished, only to rise again in the late 1950s and early 1960s in the form of independent, more radical movements.

The recent Mexican experience shows that when the land reform programme is not sufficiently effective and the established peasant organisation has been unable to satisfactorily channel or appease renewed peasant unrest, radical, independent peasant organisations will continue to spring up and new waves of peasant discontent may sweep the countryside.

INDEX

Achim, Andreas, 306
Adelman, I., 275n
Afghanistan, 360, 366, 367, 368
Africa
  trade union formation, 54, 63
  see also Developing countries
Agrarian democracy, 263, 286–7
Agrarian reform, see Reform,
  agrarian
Agricultural workers' organisations
  Latin America, 396, 397, 401–2
  North Africa and Asia, 374–7
Agriculture
  medieval England, 109–15, 137
  Poland, 323–4, 326
  Spain, 158, 167–71, 182–4
  Russia, 205–6, 207n
Aims, peasant, 33–5, 45, 145–6
  developing countries, 50, 356, 357,
    361–4, 370–3, 375–7
  Eastern Europe, 279, 293, 297–300,
    302, 305, 312–14, 324–5, 330,
    334, 345–6
  England, 114–15, 115–20, 127, 131,
    141
  Latin America, 385, 394–5, 401,
    408, 409
  medieval Europe, 76–8, 87, 89, 93
  Russia, 198–9, 208, 213, 219–30, 241
  Spain, 176–80, 182, 187
Akhramovich, R. T., 366n, 368n
Alcoy, 190
Alefirenko, P. K., 218, 220n, 256
Alexander, John T., 256
Alexandrov, Yu. G., 14, 43, 353n
Alfonso XII of Spain, 163
Algeria, 30, 31, 53, 353, 368, 374–5
Alien domination, 53–4; see also
  Colonialism; National liberation
    struggle
Alishev, Ataman, 242, 249

Alitovski, S. N., 360n, 372n
Allies, peasants', 27, 59–62, 64
  Africa and Asia, 354–5, 364, 376–7
  England, 105, 122–7, 132–4
  Eastern Europe, 303–4, 309, 322,
    330, 336–42
  Latin America, 393, 404, 406
  Russia, 194, 213, 220n, 232n, 235–9
  see also Social banditry
Almond, Gabirel, 11n
Amaru, Tupac, 379
Anarchism, 40, 162
Anarcho-internationalism, 161, 164–7
Anarcho-syndicalism, 262, 264, 311
Andalusia, 161, 172–3, 177–8, 180,
  187, 190, 192
Andreas, Bert, 174n
Andrushchenko, A. I., 201n, 220n,
  237n, 238n, 249n, 255
Antezana, L., 394n
Anti-colonialism, 5, 352–3
Apathy, 56–7
Ardévol, José Termes, 165n, 191
Armies, peasant, 48, 337; see also
  Pugachev's Cossack revolt
Arnold of Brescia, 88
Arques, 83
Arslanov, Kinzya, 197
Arze, José Antonio, 407
Asia, see Developing countries
Astrakhan, 252
Azerbaijan, Iranian, 353

Bacon, Sir Roger, 133
Baginski, K., 333
Bakunin, M., 164–6, 187–8
Ball, John, 89, 97, 124, 129–30, 135–6
Bampton, Thomas, 118n
Banditry, social, 4, 40, 142–57, 212
  England, 104, 116, 118
  Russia, 211–12, 233

Index